MAX-PLANCK-INSTITUT
FÜR AUSLÄNDISCHES ÖFFENTLICHES RECHT
UND VÖLKERRECHT

Beiträge zum ausländischen öffentlichen Recht und Völkerrecht

Begründet von Viktor Bruns

Herausgegeben von
Armin von Bogdandy · Anne Peters

Band 280

Elisabeth Veronika Henn

International Human Rights Law and Structural Discrimination

The Example of Violence against Women

Springer

ISSN 0172-4770 ISSN 2197-7135 (electronic)
Beiträge zum ausländischen öffentlichen Recht und Völkerrecht
ISBN 978-3-662-58676-1 ISBN 978-3-662-58677-8 (eBook)
https://doi.org/10.1007/978-3-662-58677-8

This Springer imprint is published by the registered company Springer-Verlag GmbH, DE, part of Springer Nature.
The registered company address is: Heidelberger Platz 3, 14197 Berlin, Germany

Preface and Acknowledgments

Structural discrimination is increasingly being debated in different disciplines. International courts and other international actors, too, have started drawing attention to pre-existing social structures and inequalities when addressing and redressing human rights violations. However, so far, academic legal research has paid little attention to this gentle turn in international human rights law and practice. This study addresses this gap by providing a systematic analysis of how international (human rights) law responds to violence against women because of structural discrimination against them. More precisely, it analyzes whether the subjective dimension of the prohibition to discriminate may be used to combat structural discrimination through proceedings before international human rights courts.

This book was prepared as a PhD thesis during my time as a research associate at the law faculty of the University of Potsdam (Germany) and defended in March 2018. It considers legal developments, jurisdiction and literature that have been published until March 2017.

The study is the result of several years of research, adventure, personal challenges and human encounters. I therefore offer my gratitude to many colleagues, friends and family members.

I wish to express my sincere gratitude to my PhD supervisor Professor Andreas Zimmermann LL.M. (Harvard). He provided me with both great freedom and advice and was always open to discussions and new ideas. I also express my gratitude to Professor Beate Rudolf who accepted to be part of the jury as an expert in women's rights and discrimination. I would also like to thank Professor Francesco Francioni and Professor Nehal Bhuta at the European University Institute not only for mentoring me during my stay as a visiting researcher in 2013 but also for encouraging me to take a closer look at sexualized violence in armed conflicts. I also would like to thank Professor Maarit Jänterä-Jareborg who directed our research group at the Hague Academy of International Law in 2014 on 'Women's Right and the Elimination of Discrimination'. Our discussions were very inspiring and heavily influenced my thinking, as well as the approach taken in my thesis. I also extend my gratitude to the editors of the 'Black Series' of the Max-Planck-Institute for

Comparative Law and International Law: Professor Anne Peters LL.M. (Harvard) and Professor Armin von Bogdandy for accepting this thesis for publication.

Finally, I would like to thank all those who crossed my path during the years of writing this thesis. Special appreciation is offered to my friend and colleague Professor Jelena Bäumler for her enthusiasm and astute feedback. I am particularly grateful to my partner; my friends Mai-Anh and Hanne; my aunts Anne and Martine; and most of all, to my mother.

Berlin, Germany
October 2018

Elisabeth Veronika Henn

Contents

Abbreviations and Acronyms

ACHR	American Convention of Human Rights
ACHPR	African Charter on Human and Peoples' Rights
AP I, II	First (Second) Protocol Additional to the Geneva Conventions of 1949
Belém do Pará Convention	Inter-American Convention on the Prevention, Punishment, and Eradication of Violence against Women
CEDAW	UN Convention on the Elimination of All Forms of Discrimination against Women
CIA	Central Intelligence Agency
CoE	Council of Europe
CRPD	Convention on the Rights of Persons with Disabilities
(CR)SV	(Conflict-related) sexualized violence
CRC	Convention on the Rights of the Child
CSW	Commission on the Status of Women
DAW	Discrimination against women
DRC	Democratic Republic of the Congo
DSU	Dispute Settlement Understanding
ECHR	European Convention of Human Rights
ECtHR	European Court of Human Rights
ECV	European Convention on the Compensation of Victims of Violent Crimes
FRY	Former Republic of Yugoslavia
GR	General Recommendation
GC I–IV	Geneva Conventions of 1949
HRC	Human Rights Committee
HRL	Human Rights Law
IACtHR	Inter-American Court of Human Rights
IAComHR	Inter-American Commission on Human Rights
ICC	International Criminal Court

ICCPR	International Covenant on Civil and Political Rights
ICJ	International Court of Justice
ICL	International Criminal Law
ICPPED	International Convention for the Protection of All Persons from Enforced Disappearance
ICTY	International Criminal Tribunal for the Former Yugoslavia
ICTR	International Criminal Tribunal for Rwanda
IDP(s)	Internally Displaced Person(s)
IHL	International Humanitarian Law
IO	Intergovernmental Organization
Istanbul Convention	Council of Europe Convention on preventing and combating violence against women and domestic violence
MESECVI	Follow-Up Mechanism on the Implementation of the Convention of Belém do Pará
Refugee Convention	Convention relating to the Status of Refugees
OPCRCAC	Optional Protocol to the Convention on the Rights of the Child on the Involvement of Children in Armed Conflict
RPE	Rules of Procedure and Evidence (ICC)
UDHR	Universal Declaration of Human Rights
UNGA	General Assembly of the United Nations
UNHRC	Human Rights Committee of the United Nations
UNSC	Security Council of the United Nations
UNSG	Secretary General of the United Nations
VAW	Violence against women
VCLT	Vienna Convention on the Law of Treaties
WPS	Women, Peace and Security
wfr	With further references

Chapter 1
Introduction

A. Background of the Research and Subject Matter

Being more sensitive to pre-existing structures and inequalities when addressing and redressing human rights violations, international actors have started drawing attention to *structural discrimination*.[1] As a social phenomenon, structural discrimination against specific social groups is characterized by its omnipresence in all spheres of life, 'resulting in a situation where the prohibition of discrimination in any one of these spheres or, indeed in all of them, will not suffice to ensure effective equality'.[2] It occurs 'when the rules of a society's major institutions consistently produce disproportionately disadvantageous outcomes for the members of certain salient social groups and the production of such outcomes is unjust'.[3] It is mostly rooted in historically unequal power relations between members of different social groups and is unintentionally perpetuated by symbols, customs, sublimed assumptions of

[1]CERD, *General recommendation No. 34*, 11 October 2011, paras 6; IACtHR, *González v. Mexico (Cotton Field Case)*, Judgment (Preliminary Objection, Merits, Reparations, and Costs), 16 November 2009, para. 450; CESCR, *General Comment No. 20*, 02 July 2009, para. 39, referring to 'systemic discrimination'; CEDAW Committee: *General Recommendation No. 30 on women in conflict prevention, conflict, and post conflict situations*, 18 October 2013, paras 77, 79; *Report on Mexico produced by the Committee on the Elimination of Discrimination against Women under article 8 of the Optional Protocol to the Convention, and reply from the Government of Mexico*, 27 January 2005, para. 34; *Consideration of reports submitted by state parties under article 18 of the Convention on the Elimination of All Forms of Discrimination against Women*, 18 September 2006, para. 232; *Consideration of reports submitted by state parties under article 18 of the Convention*, 15 May 2014, para. 134; *List of issues and questions in relation to the combined seventh and eighth periodic reports of Spain*, 17 November 2014, para. 9.

[2]Schutter, *International human rights law*, 2014, p. 732.

[3]Altman, 'Discrimination', in Zalta, para. 2.3.

E. V. Henn, *International Human Rights Law and Structural Discrimination*, Beiträge zum ausländischen öffentlichen Recht und Völkerrecht, https://doi.org/10.1007/978-3-662-58677-8_1

subordination and dominance, and stereotypes, socio-political as well as economic structures. Thus, particularly women, people of color or African descent, Roma and people with disabilities, are likely to encounter structural discrimination.[4]

To give but some examples for the increasing awareness among international actors on structural discrimination, attention should be drawn to the UN Secretary General, the European Court of Human Rights (ECtHR) and Inter-American Court of Human Rights (IACtHR).

In 2014, the UN Secretary General issued a guidance note on reparation for victims of conflict-related sexualized violence. Referring to human rights provisions encompassing the right to an effective remedy, he urged States to establish administrative and judicial mechanisms that enable the enforcement of transformative reparations. Accordingly, such reparations should not 'reinstate or reinforce the *structural* conditions within society that uphold [sexualized violence] and beliefs and that inform [its] perpetration'.[5] Rather they should subvert *pre-existing inequalities and structures* such as gender stereotypes concerning female subordination, sexual entitlement, masculinity and constructions of gender, and sexual identity around power and domination.[6]

---

[4]Schutter, *International human rights law*, 2014, p. 733; Holtmaat, 'Article 5', in Rudolf/Freeman/Chinkin, 2012, p. 155; Thornberry, *The International Convention on the Elimination of All Forms of Racial Discrimination*, 2016, pp.116; CERD, *General recommendation No. 34*, 11 October 2011, paras 6, where the Committee establishes: 'Racism and structural discrimination against people of African descent, rooted in the infamous regime of slavery, are evident in the situations of inequality affecting them and reflected, inter alia, in the following domains: their grouping, together with indigenous peoples, among the poorest of the poor; their low rate of participation and representation in political and institutional decision-making processes; additional difficulties they face in access to and completion and quality of education, which results in the transmission of poverty from generation to generation; inequality in access to the labour market; limited social recognition and valuation of their ethnic and cultural diversity; and a disproportionate presence in prison populations. The Committee observes that overcoming the structural discrimination that affects people of African descent calls for the urgent adoption of special measures (affirmative action), as established in the International Convention on the Elimination of All Forms of Racial Discrimination (arts. 1, para. 4, and 2, para. 2).'

[5]Emphasis added. UNSG, *Reparations for Conflict-Related Sexual Violence*, August 1, 2014, p. 8.

[6]The UNSG held: 'Sexual violence often results from and perpetuates patterns of pre-existing structural subordination and discrimination for both men and women. For women, it is often rooted in beliefs about women's subordination and male sexual entitlement, combined with the disregard for the equal enjoyment of human rights by women. Sexual violence against men is also rooted in stereotypes about masculinity and constructions of gender and sexual identity around power and domination. These inequalities can also aggravate the consequences of the crime. Reparations should strive to have a transformative effect on these inequalities, rather than reinstate or reinforce the structural conditions within society that uphold such practices and beliefs and that inform the perpetration of sexual violence. Reparations have the potential to trigger important changes even if they alone cannot transform the root causes of conflict-related sexual violence or the structural conditions that made such violence possible', UNSG, *Reparations for Conflict-Related Sexual Violence*, 01 August 2014, pp. 1, 6. In 2015, the International Criminal Court took up this idea. When ordering the modalities of reparations, the Court held that reparations 'with a symbolic, preventative or transformative value, may also be appropriate'. ICC, *Prosecutor v. Thomas Lubanga Dyilo*, Appeals Chamber, Judgment on the Appeals against the 'Decision establishing

Moreover, on 29 January 2013, the European Court of Human Rights (ECtHR) ruled in *Horváth and Kiss v. Hungary* that the Hungarian educational system was discriminatory against Roma children. Like many Roma children in Hungary, the applicants had been misdiagnosed and thus assigned to a remedial, in fact segregated, school for children with special educational needs during their primary education. The applicants alleged that their placement in this special school amounted to racial discrimination in the enjoyment of their right to education. When ruling in the case, the Court not only considered statistics indicative of *indirect discrimination* against Roma children as its Grand Chamber had previously done in *DH v. Czech Republic*,[7] it also considered the systemic character of the problem, that is, the societal context of historically grown structures clearly putting the members of the Roma community at a disadvantage. When finding a violation of the applicants' rights, the Court established that because of their past history of discrimination and prejudice 'the State's margin of appreciation is substantially narrower and it must have very weighty reasons for the restrictions in question'.[8]

Finally, in *González v. Mexico* (Cotton Field case), a case concerning gender-based homicides of women, the Inter-American Court of Human Rights referred to reparation measures that

> (i) question and, by means of special measures, are able to modify, the status quo that causes and maintains violence against women and gender-based murders;
> (ii) have clearly led to progress in overcoming the unjustified legal, political, social, formal and factual inequalities that cause, promote or reproduce the factors of gender-based discrimination, and
> (iii) raise the awareness of public officials and society on the impact of the issue of discrimination against women in the public and private spheres.[9]

The UNSG's guidance note, *Horváth and Kiss v. Hungary* and the Cotton Field case are only a few examples indicative of an increasing awareness among international actors for the societal and structural background that has led to the entanglement of various forms of discrimination against specific groups.[10] At first glance, this contextualized and group-related approach is surprising because

the principles and procedures to be applied to reparations' of 7 August 2012 with amended order for reparations (Annex A) and public annexes 1 and 2, 03 March 2015, Annex A, para. 34.

[7]ECtHR, *DH v. Czech Republic* [GC], Judgment, 13 November 2007, para. 188, 209.

[8]ECtHR, *Horváth and Kiss v. Hungary*, Judgment, 29 January 2013, paras 128, 104-129.

[9]IACtHR, *González v. Mexico (Cotton Field Case)*, Judgment (Preliminary Objection, Merits, Reparations, and Costs), 16 November 2009, para. 495.

[10]See also CEDAW Committee: *General Recommendation No. 30 on women in conflict prevention, conflict, and post conflict situations*, 18 October 2013, para. 77; *Report on Mexico produced by the Committee on the Elimination of Discrimination against Women under article 8 of the Optional Protocol to the Convention, and reply from the Government of Mexico*, 27 January 2005, para. 34; *Consideration of reports submitted by state parties under article 18 of the Convention on the Elimination of All Forms of Discrimination against Women*, 18 September 2006, para. 232; *Consideration of reports submitted by state parties under article 18 of the Convention*, 15 May 2014, para. 134; *List of issues and questions in relation to the combined seventh and eighth periodic reports of Spain*, 17 November 2014, para. 9.

international human rights have primarily been conceptualized as individual rights of a specific right holder. However, when taking a closer look to group-specific human rights conventions and jurisprudence, it appears that for its effectiveness, the international human rights system requires and already offers, under certain circumstances, some solutions to systemic problems, thus adding an additional, contextualized perspective to the individual focus of human rights violation. For instance, on historically grown discrimination against women, the Council of Europe Convention on preventing and combating violence against women and domestic violence (Istanbul Convention) and the Inter-American Convention on the Prevention, Punishment and Eradication of Violence Against Women (Belém do Pará Convention), as well as the UN Convention on the Elimination of Discrimination against Women (CEDAW), address gender stereotypes and hierarchies as root causes for gender-based discrimination and violence, encouraging or obliging state parties to take general and special measures (affirmative actions).[11]

To date, academic legal research has paid little attention to the gentle turn in international human rights law and practice addressing structural discrimination.[12] The academic debate has largely focused on the political power of (mostly constitutional) courts and the judicialization of politics, that is, on whether courts should address 'core moral predicaments, public policy questions, and political controversies'[13] and on whether they are lacking legitimacy by doing so.[14] This debate continues to be very crucial.

Yet, international human rights courts and bodies do, in fact, consider structural causes of discrimination when ruling on State practice failing to comply with human rights standards. Thus, the question arises to what extent the existing international human rights system addresses and requires state parties to overcome structural discrimination. To deepen the legal discussion on structural discrimination, it appears appropriate to start with an examination of the distinct responses given to each group potentially affected by structural discrimination.[15]

---

[11]See below, Chap. 6 A.

[12]But see, Schutter, *International human rights law*, 2014, pp. 732; Thornberry, *The International Convention on the Elimination of All Forms of Racial Discrimination*, 2016, pp. 116; Smekal/Sipulova, 'DH v. Czech Republic Six Years Later', (2014) 32 *Neth. Q. Hum. Rts.*, analyzing the consequences of *DH v. Czech Republic* concerning Roma discrimination in the educative system of the respondent State.

[13]Hirschl, 'The Judicialization of Politics', in Whittington/Kelemen/Caldeira, 2008.

[14]For an overview, see Whittington/Kelemen/Caldeira (eds.), *The Oxford handbook of law and politics*, 2008. On the US American debate, see Silverstein, *Law's allure*, 2009. As pointed out by *Wendy Brown,* the trend of courts assuming both, a power-limiting function and a legislative one, may raise democratic concerns. According to her, this is close to 'governance by courts', which subverts democracy, Brown, 'We are all democrats now…', in Agamben et al., 2012, p. 60. See also Bogdandy/Venzke, *In wessen Namen?*, 2014, addressing this problem concerning international courts and suggesting some democratic solutions.

[15]It should be noted that while the (legal) denomination of these groups constructs dividing lines between groups of people, thereby suggesting clear group identities, it is reflective of existing power structures.

The following analysis focuses on discrimination against women and girls (hereafter women always include girls, too).[16] More precisely, the study focuses on violence against women[17] because its wide occurrence reveals and demonstrates structural discrimination against women. Today, it is internationally recognized that violence against women is 'a manifestation of historically unequal power relations between men and women, which have led to domination over and discrimination against women by men and to the prevention of the full advancement of women'.[18] Globally prevalent gender concepts such as weak and passive femininity and subordination, on the one hand, and masculine sexual entitlement and dominance, on the other hand, allow for gender-based violence not only within matrimony but also at the workplace, on the street or within the community.[19] Historical, social and economic structures of gender inequality, hierarchies and stereotypes are the precondition for, and causes of, violence against women. These structures are deeply rooted within each society. It is thus not astonishing that violence against women 'persists in every country in the world'.[20] It can result in disadvantages in all fields of

---

[16]As it is evident that the term 'women' includes girls, too, the CEDAW Committee noticed that the CEDAW not only applies to women, but also to girls, see CEDAW, *General Recommendation No. 28 on the core obligations of state parties under article 2 of the CEDAW*, 2010, para. 21.

[17]While focusing on violence against women may further stigmatize women (Kapur, 'Tragedy of Victimization Rhetoric', (2002) 15 *Harv. Hum. Rts. J.*), and reinforce discourses on weak feminity (Engle, 'The force of shame', in McGlynn/Munro, 2010) and whereas gender-specific policies risk to aggravate essentialisms and gender stereotypes (Ní Aoláin/O'Rourke/Swaine, 'Transforming Reparations for Conflict-Related Sexual Violence', (2015) *Harv. Hum. Rts. J.*, p. 112), applying a root causes-centred approach sensitive to structural discrimination against women 'intrinsically challenges aspects of everyday life that are taken for granted, and necessitates a shift of focus from a victimization-oriented approach to one of empowerment'. The United Nations Special Rapporteur on Violence against Women, *15 Years of the United Nations Special Rapporteur on Violence against Women, its causes and consequences*, 2009, p. 35.

[18]UNGA Res. 48/104, *Declaration on the Elimination of Violence against Women*, 20 December 1993, para. 6; Preamble of the 2011 Council of Europe Convention on preventing and combating violence against women and domestic violence (Istanbul Convention); Art. 6 and Preamble of the 1994 Inter-American Convention on the Prevention, Punishment and Eradication of Violence against Women (Convention of Belém do Pará). *Cf.* also UNSG, *In-Depth-Study on All Forms of Violence Against Women*, 2006, pp. 28; UNHRC, *Report of the Special Rapporteur on violence against women, its causes and consequences, Rashida Manjoo*, 02 May 2011, paras 40, 65; UN Women, Commission on the Status of Women, *Agreed Conclusions on the prevention and elimination of violence against women and girls 2013*, 15 March 2013, para. 10.

[19]The United Nations Special Rapporteur on Violence against Women, *15 Years of the United Nations Special Rapporteur on Violence against Women, its causes and consequences*, 2009, *passim.*

[20]UN Women, Commission on the Status of Women, *Agreed Conclusions on the prevention and elimination of violence against women and girls 2013*, 15 March 2013, para. 10. See also WHO et al., *Global and regional estimates of violence against women*, 2013; United Nations Statistics Division, *The World's Women 2015, Trends and Statistics*; for recent numbers on gender-based violence in EU member States, see European Union Agency for Fundamental Rights, *Violence against women*, March 2014.

a victim's life and thus influence her life course,[21] but it also affects the life of women that have not been aggressed so far.

B. Research Questions and Roadmap

Against this backdrop, the book focuses on State responsibility[22] for human rights violations regarding violence against women. It will be analyzed whether different international and regional human rights frameworks require from state parties to take a root cause-sensitive and transformative approach to violence against women as an expression and result of structural discrimination. As conflict-related sexualized violence against women is considered here to be the '*continuum*' of 'ordinary' gender-based violence of all kinds that occurs both in peacetime settings and during conflict,[23] attention will be payed to all kinds of gender-based violence, whether it occurs in peacetime or in conflict-related settings.

A State can be directly responsible for discrimination and violence against women (VAW) committed by its agents, which, then, constitutes a violation of *negative* human rights obligations. Within the context of structural discrimination and in settings such as violence against women, where the greater number of perpetrators are private actors whose acts cannot directly be attributed to a State, *positive* State obligations are however far more crucial. Accordingly, a State may have

---

[21]Wolff/De-Shalit, *Disadvantage*, 2007; Mortimer/Shanahan (eds.), *Handbook of the life course*, 2006; Nussbaum, *Women and human development*, 2000; Henn, 'Gender injustice, discrimination, and the CEDAW: A women's life course perspective', in Jänterä-Jareborg/Tigroudja, 2016.

[22]When reading this term, a general international lawyer might immediately think of the international liability *between States*. Regional human rights courts and other actors, however, have used this term to broaden 'the scope of substantive legal obligations' (Evans, 'State Responsibility and the European Convention on Human Rights', in Fitzmaurice/Sarooshi, 2004, p. 140). When doing so, they often refer to obligations on the primary level but also to the legal consequences of a violation as codified in Part Two of the ILC Articles on the Responsibility of States for Internationally Wrongful Acts. For example, the ECtHR held in a case relating to lethal domestic violence that '[w]hile the Court cannot conclude with certainty that matters would have turned out differently and that the killing would not have occurred if the authorities had acted otherwise, it reiterates that a failure to take reasonable measures which could have had a real prospect of altering the outcome or mitigating the harm is sufficient to engage the responsibility of the State'. ECtHR, *Opuz v. Turkey*, Judgment, 09 June 2009, para. 136. For the IACtHR, see IACtHR, *González v. Mexico (Cotton Field Case)*, Judgment (Preliminary Objection, Merits, Reparations, and Costs), 16 November 2009, para. 172, where the Court held that '[a]n illegal act which violates human rights and which is initially not directly imputable to a State (e.g., because it is the act of a private person or because the person responsible has not been identified) can lead to international responsibility of the State, not because of an act itself, but because of the lack of due diligence to prevent the violation or to respond to it as required by the Convention'.

[23]Rehn/Sirleaf, *Women, war and peace*, 2002, p.10; Cockburn, 'The continuum of violence: a gender perspective on war and peace', in Giles/Hyndman, 2004; UNHRC, *Report of the Special Rapporteur on violence against women, its causes and consequences*, 13 May 2013, para. 63.

to generally prevent human rights-infringing settings and to protect specific individuals against abuses. Moreover, States may also be obliged to progressively modify legal, administrative or societal structures and to weaken the effect of disadvantaging societal institutions[24] by special measures and affirmative actions[25] and otherwise.

The question therefore arises whether and to what extent human rights provisions require from States to address structural discrimination, and, more precisely, gender hierarchies and stereotypes as root causes for gender-based violence. To answer this question, the book analyzes whether international human rights law requires from state parties pursuing a root cause-sensitive and transformative approach to structural discrimination against women in general, and to prevention, protection and reparation of violence against women in particular; whether such structural obligations are enforceable through individual complaints; whether international courts and (quasi)judicial bodies have suitable tools for addressing the systemic discrimination and occurrence of violence against women and its underlying root causes; and the limits to a transformative approach.

These questions will be addressed, first by examining the *primary obligations* of States to respect, protect and fulfill human rights concerning violence against women. Secondly, largely focusing on the practice of the European and Inter-American Courts of Human Rights (ECtHR and IACtHR), it analyzes the transformative potential of *secondary obligations* with regard to violence against women.[26]

[24] Shelton/Gould, 'Positive and Negative Obligations', in Shelton, 2010, p. 565; Chinkin, 'Addressing violence against women in the Commonwealth within states' obligations under international law', (2014) 40 *Commonwealth Law Bulletin*, p. 479.

[25] Schutter, *International human rights law*, 2014, pp. 733; Thornberry, *The International Convention on the Elimination of All Forms of Racial Discrimination*, 2016, pp. 116.

[26] When referring to 'primary' and 'secondary' human rights obligations, reference is made to the category of 'primary and secondary rules'. Primary rules are substantive provisions such as human rights that may be encompassed by both international treaties and customary law. Whether an act must be considered a breach of a primary rule depends on the specific content of the rule and of the specific circumstances of the case. (See Crawford, 'State Responsibility', in Wolfrum, 2012, para. 2.) Secondary rules provide for the legal consequences of the breach of a primary duty. This categorization is known from continental jurisprudence (Ross, *On law and justice*, 2009, para. 45) and similarly suggested by H.A.L. Hart's concept of law (Hart, *The concept of law*, 2012; see also Crawford, *State responsibility*, 2013, p. 64). International law has incorporated this dual categorization, see ILC Articles on the Responsibility of States for Internationally Wrongful Acts (ILC Articles), according to which a State's breach of a primary duty owed to another state gives rise to responsibility (ILC, *Draft articles on Responsibility of States for Internationally Wrongful Acts with commentaries*, 2001, General Commentary, p. 31). On secondary-level obligations under treaty law (on international customary law, see Echeverria, 'Do victims of torture and other serious human rights violations have an independent and enforceable right to reparation?', (2012) 16 *The International Journal of Human Rights*, pp. 702) some human rights conventions foresee a monitoring body endowed with the capacity to award reparations, e.g. Arts 41 ECHR and 63 ACHR. These provisions are *lex specialis* to the rules codified in the ILC Articles, see Crawford (ed.), *The ILC Draft Articles on Responsibility of States for Internationally Wrongful Acts*, Art. 55, p. 140).

The analysis proceeds as follows. Part I sets the analytical framework. Chapter 2 introduces the basic terms and international legal concepts on violence against women as a form of discrimination. Based on different approaches taken to causes of gender-based and conflict-related violence, it explains why there is a need for a transformative approach sensitive to the root causes of gender-based violence, and thus structural discrimination.

Chapter 3 explores the international legal framework applicable to State responsibility for gender-based violence against women. This encompasses international humanitarian law (IHL) and human rights law (HRL).

Part II analyzes how human rights obligations both at the primary and secondary level respond to violence against women as an expression of structural discrimination. Chapter 4 draws on the normative basis and theoretical distinction of positive obligations.

Chapter 5 explores on the questions, firstly, when positive obligations apply and, secondly, to what extent a State has obligations to act. It therefore particularly analyzes recent jurisprudence of the ECtHR, the IACtHR and the ICJ and, simultaneously, further develops human rights theory of positive obligations. Eventually, this chapter draws on possible factors required to establish a violation of positive obligations.

Chapter 6 categorizes potential measures to be taken for a State to comply with its positive obligations. Drawing on existing primary obligations under CEDAW, the Istanbul and the Belém do Pará Conventions, this chapter distinguishes between short-term measures, on the one hand, and long-term measures that address the root causes, on the other hand. It then discusses the content of positive human rights obligations under customary law.

Chapter 7 explores whether the practice of the ECtHR and the ACtHR on secondary obligations or otherwise has the potential to address the root causes of gender-based violence. It first draws on the international plea for transformative reparation to victims of human rights violations and international crimes. It then explores the distinct concepts of victim/injured party before the Courts. The chapter then analyzes the European and Inter-American practice both concerning their transformative potential and limits as well as their theoretical embedding.

C. On the Sources of Law Used and the Approach Taken

To analyze whether and to what extent the international legal framework foresees legal responses as to taking a root cause-sensitive and transformative approach to violence against women as an expression of structural discrimination, this study examines the different obligations encompassed by international and regional human rights treaties prohibiting discrimination, in general, or against women, in particular. Attention is paid to CEDAW, ACHR, ECHR, the above-mentioned Belém do Pará and Istanbul Conventions, as well as to a series of pertinent soft law instruments. The

African human rights system including the Maputo Protocol, as well as other treaties such as the CAT, ICCPR, ICERD and the CRC, is only mentioned fragmentarily.

Moreover, taking a comparative perspective, the study analyzes relevant jurisprudence, concluding observations and general recommendations of the IACtHR, the ECtHR, the ICJ and the CEDAW Committee. In this context, it should be noted that while the binding force of international court decisions is limited to the parties of the case in question,[27] the content of these decisions is reflective of how the relevant (quasi-)judicial body interprets the treaty it has the competence to adjudicate upon. Therefore, in future cases, other contracting parties to a convention may find themselves to be bound by standards established in a judgment regarding a case they were no parties to. However, as international courts' decisions are subsidiary means for the determination of rules of law under Article 38 (d) ICJ Statute,[28] international courts may even and in fact do 'borrow' arguments from one other,[29] thereby adding 'to the legitimacy of [a] judgment'.[30] Thus, standards set and obligations found by one court may even be applied by another court.

---

[27] *Cf.*, e.g., Art. 59 ICJ-Statute; Art. 3 (2) third sentence DSU; Art. 46 (1) ECHR; Art. 68 ACHR.

[28] Art. 38 (1) (d) ICJ Statute holds that 'subject to the provisions of Article 59, judicial decisions [are] subsidiary means for the determination of rules of law.'

[29] Boyle/Chinkin, *The making of international law*, 2007, pp. 266, 297.

[30] Simma, 'Universality of International Law from the Perspective of a Practitioner', (2009) 20 *EJIL*, p. 279. They set precedents that exercise a 'semantical power' on the legal discourses, thereby generating and, eventually, stabilizing normative expectations, Bogdandy/Venzke, *In wessen Namen?*, 2014, pp. 20, 42–136, 150–161; Staton/Moore, 'Judicial power in domestic and international politics', (2011) 65 *International Organization*; Boyle/Chinkin, *The making of international law*, 2007, pp. 266, 297.

The practice of borrowing arguments has, however, to be distinguished from another practice of the ECtHR and the IACtHR: In particular with regard to the interpretation of non-discrimination, these courts have argued with treaties the respondent State was no party to (e.g., for the ECtHR, see ECtHR, *Glor v. Switzerland*, Judgment, 30 April 2009, para. 53. Here, the Court held that the Convention on the Rights of Persons with Disabilities expresses 'a European and worldwide consensus on the need to protect people with disabilities from discriminatory treatment'. However, the UNGA adopted this convention only after the relevant facts of the case took place. Additionally, the respondent State had not ratified this convention at the time of the judgment. In ECtHR, *Mazurek v. France*, Judgment, 01 February 2000, para. 49, the Court referred to the Convention on the Legal Status of Children born out of Wedlock as evidencing the 'great importance' attached to the equal legal treatment of these children. However, this convention had been ratified by one-third of the member States of the CoE and, most importantly, not by the respondent State; see also, Harris et al., 'The European Convention on Human Rights in Context', in Harris et al., 2014, p. 11. For the IACtHR, see, e.g., IACtHR, *Yakye Axa Indigenous Community v. Paraguay*, Judgment (Merits, Reparations and Costs), 17 June 2005, para. 126; IACtHR, *Tibi v. Ecuador*, Judgment (Preliminary Objections, Merits, Reparations and Costs), 07 September 2004, para. 144; IACtHR, *Gómez-Paquiyauri Brothers v. Peru*, Judgment (Merits, Reparations and Costs), 08 July 2004, para. 164; IACtHR, *'Street Children' (Villagrán-Morales et al.) v. Guatemala*, Judgment (Merits), 19 November 1999, paras 192–193). This approach raises serious concerns, as it is in conflict with the rule under Article 31 (3) (c) VCLT. Article 31 (3) (c) VCLT only allows considering 'any relevant rules of international law applicable in the relations between the parties'. Where a State is not party to a treaty, it should not be bound to its provisions by way of an international court's judgment. On 'systemic integration', see ILC, *Fragmentation of International Law*, 13 April 2006, pp. 206.

Part I
Analytical Scope and International Legal Framework

Chapter 2
Basic Terms and Concepts

This chapter aims at setting the agenda for the analysis of State responsibility under human rights law for violence against women as an expression of structural discrimination. It therefore discusses terminologies applied within the context of violence against women, theories on the causes of violence against women, as well as legal and philosophical concepts of discrimination and equality.

Different terminologies have been applied at the international level to address violence against women either exclusively as a human rights issue or jointly with other forms of violence as a security issue. This chapter therefore first explains the term 'gender-based violence' and the different approaches to sexual(ized) violence both in 'conflict-related' and non-conflict settings (A.).

Secondly, as the awareness for root causes of human rights violations significantly impacts the effectiveness of human rights protection policies, this chapter outlines the psycho-biological, political and sociological approaches that have been put forward to explain why violence against women occurs. Adopting sociological findings and the life course theory, it will be shown by an 'iceberg model' that human rights policies combating violence against women are more likely to succeed, if they account for the entanglement of violence against women with socio-political and economic inequalities and discrimination, gender stereotypes and hierarchization as root causes of violence against women (B.).

Finally, as violence against women has internationally been characterized as a form of gender-based *discrimination*, the chapter discusses the concepts of direct, indirect and structural discrimination. While discrimination and equality are often considered to constitute two sides of the same coin, the chapter reveals, by discussing formal, substantive and transformative equality, that this assumption is somewhat misleading. The traditional concepts of discrimination and equality fall short in addressing structurally discriminatory settings and feign to be neutral, being historically biased. The shortcomings of the traditional concepts have been

E. V. Henn, *International Human Rights Law and Structural Discrimination*, Beiträge zum ausländischen öffentlichen Recht und Völkerrecht,
https://doi.org/10.1007/978-3-662-58677-8_2

addressed by the CEDAW Committee, which has integrated the concepts of structural discrimination and transformative equality into its interpretation of CEDAW (C.).

A. International Definitions of 'Gender-Based Violence' and 'Sexual(ized) Violence'

International legal documents and actors use different terms when addressing violence against women. While 'sexual(ized) violence' is often analyzed through the lens of a war-peace dichotomy and includes male victims, 'gender-based violence' refers to all kinds of violence against women that is committed on grounds of their gender.

I. Violence Against Women as 'Gender-Based Violence'[1]

The internationally established term 'gender-based violence' is used to refer to all kinds of violence directed against women because of their gender.[2] While intersex and transgender persons also experience violence because of their gender, the term gender-based violence as commonly used does not address this problem.[3]

There are different international legal definitions of 'gender-based violence' that, however, only differ slightly. Generally said, the term encompasses any kind of physical, psychological and sexualized violence whereby the perpetrator or ruling

[1]An earlier version of this section has been published in Henn, 'Gender injustice, discrimination, and the CEDAW: A women's life course perspective', in Jänterä-Jareborg/Tigroudja, 2016.

[2]Under the international legal framework, gender is understood as the socially constructed roles, behaviors, activities and attributes that a given society considers appropriate for the different sexes. These roles can change over time, place and life stage. While the term 'gender' traditionally is put in contrast with sex, this distinction is criticized by later theorists for being inadequate, see Cahill, *Rethinking rape*, 2001, p. 105, *passim*. For a critical analysis of the dichotomy of the categories man-woman in human rights law, see Elsuni, *Geschlechtsbezogene Gewalt und Menschenrechte*, 2011, pp. 139–152.

[3]When referring to women, the international concepts of 'gender-based violence' assumes a binary and heteronormative sex system. This analytical scope thus excludes not only male victims but also intersex persons as well as people whose mode of life differs from the hetero-normative standard and respective expectations towards gender roles but who, too, experience gender-based violence. Indeed, the international legal discourse by and large operates within a binary sex system consisting of 'women' and 'men' only. Hence, the focus of 'gender-based violence' on female victims may not only be because of gender-based violence affects 'women' in number more than 'men'. From a theoretical perspective, such an approach can also be understood as the very construction and/or perpetuation of existing social power structures and hierarchies. For details, see Elsuni, *Geschlechtsbezogene Gewalt und Menschenrechte*, 2011, pp. 140, 237, *passim*.

institution intentionally, traditionally or subliminally acts because of the persons perceived or ascribed sexuality or gender.

1. International Definitions

In 1992, the Committee of the UN Convention on the Elimination of Discrimination against Women (hereafter CEDAW Committee) defined gender-based violence as

> violence that is directed against a woman because she is a woman or that affects women disproportionately.[4] It includes acts that inflict physical, mental or sexual harm or suffering, threats of such acts, coercion and other deprivations of liberty. [In the Committee's understanding, gender-based violence] impairs or nullifies the enjoyment by women of human rights and fundamental freedoms under general international law or under human rights conventions [and constitutes] discrimination within the meaning of Article 1 [CEDAW].[5]

Latter definitions merely added some aspects. While the definition adopted by the UNGA is nearly identical to the definition suggested by the CEDAW Committee,[6] the definition under the above-mentioned Belém do Pará Convention, which entered into force in 1995, additionally recalls that this type of violence occurs both in the public and in the private sphere.[7] Nearly two decades later, the Istanbul Convention further broadened the understanding of gender-based violence to 'all acts of gender-based violence that result in, or are likely to result in, physical, sexual, psychological or economic harm or suffering'.[8]

2. Scenarios of Violence Against Women

Gender-based violence directed against women encompasses physical, psychological and sexual violence that occurs in the family, within the community or is committed or condoned by State actors. It includes battery, (marital) rape and incest; forced and organized marriage; honor crimes; female infanticide and sex selective abortion[9]; sterilization and female genital mutilation and other traditional practices harmful to women; non-spousal violence and violence related to exploitation; intimidation and harassment on the street, at work, in educational institutions and

---

[4]See WHO et al., *Global and regional estimates of violence against women*, 2013; Stark/Ager, 'A systematic review of prevalence studies of gender-based violence in complex emergencies', (2011) 12 *Trauma, Violence, & Abuse*; United Nations Statistics Division, *The World's Women 2015, Trends and Statistics*, pp. 142.

[5]CEDAW, *General Recommendation 19*, 1992, paras 6, 7.

[6]UNGA Res. 48/104, *Declaration on the Elimination of Violence against Women*, 20 December 1993; see also Chinkin, 'Violence Against Women', in Rudolf/Freeman/Chinkin, 2012, at 453.

[7]Art. 1 Belém do Pará Convention.

[8]Emphasis added, Art. 3 (a) Istanbul Convention.

[9]Female selective abortion is a common practice in a significant number of States. On Asian trends, see Miller, 'Female-Selective Abortion in Asia', (2001) 103 *American Anthropologist*.

elsewhere; trafficking in women[10]; exploitation in prostitution and pornography; everyday sexism; but also practices such as witch hunting, acid throwing, stoning, female circumcision and dowry-related violence and death.[11]

II. Non-conflict and Conflict-Related Sexual(ized) Violence Against Women and Men

Before discussing the different concepts of sexual(ized) violence, it is important to have a look at the adjectives 'sexual' and 'sexualized'. The term 'sexualized violence' acknowledges that the actor of rape and similar crimes has the central (and sole) agency in the moment of abuse. In contrast, from an etymological standpoint, the term 'sexual violence' is only adequate if we consider rape and other forms of this type of violence to be *sexual* activities. In Western societies of the nineteenth (and twentieth) century, this view was widely held on rape exercised by a man upon a woman's body. Besides being considered a sexual activity (of the perpetrator), rape was considered an attack on the man's or family's property and on the woman's honor, but not on her sexuality.[12] Yet, an activity that is exercised in the presence of more than one person can only be *sexual* if it is a shared and common endeavor. Otherwise, this activity, the power thereby exercised and the harm that potentially ensues from it, are *sexualized,* abusing the victim's sexuality. Although views on this issue have changed in the last decades acknowledging—at least at the international level—that this form of violence cannot be a sexual activity, the misleading term *sexual* continues to be applied within the UN and by international courts.[13] This terminology may also be explained by early attempts to respond to rape and other forms of sexualized violence under international humanitarian law. The wording of this legal framework still reflects the old approach to women's non-sexuality but honor.[14] The legally fixed term notwithstanding, for etymological

---

[10]Inglis, 'Expanding International and National Protections Against Trafficking for Forced Labour Using a Human Rights Framework', (2001) 7 *Buff. Hum. Rts. L. Rev.*

[11]CEDAW, *General Recommendation 19*, 1992; UNSG, *In-Depth-Study on All Forms of Violence Against Women*, 2006; Chinkin, 'Violence Against Women', in Rudolf/Freeman/Chinkin, 2012, pp. 454–462.

[12]For a legal analysis of the perception of rape in the nineteenth century, see Inal, *Looting and rape in wartime*, 2013, p. 77.

[13]See, e.g., IACtHR: In a context of massive lethal violence against women in Mexico (femicide), the Court considered that sexualized violence 'involves acts of a *sexual* nature, committed against a person without their consent, and that in addition to the physical invasion of the human body, they may include acts which do not involve penetration or even any physical context'. IACtHR, *Rosendo Cantú y otra v. Mexico*, Judgment, 31 August 2010, para. 109, emphasis added. See also IACtHR, *Contreas and others v. El Salvador*, Judgment (Merits, Reparations and Costs), 31 August 2011, para. 101.

[14]Inal, *Looting and rape in wartime*, 2013, *passim.*

reasons the term 'sexualized violence' will be used hereafter. It neither implies a difference in facts nor in its legal assessment from acts and situations described by the term 'sexual violence'.

1. Sexualized Violence Under the WHO

In its World report on violence and health of 2002, the World Health Organization (WHO) issued a definition of sexualized violence which reflects the scope and health consequences of sexualized violence against women and men. The framework does not mention violence directed against intersexual and transgender persons, notwithstanding that these groups are highly affected by such acts, too.

According to the WHO, sexualized violence is 'any act, attempt to obtain a sexual act, unwanted sexual comments or advances, or acts to traffic, or otherwise directed against a person's sexuality using coercion, by any person regardless of their relationship with the victim, in any setting'.[15] This definition encompasses a range of offenses, including a completed coercive or non-consensual sexual intercourse, an attempted non-consensual sex act, abusive sexual contact and non-contact sexual abuse such as threatened sexual violence, verbal sexual harassment,[16] which may occur in the 'private' and 'public' sphere both in peacetime and during armed conflicts.

2. Conflict-Related Sexualized Violence

In contrast to 'sexual violence' as understood by the WHO, the concept of 'conflict-related sexual violence' is much narrower. It is under its 'Women, Peace and Security' (WPS) agenda,[17] that the UN Security Council has specifically addressed 'conflict-related sexual violence' as an international peace and security issue. The WPS has gathered together 13 UN entities under the umbrella of 'UN Action against Sexual Violence in Conflict' (UN Action).

According to UN Action, 'conflict-related sexual violence' includes the following acts committed both against women and men[18]: rape, forced impregnation, forced

[15]WHO, *World Report on Violence and Health*, 2002, p. 149.

[16]Saltzman/Basile, *Sexual Violence Surveillance*, Centre for Disease Control and Prevention, Atlanta, Georgia et al., 2009.

[17]The 'Women, Peace and Security' (WPS) agenda refers to a group of non-binding UNSC resolutions, including resolutions 1325 (200), 1820 (2008), 1888 (2009), 1889 (2009), 1960 (2010), 2106 (2013) and 2122 (2013). The WPS aims *at inter* alia preventing and protecting against sexualized violence against women.

[18]While women are mostly concerned by these crimes, conflict-related sexualized abuse on male victims and intersex persons is more prevalent than it has been commonly acknowledged. Boys are at risk to be abused by soldiers, fighters and peacekeepers and to be kidnapped to serve as sex slaves in the abuser's household. Men and boys are at risk to suffer rape especially in prison or within the

sterilization, forced abortion, forced prostitution, sexual exploitation, trafficking, sexual enslavement, forced circumcision, castration, forced nudity or any other form of sexualized violence of comparable gravity mostly committed by non-partners and outside of the family.[19]

Being based on international criminal law, this framework only encompasses sexualized violence that constitutes a crime against humanity or a war crime. Put simply, it needs to be committed as part of a widespread or systematic attack directed against a civilian population, or it needs to occur 'in a conflict or post-conflict setting, [having] a direct or indirect causal link[20] with the conflict itself' and being committed by parties to the conflict. To constitute a war crime, 'the existence of conflict must [play] a substantial part in the perpetrator's ability or decision to commit [the crime], the manner in which it was committed or the purpose for which it was committed'.[21]

Thus, the thematic focus on conflict-related violence is limited to regions haunted by war or similar settings. In practice, this has entailed that most political efforts at the international level concentrate on the most blatant forms of sexualized violence. However, studies evidence that intimate partner violence, too, significantly increases in conflict and conflict-like settings[22] and violation by an intimate may be as

battalion, or are targeted for their sexual orientation. Men also run the risk of genital mutilation, enforced sterilization or of being forced to mutilate other detainees in public. In custody, it is likely that they are forced to display publicly fellatio or other sexual acts with other males, as it happened in Abu Ghraib or during the Balkan Wars. These humiliating acts may not only be deeply traumatizing, they also break with myths of strong masculinities. The emasculating effect increases the probability of post-traumatic sexualized aggression against others, particularly women. For details, see Mouthaan, 'Sexual Violence against Men and International Law', (2013) 13 *Int'l Crim. L. Rev;* Lewis, 'Unrecognized victims: Sexual violence against men in conflict settings under international law', (2009) 27 *Wis. Int'l L.J;* Sivakumaran, 'Sexual Violence Against Men in Armed Conflict', (2007) 18 *EJIL*; Christian et al., 'Sexual and gender based violence against men in the Democratic Republic of Congo', (2011) 27 *Medicine, conflict and survival*; Onyango/Hampanda, 'Social constructions of masculinity and male survivors of wartime sexual violence', (2011) 23 *International Journal of Sexual Health*; The World Bank, *World Development Report 2011*, 2011.

[19]Stop rape now—UN Action against Sexual Violence in Conflict, *Analytical and Conceptual Framing of Conflict-related Sexual Violence*, June 2011.

[20]A link to the conflict can be established by temporal, geographical and causal elements such as 'the perpetrator's status as a belligerent party; the proliferation and use of small arms and light weapons; the breakdown of law and order; the militarization of sites of daily activity such as fuel and water collection; cross-border consequences such as displacement, trafficking or economic disruption; the (sometimes deliberate) spread of HIV; and the targeting of ethnic, sectarian or other minorities or of populations in contested territory affording an economic, military or political advantage, including in violation of a ceasefire agreement'.

[21]ICTY, *Kunarac, Kovač and Vuković*, Appeals Chamber, Judgment, 12 June 2002, para. 58. Stop rape now—UN Action against Sexual Violence in Conflict, *Analytical and Conceptual Framing of Conflict-related Sexual Violence*, June 2011.

[22]Stark/Ager, 'A systematic review of prevalence studies of gender-based violence in complex emergencies', (2011) 12 *Trauma, Violence, & Abuse*, pp. 130–132.

devastating as violation by an unknown perpetrator.[23] Whether used in peacetime or during war, it serves as a humiliating weapon of demoralization.[24] By focusing on conflict-related sexualized violence, the international debates and respective policies run the risk to lose sight for the wider structurally discriminatory context of gender-based violence. This is particularly problematic, because domestic approaches, too, have tended to be largely limited to *re*-acting to gender-based violence.[25]

III. Conclusion: Gender-Based and Sexualized Violence

The different terms currently used at the international level are reflective of parochial strategies to combat violence against women. The term (conflict-related) sexualized violence focuses on the most blatant forms of violence committed against both women and men. This concept risks to concentrate international and domestic efforts to combat sexualized violence only, thereby ignoring the root causes for gender-specific violence more generally. In turn, the term gender-based violence is used to refer to violence committed against women only, thereby excluding intersex and transgender persons who also experience violence because of their non-conform gender. Hereafter, the term 'violence against women' refers to all kind of gender-based violence directed against women.

B. Causes of Violence Against Women

A common feature of today's human rights discourse are root causes.[26] If root causes are explored, acknowledged and integrated into human rights protection policies, the argument goes, their prospect of being successful and effective in preventing human rights abuses increases significantly. In fact, this also holds true for violence against women.

This section therefore explores the different individualistic, political and sociological approaches that try to explain the occurrence of gender-based violence both in conflict-related and in non-conflict-related settings. As will be seen, they well

---

[23]McWilliams/Ni Aolain, '"There is a War Going on You Know": Addressing the Complexity of Violence against Women in Conflicted and Post Conflict Societies', (2013) 1 *Transitional Justice Review*, p. 12.

[24]McWilliams/Ni Aolain, '"There is a War Going on You Know": Addressing the Complexity of Violence against Women in Conflicted and Post Conflict Societies', (2013) 1 *Transitional Justice Review*, p. 12.

[25]UNCHR, *Integration of the human rights of women and the gender perspective*, 20 January 2006, Summery and para. 46; UN Department of Social and Economic Affairs—Division for the Advancement of Women, *Handbook for legislation on violence against women*, 2010.

[26]Marks, 'Human rights and root causes', (2011) 74 *The Modern Law Review*.

reflect a common problem of today's discussions on human rights violations. As *Susan Marks* put it: 'In the first place, the investigation of causes is halted too soon. Secondly, effects are treated as though they were causes. And thirdly, causes are identified, only to be set aside.'[27]

I. Individual Reasons

Drawing from biological and psychological theories, individualistic approaches focus on the individual circumstances of the perpetrator.[28] Applying a (most questionable)[29] naturalistic view that relies on the 'objectivity' of biology and anatomy, some approaches postulate, for example, that men are more likely to display (sexualized) violent behavior, *inter alia*, because of their increased level of testosterone. Until the 1970s, it was even held that men qua men are able to be rapist and women qua women are 'rapable' because of their biologic anatomy.[30]

II. Political Goals in Conflict Settings

On conflict-related settings, different political factors and goals have been said to contribute to the increase or decrease of sexualized violence.[31] Accordingly, sexualized violence has been observed to increase simultaneously with the militarization and the proliferation of weapons.[32] Furthermore, it has been observed that sexualized violence may also be used as an instrument of genocide and a tactic of war to dominate and to relocate ethnic groups. It is not only an attack on the individual, but serves to destabilize and humiliate the collective.[33] Offenders may also pursue masculinist and/or nationalistic goals if their acts are directed against women in particular.[34] When female rape is perceived as an attack on the family's and the

[27]Marks, 'Human rights and root causes', (2011) 74 *The Modern Law Review*, p. 70.

[28]UNHRC, *Report of the Special Rapporteur on violence against women, its causes and consequences, Rashida Manjoo*, 02 May 2011, para. 33. For psychological models, see Ward/Polaschek/Beech, *Theories of Sexual Offending*, 2006.

[29]See a detection and falsification of naturalistic arguments, Cahill, *Rethinking rape*, 2001, pp. 22.

[30]*Cf.* Cahill, *Rethinking rape*, 2001, p. 22.

[31]Wood, 'Rape During War is Not Inevitable', in Bergsmo/Skre/Wood, 2012.

[32]Rehn/Sirleaf, *Women, war and peace*, 2002, p. 11.

[33]Unsurprisingly, we often find historical expressions such as 'The rape of Nanking', 'The rape of Russia' or 'The rape of Iraq', see Inal, *Looting and rape in wartime*, 2013, p. 222, fn. 9.

[34]Buss, 'Rethinking "Rape as a Weapon of War"', (2009) 17 *Feminist Legal Studies*, pp. 148–149 wfr; see also Rubio-Marín, 'Gender and Collective Reparation in the Aftermath of Conflict and Political Repression', in Rubio-Marín, 2009, pp. 389 f.

husband's honor, reputation and property,[35] sexual offending may constitute a meta-communication between the male enemies. The conquering soldiers may 'communicate the (enduring) political power of the perpetrator over the victim'[36] and remind the defeated group of the victory. Raping of women is also perceived as a 'spoils of war'[37] for the male vanquishers.[38] All these acts can function as a means for territorial, cultural or security control.

However, by describing potential political motives of 'conflict-related' violence *stricto sensu*, these approaches focus on the *functions* that sexualized violence performs in conflicts. They thus question this kind of violence but fail to direct their attention on *why* this specific kind of violence is conceivable. They ignore the circumstances that systematically cause and sustain aggressive 'male' behavior and 'female vulnerabilities'.

III. Societal Factors

In 2006, an expert commission at the UN level identified risk factors that have an impact on the occurrence of violence against women. Composed by more than 100 experts from all continents, the commission identified four main factors: the use of violence in conflict resolution on the family, community and State level; legal doctrines protecting the privacy of the home and family; State inaction to comply with human rights obligations towards women; and individual risk factors that, in my view, appear to be the result of structural inequalities based on the intersection of discriminatory grounds of gender, race, ethnicity, social and economic status, nationality, immigrant status, disabilities and sexual orientation.[39]

While the first three factors, that is, the use of violence in conflict resolution, the private-public dichotomy and State inaction, evidently play a role in the occurrence of violence against women, it appears that here again effects have been treated as though they were causes. The question arises why a society falls back on violence as

[35]Rubio-Marín, 'Gender and Collective Reparation in the Aftermath of Conflict and Political Repression', in Rubio-Marín, 2009, p. 390. For a historical analysis, see Eriksson, *Defining rape*, 2011.

[36]Leatherman, *Sexual violence and armed conflict*, 2011, p. 47; see, also Rubio-Marín, 'Gender and Collective Reparation in the Aftermath of Conflict and Political Repression', in Rubio-Marín, 2009, p. 389; Walker, 'Gender and Violence in Focus', in Rubio-Marín, 2009; Brownmiller, *Against our will: Men, Women and Rape*, 1975, p. 38.

[37]Meron, 'Rape as a Crime under International Humanitarian Law', (1993) 87 *AJIL*; UNCHR, *Contemporary Forms of Slavery*, 06 June 2000, p. 6; Brownmiller, *Against our will: Men, Women and Rape*, 1975, p. 38.

[38]Askin, *War crimes against women*, 1997, p. 28; Elshtain, *Women and War*, 1987; UNCHR, *Action visant à encourager et développer davantage le respect des droits de l'homme et des libertés fondamentales et, notamment, question du programme et des méthodes de travail de la Commission*, 26 January 1998, para. 12.

[39]UNSG, *In-Depth-Study on All Forms of Violence Against Women*, 2006, paras 92-100.

a means of conflict resolution, why it upholds the 'private-public dichotomy' and why the State omits effective human rights policies in favor of women.

IV. Hierarchies–Gender Stereotypes–Discrimination–Violence: A Continuum

In contrast to earlier approaches, socio-philosophical researches on violence against women suggest to take a more holistic perspective. Accordingly, gender hierarchies and stereotypes, as well as structural inequalities, are at the roots of violence and discrimination against women.[40] Along these lines, it has internationally been acknowledged that social, religious, economic and cultural institutions and practices discriminatory against women perpetuate historical gender hierarchies which fuel the widespread occurrence and acceptance of multiple forms of physical, mental and structural violence against women.[41] Violence against women is thus the result of 'gender discrimination [that shapes] social, economic, cultural and political structures, rather than being independent of them'.[42] The creation and use of 'harmful' gender stereotypes, beliefs of women's inferiority, subordination and male dominance[43] become 'one of the causes and consequences of gender-based violence against women'.[44] They impair women's health, economic and social security, political participation and thus women's possibilities and life perspectives.[45]

---

[40]For some, see Bourdieu, *La domination masculine*, 2002; MacKinnon, 'Auf dem Weg zu einer neuen Theorie der Gleichheit', (1994) *KritV*, pp. 364; MacKinnon, *Women's lives, men's laws*, 2007, pp. 48; Young, *Justice and the politics of difference*, 1990 (2011); see also UNSG, *In-Depth-Study on All Forms of Violence Against Women*, 2006, pp. 28; UNHRC, *Report of the Special Rapporteur on violence against women, its causes and consequences, Rashida Manjoo*, 02 May 2011, paras 40, 65; UNHRC, *Report of the Special Rapporteur on violence against women, its causes and consequences, Rashida Manjoo*, 22 April 2010; UNHRC, *Report of the Special Rapporteur on violence against women, its causes and consequences*, 13 May 2013; Saris/Lofts, 'Reparation Programmes: A Gender Perspective', in Stephens/Ferstman/Goetz, 2009, p. 88.

[41]UNHRC, *Report of the Special Rapporteur on violence against women, its causes and consequences, Rashida Manjoo*, 02 May 2011, para. 35; UNGA Res. 48/104, *Declaration on the Elimination of Violence against Women*, 20 December 1993; UNSG, *In-Depth-Study on All Forms of Violence Against Women*, 2006, para. 30; The United Nations Special Rapporteur on Violence against Women, *15 Years of the United Nations Special Rapporteur on Violence against Women, its causes and consequences*, 2009, p. 34.

[42]The United Nations Special Rapporteur on Violence against Women, *15 Years of the United Nations Special Rapporteur on Violence against Women, its causes and consequences*, 2009, p. 34.

[43]On the concept of male dominance, see Bourdieu, *La domination masculine*, 2002; Attia/Köbsell/Prasad (eds.), *Dominanzkultur reloaded*, 2015.

[44]IACtHR, *González v. Mexico (Cotton Field Case)*, Judgment (Preliminary Objection, Merits, Reparations, and Costs), 16 November 2009, para. 401.

[45]UNSG, *In-Depth-Study on All Forms of Violence Against Women*, 2006, pp. 28; UN Women, Commission on the Status of Women, *Agreed Conclusions on the prevention and elimination of violence against women and girls 2013*, 15 March 2013, paras 19; UNHRC, *Report of the Special*

Before the backdrop of women being more likely to be structurally disadvantaged, it is not surprising that women's position worsens during economic and humanitarian crises.[46] It is quite evident that the blatant violence that women experience during war is not only the result of the conditions of conflict but directly linked to their general living conditions before the conflict.[47] Conversely, the excessive sexualized violence in conflict-related settings is the 'continuum' of any form of discrimination and violence against women in peacetime settings.[48]

1. Gender Injustice in a Nutshell: The Iceberg-Model Through a Life Course Perspective

Indeed, the structural interconnections between violence against women, gender-based discrimination in the social, economic, cultural, political and civil fields of life, as well as gender stereotypes and hierarchies as basic social institutions can be illustrated by an 'iceberg-model of gender injustice'. It consists of a three-layered pyramid, where gender stereotypes and hierarchization are at the ground level, discrimination against women (DAW) in all fields of life is at the second level and violence against women (VAW) is the tip of the pyramid. While this model can also apply to other forms of group-based discrimination, hereafter it shall illustrate the example of women.

Highly simplifying these interconnections, the iceberg-model does not aim at illustrating linear relations but at visualizing theses interconnections. It may facilitate the analysis of root causes and thus the making of policies that consider these interconnections. However, this model does not exempt us to specifically identify *context-specific causes* and connections for each State and region.[49] Mapping

Rapporteur on violence against women, its causes and consequences, 13 May 2013, paras 16; IACtHR, *Velásquez Paiz et al. v. Guatemala*, Judgment (Preliminary Objections, Merits, Reparations and Costs), 19 November 2015, para. 180.

[46]UN Women, Commission on the Status of Women, *Elimination and prevention of all forms of violence against women and girls*, 15 March 2013, para. 32.

[47]Rehn/Sirleaf, *Women, war and peace*, 2002, p. 10.

[48]Rehn/Sirleaf, *Women, war and peace*, 2002, p.10; Cockburn, 'The continuum of violence: a gender perspective on war and peace', in Giles/Hyndman, 2004; UNHRC, *Report of the Special Rapporteur on violence against women, its causes and consequences*, 13 May 2013, para. 63. But see, Kelly/Azuero Quijano, 'A Tale of Two Conflicts', in Bergsmo/Skre/Wood, 2012, pp. 487. The authors claim that the continuum approach cannot explain the occurrence of types of sexualized violence, particularly taboos such as incest and public rape, which did not exist before the conflict. However, they compare gender rape to non-gender-specific murder (p. 489) and refer to the lack of continuity claims concerning this crime to falsify this approach. It appears that the authors have a blind spot not having considered structural inequalities.

[49]The systematic collection, disaggregation (by gender, age and other characteristics), analysis and dissemination and use of data are for such an endeavor, see UN Women, Commission on the Status of Women, *Elimination and prevention of all forms of violence against women and girls*, 15 March 2013, paras 127.

context-specific causes is, although very challenging,[50] important for both preventing and repairing harm. As will be shown, a useful tool that allows for a context-specific analysis is the *life course perspective* which is increasingly used in social science.[51] This is because one discriminatory act may be 'corrosive' during the course of a person's life and thus affect all areas of life.[52] It can be a barrier to and may violate various human rights both at the moment of the violation and in the long run.[53] The earlier a violation of rights occurs, the more disadvantaged and more likely to encounter further discrimination and injustice she will be (Fig. 2.1).

2. Ground-Level of the Iceberg: Hierarchization and Stereotypes[54]

On the ground level of this pyramid-shaped iceberg, there are 'harmful'[55] gender stereotypes and social hierarchization that are at work from the very beginning of a woman's life. Gender stereotypes, which CEDAW considers to be

---

[50]Ní Aoláin/Haynes/Cahn, *On the Frontlines: Gender, War, and the Post-conflict Process*, 2011.

[51]To analyze inequalities, social injustice and discrimination of certain groups, it is increasingly recognized that applying the perspective of an entire life course and not of one specific point in time or area of life, thus considering critical life events and decisions taken at different stages of life, is a useful tool for developing appropriate policies. It facilitates the analysis of the inter-connections between different forms of discrimination and injustice. For details on the life course theory, Mortimer/Shanahan (eds.), *Handbook of the life course*, 2006. Applying the life course perspective, see, e.g., ILO, *Gender equality at the heart of decent work*, 2009, and the German's Government Report on the Equality of Women and Men: Bundesministerium für Familie Senioren Frauen und Jugend, *Neue Wege - Gleiche Chancen*, 16 June 2011, p. 39. According to the CEDAW Committee, CEDAW also reflects the life-cycle approach, CEDAW Committee, *General Recommendation No. 30 on women in conflict prevention, conflict, and post conflict situations*, 18 October 2013, para. 7.

[52]Wolff/De-Shalit, *Disadvantage*, 2007; Nussbaum, *Women and human development*, 2000; UNSG, *In-Depth-Study on All Forms of Violence Against Women*, 2006, paras 156.

[53]UNGA, *Violence against women, its causes and consequences*, 07 August 2014; for the impact of violence on economic and political rights, see UNHRC, *Accelerating efforts to eliminate all forms of violence against women*, 25 June 2014; Rashida Manjoo, at IAComHR, *Mesa Redonda: Violencia de género y reparaciones*, 27 October 2014, at minute 14:10; Manjoo, 'Violence against women as a barrier to the realisation of human rights and the effective exercise of citizenship', (2016) 112 *Feminist Review*.

[54]An earlier version of this text has been published in Henn, 'Gender injustice, discrimination, and the CEDAW: A women's life course perspective', in Jänterä-Jareborg/Tigroudja, 2016.

[55]In literature one often finds the term 'harmful gender stereotypes'. One might be tempted to ask which gender stereotypical assumption is 'harmful' and which is not and who, ultimately, has the sovereignty to decide upon the answer. I assume that nobody but the Real (Jacques Lacan) has the sovereignty over the interpretation on what is 'harmful'. Others may prefer to merely refer to the definition provided by Art. 5 (1) CEDAW which seems less loaded of value judgments but instead conceals social realities. Accordingly, gender stereotypes are 'prejudices and custom and all other practices which are based on the idea of the inferiority or the superiority *of either of the sexes* or stereotyped roles for men and women' (emphasis added).

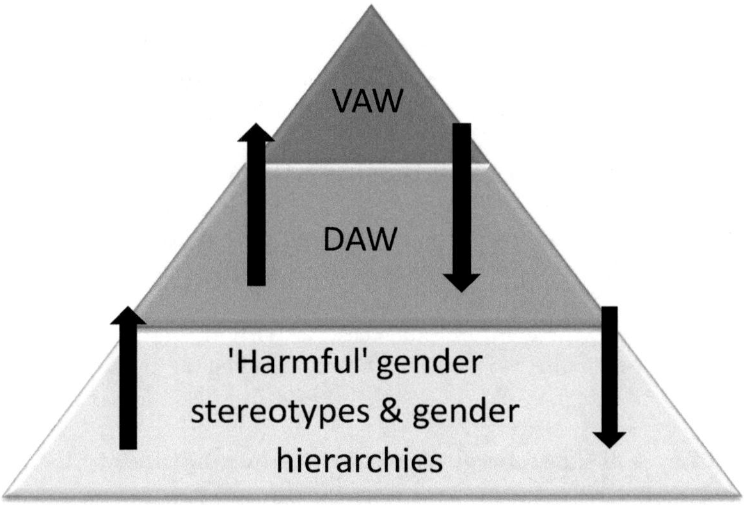

Fig. 2.1 The iceberg model of gender injustice (Henn) (An earlier version of this 'iceberg model' has been published in Henn, 'Gender injustice, discrimination, and the CEDAW: A women's life course perspective', in Jänterä-Jareborg/Tigroudja, 2016)

> prejudices and custom and all other practices which are based on the idea of the inferiority or the superiority of either of the sexes or stereotyped roles for men and women[56]

in particular concerning women's family role and body, restrict women's possibilities and life perspectives.

For example, it seems that *the* gender-stereotypical prejudice most women encounter concerns their (potential) maternal status and its structural degradation. They are discriminated against because they are or are not mothers or because they may have children in the future. If they do not want or cannot have children, this is questioned and they will be judged upon this fact or rejected. If there is still a chance that they will have children, this can affect the probability of her family to invest in her education or her employment prospects, prospects for promotion, wage increases and, consequently, a secure pension. If they have children they may be given less responsibility outside of the home (independently of whether they wish so or not), they may be referred to part-time jobs, be economically dependent on their partners or others, have less social security, pension and be at higher risk of poverty, especially in old age. In turn, when being dependant, persons tend to accept oppressive circumstances such as domestic violence.[57]

Another example of how gender stereotypes and beliefs of women's inferiority affect their life chances and capabilities is the occurrence of sexualized crimes and their ineffective prosecution or impunity. If, for example, victims of gender-based

[56]Art. 5 (1) CEDAW.

[57]For details on domestic violence, WHO, *Preventing intimate partner and sexual violence against women*, 2010; Walker, *The battered woman syndrome*, 2009.

crimes risk stigmatization by and ostracism of the family, community or society as a whole, they may—for their own security and to avoid further harm—prefer to keep absolutely silent about incidents of discrimination and sexualized violence that they have experienced. Such a setting increases the likelihood of impunity for offenders. Likewise, if a woman, having been aggressed, reports the crime to public authorities, she runs the risk of being humiliated, ignored, not believed, not heard, laughed at, ridiculed or sent away. In some countries, she may even be raped (again) at the police office. In the *Cotton Field case* before the IACtHR, for example, the mothers who reported the disappearance of their daughters were not taken seriously, virtually berated and accused for having led their daughters go outside the family home (in one case to work, and in the other case to party at night). Allegations were leveled against the victims who were accused of leading an 'indecent lifestyle'.[58]

3. Second Layer of the Iceberg: Discrimination in All Fields of Life[59]

The second level of the iceberg model consists of countless forms of discrimination against women (DAW) in the social, economic, political, civil and cultural fields of life. DAW finds various expressions depending on cultural, economic and political factors and can overlap with other grounds of discrimination such as race, ethnicity, status, nationality, age and ability. The various forms of discrimination can be illustrated through a *life course perspective*.

a. Childhood

The vast majority of cultures favor boys.[60] It is thus not surprising that the girl fetus and the girl child encounter various forms of discrimination. In India and China, for example, there is a worrisome practice concerning female selective abortion and female infanticide. If a girl child survives her birth, for the first 14 years, her major needs will be the same as those of her male counterparts: They will consist of adequate nutrition, physical, mental and emotional nurturing for a healthy development, and education. However, girls are at higher risk of malnutrition[61] and, on a

[58]See some misogynist responses given by officials, IACtHR, *Velásquez-Rodriguez v. Honduras*, Judgment (Merits), 29 July 1988, paras. 153, 198, 199, 202.

[59]This section has first been published with "The Hague Academy of International Law": Henn, 'Gender injustice, discrimination, and the CEDAW: A women's life course perspective', in Jänterä-Jareborg/Tigroudja, 2016. This contribution is the outcome of the Academy's Centre of Studies and Research.

[60]ILO, *Gender equality at the heart of decent work*, 2009, p. 43.

[61]Neumayer/Plümper, 'The gendered nature of natural disasters', (2007) 97 *Annals of the Association of American Geographers*, pp. 551–566; UNSG, *Report of the Secretary-General on the review of the implementation of the Beijing Declaration and Platform for Action and the outcome of the twenty-third special session and its contribution to shaping a gender perspective in the realization of the Millennium Development Goals*, 08 February 2010, para. 26.

global level, more likely to drop out of school, especially at secondary level.[62] Factors influencing school dropout are *inter alia* early marriage, the absence of secure and affordable means of transport, the girl child's contribution to economic activities and household, and precarious situations with limited resources where preference is given to boys. Causes underlying these factors can be ascribed to traditional gender stereotypes that are strengthened by custom, religion and culture.[63]

Along these lines, the CEDAW Committee has urged States to modify directly discriminatory laws banning teenager mothers but not fathers from secondary schools.[64] The Committee also criticized public measures such as the ban on religious dress (burqa, hijab and headscarf) in public,[65] the requirement of purchasing school uniforms and the levying of administrative fees as indirect discrimination against girls. These measures are more likely to affect girls because of custom and misogynist prejudices,[66] that is, beliefs or subliminal assumptions that men qua men are much better than women.[67] With such private and public behaviors and measures, it is not surprising that global female illiteracy is twice as high as male

---

[62]In 2006, two-third of the 187 countries for which data was available have achieved gender parity in primary education, UNSG, *Report of the Secretary-General on the review of the implementation of the Beijing Declaration and Platform for Action and the outcome of the twenty-third special session and its contribution to shaping a gender perspective in the realization of the Millennium Development Goals*, 08 February 2010, paras 45.

[63]Chamblee, 'Rhetoric or Rights: When Culture and Religion Bar Girls' Right to Education', (2003) 44 *Virginia Journal of International Law*.

[64]CEDAW CO Suriname, A/57/38, 27th Session (2002), para. 57.

[65]Both the prohibition and the obligation of wearing religious dresses also affect the right to participate in social and public life, Rudolf, 'Article 13', in Rudolf/Freeman/Chinkin, 2012, p. 348. See, however, the ECtHR Grand chamber judgment of 1 July 2014, *S.A.S. v. France*, where the court held that the French ban on wearing in public clothing designed to conceal one's face does not violate the accessory right to be free of discrimination under Article 14 ECHR together with Article 8 and 9 ECHR. See, at para. 161: 'The Court reiterates that a general policy or measure that has disproportionately prejudicial effects on a particular group may be considered discriminatory even where it is not specifically aimed at that group and there is no discriminatory intent (. . .). This is only the case, however, if such policy or measure has no "objective and reasonable" justification, that is, if it does not pursue a "legitimate aim" or if there is not a "reasonable relationship of proportionality" between the means employed and the aim sought to be realized (ibid., § 196). In the present case, while it may be considered that the ban imposed by the Law of 11 October 2010 has specific negative effects on the situation of Muslim women who, for religious reasons, wish to wear the full-face veil in public, this measure has an objective and reasonable justification for the reasons indicated previously (see paragraphs 144-159 above).'

[66]Banda, 'Article 10', in Rudolf/Freeman/Chinkin, 2012, pp. 273–274.

[67]*Cf.* the definition of misogynist, Cambridge Advanced Learner's Dictionary & Thesaurus, Cambridge University Press, available online, http://dictionary.cambridge.org/dictionary/english/misogynist.

illiteracy.[68] Even if discrimination against girls seems to be more prevalent in developing countries, it is also common in developed countries that girls do not find within their family or among their teachers the necessary emotional support to fully tap into their potential.

b. Adolescence and Youth

Depending on the level of industrialization of the country and the individual's social situation, the adolescence and youth (from 14 to 24 years) of girls and young women will be a period of further education and training, and the entrance in the labor market. Alternatively or simultaneously, it may be characterized by maternity, which often implies matrimony. Characteristic for this period are thus the need for access to sex-specific healthcare services, opportunities for higher education and the confinements of rights through and within matrimony and motherhood.

During the adolescence and youth, access to and knowledge about the existence of reproductive and sexual health services, enabling family planning and a development of a positive, safe, pleasurable and respectful approach to sexuality,[69] are particularly important for the adolescent girl's independent socioeconomic development and for combating the gender dimension of the HIV/AIDS pandemic and other sexually transmitted diseases.[70] Yet, information, access to healthcare and safety in this regard often remain out of reach, particularly to adolescent girls living in rural areas[71] or in weak financial positions. One of the most common discriminatory institutions, and one that attracts continual criticism by the Committee, are laws that criminalize abortion—regardless of the expectant mother's age or health, or the occurrence of rape—driving women into unsafe abortion and increasing the risk of maternal mortality and morbidity.[72]

Whether a young woman will be able to make use of her practical and intellectual capacities depends largely on the support she gets from public authorities and her social network, that is, her family, teachers and her husband, who need to acknowledge women's right to education and not to hold her back and/or discourage her.[73]

---

[68] UNSG, *Report of the Secretary-General on the review of the implementation of the Beijing Declaration and Platform for Action and the outcome of the twenty-third special session and its contribution to shaping a gender perspective in the realization of the Millennium Development Goals*, 08 February 2010, para. 69.

[69] WHO, Developing Sexual Health Programmes—A framework for action, (2010), http://www.who.int/reproductivehealth/publications/sexual_health/rhr_hrp_10_22/en/, accessed 30 January 2017.

[70] Cook/Undurraga, 'Article 12', in Rudolf/Freeman/Chinkin, 2012, p. 323; CEDAW, *General Recommendation No. 24 on article 12 of CEDAW*, 1999.

[71] Banda, 'Article 14', in Rudolf/Freeman/Chinkin, 2012, p. 366.

[72] Cook/Undurraga, 'Article 12', in Rudolf/Freeman/Chinkin, 2012, p. 322.

[73] For a US-American perspective on the role of the husband, see Slaughter, *Why Women can't still have it all*, 2012.

Yet, as to various gender stereotypes, (higher) education of girls and young women in fields other than the traditional ones often lacks acceptance, promotion and support. 'Female occupations' are often less well paid, so that a second salary may be required.[74] This in turn reinforces the need to marry.[75]

The vast majority of women marry at some point in their life. Even nowadays, custom, religious belief or ethnic origin can mean that women cannot always choose whether, when and whom they marry. They also may live within polygamist structures that are considered to be discriminatory against women under CEDAW.[76] Although the legal, social, economic and religious consequences of marriage and maternity have an enormous impact on women's life course, on their opportunities and thus their equality,[77] they often are insufficiently addressed by States and ignored by individuals, lacking information, the willingness, or courage to take them seriously.[78] If women do not marry, but live *de facto* in a union—which has become more common in developed countries—the non-regulation of *de facto* families and shared responsibilities may not only affect the child's rights but also impair the women's independence and social security, particularly where the relationship subsequently breaks down.[79]

As balancing reproductive work and paid work is a key factor in public and political participation, the early adulthood is the most formative period for women's prospects of participatory equality over the course of their life. As to lasting stereotypical concepts of women as 'homemakers',[80] it is not surprising that, notwithstanding the increased *de jure* equality on political rights, there is much to be improved when it comes to participatory equality in practice. To give an example, in 2009, women held only 18.8% of the world's seats in single/lower chambers of parliaments.[81] This is nothing compared to the necessary critical mass. Although it is said to require at least 30–35% of women for women to exercise an impact on the content of decisions and the political style,[82] one must seriously doubt whether in

[74]For examples and reports, see Banda, 'Article 14', in Rudolf/Freeman/Chinkin, 2012, pp. 260.

[75]Freeman, 'Article 16', in Rudolf/Freeman/Chinkin, 2012, p. 423.

[76]CEDAW, *General Recommendation No. 21*, 1994, paras 16, 27.

[77]CEDAW, *General Recommendation No. 21*, 1994, paras 25. Laws on the allocation of property after divorce may leave women homeless, see Banda, 'Article 14', in Rudolf/Freeman/Chinkin, 2012, p. 377.

[78]Freeman, 'Article 16', in Rudolf/Freeman/Chinkin, 2012, p. 411, wfr.

[79]CEDAW, *General Recommendation No. 29 on article 16 of CEDAW*, 26 February 2013, para. 30.

[80]Raday, 'Article 11', in Rudolf/Freeman/Chinkin, 2012, p. 304, emphasis added.

[81]UNSG, *Report of the Secretary-General on the review of the implementation of the Beijing Declaration and Platform for Action and the outcome of the twenty-third special session and its contribution to shaping a gender perspective in the realization of the Millennium Development Goals*, 08 February 2010, para. 218.

[82]CEDAW, *General recommendation No. 23 on women in political and public life*, para. 16.

practice such a quota is indeed enough to create an atmosphere that welcomes women's participation.

c. Adulthood

On a global level it can be stated that upon reaching adulthood, women become increasingly responsible for all chores related to household management, particularly child rearing and caretaking of other dependent members of the family (children, senior, impaired, etc.). Yet, 'their work in the family remains largely invisible, it is not accounted for in gross national products, and [not being valued in discourse and in practice] does not give women (economic) empowerment'.[83] At the same time, this is the age when employment opportunities might offer women the chance of economic independence and social empowerment, beyond or besides the woman's family status. Simply put, at this phase of her life, a woman is confronted with increased family responsibility, while also seeking to enhance her social and economic status in the world of employment and careers. This dichotomy characterizes female adulthood and the relevant forms of discrimination that women face in their professional lives.

On the right to work, on a global level women are confronted with both direct and indirect discrimination.[84] First, women receive a remuneration, which, both in the public and private sectors, often seems to be more an act of mercy on the part of the employer rather than recognition of the real value of their job. This is true not only in cases where women capitalize on their educational skills and abilities in the care sector (simply put, activities that actually cover essential needs of a community/society/State's sustainable existence). This also holds true when they capitalize on their ability and skills in sectors other than the traditionally 'female' ones or assume unpaid work in family enterprises.[85] Also outside the typical 'female sectors', women's right to work and equality is infringed by remunerations that are significantly less in comparison with male colleagues having the same position (gender pay gap).[86]

Second, besides the horizontal occupational segregation between women and men, the global labor market is also characterized by a vertical occupational segregation. Women are discriminated against on grounds of marriage, potential pregnancy and maternity and are denied jobs, promotion and further training because of

---

[83]Schöpp-Schilling, 'Impediments to Progress: The Formal Labor Market', in Schöpp-Schilling/Flinterman, 2007, p. 161. On the Western dilemma between the so-called unpaid 'women's work' and its economic valorization, see Wright, 'Women and the Global Economic Order', (1994) 10 *Am. U.J. Int'l L. & Pol'y*, p. 869; CEDAW, *General Recommendation No. 17.*

[84]See, Art. 11 (1), (2) CEDAW.

[85]CEDAW Committee, General Recommendation No. 16 on unpaid women workers in rural and urban family enterprises (1991).

[86]CEDAW Committee, General Recommendation No. 13 on equal remuneration for work of equal value (1989).

fears of parental responsibilities, which are said to only impede their working capacity and flexibility and not that of fathers. It is thus the traditional assumption of women being primarily responsible for the family that often hinders their participation and advancement to key roles in private companies, institutions and the public sector. In developed countries, this traditional approach to women's roles is unintentionally perpetuated by social regulations aiming to promote equality on the labor market and to reconcile family and working life.[87]

As to the structural and social framework, much more commonly than men, women may interrupt their careers for procreative work for certain periods of time and accept part-time jobs to take care of the family. The hourly wage of part-time jobs is often smaller. The foundation of a family is therefore the moment where women's socio-economic dependency on their partners and the risks of their career's stagnation increase significantly.[88] Yet, statistically men have a lower life expectation and the marriage or relationship may dissolute at some point. It is the woman who bears the economic burden of the consequences of the dissolution of family relations. Whereas men experience smaller or even minimal income losses after the dissolution of a relationship, women often experience a significant drop of revenue and an increased dependence on social welfare or private support.[89] This holds particularly true when a woman has carried the primary burden of household chores and only worked outside the home on a part-time basis, if at all, or turned down career opportunities to care for the children. When public social systems calculate the amount of benefits and organize their distribution based on the woman's partner or marital status, presuming the man to be the head of the household,[90] the risk of poverty increases even more. Therefore, women (and their children) depend more often than men from social networks beyond public structures, particularly in case of divorce, separation or death of their husband. The fear of dependence of others and poverty are factors among others that make women endure domestic violence.

With that framework in place, poverty of women is foreseeable. It is not surprising that global poverty is increasingly feminized.[91] Specific groups are more likely

[87]To give an example, in Germany, mechanisms like the long established spousal tax splitting (*Ehegattensplitting)*, see Wersig, *Der lange Schatten der Hausfrauenehe*, 2013, the child care subsidy (*Betreuungsgeld*) and even the parental leave (*Elternzeit*), as currently framed, incentivize the stereotype of mothers being the (primary) family caretakers. Depending on the provision's design, parental leave allows for a temporary family time, a reduced salary and the right to return to the same job. It exists *inter alia* in Canada, Norway, Sweden, Luxembourg, Czech Republic and Finland, Raday, 'Article 11', in Rudolf/Freeman/Chinkin, 2012, p. 301 wfr. However, if law does not provide sufficient incentives, men may seldom take this opportunity, also for want of acceptance on the labor market. CEDAW, *Concluding Observation of the Committee on the Elimination of Discrimination against Women, Germany*, 10 February 2009, paras. 27-30, 37-38.

[88]CEDAW, *General Recommendation No. 29 on article 16 of CEDAW*, 26 February 2013.

[89]CEDAW, *General Recommendation No. 29 on article 16 of CEDAW*, 26 February 2013, para. 4.

[90]Rudolf, 'Article 13', in Rudolf/Freeman/Chinkin, 2012, pp. 349–351.

[91]ILO, *Gender equality at the heart of decent work*, 2009, para. 58.

to be living in poverty, including female farmers, older women, rural women,[92] women working in the informal sector, single mothers, female migrant workers,[93] displaced and refugee women, and women with disabilities.[94] This is not only because of family obligations and lack of independent social protection but, in many cases, also because of the lack of access to land,[95] to property, inheritance and financial services[96] (often because of limited legal subjectivity),[97] and because of the structure of the global market[98] and a higher exposition to risks of volatile food prices, climate change and environmental destruction.

d. Senior Years +65

As disadvantages tend to accumulate over time, older women in particular face an accumulation of disadvantages. A range of factors, such as the quality of her education, the quantity of paid and unpaid work, the choice of husband and number of children, the occurrence of divorce or the partner's death, will determine whether a woman will have a secure pension and health security, or be affected by poverty during her senior years.[99] Having worked in the unpaid and/or informal realm such as in family enterprises,[100] the households (of others) or within agriculture[101] and thus not having contributed to a central scheme, older women depend on their

[92]Banda, 'Article 14', in Rudolf/Freeman/Chinkin, 2012.

[93]CEDAW Committee, General Recommendation No. 26 on women migrant worker (2008).

[94]UNSG, *Report of the Secretary-General on the review of the implementation of the Beijing Declaration and Platform for Action and the outcome of the twenty-third special session and its contribution to shaping a gender perspective in the realization of the Millennium Development Goals*, 08 February 2010, para. 18; CEDAW, *General Recommendation No. 18.*

[95]Banda, 'Article 14', in Rudolf/Freeman/Chinkin, 2012, p. 374.

[96]UNSG, *Report of the Secretary-General on the review of the implementation of the Beijing Declaration and Platform for Action and the outcome of the twenty-third special session and its contribution to shaping a gender perspective in the realization of the Millennium Development Goals*, 08 February 2010, para. 19; Manji, 'Eliminating Poverty? "Financial Inclusion", Access to Land, and Gender Equality in International Development', (2010) 73 *The Modern Law Review*; Rudolf, 'Article 13', in Rudolf/Freeman/Chinkin, 2012, pp. 351; Banda, 'Article 14', in Rudolf/Freeman/Chinkin, 2012, p. 374.

[97]Goonesekere, 'Article 15', in Rudolf/Freeman/Chinkin, 2012.

[98]Stewart, 'Who Do We Care About?', (2007) 58 *Northern Ireland Legal Quarterly*; Bedford, 'Gender and institutional strengthening', (2009) 15 *Contemporary Politics*; Pahuja, 'Trading Spaces: Locating Sites for Challenge Within International Trade Law', (2000) 14 *Australian Feminist Law Journal.*

[99]CEDAW Committee, General recommendation No. 27 on older women and their human rights, 2010.

[100]Banda, 'Article 14', in Rudolf/Freeman/Chinkin, 2012, p. 369 wfr.

[101]Banda, 'Article 14', in Rudolf/Freeman/Chinkin, 2012, p. 369.

husband's pension.[102] If she is divorced or separated or is a widow, she is at high risk of poverty. Where she has worked in the formal sector but taken time off and/or a part-time job to care for the family, a woman's pension in one country (linked to earnings during active life, not (adequately) accounting child caring and retirement being obligatory at a certain age) will often be smaller than that of her male compatriots. Women are also discriminated against when pension benefits are calculated based on life expectancy[103] and face, especially in developing countries, further disadvantages on becoming a widow.[104] Thus, elder women more often than men depend on the existence of private social networks.

4. Third Layer and Tip of the Iceberg: Gender-Based Violence

As shown through the life course perspective on gender-based discrimination, human rights violations because of hierarchizing structures have an effect on the distribution of power and resources. Hence, discrimination against women constitutes an additional condition of possibility for gender-based violence—as the third layer of the iceberg.

Acts of physical or mental violence may in first instance violate the rights to life, security and integrity, and to freedom of torture and other cruel, inhuman or degrading treatment or punishment. In the long run, this violence may also impair the enjoyment of social, economic, political and cultural rights of the one having been aggressed. However, as to the omnipresent threat of gender-based violence and its repercussions on its daily life, preventing most women from enjoying a life free from fear, all women are potentially concerned and affected.[105]

V. Conclusion: Need for a Transformative Approach to Violence Against Women

As shown, from a structural perspective, violence against women, gender stereotypes and hierarchies, and other forms of gender-based discrimination in all fields of life are very much entangled. Their structural interrelations can be illustrated by an

---

[102] In 2013, the global sex ratio was 62 to 100 women in the age group 80 or over, see UN Department of Economic and Social Affairs, World Population Ageing 2013, available under http://www.un.org/en/development/desa/population/publications/ageing/WorldPopulationAgeingReport2013.shtml, accessed 30 January 2017, p. 33.

[103] Raday, 'Article 11', in Rudolf/Freeman/Chinkin, 2012, p. 303; European Court of Justice, *Association Belge des Consommateurs Test-Achats and Others v. Conseil des ministres* (Grand Chamber), Judgment, 01 March 2011.

[104] Owen, 'Human rights of widows in developing countries', in Askin/Koenig, 1999-2001.

[105] Cahill, *Rethinking rape*, 2001, pp. 143; Tiroch, 'Violence against Women by Private Actors', (2010) 14 *Max Planck UNYB*, p. 368 wfr.

'iceberg-model of gender injustice'. Accordingly, immanent and direct, often sexualized violence against women, which in war time garnishes much media and UN attention, is merely the tip of a much larger iceberg and the continuum of structures existing in peacetime. Conflict-related sexualized violence can hardly be combated if it is conceptualized as an individual crime committed in conflict settings against an individual person only. Thus, the analytical scope of and ensuing policies aiming at directly combating 'conflict-related' sexualized violence as under the UN framework do not suffice to effectively prevent its occurrence.[106] It is a parochial approach that ignores pre-existing patterns of and masks the root causes for gender-based violence that already exist in 'non-conflict settings'. It condemns the endeavor to *eliminate* (as the title of CEDAW promises) discrimination against women, including gender-based violence, from the very outset.

Hence, the following analysis focuses on violence against women both in peacetime and conflict-related settings. To be effective, legal and administrative measures aiming at preventing discrimination and violence against women must consider the entanglement of violence and discrimination against women in all fields of life in the respective society, as well as gender-stereotypes and hierarchies. While international courts, when establishing a violation of the prohibition not to discriminate, usually limit their examination to one discriminatory ground (e.g. gender),[107] it is crucial to identify the intersection of gender-based discrimination with other discriminatory grounds such as skin color (race), age, class and disability.[108] Human rights policies of prevention, protection and reparation need to echo the identified root causes of gender-based violence against women and should include all areas and stages of life.[109]

---

[106]Olugbuo, 'Thematic Prosecution of International Sex Crimes and Stigmatisation of Victim and Survivors', in Bergsmo, 2012, pp. 131–133.

[107]Charlesworth, 'Concepts of Equality in International Law', in Huscroft/Rishworth, 2002, p. 144; Rubio-Marín/Möschel, 'Anti-Discrimination Exceptionalism', (2015) 26 *EJIL*.

[108]Chinkin, 'Violence Against Women', in Rudolf/Freeman/Chinkin, 2012, p. 464. A one-dimensional perspective entails that settings of *multidimensional* and *intersectional* discrimination are ignored. However, where one discriminatory ground intersects with other axes of discrimination, the harmful consequences of violence increase significantly. Crenshaw, 'Demarginalizing the intersection of race and sex', (1989) *Univ. Chicago Legal Forum*; Grabham et al. (eds.), *Intersectionality and beyond: Law, power and the politics of location*, 2008; Elsuni, *Geschlechtsbezogene Gewalt und Menschenrechte*, 2011, pp. 213.

[109]*Cf.* UNCHR, *Integration of the human rights of women and the gender perspective*, 20 January 2006, para. 16.

C. Violence Against Women as Discrimination: International Legal Approaches and Their Shortcomings

Having drawn on the social reasons for and root causes of violence against women, it is necessary to analyze how violence against women is addressed by human rights law. Until the late 1980s, violence against women had gone unnoticed within the leading international human rights discourse. During the 'UN Decade for Women', that is, the 1980s, it was rather perceived as a criminological and social evil.[110] As a human rights issue, it has first been addressed by national and international women's movements and later by international organizations and institutions.[111]

In 1992, the CEDAW Committee conceptualized violence against women as a form of *discrimination*.[112] Subsequently, this approach was widely adopted by international and regional human rights instruments and actors.[113] Accordingly, violence against women is discrimination, first, when it is committed by State actors. Moreover, violence perpetrated by non-State actors constitutes discrimination insofar as a State omits to take necessary measures to prevent and protect against it.[114] Along these lines, the HRC held that the principle of equality between women and men under Article 3 ICCPR[115] requires the particular protection of women against sexualized violence during armed conflicts.[116]

However, the question arises what exactly the concepts of discrimination and equality designate. Philosophical and political concepts of equality and discrimination have been discussed for thousands of years[117] and taken up by domestic and international law.[118] On violence against women, the underlying concepts of

[110]Chinkin, 'Violence Against Women', in Rudolf/Freeman/Chinkin, 2012, pp. 444.

[111]For details on how the perception of violence against women evoluted, see Chinkin, 'Violence Against Women', in Rudolf/Freeman/Chinkin, 2012, pp. 444; Antrobus, *The Global Women's Movement*, 2004, p. 91.

[112]CEDAW, *General Recommendation No. 19 on violence against women*, 1992, para. 6.

[113]UNGA Res. 48/104, *Declaration on the Elimination of Violence against Women*, 20 December 1993, para. 6; 1994 Inter-American Convention on the Prevention, Punishment and Eradication of Violence against Women (Convention of Belém do Pará); Fourth World Conference on Women, *Beijing Declaration and Platform for Action*, 1995; UNSG, *In-Depth-Study on All Forms of Violence Against Women*, 2006; UNHRC, *Report of the Special Rapporteur on violence against women, its causes and consequences, Rashida Manjoo*, 02 May 2011; 2011 Council of Europe Convention on preventing and combating violence against women and domestic violence (Istanbul Convention); UN Women, Commission on the Status of Women, *Agreed Conclusions on the prevention and elimination of violence against women and girls 2013*, 15 March 2013.

[114]For details, see Chaps. 4 and 5.

[115]Art. 3 ICCPR reads as follows: The state parties to the present Covenant undertake to ensure the equal right of men and women to the enjoyment of all civil and political rights set forth in the present Covenant.

[116]UN Human Rights Committee, *General Comment No. 28*, 29 March 2000.

[117]For an overview, Gosepath, 'Equality', in Zalta.

[118]Charlesworth, 'Concepts of Equality in International Law', in Huscroft/Rishworth, 2002; Schutter, *International human rights law*, 2014, pp. 635.

equality and discrimination significantly impact the way it is combated, prevented and, eventually, remedied.

The following section therefore discusses, first, the different legal and philosophical concepts of discrimination and equality. It will be shown that traditional legal approaches tend to be formalistic, while later structural and transformative concepts allow to better address the root causes of inequalities of specific social groups (I.). The section then focuses on the innovative, and indeed structural, approaches taken to discrimination and equality both by CEDAW and the CEDAW Committee (II.).

I. Concepts of Discrimination and Equality[119]

There are different terms used to refer to equality and discrimination both in philosophy and within the human rights context: direct, indirect and structural discrimination and formal, substantive and transformative equality. While equality and discrimination are often considered to constitute two sides of the same coin, discrimination implying absence of equality and equality implying absence of discrimination,[120] this section shows that this legal understanding is too simplistic.

1. Concepts of Discrimination

a. Legal Concepts: Direct and Indirect Discrimination

Within legal doctrine, discrimination can be *direct or indirect.* There is direct discrimination when laws, practices or social beliefs explicitly refer to sex or other discriminatory grounds as a basis for differential treatment. When direct discrimination is inscribed in law, it is also referred to as *de jure* discrimination. There is indirect discrimination when practices and laws seeming to apply neutral criteria *de facto* have a disproportionately disadvantageous impact on one particular group.[121] While explicitness and intention characterize the legal concept of direct discrimination, indirect discrimination generally lacks intention. If there is no legitimate aim and/or reasonable relation of proportionality between means and aim, the respective act is considered discriminatory.[122] However, the prohibition of discrimination does not outlaw differential treatment which aims at correcting 'factual inequalities' between different social groups. Rather, as the ECtHR held, 'in

[119]An earlier version of this section has been published in 2016: Henn, 'Gender injustice, discrimination, and the CEDAW: A women's life course perspective', in Jänterä-Jareborg/Tigroudja, 2016.

[120]Charlesworth, 'Concepts of Equality in International Law', in Huscroft/Rishworth, 2002, pp. 145, wfr; see also Nikolaidis, *The right to equality in European human rights law*, 2015, p. 29.

[121]Byrnes, 'Article 1', in Rudolf/Freeman/Chinkin, 2012, p. 65.

[122]Altman, 'Discrimination', in Zalta, paras 2.1-2.2.

certain circumstances a failure to attempt to correct inequality through different treatment may in itself'[123] constitute discrimination.

b. Structural Discrimination: Contextualized Perspective for Effective Anti-discrimination Policies

The legal concept of indirect discrimination allows for considering inequalities that are not the result of a specific intend but rather the outcome of whatever kind of effect concerning the members of a social group. It has therefore become common practice of the ECtHR to shift the burden of proof to the respondent State, where statistics provided by the claimant indicate a *prima facie* case of indirect discrimination.[124] Yet, the concept of indirect discrimination does, in principle, not address cross-cutting forms of discrimination against members of one specific group in various spheres of life, 'resulting in a situation where the prohibition of discrimination in any one of these spheres or, indeed in all of them, will not suffice to ensure effective equality'.[125] Rather, the concept of indirect discrimination has been limited to the establishment of an unequal outcome about one specific aspect.

Considering *de facto* structurally discriminatory circumstances can increase the effectiveness of human rights and the prohibition of discrimination against specific groups.[126] As said above, structural discrimination occurs 'when the rules of a society's major institutions consistently produce disproportionately disadvantageous outcomes for the members of certain salient social groups and the production of such outcomes is unjust'.[127] These institutions include 'family relations, property ownership and exchange, political powers and responsibilities'.[128] Structural discrimination thus refers to settings under which rights and opportunities, available to one group, are constantly less or not available to another group because of legal and social rules, attitudes and behavior of institutions and other societal structures.[129] Thus, in contrast to indirect discrimination, the concept of structural discrimination considers both a wider societal context of discrimination and a multitude of persons, who share a characteristic which is socially considered as relevant. To be sure, most cases that constitute structural discrimination are already encompassed by the current concept of indirect discrimination. However, the concept of structural discrimination

---

[123] *Cf.*, e.g., ECtHR, *Horváth and Kiss v. Hungary*, Judgment, 29 January 2013, para. 101.

[124] E.g., ECtHR, *DH v. Czech Republic* [GC], Judgment, 13 November 2007, paras 175-180; ECtHR, *Opuz v. Turkey*, Judgment, 09 June 2009, paras 189. On the use of statistics in cases of discrimination, see European Union Agency for Fundamental Rights, *Handbook on European non-discrimination law*, 2011, p. 129.

[125] Schutter, *International human rights law*, 2014, p. 732.

[126] *Cf.* Schutter, *International human rights law*, 2014, pp. 732.

[127] Altman, 'Discrimination', in Zalta, para. 2.3.

[128] Altman, 'Discrimination', in Zalta, para. 2.3; UNHRC, *Report of the Special Rapporteur on violence against women, its causes and consequences*, 13 May 2013, paras 26.

[129] Altman, 'Discrimination', in Zalta, para. 2.3.

can deepen the understanding for causes and entanglements of various forms of social injustice.

In fact, group-specific human rights conventions and some international legal actors increasingly take a contextualized approach, referring to structural discrimination.[130] To give but the example of CEDAW, its Article 5 incorporates the idea of structural discrimination[131] requiring from contracting parties to eliminate social structures such as prejudices and customs and all other practices 'which are based on the idea of the inferiority or the superiority of either of the sexes or on stereotyped roles for men and women'.[132] Along these lines, the CEDAW Committee has applied a structural perspective. When considering the obligations of States relating to conflict prevention and sexualized violence against women, for example, it explicitly called for attention to be drawn to 'the underlying structural sex and gender-based discrimination'.[133]

As will be shown,[134] it is in the context of positive human rights obligations that the awareness for and acknowledgement of the structural occurrence of disadvantages can positively influence the conceptualization of effective prevention and protection policies aiming at complying with primary obligations. Legislative and administrative practice may be able to transform societal structures that reinforce, perpetuate and enable discrimination against socially disadvantaged groups. On violence against women, integrating the concept of structural discrimination into its legal understanding as discrimination can help to unveil its connection with gender stereotypes, hierarchization and gender-based discrimination in the

---

[130]Introduction. Schutter, *International human rights law*, 2014, pp. 732 wfr; Thornberry, *The International Convention on the Elimination of All Forms of Racial Discrimination*, 2016, p. 116, *passim;* see also the references in Chap. 1.

[131]Holtmaat, 'Article 5', in Rudolf/Freeman/Chinkin, 2012, pp. 143.

[132]Holtmaat, 'Article 5', in Rudolf/Freeman/Chinkin, 2012, p. 143. Art. 5 reads as follows: state parties shall take all appropriate measures: (a) To modify the social and cultural patterns of conduct of men and women, with a view to achieving the elimination of prejudices and customary and all other practices which are based on the idea of the inferiority or the superiority of either of the sexes or on stereotyped roles for men and women; (b) To ensure that family education includes a proper understanding of maternity as a social function and the recognition of the common responsibility of men and women in the upbringing and development of their children, it being understood that the interest of the children is the primordial consideration in all cases.

[133]CEDAW Committee, *General Recommendation No. 30 on women in conflict prevention, conflict, and post conflict situations*, 18 October 2013, para. 77. See also CEDAW, *Report on Mexico produced by the Committee on the Elimination of Discrimination against Women under article 8 of the Optional Protocol to the Convention, and reply from the Government of Mexico*, 27 January 2005, para. 34; CEDAW, *Consideration of reports submitted by state parties under article 18 of the Convention on the Elimination of All Forms of Discrimination against Women*, 18 September 2006, para. 232; CEDAW, *Consideration of reports submitted by state parties under article 18 of the Convention*, 15 May 2014, para. 134; CEDAW, *List of issues and questions in relation to the combined seventh and eighth periodic reports of Spain*, 17 November 2014, para. 9; and the examples given in the introduction. See also CERD, *General recommendation No. 34*, 11 October 2011, paras 6.

[134]Chapters 6 and 7.

economic, social and procreative field. Finally, reparative and general measures as ordered by the IACtHR and taken by respondent States in the execution of a judgment of the ECtHR may be better conceptualized when considering a structural perspective.

2. Concepts of Equality

a. Legal Concepts: Formal and Substantive Equality

The term *formal equality* is generally used in law to refer to the Aristotelian notion of equality, which requires, on the one hand, that persons who are alike or similarly situated on a normatively relevant aspect are treated identically on this aspect.[135] On the other hand, the Aristotelian approach to equality allows for or even requires an unequal treatment of persons in proportion to their difference (*substantive equality*).[136] It follows therefrom that unequal treatment of equals or similarly situated persons or equal treatment of unequally situated persons requires an appropriate and 'objective' justification.[137] Unlike treatment is thus not automatically unlawful. To the contrary and depending on the circumstances, unequal treatment may even be mandatory and impose positive obligations if persons are found in different situations.[138]

Hence, equality means identical treatment of like persons (formal equality), on the one hand, and differential treatment of unlike persons (substantive equality), on the other hand. Whether persons are equally situated or not is established through the comparison of specific characteristics. As equality so understood requires a standard of comparison, there is always one privileged group or individual of reference to whom the other disadvantaged group or individual seeks to be equalized.[139]

Remarkably, this approach does not in principle indicate when a person's situation can be considered different from or equal to another, and, if considered different, to what extent the treatment should differ.[140] As *Cathrin MacKinnon* observed, the

[135]Byrnes, 'Article 1', in Rudolf/Freeman/Chinkin, 2012, p. 53.

[136]Byrnes, 'Article 1', in Rudolf/Freeman/Chinkin, 2012, p. 54.

[137]Gosepath, 'Equality', in Zalta, para. 2.1.

[138]E.g., ECtHR, *Case 'relating to certain aspects of the laws on the use of languages in education in Belgium' v. Belgium*, Judgment (Merits), 23 July 1968, p. 34, para. 10; ECtHR, *Thlimmenos v. Greece* [GC], Judgment, 06 April 2000. On the evolution of the Court's interpretation of Art. 14 ECHR, see Nikolaidis, *The right to equality in European human rights law*, 2015, on positive obligations, see p. 73; Rubio-Marín/Möschel, 'Anti-Discrimination Exceptionalism', (2015) 26 *EJIL*.

[139]Elsuni, *Geschlechtsbezogene Gewalt und Menschenrechte*, 2011, p. 224.

[140]Arnardóttir, *Equality and non-discrimination under the European Convention on Human Rights*, 2003, pp. 9–12; Byrnes, 'Article 1', in Rudolf/Freeman/Chinkin, 2012, p. 54. For an attempt to conceptualize equality as a prohibition of hierarchization, see Baer, *Würde oder Gleichheit?*, 1995 and to conceptualize the prohibition of discrimination as a right to be from hierarchization Elsuni,

void created by this normative indeterminacy and conceptual openness risks to be filled by judgments of any kind.[141] As long as the discourse explicitly considered white, heterosexual, bourgeois men exempt from disability to be superior over all other groups, this concept was able to justify countless explicitly differential treatments. It served as a basis for colonialism, Apartheid, racial segregation in the US and even for Nazi atrocities.[142]

To hinder such abuses, the UN Charter[143] and today's international human rights provisions on equality—again being conceptualized in the spirit of Aristotelian equality—expresses the belief that all human beings are equal (although not equally situated) and, consequently, prohibit the use of particular characteristics of individuals and groups as a basis of differentiation.[144]

b. Transformative Equality: Adding a Forward Looking Element

In view of the above described social structures of dominance, stereotypes and hierarchies, it has been suggested that seeking equality should not merely mean removing barriers to women's opportunities and seeking for an allegedly 'gender-neutral future (. . .) allowing women into a male-defined world'.[145] Instead, a real form of equality would require a transformation restructuring the society, redistributing power and resources, and transforming institutional structures.[146] To achieve this so-called *transformative equality*, it would be necessary to actively and positively draw attention to other perspectives than the dominant view, to women's 'capabilities'[147] and to participatory procedures that respond to women's needs. Transformative equality would also imply that characteristics prevalently perceived as female-like would not be undervalued as compared to male ones. As will be seen below, the idea of transformative equality has been taken up by the CEDAW Committee.

Geschlechtsbezogene Gewalt und Menschenrechte, 2011; Sacksofsky, *Das Grundrecht auf Gleichberechtigung*, 1996.

[141]MacKinnon, *Women's lives, men's laws*, 2007, p. 48.

[142]Ibid., pp. 46.

[143]*Cf.* Article 1 UN Charter and its Preamble.

[144]Byrnes, 'Article 1', in Rudolf/Freeman/Chinkin, 2012, p. 53; Charlesworth, 'Concepts of Equality in International Law', in Huscroft/Rishworth, 2002.

[145]Fredman, 'Beyond the Dichotomy of Formal and Substantial Equality', in Boerefijn, 2003, p. 115.

[146]Fredman, 'Beyond the Dichotomy of Formal and Substantial Equality', in Boerefijn, 2003, p. 115.

[147]When referring to capabilities and choices, Fredman relies on the capabilities approach developed by Martha Nussbaum and Amartya Sen, Nussbaum, *Women and human development*, 2000; Nussbaum/Sen, *The quality of life*, 1993.

II. Approaches to Equality and Non-discrimination Under CEDAW

In view of the subject matter, the following section focuses on the definition of discrimination adopted by CEDAW and its Committee. While various international provisions have conceived discrimination on grounds of sex as arbitrary, unfair and/or unjustifiably distinct treatment of women and men or men and women,[148] CEDAW has taken a more specific approach. Bearing in mind the root causes of discrimination, the CEDAW Committee has interpreted this definition because of a need for social transformation.[149]

1. Definition of Discrimination Under Article 1 CEDAW

Article 1 CEDAW provides for a definition of discrimination against women. Accordingly, discrimination against women is any

> distinction, exclusion or restriction made on the basis of sex[150] which has the effect or purpose of impairing or nullifying the recognition, enjoyment or exercise by women, irrespective of their marital status, on a basis of equality of men and women, of human rights and fundamental freedoms in the political, economic, social, cultural, civil or any other field.

This definition reflects that women experience various forms of unjustifiably distinct treatment which affect the possibility to enjoy human rights simply because they are women. The language and the history of Article 1 indicate that it covers both direct and indirect discrimination.[151]

However, the definition includes two critical points: first, concerning the reference made to the equal treatment *on a basis of equality of men and women*, CEDAW appears to aim at allowing 'women eventually to perform exactly like men',[152] confining those rights on women that men already have and thus embracing equality as 'sameness'.[153] Such an approach is problematic, because it may entail that the scope of equalized action is restricted to the 'public sphere' where men have traditionally had their ambit of action. This limitation could explain why violence

[148]For an overview, see Schutter, *International human rights law*, 2014, pp. 635.

[149]For details, see Byrnes, 'Article 1', in Rudolf/Freeman/Chinkin, 2012, p. 57; Rudolf, 'Menschenrechte und Geschlecht - eine Diskursgeschichte', in Lembke, 2014, pp. 35; Charlesworth, 'Concepts of Equality in International Law', in Huscroft/Rishworth, 2002.

[150]The CEDAW definition encompasses 'gender-based' discrimination, CEDAW, *General Recommendation No. 28 on the core obligations of state parties under article 2 of the CEDAW*, 2010; see also Byrnes, 'Article 1', in Rudolf/Freeman/Chinkin, 2012, p. 59; Chinkin/Freeman, 'Introduction', in Rudolf/Freeman/Chinkin, 2012, p. 15.

[151]*Cf.* Byrnes, 'Article 1', in Rudolf/Freeman/Chinkin, 2012, pp. 65.

[152]Charlesworth/Chinkin, *The Boundaries of International Law*, 2000, pp. 230–232.

[153]Charlesworth, 'Concepts of Equality in International Law', in Huscroft/Rishworth, 2002, p. 146.

against women occurring in the 'private sphere' is not explicitly touched upon by the convention's text itself.[154]

Secondly, the approach to equality as provided by Article 1 has mostly been interpreted by States[155] as to limit the 'meaning of equality to a guarantee of equal opportunity' instead of an equality of outcome.[156] This is problematic because the

> approach of insisting that women and men be treated similarly falters when women and men are not in the same position either because of physical difference or because of structural disadvantage. (. . .) In dealing with individual cases of discrimination rather than structural inequality, the principle of equal opportunity can solve a limited number of discrete problems and fails to address the underlying causes of sex discrimination. (. . .) The principle of equal opportunity (. . .) is "inadequate to criticise and transform a world in which the distribution of (social) goods is distributed along gender lines."[157]

Hence, if the understanding of equality under Article 1 CEDAW is limited to equality of opportunity, it leaves little leeway to transformative equality.

2. Authoritative Interpretation of Article 1: General Recommendation No. 25

In its General Recommendation No. 25 relating to the interpretation of temporary special measures under Article 4 (1) CEDAW (hereafter GR 25), the CEDAW Committee took the view that the Convention encompasses a broad approach to discrimination and equality. The Committee held that

> Firstly, state parties' obligation is to ensure that there is no direct or indirect discrimination against women in their laws and that women are protected against discrimination — committed by public authorities, the judiciary, organizations, enterprises or private individuals — in the public as well as the private spheres by competent tribunals as well as sanctions and other remedies. Secondly, state parties' obligation is to improve the de facto position of women through concrete and effective policies and programmes. Thirdly, state parties' obligation is to address prevailing gender relations and the persistence of gender-based stereotypes that affect women not only through individual acts by individuals but also in law, and legal and societal structures and institutions.
>
> 8. In the Committee's view, a purely formal legal or programmatic approach is not sufficient to achieve women's de facto equality with men, which the Committee interprets as substantive equality. In addition, the Convention requires that women be given an equal start and that they be empowered by an enabling environment to achieve equality of results. It is not enough to guarantee women treatment that is identical to that of men. Rather, biological as

---

[154] CEDAW explicitly mentions prostitution as a form of violence against women that generally occurs in the 'public sphere'; Charlesworth/Chinkin, *The Boundaries of International Law*, 2000, pp. 232.

[155] Byrnes, 'Article 1', in Rudolf/Freeman/Chinkin, 2012, p. 66.

[156] Charlesworth, 'Concepts of Equality in International Law', in Huscroft/Rishworth, 2002, pp. 145.

[157] Charlesworth, 'Concepts of Equality in International Law', in Huscroft/Rishworth, 2002, p. 145, referring to an unpublished work of Nicola Lacey (1987).

> well as socially and culturally constructed differences between women and men must be taken into account. Under certain circumstances, non-identical treatment of women and men will be required in order to address such differences. Pursuit of the goal of substantive equality also calls for an effective strategy aimed at overcoming underrepresentation of women and a redistribution of resources and power between men and women.
>
> 9. Equality of results is the logical corollary of de facto or substantive equality. These results may be quantitative and/or qualitative in nature; that is, women enjoying their rights in various fields in fairly equal numbers with men, enjoying the same income levels, equality in decision-making and political influence, and women enjoying freedom from violence.
>
> 10. The position of women will not be improved as long as the underlying causes of discrimination against women, and of their inequality, are not effectively addressed. The lives of women and men must be considered in a contextual way, and measures adopted towards a real transformation of opportunities, institutions and systems so that they are no longer grounded in historically determined male paradigms of power and life patterns.[158]

Hence, the Committee assumes that CEDAW not only encompasses the traditional concepts of equality and discrimination, but also the above discussed concept of transformative equality.[159] It calls for a contextualized, root cause-sensitive approach.

Whereas general recommendations are non-binding, they are the authoritative interpretation of CEDAW, giving guidance to state parties in applying it consistently.[160] State parties are thus invited to take a root cause-sensitive and contextualized perspective and to apply the concept of transformative equality when adopting special measures under Article 4 CEDAW.[161] Along these lines, in subsequent State reporting procedures, the Committee has drawn attention to the wider, structurally discriminatory context.[162]

III. Conclusion

If one sticks to the traditional understandings of, first, discrimination as being direct or indirect and, second, equality being formal or substantive, equality and discrimination indeed appear to constitute two sides of the same coin. However, the concept

---

[158] CEDAW, *General Recommendation No. 25 on article 4, paragraph 1, of the Convention on the Elimination of All Forms of Discrimination against Women, on temporary special measures*, 2004, paras 7.

[159] *Cf.* also, Cusack/Pusey, 'CEDAW and the Rights to Non-Discrimination and Equality', (2013) 14 *Melb. J. Int'l L.*, p. 11; Byrnes, 'Article 1', in Rudolf/Freeman/Chinkin, 2012, p. 55.

[160] Chinkin/Freeman, 'Introduction', in Rudolf/Freeman/Chinkin, 2012, p. 21.

[161] See Chap. 6 A II.

[162] E.g., CEDAW Committee, *General Recommendation No. 30 on women in conflict prevention, conflict, and post conflict situations*, 18 October 2013, para. 77; CEDAW, *List of issues and questions in relation to the combined seventh and eighth periodic reports of Spain*, 17 November 2014, para. 9; CEDAW, *Consideration of reports submitted by state parties under article 18 of the Convention on the Elimination of All Forms of Discrimination against Women*, 18 September 2006, para. 232; CEDAW, *Consideration of reports submitted by state parties under article 18 of the Convention*, 15 May 2014, para. 134.

of transformative equality and a contextualized approach to structurally discriminatory settings add an additional perspective. Structural discrimination allows for broadening the perspective for past and present social structures in which human rights abuses are embedded,[163] whereas transformative equality rather takes a forward-looking approach. In the context of group-based discrimination, the concepts of structural discrimination and transformative equality may rectify conceptual disadvantages the traditional approaches to discrimination often entail. This is because the concept of indirect discrimination is limited to the establishment of an unequal outcome about one specific aspect. Group-based discrimination is not limited to one specific aspect of a different *de facto* treatment though, but rather rooted in historically grown disadvantageous structures. It is thus far more complex. As acknowledged by the CEDAW Committee, integrating a structural perspective into the understanding of discrimination and adopting a transformative view can be a tool for improving the effectiveness of human rights protection policies.

[163]On discrimination against Roma, see, e.g., ECtHR, *Horváth and Kiss v. Hungary*, Judgment, 29 January 2013, paras 104, 128.

Chapter 3
The Legal Frameworks Applicable to Violence Against Women

When taking a structural approach to State responsibility for all kinds of violence against women both in peacetime and in conflict-settings, the first question to be solved relates to the applicable law. While it is historical to claim that international humanitarian rules (hereafter IHL) are the only international norms that apply during armed conflicts, today's concerns focus on the relationship between the different branches of law. Concerning State responsibility for violence against women, the potential norm conflict emerges between different provisions encompassed by IHL and human rights law.

This chapter therefore analyzes the relationship between these two branches in view of provisions that relate to gender-based violence against women. To do so, it needs to give an overview of humanitarian rules. In section A, this chapter first shows that IHL merely addresses the 'top of the tip of the iceberg'. It neither touches upon lesser forms of gender-based violence nor on the structural root causes. Rather, under its provisions not even all acts of *sexualized* violence amount to a violation of IHL.[1] IHL is limited to the prohibition of sexualized violence that reaches a certain threshold of gravity and has a nexus with the conflict itself. For some of these settings, IHL additionally formulates positive obligations. Section B of this chapter then analyzes the scope of application of human rights and discusses those human rights treaties and international soft law instruments that address violence against women.

[1] *Cf.* Gaggioli, 'Sexual violence in armed conflicts', (2014) 96 *IRRC*, p. 514.

E. V. Henn, *International Human Rights Law and Structural Discrimination*, Beiträge zum ausländischen öffentlichen Recht und Völkerrecht, https://doi.org/10.1007/978-3-662-58677-8_3

A. Humanitarian Rules Applicable in Armed Conflicts: Addressing the Tip of the Iceberg

I. Early Developments

International humanitarian law has long been reluctant to explicitly address and prohibit rape, sexual slavery, forced prostitution, forced impregnation, forced abortion and torture in war time by any international treaty. Until the middle ages, female rape was permissible under the rules and customs of war.[2] At that time *male* rape was not regulated.[3] The first to conclude that female rape in wartime should be prohibited (and eventually generally punished) was *Hugo Grotius* in his 'On the law of war and peace' of 1625.[4]

Two and a half centuries later, the *Lieber Code* of 1863[5] reflected Grotius' ideas. This document, originally known as 'Instructions for the Government of Armies of the United States in the Field', served as a field manual. Under its Article 44

> [a]ll wanton violence committed against persons in the invaded country ... all rape, wounding, maiming, or killing of such inhabitants, [were] prohibited under the penalty of death, or such other severe punishment as may seem adequate for the gravity of the offense.

While not being an international document *stricto sensu*, the Lieber Code served as a draft for future conventions.[6]

Subsequently, the rule explicitly prohibiting and sanctioning rape was not included in the Brussels Declaration of 1874, even though—with regard to other rules—it heavily relied on the Lieber Code. Instead, it stipulated that the 'honour of women and the rights of the family have to be respected'.[7] From a contemporary perspective, this wording appears euphemistic. From an inter-temporal perspective, one may argue that the use of the term 'honour' can be explained by its entirely different connotation at the time, where it 'was considered [a] highly important constraint (. . .) in war and (. . .) at the core of IHL rules in 1949 and before'.[8] Yet, it must also be seen in its social context of a tabooed sexuality and of women being considered rather the property of men than independent individuals.[9]

---

[2]For details, see Askin, *War crimes against women*, 1997, pp. 19–30.

[3]Even nowadays male rape continues to be an underreported issue, see Sivakumaran, 'Sexual Violence against Men in Armed Conflict', (2007) 18 *EJIL* and Sivakumaran, 'Prosecuting Sexual Violence against Men and Boys', in Brouwer/Ku/van Herik, 2013.

[4]Grotius, *De Jure Belli Ac Pacis Libri Tres*, 1625, p. 656–657.

[5]Askin, *War crimes against women*, 1997, p. 36.

[6]Vöneky, 'Der Lieber's Code und die Wurzeln des modernen Kriegsvölkerrechts', (2002) 62 *ZaöRV*, pp. 424.

[7]Para. 38. The original version in French declares that 'l'honneur et les droits de la famille (. . .) doivent être respectés'. Actes de la Conférence de Bruxelles de 1874, p. 60.

[8]Gaggioli, 'Sexual violence in armed conflicts', (2014) 96 *IRRC*, p. 512.

[9]For details, see Inal, *Looting and rape in wartime*, 2013.

This blurred wording was taken up in Article 46 of the Hague Regulations annexed to the Conventions respecting the Laws and Custom of the War on Land 1907.[10] While during the drafting conferences in 1899 the Belgian delegate had objected that the Draft Article would be far too vague, other participants held that there would be neither a necessity nor a possibility to 'define more in detail the sense of this Article, the purport of which [would] be evident'.[11] The reason for such reluctance could not only be the sensibility on explicitly naming the French word *viol* (rape) being considered vulgar at that time.[12] It could also be suggested that there was a general reluctance on the part of States in explicitly prohibiting behavior and ordering measures they believed they could not comply with. Instead, they tried to make provisions as blurred as possible.[13] In this very same spirit, the Geneva Convention on Prisoners of War of 1929 vaguely holds in its Article 3 that 'prisoners of war are entitled to respect for their persons and honour' and that 'women shall be treated with all consideration due to their sex'.

II. Today's Humanitarian Rules

The majority of today's international treaties on humanitarian rules applicable in armed conflict has been adopted after the Second World War. The protection provided against sexualized violence depends, in principle, on whether the conflict is of an international or non-international character. Even though there is no explicit nexus requirement to be found in IHL provisions, acts of sexualized violence occurring during an armed conflict are only encompassed by IHL if they have a sufficient link with the conflict.[14] Other crimes and offences not covered by IHL are partly addressed by international criminal law,[15] and largely or entirely encompassed by domestic law and international human rights law.

1. Protection During International Armed Conflicts

Humanitarian provisions relevant to this research and applicable to international armed conflicts are foreseen in the Fourth Geneva Conventions of 1949 relative to

[10]Adams, *Der Tatbestand der Vergewaltigung im Völkerstrafrecht*, 2013, p. 102 wfr.

[11]Scott (ed.), *The Proceedings of the Hague Peace Conferences*, 1920, p. 488.

[12]Inal, *Looting and rape in wartime*, 2013, p. 66.

[13]Inal, *Looting and rape in wartime*, 2013, p. 66.

[14]Gaggioli, 'Sexual violence in armed conflicts', (2014) 96 *IRRC*, pp. 514; ICTY, *Kunarac, Kovač and Vuković*, Appeals Chamber, Judgment, 12 June 2002, para. 58.

[15]This relates to crimes against humanity which requires that they are 'committed as part of a widespread or systematic attack directed against any civilian population, with knowledge of the attack', *cf.* Art. 7 Rome Statute of the ICC.

the protection of civilian persons in time of war (GC IV), the Third Geneva Convention of 1949 relative to the protection of Prisoners of War (POW Convention) and the Additional Protocols to the Geneva Conventions of 1949, and relative to the Protection of Victims of International Armed Conflicts (AP I). With 196 (GC IV) and 173 (AP I) state parties, these documents are said to largely reflect customary law in international armed conflicts.[16] However, it cannot be neglected that some relevant States, such as India, Israel and the United States of America, are no contracting parties to AP I.

a. The Geneva Convention IV

At the beginning of the post-Second World War period, significant improvement on to the protection against sexualized violence during armed conflict was reached thanks to the International Committee of the Red Cross (ICRC) and the International Alliance of Women (IAW).[17]

1) Articles 27 and 32 GC IV

During the drafting process of the Geneva Conventions, the ICRC recalled the mass rapes and forced sexualized slavery during the Second World War[18] and drew attention to the weakness of Article 46 of the Hague Regulations.[19] Consequently, the ensuing provision which is still in force today explicitly mentions female rape. Article 27 of the Fourth Geneva Convention says:

1. Protected persons [under this Convention] are entitled, in all circumstances, to respect for their persons, their honour, their family rights, their religious convictions and practices, and their manners and customs. They shall at all times be humanely treated, and shall be protected especially against all acts of violence or threats thereof and against insults and public curiosity.
2. Women shall be especially protected against any attack on their honour, in particular against rape, enforced prostitution, or any form of indecent assault.

Remarkably, the first paragraph stipulates a principle of absolute, non-discriminatory respect for the human person which is the leitmotiv of the Geneva Conventions.[20] Referring to the right of respect, the norm particularly covers

[16] Doswald-Beck/Henckaerts (eds.), *Customary international humanitarian law*, 2005.

[17] For details, see Inal, *Looting and rape in wartime*, 2013, p. 97.

[18] Totsuka, 'Commentary on a Victory for "Comfort Women"', (1999) 8 *Pacific Rim Law and Policies Journal*; Grossmann, 'The "Big Rape": Sex and Sexual Violence, War and Occupation in Post-World-War II Memory and Imagination', in Heineman, 2011. The crimes perpetrated by French and American soldiers after 1945 have only recently been explored, see Gebhardt, *Als die Soldaten kamen*, 2015.

[19] For details, see Inal, *Looting and rape in wartime*, 2013, pp. 93–94 wfr.

[20] See already Pictet (ed.), *The Geneva Conventions of 12 August 1949 - Commentary*, 1958, Art. 27, p. 204.

the right to physical, moral and psychological integrity of those in the hands of a party to the conflict.[21] Article 27 also establishes a due diligence obligation to ensure the safety and protection of civilians against acts by all kind of actors.[22] It does, however, not specify what kind of measures the Adversary State needs to take to comply with this provision.

The second paragraph goes into details regarding the *protection* required against specific crimes committed against women and attaining a certain gravity threshold. In the context of rape and enforced prostitution, the provision's text still refers to a woman's *honour* but not to dignity. It also remains unclear on what exactly means 'rape' because there was at the time no internationally accepted definition of this crime.[23] Thus, this norm leaves a wide margin of appreciation on substantial issues.[24] Article 27 (2) also evidences that, in contrast to other explicitly prohibitive humanitarian norms such as those on torture, corporal punishment, pillage and taking of hostage,[25] state parties did not explicitly agree to *prohibit* rape and other sexualized crimes. However, if Article 27 (2) is read in conjunction with Article 32 GC IV,[26] it appears that rape and other forms of sexualized violence committed under the authority of a contracting party[27] are prohibited.[28] Article 32 stresses the principle of absolute respect for the human person expressed in Article 27 and aims to ensure that every human person receives human treatment.[29]

2) Positive Obligations Under the Grave Breaches Regime

Further protection against sexualized violence is provided by the grave breaches regime under Articles 146, 147 GC IV. Grave breaches are considered willful killing of protected persons, torture or inhuman treatment, willfully causing great suffering or serious injury to body or health, as well as the taking of hostages and

---

[21]Pictet (ed.), *The Geneva Conventions of 12 August 1949 - Commentary*, 1958, Art. 27, p. 201.

[22]David, *Principes de droit des conflits armés*, 2012, p. 548; Eritrea-Ethiopia Claims Commission, *Partial Award, Civilians Claims Ethiopia's Claim Nr. 5, between The Federal Democratic Republic of Ethiopia and The State of Eritrea*, 17 December 2004, paras 98–99.

[23]For today's definition under international criminal law, see Gaggioli, 'Sexual violence in armed conflicts', (2014) 96 *IRRC*, pp. 507.

[24]Inal, *Looting and rape in wartime*, 2013, p. 98.

[25]*Cf.* Arts 29, 33, 34 GC IV.

[26]Art. 32 reads as follows: 'The High Contracting Parties specifically agree that each of them is prohibited from taking any measure of such a character as to cause the physical suffering or extermination of protected persons in their hands. This prohibition applies not only to murder, torture, corporal punishment, mutilation (. . .), but also to any other measures of brutality whether applied by civilian or military agents.'

[27]Pictet (ed.), *The Geneva Conventions of 12 August 1949 - Commentary*, 1958, Art. 32, p. 221. Sexualized acts committed by other persons continue to be subjected to the domestic criminal law only.

[28]See also Adams, *Der Tatbestand der Vergewaltigung im Völkerstrafrecht*, 2013, p. 105.

[29]Pictet (ed.), *The Geneva Conventions of 12 August 1949 - Commentary*, 1958, Art. 32, pp. 221–222.

unlawful confinement of persons protected under Article 4.[30] While rape and similar acts are not explicitly mentioned, it is generally acknowledged that acts of sexualized violence constitute grave breaches of international humanitarian law. By applying a textual approach (Article 31 VCLT), rape, sexualized slavery and other forms of sexualized violence can be subsumed under the prohibited acts of inhuman treatment, willful causing of great suffering or serious injury to body or health, torture and unlawful confinement.[31] While the *travaux préparatoires* indicate that the drafters of Article 147 GC IV did not discuss whatever form of sexualized violence separately (which may be because of the social-normative framework of the time which did not ease a discussion on that subject), the historical method of interpretation (Art. 32 VTC) is merely a subsidiary method unnecessary in this case.[32]

Under Article 146, state parties have positive obligations that go beyond the simple obligation to ensure respect as foreseen under common Articles 1 GCs and 1 (1) AP I.[33] Accordingly, States have to enact any legislation necessary to provide effective penal sanctions for persons allegedly committing or ordering to be committing grave breaches; they also must search for persons alleged to have committed breaches of the Convention and to bring such persons 'regardless of their nationality' before its own courts, or to hand them over for trial to other contracting parties. Simply put, state parties must criminalize grave breaches[34] under domestic laws

[30]See below.

[31]ICTY, *Prosecutor v. Furundžija*, Trial Chamber, Judgment, 10 December 1998, para. 168; for an overview on domestic and international practice regarding the prohibition of rape under international humanitarian law, see Doswald-Beck/Henckaerts (eds.), *Customary International Humanitarian Law*, 2005, Part II, paras 1555, 1723. *Cf.* also Gaggioli, 'Sexual violence in armed conflicts', (2014) 96 *IRRC*; Adams, *Der Tatbestand der Vergewaltigung im Völkerstrafrecht*, 2013, p. 109; Gardam/Jarvis, *Women, armed conflict, and international law*, 2001; Pilch, 'The Crime of Rape in International Humanitarian Law', (1998) 9 *USAF Acad. J. Legal Stud;* UNCHR, *Action visant à encourager et developper davantage le respect des droits de l'homme et des libertés fondamentales et, notamment, question du programme et des méthodes de travail de la Commission*, 26 January 1998; ICRC, Update on the Aide-Memoire on rape committed during the armed conflict in ex-Yugoslavia, of 3 December 1992; Meron, 'Rape as a Crime under International Humanitarian Law', (1993) 87 *AJIL*, pp. 426; Pictet (ed.), *The Geneva Conventions of 12 August 1949 - Commentary*, 1958, Art. 147, p. 598.

[32]But see Inal, *Looting and rape in wartime*, 2013, p. 102.

[33]These provisions read as follows: 'The High Contracting Parties undertake to respect and *to ensure respect* for this Protocol in all circumstances' (emphasis added). On the question whether this obligation relates to actors among the state's own population only or also to third States, see David, *Principes de droit des conflits armés*, 2012, p. 643.

[34]As suggested by Rule 156 of the ICRC-Customary Law Study, it is in the context of an international armed conflict that sexualized violence, in particular rape, sexual slavery, enforced prostitution and enforced pregnancy, which reach the threshold of a grave breach, amount to war crimes if the act is directed against protected persons. Doswald-Beck/Henckaerts (eds.), *Customary international humanitarian law*, 2005, Rule 156. It should be noted, however, that under today's international treaty law sexualized crimes failing to reach the grave breaches threshold or being directed against victims not falling under the category of protected persons can also be prosecuted as war crime, see Gaggioli, 'Sexual violence in armed conflicts', (2014) 96 *IRRC*, p. 527.

and are obliged to investigate, prosecute and punish perpetrators ex officio.[35] It is clear though that the obligation to adopt criminal legislation relating to grave breaches 'must be put into effect in peacetime in anticipation' of war.[36] While state parties first adopted legislation concerning grave breaches at the domestic level, international war crimes including sexualized crimes were later codified at the international level, *inter alia* under the Rome-Statute.[37]

In conclusion, there are negative and positive obligations to be found under GV IV concerning sexualized violence. Articles 27 and 32, 146, 147 oblige contracting parties to actively protect civilians against all forms of sexualized violence the commission of which is prohibited, to enact at the domestic level criminal laws and to prosecute perpetrators.

3) Scope of Application

Articles 27 and 32, 146, 147 do not protect all persons potentially affected by sexualized violence during an armed conflict. Their application is limited to those persons who are covered by Article 4 GC IV, that is, persons who are 'in the hands of a Party to the conflict or Occupying Power of which they are not nationals'.[38] It follows therefrom that the population of a State in conflict is not protected against

[35] David, *Principes de droit des conflits armés*, 2012, p. 936.

[36] Pictet (ed.), *The Geneva Conventions of 12 August 1949 - Commentary*, 1958, p. 591. See, e.g., the German Criminal Code for International Crimes (Völkerstrafgesetzbuch vom 26. Juni 2002 (BGBl. I S. 2254), available under http://www.gesetze-im-internet.de/vstgb/BJNR225410002.html, accessed 16 January 2016. For further national legislation, see references at Doswald-Beck/Henckaerts (eds.), *Customary international humanitarian law*, 2005, Rule 165, p. 585, fn. 84.

[37] As has been resumed by 'UN Action against Sexual Violence in Conflict', the 'statutes and case law of the International Tribunals for the Former Yugoslavia and Rwanda, the Special Court for Sierra Leone, the Extraordinary Chambers in the Courts of Cambodia, and the ICC Rome Statute, when taken collectively, define sexual violence to encompass: rape, sexual slavery, forced prostitution, forced impregnation, enforced sterilization and any other form of sexual violence of comparable gravity, which may include indecent assault, trafficking, inappropriate medical examinations and strip searches'. Stop rape now—UN Action against Sexual Violence in Conflict, *Analytical and Conceptual Framing of Conflict-related Sexual Violence*, June 2011. Sexualized violence so understood is prosecuted **as war crime** 'when committed in the context of and associated with an armed conflict', as crime 'against humanity when committed in the context of a widespread or systematic attack on a civilian population' which does not necessarily occur within the context of an armed conflict; 'and/or as an act of genocide when committed with the intent to destroy an ethnic, religious, national or racial group in whole or in part' (footnotes omitted). See Global Summit to End Sexual Violence in Conflict, *International Protocol on the Documentation and Investigation of Sexual Violence in Armed Conflicts*, June 2014, p. 17. For details, see Bergsmo (ed.), *Thematic prosecution of international sex crimes*, 2012; Bergsmo/Skre/Wood (eds.), *Understanding and proving international sex crimes*, 2012.

[38] *Cf.* Art. 4 and Pictet (ed.), *The Geneva Conventions of 12 August 1949 - Commentary*, 1958, p. 46.

aggressions by members of the own armed forces and by forces of third States that assist the former State.[39]

b. The Prisoner of War Convention (POW/GC III) of 1949

Under Article 14, all prisoners of war (POW) 'are entitled in all circumstance to respect for their [physical] and [moral] person and honour'. Article 130 also establishes a grave breaches regime which applies *inter alia* to torture or inhuman treatment and willfully causing of great suffering or serious injury to body or health. However, while Articles 25, 29, 88, 97 grant to female prisoners separated dormitories, conveniences and supervision by women when under disciplinary punishment, decreasing the risk to be sexually aggressed, the general clause contained in Article 14 also stresses that female POWs 'shall be treated with all regard to their sex and shall in all cases benefit by treatment *as favourable as that granted to men*'.[40]

c. Extending the Group of Protected Persons: Additional Protocol I of 1977

In view of the deficient protection *ratione personae*, there was a need to further develop humanitarian rules. Under Additional Protocol I (AP I) contracting parties agreed upon improving the protection against sexualized violence. The protection of civilians which has first been provided by Article 27 (1) and (2) GV IV has been significantly extended by Article 75 and 76 (1) AP I. Articles 75 and 76 extend the scope of application *ratione personae.*

1) Articles 75 AP I

Article 75[41] provides for a simple protection regime. It grants a minimum of protection against violations whether committed by civilian or by military agents

---

[39]David, *Principes de droit des conflits armés*, 2012, p. 546 wfr to relevant international jurisprudence.

[40]Arts 13, 14 POW Convention.

[41]Article 75 reads as follows: 'Fundamental guarantees: (1) In so far as they are affected by a situation referred to in Article 1 of this Protocol, persons who are in the power of a Party to the conflict and who do not benefit from more favourable treatment under the Conventions or under this Protocol shall be treated humanely in all circumstances and shall enjoy, as a minimum, the protection provided by this Article without any adverse distinction based upon race, colour, sex, language, religion or belief, political or other opinion, national or social origin, wealth, birth or other status, or on any other similar criteria. Each Party shall respect the person, honour, convictions and religious practices of all such persons. (2) The following acts are and shall remain prohibited at any time and in any place whatsoever, whether committed by civilian or by military agents: (a) violence to the life, health, or physical or mental well-being of persons, in particular: (i) murder; (ii) torture of all kinds, whether physical or mental; (iii) corporal punishment; and (iv) mutilation; (b) outrages upon personal dignity, in particular humiliating and degrading treatment, enforced prostitution and

to *all persons in the power of a party who do not benefit from a more favourable treatment* under the GCs, AP I or other provisions of international law.[42] This minimum of protection includes the prohibition of violence to the life, health, or physical or mental well-being of persons, of physical or mental torture, mutilation and outrages upon personal dignity, in particular humiliating and degrading treatment, of enforced prostitution and any form of indecent assault.

For the scope of application, a person's nationality is irrelevant for her to be entitled to a minimum of protection.[43] Admittedly, no consensus could be reached during the drafting procedure as to whether Article 75 should explicitly cover the belligerent State's *own* nationals.[44] Nevertheless, because of the further wording, object and purpose and normative environment of Article 75, the latter applies to own nationals, too.

First of all, the wording in place ('persons who are in the power') leaves the question open. The non-inclusion of an explicit reference to own nationals may be interpreted in both ways.[45] This is—secondly—where Article 72 comes into play. It stipulates:

> The provisions of this Section are additional to the rules concerning humanitarian protection of civilians and civilian objects in the power of a Party to the conflict contained in the Fourth Convention, particularly Parts I and III thereof, as well as to other applicable rules of international law relating to the protection of fundamental human rights during international armed conflict.

The provision explicitly states that the present section, which includes Article 75, is 'additional' to the Fourth Convention and to fundamental human rights as applicable during international armed conflict. Under Article 4 GC IV, the latter only applies to persons 'in the hands of persons a Party to the conflict or Occupying Power of which they are not nationals'. Thus, if the present section is conceptionalized as adding normative content to the Fourth Convention, it may have a larger scope and include own nationals, too.

Thirdly, the fact that under Article 72 the present section adds to human rights, points towards a universal approach including own nationals. Adding to human rights means, in the ordinary sense, maintaining their basic protection. International

---

any form of indecent assault; (c) the taking of hostages; (d) collective punishments; and (e) threats to commit any of the foregoing acts. (...) (8) No provision of this Article may be construed as limiting or infringing any other more favourable provision granting greater protection, under any applicable rules of international law, to persons covered by paragraph 1.'

[42]Art. 75 (1) and (8); Pictet et al. (eds.), *Commentary on the Additional Protocols of June 8 1977 to the Geneva Conventions of 12 August 1949*, 1987, para. 3040.

[43]For details see, Pictet et al. (eds.), *Commentary on the Additional Protocols of June 8 1977 to the Geneva Conventions of 12 August 1949*, 1987, paras 3022.

[44]David, *Principes de droit des conflits armés*, 2012, p. 546; Pictet et al. (eds.), *Commentary on the Additional Protocols of June 8 1977 to the Geneva Conventions of 12 August 1949*, 1987, para. 3017.

[45]Pictet et al. (eds.), *Commentary on the Additional Protocols of June 8 1977 to the Geneva Conventions of 12 August 1949*, 1987, para. 3018.

human rights have, right from the start, been seen as rights of citizens against their State. There is no reasonable, non-arbitrary explanation why States should be allowed to exclude their own nationals from core guarantees such as protection from murder, torture or enforced prostitution and any form of indecent assault (Art. 75 (2) lit. a and b). This also holds true from a humanitarian law perspective. The protection of human integrity is a priority goal and, with due regard to the importance of the said guarantees, there is no reason, especially not one of military necessity, to rule otherwise.

Finally, the prohibition of recruiting children under the age of 15 years in Art. 77 (2), which is situated in the same section as Article 75, does only make sense when applied to own nationals, too.[46]

From these arguments, it seems negligible that Article 73 explicitly extends the scope of protection of Part I and III of the Fourth Convention to stateless persons or refugees, which could mean *mutatis mutandis* that an application to own nationals needed an explicit clause in that sense, too.

2) Articles 76 AP I

Under Article 76 (1) 'women shall be the object of special respect and *shall be protected* in particular against rape, forced prostitution and any other form of indecent assault'.[47] It finally omits a reference to women's 'honour'. Most importantly, it does not only apply to 'women affected by the armed conflict but all women who are in the territory of Parties involved in the conflict, and to others; to women protected by the fourth Convention and to those who are not'.[48] Paragraphs 2 and 3 additionally foresee particular protection for pregnant women and mothers of dependent children who are arrested, detained, interned or convicted for reasons related to the armed conflict.

3) No Supplementary Protection Under the Grave Breaches Regime

Article 85 AP I also provides for a grave breaches regime supplementary to the one under the GCs. In contrast to the broad protection *ratione personae* provided by Article 76 AP I to all women on the territory of the conflicting State, the beneficiaries of the grave breaches regime are limited to persons protected under Article 4 GC IV.[49] Hence, this regime adds nothing to the protection of women provided by Articles 27, 31, 146, 147 GV IV.

[46] Pictet et al. (eds.), *Commentary on the Additional Protocols of June 8 1977 to the Geneva Conventions of 12 August 1949*, 1987, para. 2915.

[47] Emphasis added.

[48] Pictet et al. (eds.), *Commentary on the Additional Protocols of June 8 1977 to the Geneva Conventions of 12 August 1949*, 1987, para. 3151.

[49] Art. 85 (2) AP I.

2. Protection During Non-international Armed Conflicts

a. Treaty Law

Treaty provisions regulating armed conflicts not of an international character and non-international armed conflicts are less complex than those relating to international armed conflicts.

The Protocol Additional to the Geneva Conventions of 1949, and relating to the Protection of Victims of Non-International Armed Conflicts (AP II) of 1977 applies to conflicts that

> take place in the territory of a High Contracting Party between its armed forces and dissident armed forces or other organized groups which, under responsible command, exercise such a control over a part of its territory as to enable them to carry out sustained and concerted military operations and to implement [the Additional Protocol II to the Geneva Conventions].[50]

AP II thus establishes a higher threshold of application than does common Article 3 GCs, which applies to all conflicts 'not of an international character'.[51]

The protection against rape and similar acts guaranteed by AP II and common Article 3 is similar to the one provided by Article 75 AP I.[52] According to common Article 3 GCs, persons taking no active part in hostilities are to be treated humanely by all parties to the conflict (including State and non-State actors). Acts such as torture, cruel treatment, mutilation and outrages upon personal dignity, in particular humiliating and degrading treatment, are in any place and at any time prohibited. As with Article 27 GC IV, it is a textual approach that indicates that sexualized violence against the population is prohibited during conflicts of a non-international character.[53] While there is no grave breaches regime for these non-international settings, it is recognized that serious violations of common Article 3 also amount to war crimes in need to be punished.[54]

---

[50]Art. 1 (1) AP II.

[51]For details, see Norris/Watkin, *Non International Armed Conflict in the Twenty-first Century*, 2012, pp. 46.

[52]Art. 75 AP I was indeed directly inspired by common Art. 3 GCs and was adopted after Art. 4 (2) AP I, see Pictet et al. (eds.), *Commentary on the Additional Protocols of June 8 1977 to the Geneva Conventions of 12 August 1949*, 1987, para. 3037.

[53]ICTY, *Prosecutor v. Furundžija*, Trial Chamber, Judgment, 10 December 1998, para. 166; Adams, *Der Tatbestand der Vergewaltigung im Völkerstrafrecht*, 2013, p. 111, wfr at fn. 303; Gaggioli, 'Sexual violence in armed conflicts', (2014) 96 *IRRC*, p. 528.

[54]E.g., ICTY, *Prosecutor v. Furundžija*, Trial Chamber, Judgment, 10 December 1998, para. 166–169; 'Article 4 of the 1994 ICTR Statute, entitled "Violations of Article 3 common to the Geneva Conventions and of Additional Protocol II", provides that the Tribunal "shall have the power to prosecute persons committing or ordering to be committed serious violations of Article 3 common to the Geneva Conventions and of Additional Protocol II thereto"', see Doswald-Beck/Henckaerts (eds.), *Customary International Humanitarian Law*, 2005, chapter 44, para. 15.

Article 4 AP II repeats the principle of human treatment without any adverse distinction founded on race, color, sex, language, religion or belief, political or other opinion, national or social origin, wealth, birth or other status. The provision forbids the same acts as common Article 3 GCs.[55] Without reference to the victim's sex or gender, Article 4 (2) lit. (e) and (f) explicitly spell out that rape, enforced prostitution and any form of indecent assault and slavery are prohibited.

b. Customary Law

Even when a State on the territory of which an internal conflict occurs is neither a contracting party to the GCs (which because of the quasi-universal ratification is rather unlikely) nor to AP II (168 state parties), protection may be provided by customary international law. On sexualized violence, State practice appears to reflect the rules as foreseen under AP II and common Article 3 GCs. Accordingly, civilians and persons *hors de combat* must be treated humanely,[56] that is, with dignity.[57] State practice also indicates that 'torture, cruel or inhuman treatment and outrages upon personal dignity, in particular humiliating and degrading treatment are prohibited'.[58] Finally, State practice shows that rape and other forms of sexualized violence are prohibited[59] and must be punished.[60]

[55]AP II Art. 4 reads as follows: '(1) All persons who do not take a direct part or who have ceased to take part in hostilities, whether or not their liberty has been restricted, are entitled to respect for their person, honour and convictions and religious practices. They shall in all circumstances be treated humanely, without any adverse distinction (…). (2) Without prejudice to the generality of the foregoing, the following acts against the persons referred to in paragraph 1 are and shall remain prohibited at any time and in any place whatsoever: (a) violence to the life, health and physical or mental well-being of persons, in particular murder as well as cruel treatment such as torture, mutilation or any form of corporal punishment; (…); (c) taking of hostages; (…); (e) outrages upon personal dignity, in particular humiliating and degrading treatment, rape, enforced prostitution and any form of indecent assault; (f) slavery and the slave trade in all their forms; (h) threats to commit any of the foregoing acts.'

[56]For a survey of relevant state practice in that regard, see Doswald-Beck/Henckaerts (eds.), *Customary International Humanitarian Law*, 2005, Rule 87. Note that this study has been criticized *inter alia* because it would weigh *opinio iuris* over state practice and because it omits to differentiate between the two types of non-international armed conflicts, Bellinger/Haynes, 'A US Government Response to the Study of the International Committee of the Red Cross Study Customary International Law', (2007) 40 *IRRC*.

[57]Doswald-Beck/Henckaerts (eds.), *Customary international humanitarian law*, 2005, p. 307, fn. 42.

[58]Doswald-Beck/Henckaerts (eds.), *Customary International Humanitarian Law*, 2005, Rule 90.

[59]Doswald-Beck/Henckaerts (eds.), *Customary International Humanitarian Law*, 2005, Rule 93.

[60]Doswald-Beck/Henckaerts (eds.), *Customary international humanitarian law*, 2005, Rule 90, pp. 325 wfr and Rule 156.

III. Conclusion

Contemporary humanitarian rules relating to sexualized violence committed in the context of an armed conflict are first of all a code of conduct for the conflicting parties. During non-international armed conflicts (AP II) and conflicts not of an international character (common Article 3), sexualized violence is prohibited under common Article 3 GCs, Article 4 AP II and customary law.

Positive due diligence obligations only apply within the context of an international armed conflict and on protected persons under the grave breaches regime. States must *inter alia* adopt legislation in anticipation to the conflict, and investigate *ex officio*, prosecute and punish perpetrators of grave breaches of IHL. Because of the definition of protected persons under Article 4 GC IV, positive obligations are restricted to the enemy population and do not extent to the State's own population or other persons. As will be shown in the next section, gaps of protection and situations not encompassed by IHL have been addressed by human rights law.

B. Human Rights Treaties Applicable in Peacetime and Armed Conflicts

I. Applicability of Human Rights Treaties

Whether human rights treaties apply to violence against women depends on different factors—that is the territorial, personal, temporal and material scope of application.[61]

1. Extraterritorial Application of Human Rights Obligations

To establish the existence of State obligations, many human rights treaties require the individual to be subject to 'the jurisdiction' of the State whose responsibility is in issue.[62]

[61]See also Henckaerts, 'Concurrent Application of Humanitarian Law and Human Rights Law', in Arnold/Quénivet, 2008, pp. 252.

[62]E.g., the ACHR holds: 'state parties to this Convention undertake to respect the rights and freedoms recognized herein and to ensure to all persons subject to their jurisdiction the free and full exercise of those rights and freedoms, without any discrimination (...)' (Article 1 (1)); the ECHR states that Parties to the Convention 'shall secure to everyone within their jurisdiction the rights (...)' (Art. 1); and under the ICCPR each State Party 'undertakes to respect and to ensure to all individuals within its territory and subject to its jurisdiction the rights recognized in the present Covenant, without distinction of any kind' (Art. 2 (1)). While CEDAW, the Istanbul and the Belém do Pará Conventions contain no 'jurisdiction clause' it may be deduced from their wording that these instruments too are state-centric frameworks establishing a duty to respect, protect and fulfill human rights within their jurisdiction. This is because the majority of the obligations they establish

Traditionally, 'jurisdiction' was viewed as to be limited to conduct exercised within the State's own territory. State acts, the argument went, must be free from interferences with rights of other States.[63] This implied that 'jurisdiction' was a preliminary matter.[64] If the act in issue did not fall under the 'jurisdiction of the State', attribution of an action or an omission encroaching upon human rights was irrelevant and did not imply the responsibility of a State.

This consequence of the traditional territorial approach has been increasingly challenged. There was no reasonable ground why a State should be able to do whatever suits to it just because it is acting beyond its own territory.

a. Territorial or Personal Control as a Precondition for Extraterritorial Application

Especially on peacekeeping missions and armed operations abroad, the traditional approach therefore started shifting slightly towards holding States responsible for acts committed beyond their own territory. Because of this judicial development, today 'jurisdiction' is generally understood as an issue of effective (overall) control over the area or lieu of crime (territorial control) or control over the victim (personal control).[65] Still, extraordinary circumstances such as occupation or extraterritorial custody are required for States to have extraterritorial human rights obligations.

(such as taking legislative measures) are *per se* and logically limited to the area of influence of the State that is acting.

[63] *Cf.*, e.g., ECtHR, *Al-Skeini and others v. the UK* [GC], Judgment, 07 July 2011, para. 131.

[64] Milanović, *Extraterritorial application of human rights treaties*, 2011, p. 51; ECtHR, *Jaloud v. The Netherlands* [GC], Judgment, 20 November 2014, para. 139.

[65] ECtHR, *Bankovic and others v. Belgium and others* [GC] (dec.), 12 December 2001; CEDAW Committee, *General Recommendation No. 30 on women in conflict prevention, conflict, and post conflict situations*, 18 October 2013, para. 8; ICJ, *Case concerning Application of the International Convention on the Elimination of all Forms of Racial Discrimination (Georgia v. Russian Federation)*, Order on the Indication of Provisional Measures, 15 October 2008, pp. 353, para. 109; CERD Committee, *Consideration of reports submitted by state parties under article 9 of the Convention, Concluding observations Israel*, 09 March 2012 para. 10; UNCESCR, *Consideration of reports submitted by state parties under articles 16 and 17 of the Covenant, Concluding observations Israel*, 16 December 2011, para. 8; UNHRC, *Delia Saldias de Lopez Burgos v. Uruguay*, Communication No. 52/1979, 29 July 1981, para. 12.1; UNHRC, *Lilian Celiberti de Casariego v. Uruguay*, Communication No. 56/1979, 29 July 1981, paras 10.1; UNHRC, *Mabel Pereira Montero v. Uruguay*, Communication No. 106/1981, 31 March 1983, para. 5; UN Human Rights Committee, *General Comment No. 31*, 26 May 2004, para. 10; ICJ, *Legal Consequences of the Construction of a Wall in the Occupied Palestinian Territory*, Advisory Opinion, 09 July 2004, paras 107. On the drafting history of the ICCPR, see the discussion of the preliminary draft in the Commission on Human Rights, UN Doc. E/CN.4/SR.194, para. 46; and United Nations, Official record of the General Assembly, Tenth Session, Annexes, A/2929, Part II, Chap. V, para. 4 (1955); see also Milanović, *Extraterritorial application of human rights treaties*, 2011; Pasqualucci, *The practice and procedure of the Inter-American Court of Human Rights*, 2013, pp. 146; Wenzel, 'Human Rights, Treaties, Extraterritorial Application and Effects', in Wolfrum, 2012.

Thus, it is only under exceptional circumstances that a State act performed outside the State's territories can constitute an exercise of jurisdiction.[66]

b. Extraterritorial Application of Positive Obligations

As to the particular relevance of positive human rights obligations in the context of violence against women, attention should be drawn here to the fact that today's approach towards 'jurisdiction', understood as *personal* or *territorial* control, has a distinct effect on positive and negative human rights obligations.[67] As *Marco Milanović* pointed out, positive obligations requiring actions to be taken for the State to comply with them can only apply where the State has *effective control over an area*, *viz.* over the State's own territory, occupied territory or over a place or small area such as an extraterritorial prison: when a State has control over the victim, it is quite likely, however not mandatory, that the alleged human rights violation overlaps with the facts establishing control. A total overlap of the facts establishing personal control and the facts constituting the violation will most likely correspond to a violation of the negative obligation to respect. In turn, an omission constituting the human rights violation in question will not overlap with the facts establishing control over an area. Hence, when applying the general principle of territorial or personal control to State omissions and thus to positive obligations requiring a State to take action, one can but conclude that unlike negative obligations, positive obligations are by and large territorially bound.[68]

c. Positive Obligations Having an Extraterritorial Effect

These principles of extraterritorial application of human rights as outlined above, however, do not apply where acts of States have extraterritorial *effects*. Rather, acts of States producing an effect outside of the territory of or occupied territory may amount to exercise by them of their jurisdiction.[69]

---

[66]See, e.g., ICJ, *Legal Consequences of the Construction of a Wall in the Occupied Palestinian Territory*, Advisory Opinion, 09 July 2004, para. 111; ECtHR, *Jaloud v. The Netherlands* [GC], Judgment, 20 November 2014, para. 139; ECtHR, *Al-Skeini and others v. the UK* [GC], Judgment, 07 July 2011, para. 139; ECtHR, *Rantsev v. Cyprus and Russia*, Judgment, 07 January 2010, para. 307; ECtHR, *Bankovic and others v. Belgium and others* [GC] (dec.), 12 December 2001, para. 67.

[67]Milanović, *Extraterritorial application of human rights treaties*, 2011, pp. 51.

[68]Ibid. *Milanović* therefore concludes that 'jurisdiction' should be understood as territorially unbound with regard to negative obligations. With regard to positive obligations, the application of human rights treaties should be limited to situations where the state has '*de facto* the effective control over areas and places' (p. 209). Conversely, 'jurisdiction' shall only refer to territorial control (and not territory) where positive obligations come into question (pp. 209). See also Hakimi, 'State Bystander Responsibility', (2010) 21 *EJIL, 361*. For a different analysis, see Heijer/Lawson, 'Extraterritorial human rights and the concept of "jurisdiction"', in Langford, 2013, pp. 153.

[69]E.g., ECtHR, *Ilaşcu v. Moldova and Russia* [GC], Judgment, 08 July 2004, para. 314.

For example, the CEDAW Committee held in its GR 30 relating to positive obligations that States have the obligation 'to regulate the activities of domestic non-State actors, within their effective control, who operate extraterritorially'.[70] Here, the legislative activity, required for a State to comply with its duty, can be exercised within its territorial control having, however, an extraterritorial effect on the enjoyment of human rights. In such settings, it is difficult to see where a conflict of extraterritorial jurisdiction with the territorial jurisdiction of another State could arise.

To the same token, the ICJ held in its *Case concerning the application of the Convention of Prevention and Punishment of the Crime of Genocide* (hereinafter *Genocide case*), that the obligations under the Genocide Convention, including the obligation to prevent genocide, 'are not on their face limited by territory'.[71] Although the Genocide Convention does not include a 'jurisdiction clause' and although the Court explicitly did not want to establish a general rule on positive obligations, it is worthwhile looking at this judgment[72]: neither did the massacres occur in the territory of the respondent State, Serbia, but next to its borders, nor had it sufficient control over the territory or the Serbian paramilitary groups that were controlling the region around Srebrenica.[73] Similar to the ECtHR in the *Ilascu case*,[74] the ICJ developed criteria useful to assess whether there is an influential relationship between the State and the abuser 'tantamount as to oblige the State to protect and prevent genocide to occur'.[75]

---

[70]CEDAW Committee, *General Recommendation No. 30 on women in conflict prevention, conflict, and post conflict situations*, 18 October 2013, paras 8.

[71]ICJ, *Case concerning application of the Convention of Prevention and Punishment of the Crime of Genocide (Bosnia and Herzegovina v. Serbia and Montenegro)*, Judgment, 26 February 2007, para. 183.

[72]As the Court held: 'The decision of the Court does not, in this case, purport to establish a general jurisprudence applicable to all cases where a treaty instrument, or other binding legal norm, includes an obligation for States to prevent certain acts. Still less does the decision of the Court purport to find whether, apart from the texts applicable to specific fields, there is a general obligation on States to prevent the commission by other persons or entities of acts contrary to certain norms of general international law. The Court will therefore confine itself to determining the specific scope of the duty to prevent in the Genocide Convention, and to the extent that such a determination is necessary to the decision to be given on the dispute before it.' ICJ, *Case concerning application of the Convention of Prevention and Punishment of the Crime of Genocide (Bosnia and Herzegovina v. Serbia and Montenegro)*, Judgment, 26 February 2007, para. 429.

[73]ICJ, *Case concerning application of the Convention of Prevention and Punishment of the Crime of Genocide (Bosnia and Herzegovina v. Serbia and Montenegro)*, Judgment, 26 February 2007, para. 183.

[74]ECtHR, *Ilaşcu v. Moldova and Russia* [GC], Judgment, 08 July 2004, para. 392, finding that Russia had 'decisive influence', and that the separatists 'survive[d] by virtue of [Russia's] military, economic, financial, and political support'.

[75]ICJ, *Case concerning application of the Convention of Prevention and Punishment of the Crime of Genocide (Bosnia and Herzegovina v. Serbia and Montenegro)*, Judgment, 26 February 2007, para. 430. Emphasis added. Accordingly, it is crucial whether there are political, military and financial or other links and support enabling the state 'to influence effectively the action of persons

While this judgment has largely been understood as to establish extraterritorial duties on the prevention of genocide,[76] it appears that this interpretation is not mandatory (and could not be extended to other violations of rules not constituting *ius cogens*). The Court did not explicitly refer to extraterritorial measures the respondent State should have taken to comply with its positive duty. Rather, it can be held that reference was implicitly made to measures that the State, having decisive influence on the abusers, should have taken in view of their prospect to exercise an extraterritorial *effect*.

d. Conclusion: Extraterritorial Application and Effects of Positive Obligations

As international human rights law stands today, jurisdiction is generally understood as territorial control or control over the victim. Human rights treaties thus apply first and foremost on the State's own territory and, under exceptional circumstances, extraterritorially. Extraterritorial obligations to take positive measures only exist to a very limited extent, because they are, by and large, territorially bound. However, the rules on the extraterritorial application of human rights must not be confounded with settings, where a State must take measures on its own territory because it exercises decisive influence on abusers acting abroad. Consequently, and as will be shown below, positive obligations of cooperation are decisive to address transborder situations of discrimination and violence against women.

2. Personal Scope of Application or Attribution

Human rights (conventions) are, in principle, only binding upon States (parties to a convention) in relation to individuals. Consequently, human rights obligations only

likely to commit' the crimes. This capacity depends on the *de jure* and *de facto* relationship between the state and the abuser as well as on the 'geographical distance' of the state whose responsibility is in issue and the scene of the events.

[76] For example, in his separate opinion, Judge *Tomka* drew attention to the fact that 'a broad construction of [the obligation to prevent] would mean that preventive action undertaken by one *state in the territory of another* should be viewed as lawful'. Implicitly referring to the 'responsibility to protect' which has no legal force, he recalled that 'in practice, unilateral or plurilateral actions undertaken without the authorization of the Security Council still remain controversial', ICJ, *Case concerning application of the Convention of Prevention and Punishment of the Crime of Genocide (Bosnia and Herzegovina v. Serbia and Montenegro)*, Judgment, 26 February 2007, Separate opinion Judge Tomka, para. 66. See also Ryngaert, 'Jurisdiction: Towards a reasonable test', in Langford, 2013, p. 203; Hakimi, 'State Bystander Responsibility', (2010) 21 *EJIL*, p. 346, fn. 27. On the extraterritorial application of positive human rights obligations, see also Schutter et al., 'Commentary to the Maastricht Principles on extraterritorial obligations of states in the area of economic, social and cultural rights', (2012) 34 *Hum. Rts. Q.*, Principles No. 3 and 9. These principles have been developed by a think-tank and are non-binding. However, as an international expert opinion, the Maastricht Principles may function as subsidiary means for the determination of rules of law, Art. 38 (1) lit. d of the ICJ-Statute.

apply to State acts, *viz.* State actions and omissions. As a State cannot act on its own, States can only act through natural persons, who may function as State organs, State agents or officials, or through other entities. To constitute an act of State, an action or omission of such person must thus be attributable to a State.

The international rules on the attribution of internationally wrongful acts are codified in the International Law Commission's *Articles on Responsibility of States for Internationally Wrongful Acts* (hereafter ILC Articles).[77] These rules, and particularly those relevant hereafter, largely codify customary international law. The Articles differentiate between the question of attribution of an internationally wrongful act (Part One of the Articles) and the legal consequences of a breach of a State's primary obligation (Part Two). Part One expresses the general principles of attribution of an internationally wrongful act of State and does not only apply to interstate relations but also to relations with other actors.[78] They apply to human rights settings as well.[79]

Under Article 4, an act (action or omission) is attributable to a State, first, if the conduct is exercised by one of its State organs.

Secondly, under Article 7 ILC Articles, a conduct is attributable to the State if a person or entity empowered by internal law to exercise elements of the governmental authority is *acting in that capacity* even if it exceeds its authority or contravenes instructions.[80] Consequently, the provision distinguishes between personal ('private') acts and 'public' acts, that is, 'acts within the scope of (alleged) authority'[81] which is particularly relevant for acts of sexualized violence.

The underlying distinction between private and public/official acts as made by Article 7 does, however, not necessarily apply to human rights violations committed in the context of an armed conflict. Under Article 3 of the Convention (IV) respecting the Laws and Customs of War on Land of 1907, '[a belligerent party] shall be responsible *for all acts* committed by persons forming part of its

[77]ILC, *Draft articles on Responsibility of States for Internationally Wrongful Acts with commentaries*, 2001.

[78]*James Crawford* explains in his commentary on the Articles, that they 'do (. . .) not exclude the possibility that an internationally wrongful act may involve legal consequences in the relations between the State responsible for that act and persons or entities other than States. This follows from Article 1, which covers all international obligations of the State and not only those owed to other States.' Crawford (ed.), *The ILC Draft Articles on Responsibility of States for Internationally Wrongful Acts*, Art. 28, para. 3.

[79]See, e.g., ECtHR, *Jaloud v. The Netherlands* [GC], Judgment, 20 November 2014, para. 98.

[80]Arts 5, 7. Art. 7 ILC Articles reads as follows: 'Acts of a State organ or of a person or entity empowered to exercise elements of the governmental power are to be considered a conduct of the State if the organ, person or entity acts in that capacity, even if it exceeds its authority or contravenes instructions.' See, e.g., ECtHR, *Aydin v. Turkey* [GC], Judgment, 25 September 1997. The assumption that torture is a public act if committed by a public official, for instance in prison, should however not be transposed to the claim of immunity in a criminal proceeding, see Chinkin, 'A critique of the Public/Private Dimension', (1999) 10 *EJIL*, p. 391.

[81]Crawford, *Brownlie's Principles of public international law*, 2012, p. 550.

armed forces'.[82] Along these lines, it is acknowledged that because State agents are put in a position which allow for abuse in warlike settings,[83] a State needs to be held responsible for all abuses including sexualized violence. Article 3 is *lex specialis* to Article 7 ILC Articles.[84] Consequently, the criminal activities committed during an armed conflict by members of the armed forces of a belligerent party going round the city in their spare time raping civilians or forcing children to sexualized acts in exchange for food may well be attributed to a State.

While this generalized attribution is a historical improvement, this norm creates some loopholes insofar as it is limited to acts of members of the belligerent parties and to armed conflicts *stricto sensu*. Firstly, acts of members of armed forces of a State not party to the conflict will not be attributed to that State under the said Article 3, but only under Article 7 ILC Articles.

Secondly, it appears to be an undue result if conflict-related sexualized violence is not attributed to a State only because under IHL the conflict is considered to be terminated. It may well be that a soldier being charged with the protection of a refugee camp commit sexualized crimes.

Thirdly, under Article 8 ILC Articles an act is attributable to a State if a person is 'in fact acting on the instructions of, or under the direction or control of, that State in carrying out the conduct' (*de facto* organ). Control is exercised where 'an organ of the State gave the instructions or provided the direction pursuant to which the perpetrators of the wrongful act acted or where it exercised *effective* control over the action during which the wrong was committed'.[85] In contrast, 'overall control' as suggested by the ICTY in its well-known *Tadic case* is 'unsuitable, for it stretches

[82]Emphasis added.

[83]Sassòli, 'State Responsibility for violation of international humanitarian law', (2002) 84 *IRRC*, p. 406 wfr.

[84]Referring to this rule as customary international law, the ICJ considered in its judgment *Armed Activities on the territory of the Congo (DRC v. Uganda)* that all acts of a State's armed forces perpetrated during an armed conflict are to be attributable to that state. The Court rejected '[t]he contention that the persons concerned did not [loot natural resources] in the capacity of persons exercising governmental authority'. It held that it was without merits whether the state agents acted *ultra vires* or were given instructions. ICJ, *Armed Activities on the territory of the Congo (DRC v. Uganda)*, Judgment, 19 December 2005, paras 213–214; Doswald-Beck/Henckaerts (eds.), *Customary international humanitarian law*, 2005, Rule 149. This position is unanimously supported by scholarly writing, e.g., Sassòli, 'State Responsibility for violation of international humanitarian law', (2002) 84 *IRRC*, pp. 405–406 wfr; Crawford, *Brownlie's Principles of public international law*, 2012, p. 551.

[85]Emphasis added. ICJ, *Case concerning application of the Convention of Prevention and Punishment of the Crime of Genocide (Bosnia and Herzegovina v. Serbia and Montenegro)*, Judgment, 26 February 2007, para. 406; *Cf.* also ICJ, *Armed Activities on the territory of the Congo (DRC v. Uganda)*, Judgment, 19 December 2005, para. 160; ICJ, *Military and paramilitary activities in and against Nicaragua (Nicaragua v. United States of America)*, Judgment (merits), 27 June 1986, para. 115.

too far, almost to breaking point, the connection which must exist between the conduct of a State's organs and its international responsibility'.[86]

Finally, Article 9 ILC Articles suggests that under exceptional circumstances, an act may also be attributed to a State if a person or group of persons is in fact exercising elements of the governmental authority such as running a prison in the absence or default of the official authorities. Besides, acts committed by members of an insurrectional or other movement which later becomes the new government of a State or which succeeds in establishing a new State in part of the territory of a pre-existing State must be considered acts of that (new) State.[87] An act is also attributable to a State if and to the extent that it acknowledges and adopts a conduct as its own.[88] On gender-based violence attribution through acknowledgement is however unlikely. Ultimately, while this is not a question of attribution but responsibility, it should be noted that the responsibility of a State 'may also arise in connection with the act of another State, when an agent of the former State aids or assists an agent of the latter "in a view to facilitating the abuse"'.[89]

If under these rules actions or legally relevant omissions are attributable to a State, these acts must comply with those human rights obligations that are binding upon the respective State.

3. Particular Problems with Regard to Gender-Based Violence in Wartime: Temporal and Material Scope of Application

Under the traditional legal doctrine, persons affected by sexualized and gender-based violence during an armed conflict were not able to invoke their human rights. In times of war, the argument went, a State has no human rights obligations. However, views regarding this matter have changed over the last decades.[90] Whereas there is now quite a consensus that the application of human rights is not temporarily limited to times of peace, but instead is permanent, it still remains disputed to what extent human rights apply and how conflicting rules of human rights and humanitarian norms have to be balanced.

This section traces the development concerning the temporal and material scope of application. It first explains why human rights norms apply permanently and thus also in times of armed conflicts (temporal scope). It then discusses the relationship of

[86]ICJ, *Case concerning application of the Convention of Prevention and Punishment of the Crime of Genocide (Bosnia and Herzegovina v. Serbia and Montenegro)*, Judgment, 26 February 2007, para. 406.

[87]Art. 10 ILC Articles.

[88]Art. 11 ILC Articles.

[89]Arts 16–18 ILC Articles.

[90]Henckaerts, 'Concurrent Application of Humanitarian Law and Human Rights Law', in Arnold/ Quénivet, 2008, pp. 252.

human rights and humanitarian law (material scope) concerning sexualized and gender-based violence.

a. Temporal Restriction or Permanent Applicability

While international humanitarian law was developed for the purpose to apply to situations of armed conflicts, human rights treaties were thought to apply in peacetime but not during armed conflicts.[91] This separate development notwithstanding,[92] a temporally limited applicability of human rights is now widely rejected.[93] Rather, human rights are held to apply permanently.

When the question of the concurrent application first came up, the application of IHR treaties in wartime was said to contravene the traditional 'doctrine on the effect of war on treaties'.[94] Accordingly, in times of war treaty obligations of States would be suspended. Consequently, States would not be bound to human rights standards vis-à-vis both their own and foreign nationals subjected to their jurisdiction.[95] Later, this doctrine was said not to apply to human rights treaties simply because IHL had been developed beforehand.[96] In 2011, the International Law Commission (ILC) concluded that an armed conflict does not *ipso facto* suspend or terminate the operation of treaties between their contracting parties.[97] Accordingly, the general rules on the law of treaties do not prejudge any question that may arise from the outbreak of hostilities between States.[98] However, by their nature, human rights treaties would imply their permanent application, even if or because some rights

[91]Kolb, 'The relationship between international humanitarian law and human rights law', (1998) 38 *IRRC*.

[92]Henckaerts, 'Concurrent Application of Humanitarian Law and Human Rights Law', in Arnold/Quénivet, 2008, pp. 238.

[93]See, Ben Naftali (ed.), *International humanitarian law and international human rights law*, 2011; Dröge, 'Elective Affinities?', (2008) 90 *IRRC*; Provost, *International human rights and humanitarian law*, 2002, pp. 247–276.

[94]For a detailed and historical analyses of the debate regarding the fate of international treaties in wartime, see Vöneky, *Die Fortgeltung des Umweltvölkerrechts in internationalen bewaffneten Konflikten*, 2012, p. 193.

[95]On the extent to which States are bound to respect IHR extraterritorially, see for the Inter-American system IAComHR, *Alejandre v. Cuba*, Case 11.589, Report No. 86/99, 29 September 1999 and for the European system ECtHR, *Bankovic and others v. Belgium and others* [GC], 12 December 2001; Roxstrom, 'The NATO Bombing Case (Bancovic et al. v. Belgium at al.) and the limits of western human rights protection', (2005) 23 *B.U. Int'l L.J;* Jankowska-Gilberg, 'Das Al-Skeini-Urteil des Europäischen Gerichtshofs für Menschenrechte – eine Abkehr von Banković?', (2012) 50 *AVR*; Naert, 'The European Court of Human Rights' Al-Jedda and Al-Skeini Judgments', (2011) 50 *Military Law Review*.

[96]Ronzitti, 'Access to Justice and Compensation for Violations of the Law of War', in Francioni, 2007, p. 99.

[97]ILC, *Effects of Armed Conflicts on Treaties, with commentaries*, 2011, Art. 3.

[98]Art. 73 VCLT.

guaranteed by them can be derogated.[99] The ILC approach reflects what is nowadays widely accepted. The better arguments fight indeed for the applicability of human rights treaties during armed conflicts.

Firstly, some regional and international human rights conventions explicitly provide for non-derogable rights in times of State emergency. Other human rights treaties explicitly refer to times of war.[100] Even where there is no explicit reference to war but only to a general public emergency, such derogation clauses indicate the application of human rights treaties during armed conflicts. This is because a situation of an armed conflict itself is nothing else but a State emergency. The mere threat of war may even be considered a state of emergency.[101] Considering the provisions and practice under the ACHR, the ECHR and the ICCPR, one can conclude that State emergency generally relates to an exceptional situation that constitutes a threat to the life of the nation or to the security or independence of the State.[102] From a customary law perspective, it follows therefrom that, even during the disputed acts in question it was not a member of any human rights convention, a State is bound at least to a minimum of human rights, if derogation has been declared and somehow notified.[103] Hence, it has come to the fore that, even during armed conflicts, a minimum of 'core' rights always must be respected.

Secondly, international humanitarian law conventions make several explicit references to 'other applicable rules of international law relating to the protection of fundamental human rights during armed conflicts'.[104] For example, the above discussed 'more favourable treatment clause' under Article 75 AP I being included in different IHL treaties, it testifies to the openness of international humanitarian law to other branches of international law.[105]

Thirdly, even if IHR and IHL had been conceived as two distinct bodies of law, recent developments of international conventions and treaties—such as the Optional Protocol to the Convention on the Rights of the Child on the Involvement of Children in Armed Conflicts (OPCRCAC)—strongly bear testimony to the

---

[99]ILC, *Effects of Armed Conflicts on Treaties, with commentaries*, 2011, Art. 7 and Annex.

[100]See, e.g., Article 4 ICCPR, Article 15 ECHR, Article 27 ACHR and Article 2 (1) CAT. To give a restrictive example among IHR treaties, 'core rights' that continue to be granted under the ECHR in the case of State emergency include the right to life, the prohibition of torture, protection against slavery and the protection against retroactive criminal law.

[101]Concerning Chile (and later Paraguay), the IAComHR applied the rules governing State emergency, despite the fact that none of them was a member to the IACHR, see, IAComHR, *Report on the Situation of Human Rights in Paraguay*, 31 January 1978, p. 212 and IAComHR, *Report on the Situation of Human Rights in Chile*, 25 October 1974, p. 14.

[102]Provost, *International human rights and humanitarian law*, 2002, pp. 271 referring to the ECHR, ACHR and ICCPR.

[103]For judicial practice, see Provost, *International human rights and humanitarian law*, 2002, First Edition 2002, p. 269 wfr.

[104]Art. 72 AP I. It can remain open, whether common Art. 2 of the GCs, stating that the conventions apply in 'addition to provisions which shall be implemented in peacetime' and must be interpreted as referring to human rights provisions that subsequently came into force.

[105]Ticehurst, 'The Martens Clause and the laws of armed conflict', (1997) *IRRC*.

applicability of both human rights and IHL in international and non-international armed conflicts.[106]

Ultimately, it has become a common practice of international organizations and (quasi-)judicial bodies to apply human rights in wartime. From the 1960s onward, different United Nations organs affirmed the applicability of human rights treaties in wartime.[107] Human rights violations that occurred in the context of armed conflicts and occupation such as in former Yugoslavia, Afghanistan, Iraq, Syria and Russia have been condemned by different UN organs and national authorities.[108] Ultimately, in 1996 and 2004, in two Adversary Opinions on nuclear weapons and on the legal consequences of the construction of a wall in Palestine, as well as in the *DRC vs. Uganda case*, the ICJ made a clear statement in favor of the principal applicability of *inter alia* ICCPR, CRC, OPCRCAC and ACHRP in armed conflicts and, hence, of human rights in general.[109] On CEDAW, the Committee too clarified its territorial and extraterritorial application in armed conflicts.[110]

b. Material Scope: Normative Conflicts

1) Coexisting Norms: Applying HRL and IHL During Armed Conflicts

As shown, in times of public emergency and armed conflict, a State is bound by human rights. It is—in principle—bound by the entire *corpus* of obligations encompassed by the conventions it is a party to as well as by international customary law. However, a State may declare a derogation insofar as it is allowed to do so. A State must then comply with the formal requirements and will, nonetheless, continue to be bound by a minimum of core rights. The question then arises how (apparent) normative conflicts of obligations under IHL and IHR may be resolved.

---

[106] Dröge, 'Elective Affinities?', (2008) 90 *IRRC*, p. 507.

[107] See, e.g., UNGA Res. 60/147, *Basic Principles and Guidelines on the Right to a Remedy and Reparation for Victims of Gross Violations of International Human Rights Law and Serious Violations of International Humanitarian Law*, 21 March 2006; The African Commission on Human and People's Rights (Commission Nationale des Droits de l'Homme et des Libertés v. Chad (Communication No. 74/92), 18th Ordinary Session, 2–11 October 1995, International Human Rights Reports 4 (1997), p. 94, para. 21; CEDAW, *General Recommendation No. 28 on the core obligations of state parties under article 2 of the CEDAW*, 2010, para. 11; for further references, see Dröge, 'The Interplay Between International Humanitarian Law And International Human Rights Law In Situations Of Armed Conflict', (2007) 40 *Isr. L. Rev.*, p. 315; Provost, *International human rights and humanitarian law*, 2002, pp. 2–12.

[108] For detailed references, Henckaerts, 'Concurrent Application of Humanitarian Law and Human Rights Law', in Arnold/Quénivet, 2008, pp. 250.

[109] ICJ, *Legality of the Threat or Use of Nuclear Weapons*, Advisory Opinion, 08 July 1996, para. 25; ICJ, *Legal Consequences of the Construction of a Wall in the Occupied Palestinian Territory*, Advisory Opinion, 09 July 2004, para. 106; ICJ, *Armed Activities on the territory of the Congo (DRC v. Uganda)*, Judgment, 19 December 2005, paras 215.

[110] CEDAW Committee, *General Recommendation No. 30 on women in conflict prevention, conflict, and post conflict situations*, 18 October 2013, paras 8.

a) Formal Requirements for a Derogation of Human Rights Obligations

If a human rights convention allows for the derogation of certain rights in times of public emergency and war, the derogation must formally be declared as required under the instrument in question.[111] To suspend certain treaty obligations to the extent strictly required by the exigencies of the situation, States must officially proclaim and notify the public emergency to the competent treaty body. Only in this case, human rights obligations are limited to non-derogable ones.[112] In practice, however, derogation seems to be rare.[113]

b) Non-derogable Rights

Under all human rights regimes the right to life, and the rights to freedom from slavery or servitude, torture and inhuman treatment are protected under all circumstances.[114] States are not exempt from the obligation not to discriminate because of 'race, color, sex, language, religion, or social origin'.[115] The following ACHR additional rights are exempt from suspension: the rights of the family, of the child, to a name and nationality, the freedom of conscience and religion and the judicial guarantees encompassed by Articles 7 (6), 8 (1), 25 (1) of the ACHR, which are essential for the protection of such rights.[116] Most importantly, the legal commitment under CEDAW to women's equality cannot be suspended in wartime or otherwise.[117] It is thus consequent that CEDAW does not foresee the possibility of derogation in times of public emergency. If a State derogates from certain guarantees provided by general human rights regimes, measures adopted must be free from discrimination based on race, color, sex, language and religion or social origin.[118]

c) The Principal Rules of Normative Conflict

Whether a derogation has been declared, a coherent application of IHL and IHR requires rules of conflict. In its 1996 *Advisory Opinion on the Legality of the Threat*

[111] Henckaerts, 'Concurrent Application of Humanitarian Law and Human Rights Law', in Arnold/Quénivet, 2008, p. 253; Dröge, 'Elective Affinities?', (2008) 90 *IRRC*.

[112] Henckaerts, 'Concurrent Application of Humanitarian Law and Human Rights Law', in Arnold/Quénivet, 2008, p. 254.

[113] For the state parties to the ECHR, e.g., see Gioia, 'The Role of the European Court of Human Rights in Monitoring Compliance with Humanitarian Law in Armed Conflict', in Ben Naftali, 2011, p. 219.

[114] Art. 27 (2) ACHR; Article 15 (2) ECHR; Article 4 (2) ICCPR. The African Charter contains no provision on derogation.

[115] Art. 27 ACHR; *Cf.* also Art. 4 ICCPR; *ex neg.* Art. 15 (1) ECHR.

[116] Burgorgue-Larsen, 'The Right to Effective Remedy', in Burgorgue-Larsen/Úbeda de Torres/Greenstein, 2011, p. 680.

[117] Chinkin/Freeman, 'Introduction', in Rudolf/Freeman/Chinkin, 2012, p. 28.

[118] *Cf.* Art. 4 ICCPR; see also Art. 14 ECHR, 27 ACHR.

or Use of Nuclear Weapons, the Court held that the ICCPR 'does not cease in times of war', but that humanitarian law may provide specific rules that apply as *lex specialis*.[119] In its 2004 *Advisory Opinion on the Legal Consequences of the Construction of a Wall in the Occupied Palestinian Territory*, the ICJ more generally held that

> ...the protection offered by human rights conventions does not cease in case of armed conflict, save through the effect of provisions for derogation of the kind to be found in Article 4 of the International Covenant on Civil and Political Rights. As regards the relationship between international humanitarian law and human rights law, there are thus three possible situations: some rights may be exclusively matters of international humanitarian law; others may be exclusively matters of human rights law; yet others may be matters of both these branches of international law. In order to answer the question put to it, the Court will have to take into consideration both these branches of international law, namely human rights law and, as lex specialis, international humanitarian law.[120]

Hence, the ICJ suggested three possible relationships between norms of both bodies of law: (1) exclusive application of a IHL provision, because, for example, it deals with questions not covered by the other regime, or because it prevails over an applicable rule of the other branch; (2) exclusive application of an IHR provision because, for example, it specifies or interprets a rule of IHL or has revised an older rule of IHL; (3) simultaneous application of rules from both branches of law.[121] Consequently, neither does IHL apply *en bloc*[122] as l*ex specialis* nor does it generally derogate IHR as *legi generali.*[123]

Alongside with the *lex specialis* rule, it seems that where there is a dense body of specified humanitarian rules, which is the case for the law of international armed conflicts, it is likely that a rule of IHL applies. In turn, in non-international armed conflicts where the rules of IHL are less precise, human rights are more likely to

[119]ICJ, *Legality of the Threat or Use of Nuclear Weapons*, Advisory Opinion, 08 July 1996, para. 25.

[120]Emphasis added, ICJ, *Legal Consequences of the Construction of a Wall in the Occupied Palestinian Territory*, Advisory Opinion, 09 July 2004, para. 106. *Cf.* ICJ, *Armed Activities on the territory of the Congo (DRC v. Uganda)*, Judgment, 19 December 2005, paras 205.

[121]Sassòli, 'The Role of Human Rights and International Humanitarian Law in New Types of Armed Conflicts', in Ben Naftali, 2011, pp. 72–78.

[122]Sassòli, 'The Role of Human Rights and International Humanitarian Law in New Types of Armed Conflicts', in Ben Naftali, 2011, pp. 72.

[123]Henckaerts, 'Concurrent Application of Humanitarian Law and Human Rights Law', in Arnold/Quénivet, 2008, p. 264. Watkin, 'Controlling the use of force: a role for human rights norms in contemporary armed conflict', (2004) *AJIL*; Sassòli, 'The Role of Human Rights and International Humanitarian Law in New Types of Armed Conflicts', in Ben Naftali, 2011; Milanović, 'Norm Conflicts, International Humanitarian Law, and Human Rights Law', in Ben Naftali, 2011. See also UN Human Rights Committee, *General Comment No. 31*, 26 May 2004, para. 11.

apply.[124] In some contexts, the maxim *lex posterior derogat lex anterior* may also indicate the application of one regime.

Yet, as '[t]he source of the norm (whether treaty, custom, or general principle of international law) is not decisive for the determination of the more specific standard',[125] customary rules may also apply. The differing normative power of norms (ius cogens) may also be crucial.[126] Ultimately, conflicting norms can also be harmonized if interpreted under the principle of 'systemic integration' in a way as to render them compatible, considering the 'normal meaning, party will, legitimate expectations, good faith, and subsequent practice, as well as the "object and purpose" and the principle of effectiveness'.[127] Consequently, it largely depends on the specific case which norm of which branch of law applies.[128]

2) The Relationship Between IHL and IHR Provisions Protecting Against Conflict-Related Sexualized Violence

To establish which branch of law applies *in concreto*, one must thus examine which are the material norms potentially violated by the act in question. No conflict of norms can arise in cases of gender-based violence that lack the legally required nexus to the conflict, e.g. rape as a disciplinary sanction against soldiers, rape by civilians or domestic violence. To such cases, human rights law will apply exclusively.

However, on conflict-related sexualized violence, the relationship between IHL and IHR is highly context specific because both branches of law address the issue of sexualized violence. One can roughly distinguish between two settings: first, acts of sexualized violence covered by the grave breaches regime and, second, violence not covered by the grave breaches regime. The latter will predominantly be covered by human rights law.

a) Conflict-Related Sexualized Violence Covered by the Grave Breaches Regimes

As shown above, humanitarian rules clearly prohibit sexualized violence. IHL provides first and foremost rules of conduct for the parties to a conflict. In the context of an international armed conflict, this obligation to abstain from such violations is supplemented by a due diligence obligation to ensure the safety and protection of

[124]Milanović, 'Norm Conflicts, International Humanitarian Law, and Human Rights Law', in Ben Naftali, 2011; Abresch, 'A Human Rights Law of Internal Armed Conflict', (2005) 16 *EJIL*; Dröge, 'Elective Affinities?', (2008) 90 *IRRC*.

[125]ILC, *Fragmentation of International Law*, 18 July 2006, p. 8; see also ILC, *Fragmentation of International Law*, 13 April 2006.

[126]ILC, *Fragmentation of International Law*, 13 April 2006, pp. 166.

[127]ILC, *Fragmentation of International Law*, 13 April 2006, pp. 206, 208.

[128]*Cf.* also Milanović, 'A Norm Conflict Perspective on the Relationship between International Humanitarian Law and Human Rights Law', (2010) 14 *JCSL*.

protected persons against all kind of actors.[129] It is, however, not specified what kind of measures the Adversary State needs to take to comply with this provision. On *serious* forms of sexualized violence that fall under the grave breaches regime, whether committed by the State's own nationals or foreign nationals, States must put in place a legal framework, to instruct members of the army and to investigate, prosecute and punish *ex officio*. For such cases only, international humanitarian law clearly provides for both negative and positive obligations.

Applying the above exposed rules on norm conflicts, it appears that in such cases humanitarian rules must be interpreted from today's negative and positive human rights obligations, either as 'relevant rules of international law applicable in the relations between the parties' (Article 31 (3) (c) VCLT)[130] or, more generally, from the principle of 'systemic integration'.[131]

In turn, in international judicial practice, for reasons to be found in their jurisdictional competence and because the substantive content of IHR provisions parallels or specifies those of IHL, international courts interpret IHR in light of IHL.[132] The rules of conflicting branches and norms of law apply in the pure form where courts have the competence to adjudicate upon *all* norms binding on the parties. Human rights treaty bodies merely can base their decisions on norms they have the competence to adjudicate upon.[133] They are not entitled to assess compliance with humanitarian norms.[134] Nonetheless, under the principle of 'systemic integration' and to maintain the coherence and meaningfulness of the international legal order, such monitoring bodies consider the normative environment which includes humanitarian rules. Consequently, the respective human rights provisions are interpreted in light of

[129] Art. 27 GC IV. David, *Principes de droit des conflits armés*, 2012, p. 548; Eritrea Ethiopia Claims Commission, *Partial Award, Civilians Claims Ethiopia's Claim Nr. 5, between The Federal Democratic Republic of Ethiopia and The State of Eritrea*, 17 December 2004, paras 98.

[130] Note that this provision 'does not specify whether, in determining relevance and applicability one must have regard to all parties to the treaty in question, or merely to those in dispute'. ILC, *Fragmentation of International Law*, 13 April 2006, p. 215. If interpreted as to require another treaty concluded between all parties of the treaty in need to be interpreted, this would be useless for our concern (if not every case), as, unlike the GCs IV, no human rights treaty has 196 state parties (e.g. ICCPR 168, CEDAW 174 state parties at the time of writing). However, Article 31 (3) (c) is said to express the general principle of 'systemic integration', ILC, *Fragmentation of International Law*, 13 April 2006, pp. 206.

[131] ILC, *Fragmentation of International Law*, 13 April 2006, pp. 206.

[132] E.g., ECtHR, *Hassan vs. UK* [GC], Judgment, 16 September 2014, paras 102–106 wfr. For the IACtHR, see Tigroudja, 'The Inter-American Court of Human Rights and international humanitarian law', in Kolb/Gaggioli, 2013.

[133] E.g., Article 19 ECHR. Henckaerts, 'Concurrent Application of Humanitarian Law and Human Rights Law', in Arnold/Quénivet, 2008, p. 265.

[134] In the *Tablada case*, the IAComHR did so and received harsh criticism, see Zegveld, 'The Inter American Commission on Human Rights and International Humanitarian Law', (1998) 38 *IRRC*; Martin, 'Application du droit international humanitaire par la Cour interaméricaine des droits de l'homme', (2001) 83 *IRRC*.

humanitarian law and with due regard to the aggravated circumstances during war.[135]

Hence, when adjudicating upon violations of the right to life during hostilities, claims before a regional human rights court may fail at the substantive level if humanitarian rules allow for a conduct which human rights would prohibit as such.[136] In turn, where IHR and IHL provide the same level of protection, as is the case with conflict-related sexualized violence, a violation of the respective human right can never be justified by humanitarian rules. Neither can sexualized acts be committed by accident nor in a proportionate manner. As will be shown below,[137] even on positive obligations to investigate, prosecute and punish, both branches of law will come to the same result.

For example, in the context of an international armed conflict, soldiers pass through a village and aggress the inhabitants sexually, rape women in front of others, mutilate them and kill the remaining men. These acts are grave breaches of humanitarian law under Articles 27, 32, 147 IV of the GC IV and violate the rights to life and to be free of torture and inhuman treatment. Humanitarian law requires positive measures (investigation, etc.) to be taken. As we will see below, this is what human rights require, too—although their requirements are more precise. The applicable norms of both human rights law and IHL have the same content with no norm trumping another. Instead, the norms coexist and need to be applied simultaneously forming a cohesive body of international law. A human rights body concerned with this case can simply apply the legal regime it is competent to monitor; the interpretation of it in light of humanitarian law will lead to the same result.

b) Conflict-Related Sexualized Violence Not Being Covered by the Grave Breaches Regimes

The question arises whether there is a conflict of norms between IHL and HRL when acts of conflict-related sexualized violence are not covered by the grave breaches regime, either because the violence does not reach the gravity threshold or because it is committed against specific persons or during a conflict not of an international character.

As seen above, the simple protection regime under Articles 72, 75 (1) and (8) AP I indicates that within the context of an international armed conflict, *all persons in the power of a party* who do not benefit from a more favorable treatment under international law are protected against violations of rights that are exactly the

---

[135]For the practice of the HRC, the IAComHR, the IACtHR and the ECtHR, see Abresch, 'A Human Rights Law of Internal Armed Conflict', (2005) 16 *EJIL*; Tigroudja, 'The Inter-American Court of Human Rights and international humanitarian law', in Kolb/Gaggioli, 2013.

[136]See, e.g., ICJ, *Legality of the Threat or Use of Nuclear Weapons*, Advisory Opinion, 08 July 1996, para. 25; ECtHR, *Hassan vs. UK* [GC], Judgment, 16 September 2014, paras 102–106; Krähenmann, 'Positive obligations in human rights law during armed conflicts', in Kolb/Gaggioli, 2013, pp. 170 wfr.

[137]See PART II.

non-derogable ones under human rights treaties.[138] However, all persons under the jurisdiction of a State (including the State's own nationals) are protected by human rights and human rights treaties provide for a more favorable protection: their provision and respective interpretation are far more precise and clearly provide for positive obligations. Nonetheless, it is evident that particularly positive human rights obligations applicable in the relevant case must be interpreted with due regard to the aggravated circumstances.[139]

It thus appears that during an international armed conflict human rights obligations will predominantly determine those cases where, first, sexualized violence committed against a person in the power of a party fails to reach the gravity threshold, or, second, where the person aggressed is not a 'protected person' because she is a national of the State whose agent is the perpetrator.

However, in cases having a link to an internal conflict, human rights law appears to prevail over humanitarian law insofar as the relevant acts are acts of States. This is because IHL merely foresees very vague obligations that only refer to severe cases constituting inhuman treatment. In contrast, IHR provisions are more precise and even include positive obligations. Human rights law can thus be said to specify or interpret these humanitarian rules.

c. Conclusion

Whereas it is acknowledged that HRL applies at all times and not only in peacetime, various factors are relevant to decide to what *extent* it applies to State acts relating to conflict-related sexualized violence. It depends, first and foremost, on the context of the specific case, on whether a state of emergency has been declared and notified, and on the rules of norm conflicts applicable.

If the conditions for a public emergency are met and the State officially declares a derogation, only non-derogable human rights provisions and those under CEDAW protect against gender-based violence. If no declaration has been made, the acting State is bound by all human rights obligations guaranteed under treaties it is a party of and by customary human rights law which provides for a core of non-derogable rights.

When taking a closer look to the potential situations of conflict-related sexualized violence, it appears that many of them are not covered by IHL but by human rights provisions. This is particularly true for violence that, firstly, is committed against non-protected persons, that, secondly, fails to fulfill the gravity threshold and that, ultimately, has no nexus to the conflict. Only on grave acts of sexualized violence

---

[138] Rights to life, health, or physical or mental well-being of persons, physical or mental torture, mutilation, and outrages upon personal dignity, in particular humiliating and degrading treatment, enforced prostitution and any form of indecent assault. Art. 75 (1) and (8); Pictet et al. (eds.), *Commentary on the Additional Protocols of June 8 1977 to the Geneva Conventions of 12 August 1949*, 1987, para. 3040.

[139] See below, Chap. 5 B.

committed in the context of an international armed conflict, IHL foresees specific obligations under the grave breaches regime. However, in these cases both, the humanitarian and human rights regimes, prohibit these crimes and foresee positive obligations to prosecute perpetrators. The legal assessments of breaches will by and large come to the same result.

II. Human Rights (Instruments) Protecting Against Gender-Based Violence

This section provides an overview of the existing universal and regional human rights systems that guarantee rights potentially violated by gender-based violence. It is only in the last decades that international human rights instruments and bodies took a clear and explicit stand to violence against women. While CEDAW hardly touches upon this issue, today it is acknowledged that even general human rights instruments implicitly protect against gender-based violence. More recent treaties explicitly address violence against women and provide for detailed obligations. Accordingly, state parties have recognized that gender-based violence is a structural problem which is rooted in gender hierarchies.

1. Specific Instruments and Conventions Explicitly Addressing Violence Against Women[140]

Whilst CEDAW itself only touches upon specific forms of violence against women, CEDAW Committee and the UNGA were trailblazers taking the first important steps to creating international awareness for violence against women in the 1990s. They issued two crucial instruments that apply a holistic approach to violence against women. Subsequently, regional conventions and soft law instruments explicitly addressing gender-based violence were negotiated. Apart from the Council of Europe Convention on preventing and combating violence against women and domestic violence (Istanbul Convention), these global and regional human rights instruments largely focus on the protection of female victims only.

a. Universal Instruments and Soft Law Documents

1) CEDAW

The International Convention for the Elimination of all forms of Discrimination against Women (CEDAW) was developed by the UN Commission on the Status of

[140] An earlier version of this text has in part been published in Henn, 'Gender injustice, discrimination, and the CEDAW: A women's life course perspective', in Jänterä-Jareborg/Tigroudja, 2016.

Women and adopted by the General Assembly in 1979. It entered into force in 1981. Having 189 state parties,[141] it can be said to be a universal instrument. There is a State reporting procedure and an interstate procedure. These enforcement mechanisms have first been quite weak until the entry into force of the Optional Protocol in December 2000. The Optional Protocol expands the power of the CEDAW Committee, so that it can receive complaints of individuals or groups of individuals.[142] Complaints can even be submitted on behalf of individuals or groups, with their consent. The protocol has 106 state parties.[143] However, although CEDAW is unique in approaching issues that particularly affect women, it offers crucial structural weaknesses, such as the considerable reservation regime.[144]

CEDAW also applies to girls, because girls 'are part of the larger community of women'.[145] Under Article 6 CEDAW, state parties agreed to take all appropriate measures, including legislation, to suppress all forms of trafficking in women and exploitation of female prostitution. Article 6 is the only provision under CEDAW that explicitly addresses one form of sexualized violence. No other provision makes explicit reference to gender-based violence against women.

2) Soft Law Instruments

There are several soft law instruments calling upon States to adopt laws, policies and special measures to eliminate violence against women. Attention must be drawn to the General Recommendation No. 19 of the CEDAW Committee, to the UNGA Declaration on the Elimination of Violence against Women and to the package of UNSC resolution that are generally known as 'Women, peace and security agenda'.

---

[141]United Nations Treaty Collection, available under https://treaties.un.org/Pages/ViewDetails.aspx?src=TREATY&mtdsg_no=IV-8&chapter=4&lang=en accessed 19 January 2016. It should be noted that under Art. 27 CEDAW, the Convention is binding upon ratification or accession. Many States therefore directly proceeded to ratification without making a signature beforehand.

[142]Article 2 OP to CEDAW provides: 'Communications may be submitted by or on behalf of individuals or groups of individuals, under the jurisdiction of a State Party, claiming to be victims of a violation of any of the rights set forth in the Convention by that State Party. Where a communication is submitted on behalf of individuals or groups of individuals, this shall be with their consent unless the author can justify acting on their behalf without such consent.'

[143]United Nations Treaty Collection, available under https://treaties.un.org/Pages/ViewDetails.aspx?src=TREATY&mtdsg_no=IV-8-b&chapter=4&lang=en accessed 19 January 2016.

[144]If States declare reservations to provisions of the Convention, they are only valid if they do not contradict the very purpose of a treaty, see Art. 28 (2) CEDAW. Regarding the family rights under Article 16, for instance, the Committee considered reservations incompatible and thus invalid, as they contradict the very purpose of the Convention CEDAW, *General Recommendation No. 29 on article 16 of CEDAW*, 26 February 2013, para. 3 and General recommendation No. 20 on reservations (1992). For details, see Riddle, 'Making CEDAW Universal', (2002) 34 *Geo. Wash. Int'l L. Rev.*

[145]CEDAW, *General Recommendation No. 28 on the core obligations of state parties under article 2 of the CEDAW*, 2010, para. 21.

While they carry no legal force as such, these documents can be said to reflect an international consensus within the international community rejecting violence against women. General recommendations give authoritative guidance to the understanding and coherent interpretation and application of CEDAW by States.[146] Along these lines, the ICJ ascribes 'great weight to the interpretation adopted' by UN human rights treaty bodies.[147] States include in their periodic reports to the CEDAW Committee steps taken to combat violence against women. Domestic courts refer to these documents as expressing a legal standard which should be respected.[148] Ultimately, these documents gained importance through the frequent referral by international courts.[149]

a) CEDAW Committee: General Recommendation No. 19

In 1992, the Committee issued General Recommendation No. 19 on violence against women (hereafter GR No. 19). Therein, for the very first time, violence against women was defined at the international level. Based on the Convention's concepts of discrimination and equality, the Committee equates sexualized violence to sex- and gender-based discrimination.[150] Accordingly, sexualized violence constitutes discrimination against women when State agents commit it 'intentionally, traditionally or subliminally' against female prisoners, but not (or proportionally less) against men.[151]

The Committee urges States to 'exercise due diligence to prevent, investigate and, in accordance with national legislation, punish acts of violence against women, whether those acts are perpetrated by the State or private persons'.[152] Besides,

---

[146] Freeman/Chinkin, 'Introduction', in Rudolf/Freeman/Chinkin, 2012, p. 21.

[147] ICJ, *Ahmadou Sadio Diallo (Republic of Genuia v. Democratic Republic of Congo)*, Judgment (merits), 30 November 2010, para. 66. Although the Court referred to the HRC, this mutatis mutandis holds true for other human rights treaty bodies, see also Chinkin, 'Addressing violence against women in the Commonwealth within states' obligations under international law', (2014) 40 *Commonwealth Law Bulletin*, p. 473.

[148] For the practice of domestic courts within the Commonwealth, see Chinkin, 'Addressing violence against women in the Commonwealth within states' obligations under international law', (2014) 40 *Commonwealth Law Bulletin*, pp. 473.

[149] See, e.g., ECtHR, *M.C. v. Bulgaria*, Judgment, 04 December 2003, referring to GR No. 19 of the CEDAW Committee.

[150] Although CEDAW merely mentions distinction, exclusion or restriction made based on sex, it includes also gender-based discrimination, see Byrnes, 'Article 1', in Rudolf/Freeman/Chinkin, 2012, at 59; Chinkin/Freeman, 'Introduction', in Rudolf/Freeman/Chinkin, 2012, p. 15. In 2010, the CEDAW Committee stated in its General Recommendation No. 28 that the 'term gender refers to socially constructed identities, attributes and roles for women and men and society's social and cultural meaning for these biological differences resulting in hierarchical relationships between women and men and in the distribution of power and rights favouring men and disadvantaging women'.

[151] CEDAW, *General Recommendation 19*, 1992, para. 6.

[152] CEDAW, *General Recommendation 19*, 1992, para. 9.

when a State fails to provide for appropriate measures protecting against gendered crimes, this State may be violating its obligations ensuing from the right to non-discrimination under CEDAW. Applying a holistic approach, the Committee calls for attention on how gender hierarchies and different forms of gender-based violence against women, both in peacetime and during armed conflicts, impair or nullify women's enjoyment of human rights and fundamental freedoms.[153] On situations of armed conflicts and occupation of territories, the Committee recommends special measures that States are required to adopt to protect women against increased prostitution, trafficking in and sexual assault of women.[154]

b) UNGA Declaration on the Elimination of Violence Against Women

In 1993, the UN General Assembly adopted a resolution on the elimination of VAW which is nearly identical to GR No. 19. It enumerates a series of human rights that can be infringed by acts of (sexualized) violence against women. It underlines the prevalence of violence against women in all areas of life and its seamless ability of the various forms to increase, disappear and change over time.[155] It recalls that it is perpetrated and/or condoned in the family, in the community—defended as traditional, though harmful, practices—on the streets, at the workplace, by State officials and public institutions, in times of peace, times of transition and during armed conflicts.[156] The UNGA acknowledges that violence against women constitutes one of 'the crucial social mechanisms by which women are forced into a subordinate position compared with men' and that the reasons for violence against women being so prevalent are to be found in 'historically unequal power relations between men and women, which have led to domination over women by men [. . .]'.[157]

c) Women, Peace and Security Agenda of the UNSC

Under the women, war and security (WPS) agenda, the UNSC, the CEDAW Committee and the UNSG issued a series of non-binding documents that are central to the international discourse on violence against women.[158] In its first well-known

[153]CEDAW, *General Recommendation 19*, 1992, paras 7.

[154]CEDAW, *General Recommendation No. 19 on violence against women*, 1992, para. 16.

[155]UNGA Res. 48/104, *Declaration on the Elimination of Violence against Women*, 20 December 1993.

[156]For details, see Askin, 'Treatment of Sexual Violence in Armed Conflicts', in Brouwer et al., 2013; Inal, *"So what?" The Impact of Legalization on change on the Ground,* 2010; Eriksson Baaz/ Stern, *Sexual violence as a weapon of war?*, 2013.

[157]UNGA Res. 48/104, *Declaration on the Elimination of Violence against Women*, 20 December 1993; UNSG, *In-Depth-Study on All Forms of Violence against Women*, 2006, para. 30; see also the Preamble of the Istanbul Convention.

[158]One must distinguish between binding resolutions under Chapter VII that foresee coercive measures and resolutions under Chapter VI including *thematic* resolutions that are non-coercive. The resolutions on women, war and security apply a comparatively weak language. For the

resolution 1325 (2000), the UN Security Council called on all parties to a conflict to take special measures to protect women against gender-based violence. The resolution strongly reflects human rights obligations existing under CEDAW[159] and obligations under IHL. It emphasizes 'the responsibility of all States to put an end to impunity and to prosecute those responsible for genocide, crimes against humanity, and war crimes including those relating to sexual and other violence against women and girls'.[160] It also 'stress[ed] the need to exclude these crimes, where feasible from amnesty provisions'.[161]

The UNSC adopted supplementary resolutions that recall the human rights obligations. UNSC resolutions 1820 (2008),[162] 1888 (2009),[163] 1889 (2009),[164] 1960 (2010),[165] 2106 (2013)[166] and 2122 (2013)[167] call for women's participation in peace negotiations and peacekeeping as well as in developing responses to conflict-related sexualized violence such as judicial, legal and security-sector reforms and the enforcement of the right to a remedy.[168] Reflecting existing positive State obligations on social and economic human rights, UNSC resolution 1889 encourages post-conflict States to improve the socio-economic situation 'through education, income generating activities, access to basic services, in particular health services'.[169] These aspects indicate a timid trend towards a transformative approach.

---

discussion on whether UNSC resolutions make international law, see Talmon, 'The Security Council as world legislature', (2005) *AJIL*; Cronin/Hurd (eds.), *The UN Security Council and the politics of international authority*, 2008; Alvarez, 'Legal Perspective', in Weiss/Daws, 2008; Chinkin, 'Normative Development in the International Legal System', in Shelton, 2003.

[159]CEDAW Committee, *General Recommendation No. 30 on women in conflict prevention, conflict, and post conflict situations*, 18 October 2013, para. 25.

[160]UNSC Res. 1325 (2000), 31 October 2000, paras. 10, 11.

[161]UNSC Res. 1325 (2000), 31 October 2000, paras. 10, 11.

[162]In the 1820 resolution, the SC stressed the impact sexual violence has on peace and security and that such violence 'can significantly exacerbate situations of armed conflicts and may impede the restoration of international peace and security'. For details, see Barrow, 'UN Security Council Resolutions 1325 and 1820: constructing gender in armed conflict and international humanitarian law', (2010) 92 *IRRC*; Anderson, 'Politics by Other Means: When does Sexual Violence Threaten International Peace and Security?', (2010) 17 *International Peacekeeping*.

[163]This resolution created the office of the Secretary-General's Special Representative on Sexual Violence in Conflict.

[164]Putting an emphasis on women's agency and participation in peace-building processes.

[165]Addressing accountability gaps in UNSC resolution 1325.

[166]Addressing AIDS in conflict and post-conflict settings.

[167]Addressing women's leadership.

[168]For an analysis, see Lewis et al., *Making the normative case*, April 2015, pp. 23. See also Olugbuo, 'Thematic Prosecution of International Sex Crimes and Stigmatisation of Victim and Survivors', in Bergsmo, 2012, pp. 131–133; Tachou-Sipowo, 'The Security Council on women in war', (2010) 92 *IRRC*; Tryggestad, 'Trick or Treat? The UN and Implementation of Security Council Resolution 1325 on Women, Peace, and Security', (2009) 15 *Global Governance: a review of multilateralism and international organizations*.

[169]UNSC Res. 1889 (2009), 5 October 2009, para. 10. For details, see Lewiset al., *Making the normative case*, April 2015, pp. 23.

b. Regional Human Rights Instruments

In contrast to the above discussed soft law instruments, the existing regional instruments are binding upon state parties. Apart from the 1994 Inter-American Convention on the Prevention, Punishment and Eradication of Violence against Women (Convention of Belém do Pará) and the 2011 European Council Convention on preventing and combating violence against women and domestic violence (Istanbul Convention), there is also the 2003 Protocol to the African Charter on Human and Peoples' Rights on the Rights of Women in Africa (Maputo Protocol). They all apply to situations of armed conflicts[170] and foresee no possibility for States to derogate from their obligations in times of emergency.

1) Organization of American States: 1994 Belém do Pará Convention

The 1994 Inter-American Convention on the Prevention, Punishment and Eradication of Violence against Women (Convention of Belém do Pará or Bélem Convention) is a treaty concluded under the auspice of the Organization of American States (OAS), which unites all 35 States of the Americas. The Belém Convention has been ratified by all OAS member States apart from the United States of America and Canada. Besides establishing a State reporting system,[171] the Convention enables state parties to request an advisory opinion on the interpretation of the Convention by the Inter-American Court of Human Rights (IACtHR).[172] Under Article 12, the Inter-American Commission of Human Rights (IAComHR) has the competence to consider individual petitions containing denunciations or complaints of violations of Article 7.[173] While the text of the Convention foresees no jurisdictional competence of the Court itself, the Court found to have jurisdiction *ratione materiae* to examine alleged violations of Article 7 of the Belém do Pará Convention in those cases where the Commission forwards the case to it.[174] The Court inferred its competence from Art. 12 where reference is made to 'the norms and procedures established by the American Convention on Human Rights and the Statutes and Regulations of the Inter-American Commission on Human Rights for lodging and considering petitions'.[175]

As to its basic assumptions, the Belém do Pará Convention recalls the 'iceberg' model. In its Article 3, the Convention provides that 'every woman has the right to

[170] Art. 2 (3) Istanbul Convention; *ex negativo* Art. 9 Belém do Pará Convention.

[171] Art. 10.

[172] Art. 11.

[173] IACtHR, *González v. Mexico (Cotton Field Case)*, Judgment (Preliminary Objection, Merits, Reparations, and Costs), 16 November 2009, para. 78.

[174] Critical, see Tiroch, 'Violence against Women by Private Actors', (2010) 14 *Max Planck UNYB*.

[175] IACtHR, *González v. Mexico (Cotton Field Case)*, Judgment (Preliminary Objection, Merits, Reparations, and Costs), 16 November 2009, paras 43, 58. That was however disputed by some legal scholars and by States, see Burgorgue-Larsen/Úbeda de Torres/Greenstein (eds.), *The Inter-American Court of Human Rights*, 2011, Chapter 17, paras 17.10.

live a life free of violence in both the private and public sphere'. Under Article 6, this right includes 'the right of women to be free from all forms of discrimination' and 'the right of women to be valued and educated free of stereotyped patterns of behaviour and social and cultural practices based on concepts of inferiority or subordination'.

Article 7, 8 and 9 are the central provisions regarding measures that States must adopt to prevent VAW. While Article 7 rather focuses on legislation,[176] Article 8 relates to larger policies that aim at transforming societal patterns detrimental to women and that can effectively prevent violence against women.[177] Considering the

[176]Article 7 reads as follows: 'The state parties condemn all forms of violence against women and agree to pursue, by all appropriate means and without delay, policies to prevent, punish and eradicate such violence and undertake to: (a). refrain from engaging in any act or practice of violence against women and to ensure that their authorities, officials, personnel, agents, and institutions act in conformity with this obligation; (b). apply due diligence to prevent, investigate and impose penalties for violence against women; (c). include in their domestic legislation penal, civil, administrative and any other type of provisions that may be needed to prevent, punish and eradicate violence against women and to adopt appropriate administrative measures where necessary; (d). adopt legal measures to require the perpetrator to refrain from harassing, intimidating or threatening the woman or using any method that harms or endangers her life or integrity, or damages her property; (e). take all appropriate measures, including legislative measures, to amend or repeal existing laws and regulations or to modify legal or customary practices which sustain the persistence and tolerance of violence against women; (f) establish fair and effective legal procedures for women who have been subjected to violence which include, among others, protective measures, a timely hearing and effective access to such procedures; (g). establish the necessary legal and administrative mechanisms to ensure that women subjected to violence have effective access to restitution, reparations or other just and effective remedies; (h). adopt such legislative or other measures as may be necessary to give effect to this Convention.'

[177]Article 8 reads as follows: 'The state parties agree to undertake progressively specific measures, including programs: (a). to promote awareness and observance of the right of women to be free from violence, and the right of women to have their human rights respected and protected; (b). to modify social and cultural patterns of conduct of men and women, including the development of formal and informal educational programs appropriate to every level of the educational process, to counteract prejudices, customs and all other practices which are based on the idea of the inferiority or superiority of either of the sexes or on the stereotyped roles for men and women which legitimize or exacerbate violence against women; (c). to promote the education and training of all those involved in the administration of justice, police and other law enforcement officers as well as other personnel responsible for implementing policies for the prevention, punishment and eradication of violence against women; (d). to provide appropriate specialized services for women who have been subjected to violence, through public and private sector agencies, including shelters, counselling services for all family members where appropriate, and care and custody of the affected children; (e). to promote and support governmental and private sector education designed to raise the awareness of the public with respect to the problems of and remedies for violence against women; (f). to provide women who are subjected to violence access to effective readjustment and training programs to enable them to fully participate in public, private and social life; (g). to encourage the communications media to develop appropriate media guidelines in order to contribute to the eradication of violence against women in all its forms, and to enhance respect for the dignity of women; (h). to ensure research and the gathering of statistics and other relevant information relating to the causes, consequences and frequency of violence against women, in order to assess the effectiveness of measures to prevent, punish and eradicate violence against

detrimental effect of overlapping, multiple and intersectional forms of discrimination,[178] Article 9 provides that state parties 'shall take special account of the vulnerability of women to violence by reason of, among others, their race or ethnic background or their status as migrants, refugees or displaced persons'. Article 9 also requires special consideration to be given to 'women subjected to violence while pregnant or who are disabled, of minor age, elderly, socioeconomically disadvantaged, affected by armed conflict or deprived of their freedom'.

2) African Union: 2003 Maputo Protocol and Subsequent Instruments

The Maputo Protocol has been adopted by the Assembly of the African Union in 2003 and entered into in 2005. Until today, 36 of 54 member States to the African Union have ratified the Protocol, while an additional 15 States signed it. The protocol foresees a State reporting system by the African Commission on Human and Peoples' Rights. The African Court on Human and Peoples' Rights, in turn, has the competence to interpret the Protocol.[179]

At the substantive level, the Protocol widely reflects the UN Declaration on the Elimination of Violence against Women and CEDAW. It defines violence against women and establishes a series of positive obligations relating to the prevention and protection against violence against women. To provide but some examples, Article 2 addresses the elimination of all forms of discrimination through appropriate legislative, institutional and regulatory measures. Article 4 (2) (a), in turn, calls on States to 'enact and enforce laws to prohibit all forms of violence against women, including unwanted or forced sex, whether the violence takes place in private or public'. Finally, Article 4 (2) (c) particularly requires that States 'identify the causes and consequences of violence against women and take appropriate measures to prevent and eliminate such violence'.

However, because the Maputo Protocol was said to be ineffective on the ground, different actors issued further documents regarding violence against women. Members form the civil society drafted the *Nairobi Declaration on Women and Girls' Right to a Remedy and Reparation* which gained international importance for the promotion of meaningful reparation.[180] The African Commission on Human and

women and to formulate and implement the necessary changes; (i). to foster international cooperation for the exchange of ideas and experiences and the execution of programs aimed at protecting women who are subjected to violence.'

[178] On intersectionality, see Crenshaw, 'Mapping the margins', (1991) 43 *Stan. L. Rev;* Grabham et al. (eds.), *Intersectionality and beyond: Law, power and the politics of location*, 2008; Davis, 'Intersectionality and International Law', (2015) 28 *Harv. Hum. Rts. J.*

[179] Arts 26, 27.

[180] *Nairobi Declaration on Women and Girls' Right to a Remedy and Reparation*, 21 March 2007. See below, Chap. 7.

Peoples' Right too urged state parties to the African Convention to undertake protective and preventive measures concerning sexualized violence.[181]

Because of the massive occurrence of conflict-related sexualized violence in East African States, the protection of human rights violated by sexualized violence also became one of the central subjects to the International Conference on the Great Lakes Region.[182] This sub-regional organization adopted the legally binding[183] 2008 *Goma Declaration on Eradicating Sexual Violence and Ending Impunity in the Great Lakes Region* which provides a detailed list of measures to be taken on the national and regional level to prevent sexualized violence and to protect the human rights of women and children.[184]

3) Council of Europe: 2011 Istanbul Convention

In 2002, the Parliamentary Assembly of the Council of Europe (CoE) adopted a recommendation on the protection of women against violence, recognizing that States must 'exercise due diligence to prevent, investigate and punish acts of violence, whether those acts are perpetrated by the State or private persons, and provide protection to victims'.[185] The Parliamentary Assembly stressed the importance of additional legally binding standards of protection against gender-based violence.[186]

[181] African Commission on Human and Peoples' Rights Res. 111, *Resolution on the Right to a Remedy and Reparation for Women and Girls Victims of Sexual Violence*, 28 November 2007. Without explicitly mentioning the obligation to protect and fulfill, the Commission urged state parties to: 'Criminalise all forms of sexual violence, ensure that the perpetrators and accomplices of such crimes are held accountable by the relevant justice system; Ensure that police and military forces, as well as all the members of the judiciary receive adequate training on the principles of international humanitarian law, women's rights and the children's rights; Identify the causes and consequences of sexual violence and to take all necessary measures to prevent and eradicate it; Develop campaigns to raise public awareness on existing remedies for cases of sexual violence; Put in place efficient and accessible reparation programmes that ensure information, rehabilitation and compensation for victims of sexual violence; Ensure that victims of sexual violence have access to medical assistance and psychological support; Ensure participation of women in the elaboration, adoption and implementation of reparation programmes.'

[182] The International Conference on the Great Lakes Region is an inter-governmental organization of countries in the Great Lakes Region. Member States are Angola, Burundi, Central African Republic, Republic of Congo, Democratic Republic of Congo, Kenya, Uganda, Rwanda, Sudan, Tanzania and Zambia.

[183] Arostegui, 'Gender, conflict, and peace-building', (2013) 21 *Gender & Development*, p. 538.

[184] Full title: Goma Declaration on Eradicating Sexual Violence and Ending Impunity in the Great Lakes Region.

[185] Council of Europe, Committee of Ministers, *Recommendation Rec(2002)5 of the Committee of Ministers to member states on the protection of women against violence*, 30 April 2002; Council of Europe, *Convention on preventing and combating violence against women and domestic violence (Istanbul Convention),* 2014.

[186] Council of Europe, *Convention on preventing and combating violence against women and domestic violence (Istanbul Convention),* 2014.

In 2011, these efforts culminated in the adoption of the above mentioned Istanbul Convention. The Istanbul Convention entered into force in 2014. Until October 2018, 45 out of 47 member States to the Council of Europe signed and 33 ratified this Convention.[187]

The Convention's monitoring mechanisms consists of two different, but interacting, bodies, that is, an independent Group of Experts on Action against Violence against Women and Domestic Violence (GREVIO) and the Committee of Parties, a political body representing the state parties. GREVIO is competent to monitor the implementation of the Convention. It adopts country-by-country reports and conclusions. It may also issue general recommendations and undertake, in the case of serious or large-scale violations of the Convention, urgent inquiries. The Committee of Parties may adopt, from GREVIO reports and conclusions, specific recommendations regarding measures to be taken to implement the conclusions of GREVIO. If there is a dispute between state parties concerning the application or interpretation of the Convention, the Committee of Ministers of the Council of Europe may also establish procedures of settlement to be available for use by the parties in dispute.[188] It can thus be said that the monitoring mechanism of the Istanbul Convention is similar to the one in force under CEDAW until 2000, e.g. before the entry into force of its Optional Protocol.[189]

Whereas the Belém do Pará Convention provides for the possibility of individuals to file petitions before the Inter-American Commission and, on the Commission's discretion, also before the Inter-American Court, the Istanbul Convention lacks an individualized enforcement mechanism. *A priori*, this decreases the effectiveness of the Istanbul Convention. However, in applying Article 31 (3) (c) VCLT, the ECtHR may, in relation to contracting parties of the Istanbul Convention, interpret Article 1-6 ECHR in light of this new instrument.

Its current weak enforcement mechanisms notwithstanding, it is because of its broad material scope that the Istanbul Convention constitutes the most holistic instrument on violence against women. Compared to the Belém do Pará Convention, the Istanbul Convention differs as far as its understanding of violence, its scope of application and the measures necessary to be taken are concerned. It demonstrates how ideas have changed since the first international approaches to the subject 20 years before.

Firstly, it amplifies the international definition of violence against women[190] by acts that result in, or are likely to result in, *economic* harm or suffering.[191]

---

[187] *Cf.* CoE, Full list, Chart of signatures and ratifications of Treaty 210, http://www.coe.int/en/web/conventions/full-list/-/conventions/treaty/210/signatures, accessed 11 April 2017.

[188] Art. 74.

[189] The Optional Protocol expands the power of the CEDAW Committee, so that it can receive complaints of individuals or groups. Complains can also be submitted on behalf of individuals or groups, with their consent. The protocol has 80 signatories and 109 parties (23 April 2017).

[190] See above, Chap. 2.

[191] Article 3 (a) Istanbul Convention, emphasis added.

Secondly, its material scope also encompasses children and male victims of *domestic* violence.[192] Nonetheless, parties need to pay particular attention to women victims of gender-based violence when implementing the provisions of this convention.[193] With the ratification of the Convention, contracting parties recognize 'that the realisation of *de iure* and *de facto* equality between women and men is a key element in the prevention of violence against women'. Referring to the above-mentioned GR 19 of the CEDAW Committee and the UNGA resolution on this subject, contracting parties recall 'that violence against women is a manifestation of historically unequal power relations between women and men, which have led to domination over, and discrimination against, women by men and to the prevention of the full advancement of women'.[194] The convention thus aims at 'killing two birds with one stone': while acknowledging the structural nature of violence against women as gender-based violence,[195] and thus requiring gender-specific responses, it avoids fostering and perpetuating an essentialist image of the 'weak female victim'.

Thirdly, the Convention foresees very detailed measures necessary for the protection against, prevention and prosecution of gender-based violence and domestic violence. It generally establishes in its Article 4 (1) that parties must 'take the necessary legislative and other measures to promote and protect the right for everyone, particularly women, to live free from violence in both the public and the private sphere'. Article 7 (1) holds that States 'shall take the necessary legislative and other measures to adopt and implement *State-wide effective*, *comprehensive* and co-ordinated policies encompassing all relevant measures to *prevent and combat all forms of violence* covered by the scope of this Convention and offer *a holistic response* to violence against women'.[196] To this effect, contracting parties 'shall undertake to collect disaggregated relevant statistical data at regular intervals on cases of all forms of violence covered by the scope of this Convention' and 'support research in the field of all forms of violence covered by the scope of this Convention to study its root causes and effects, incidences and conviction rates, as well as the efficacy of measures taken to implement this Convention'.[197]

The subsequent Articles then specify in detail how these obligations must be implemented. States must take specific preventive measures (Articles 12–17) to provide support and protect victims (Articles 18–28), to modify and adopt

[192]Article 2 reads as follows: '(1) This Convention shall apply to all forms of violence against women, including domestic violence, which affects women disproportionately. (2) Parties are encouraged to apply this Convention to all victims of domestic violence. Parties shall pay particular attention to women victims of gender-based violence in implementing the provisions of this Convention.'

[193]Art. 2 Istanbul Convention.

[194]Preamble of the Istanbul Convention.

[195]Preamble of the Istanbul Convention.

[196]Emphasis added.

[197]Article 11 (1).

substantive laws (Articles 19–48), and to investigate and prosecute crimes while protecting victims and witnesses (Articles 49–58).

2. General Treaties Guaranteeing Rights That Are Impaired or Nullified by Gender-Based Violence[198]

Framing violence against women as a violation of rights was an immense success, as it shifted the discourse 'from "natural" and "inevitable" violence to a focus on the failure of state parties' obligations'.[199] Today's general international human rights framework provides for countless rights guaranteed in global and regional conventions that are recognized to be potentially violated both in the event of gender-based violence and by ineffective preventive policies.

a. Rights of Freedom Potentially Violated When Gender-Based Violence Occurs

Today, it is generally acknowledged that certain constellations of gender-based violence amount to torture, cruel, inhuman or degrading treatment or punishment,[200]

[198]An earlier version of this section has in part been published in Henn, 'Gender injustice, discrimination, and the CEDAW: A women's life course perspective', in Jantera-Jareborg/Tigroudja, 2016.

[199]Chinkin, 'Violence against Women', in Rudolf/Freeman/Chinkin, 2012, p. 451.

[200]See, e.g., ECtHR, *Aydin v. Turkey* [GC], Judgment, 25 September 1997; ECtHR, *Valiuliene v. Lithuania*, Judgment, 26 March 2013. For details, see Tiefenbrun, *Women's international and comparative human rights*, 2012, at Chapter 3; Liebling-Kalifani et al., 'Experiences of Women War-Torture Survivors in Uganda', (2007) 8 *Journal of International Women's Studies*; Edwards, 'The "Feminizing" of Torture under International Human Rights Law', (2006) 19 *Leiden JIL*; Marshall, 'Positive Obligations and Gender-based Violence: Judicial Developments', (2008) 10 *Int'l Comm. L. Rev.*, see cases at fn. 17; UNCHR, *Torture and other cruel, inhuman or degrading treatment or punishment*, 19 February 1986; UNHRC, *Report of the Special Rapporteur on Torture, and other cruel, inhuman or degrading treatment or punishment, Manfred Nowak*, 15 January 2008; Joseph/Schultz/Castan (eds.), *The international covenant on civil and political rights*, 2004; Gaggioli, 'Sexual violence in armed conflicts', (2014) 96 *IRRC*; McQuigg, 'Domestic Violence as a Human Rights Issue', (2015) 26 *EJIL*. On the question of whether torture can *de jure* only be committed by public authorities, see the concurring opinion of Judge *Cecilia Medina* in the Cotton Field Judgment, IACtHR, *González v. Mexico (Cotton Field Case)*, Judgment (Preliminary Objection, Merits, Reparations, and Costs), 16 November 2009. Owing to the absolute character of the right guaranteed, the ECtHR 'does not rule out the possibility that Article 3 of the Convention may also apply where the danger emanates from persons or groups of persons who are not public officials'. ECtHR, *Hirisi Jaama er all v. Italy* [GC], Judgment, 23 February 2012, para. 120.

or to slavery[201] which pertain to the corpus of customary law and also to *jus cogens*.[202] Acts of gender-based violence may also violate civil and political rights that are mostly non-derogable, including the rights to life,[203] to security, to physical and psychological integrity,[204] to privacy or to a private life[205] and the right to liberty. These rights are all encompassed by the non-specific human rights treaties, be they universal or regional.

As described above,[206] gender-based violence may have a particular 'domino'[207] or 'corrosive' effect for those having been aggressed, and even for those who fear to become a victim.[208] Particularly social, economic and cultural rights are inhibited in the aftermath of gender-based violence.[209] This effect is what perpetuates the structural disadvantages that women encounter. However, these indirect infringements, being the consequence of gender-based violence,[210] are best framed as harm in need to be redressed by reparation.[211]

b. Rights to Non-discrimination

As stated above, gender-based violence against women constitutes discrimination under international law.[212] Human rights guarantees providing for a right to equality and non-discrimination are to be found in a number of conventions and documents.[213] It appears to be widely accepted that the principle of non-discrimination

[201]UNCHR, *Contemporary Forms of Slavery*, 22 June 1998; ECtHR, *Rantsev v. Cyprus and Russia*, Judgment, 07 January 2010, paras 272–309.

[202]Seyler, 'Rape in Conflict: Battling the Impunity that Stifles its Recognition as a Jus Cogens Human Right Expression', (2011); UNCHR, *Contemporary Forms of Slavery*, 22 June 1998.

[203]E.g., ECtHR, *Opuz v. Turkey*, Judgment, 09 June 2009; ECtHR, *Rantsev v. Cyprus and Russia*, Judgment, 07 January 2010, paras 233.

[204]E.g., ECtHR, *M.C. v. Bulgaria*, Judgment, 04 December 2003.

[205]E.g., ECtHR, *X and Y v. The Netherlands*, Judgment, 26 March 1985; IACtHR, *Fernández Ortega and others v. Mexico*, 30 August 2010; ECtHR, *M.C. v. Bulgaria*, Judgment, 04 December 2003.

[206]Chapter 2 B.

[207]Duggan/Jacobson, 'Reparation of Sexual Violence and Reproductive Violence', in Rubio-Marín, 2009, p. 124.

[208]Wolff/De-Shalit, *Disadvantage*, 2007; UNSG, *In-Depth-Study on All Forms of Violence against Women*, 2006, paras 156.

[209]CESCR, *General Comment 16*.

[210]*Cf.* also ECtHR, *O'Keeffe v. Ireland* [GC], Judgment, 28 January 2014, para. 192.

[211]See Chap. 7.

[212]See above, Chap. 2 C.

[213]To give some examples: Art. 2 UDHR; Arts 1 (3) and 55 (c) UN Charter; Preamble of the ICERD; Arts 3 (g), 6, 8 (1) (b) ICRPD; Arts 2, 3, 4, 24, 5, 26 ICCPR; Arts 2 (2), 3, 10 (3) ICESCR; Arts 7 MWC; Art. 27 (3) GC IV; Art. 85 (4) (c) AP I; Art. 14 ECHR and Protocol 12 to the ECHR; Art. 1 (1) ACHR; Art. 2 AfrCHRP; Protocol to the African Charter on Human and Peoples' Rights on the Rights of Women in Africa (2003 Maputo Protocol). See also Cusack/Pusey, 'CEDAW and

based on sex or gender has gained customary law status.[214] However, unlike the prohibition of discrimination based on race,[215] the prohibition of sex- and gender-based discrimination appears not to be part of *jus cogens* as long as it does not constitute torture or slavery.[216]

More precisely, acts and omissions relating to gender-based violence may violate the rights to equal treatment by the law, to be free from discrimination based on sex and other, intersecting discriminatory grounds such as (ascribed) ethnicity/race and disabilities,[217] and the accessory and non-accessory rights to equality. We can consider three settings:

Firstly, where violence is disproportionally committed by State agents against women and less or not against men, it is most likely that this State violates both the accessory and non-accessory rights to equality and the right to equal protection of the law.[218]

Secondly, where neither structural measures of prevention nor appropriate measures of protection against gender-based violence are sufficiently provided by a State, this State is most likely to violate the accessory and non-accessory rights to equality and the right to equal protection of the law.[219] Ineffective prevention and protection against gender-based violence in particular constitutes a *structural* form of discrimination. Within the traditional distinction of direct and indirect

---

the Rights to Non-Discrimination and Equality', (2013) 14 *Melb. J. Int'l L;* Rubio-Marín/Möschel, 'Anti-Discrimination Exceptionalism', (2015) 26 *EJIL*; Woodward, 'From equal treatment to gender mainstreaming and diversity management', in Abels/Mushaben, 2012. Comparing EU law and the ECHR, see Nikolaidis, *The right to equality in European human rights law*, 2015. Giving guidance on how discrimination against women can be ended: Convention of Belém do Pará; Istanbul-Convention; CEDAW; UNSC Res. 1820 (2008), *On Acts of Sexual Violence against Civilians in Armed Conflicts*; UNSC Res. 1674 (2006), 28 April 2006; Fourth World Conference on Women, *Beijing Declaration and Platform for Action*, 1995; UNGA Res. 48/104, *Declaration on the Elimination of Violence against Women*, 20 December 1993; UNGA Res. 57/181, *Elimination of all forms of violence against women*, 04 February 2003; OHCHR, *Report of the Panel on Remedies and Reparation for Victims of Sexual Violence in the Democratic Republic of Congo to the High Commissioner for Human Rights*, March 2011; UNSC Res. 1325 (2000), 31 October 2000; UNGA Res. 60/1, *2005 World Summit Outcome*, 24 October 2005.

214 Chinkin/Freeman, 'Introduction', in Rudolf/Freeman/Chinkin, 2012, p. 28 wfr.

215 Frowein, 'Ius cogens', in Wolfrum, 2012, para. 6; On the gender bias of principles recognized as *jus cogens*, see Charlesworth/Chinkin, 'The Gender of Jus Cogens', (1993) 15 *Hum. Rts. Q.* and on the hierarchization the different forms of discrimination, Charlesworth, 'Concepts of Equality in International Law', in Huscroft/Rishworth, 2002, pp. 145.

216 On the *ius cogens* character of sexualized violence, see Askin, *War crimes against women*, 1997, pp. 239–242; Eriksson, *Defining rape*, 2010, pp. 372; Seyler, *Rape in Conflict,* 2011.

217 It may also violate the rights to non-discrimination encompassed in CERD, CRPD and CRC.

218 E.g., ECtHR, *T.M. and C.M. v. The Republic of Moldova*, Judgment, 28 January 2014, para. 57.

219 UN Human Rights Committee, *General Comment No. 28*, 29 March 2000, para. 31; IACtHR, *González v. Mexico (Cotton Field Case)*, Judgment (Preliminary Objection, Merits, Reparations, and Costs), 16 November 2009; ECtHR, *Opuz v. Turkey*, Judgment, 09 June 2009; IACtHR, *Fernández Ortega and others v. Mexico*, 30 August 2010, paras 184.

discrimination, the lack of appropriate policies of prevention and protection constitutes *indirect* discrimination.

Thirdly, in a post-conflict setting where neither a violation by sexualized acts nor a legally relevant failure to prevent and protect appropriately against them can be established, there is still a possibility to claim a violation of the right to equality: the non-inclusion of victims of sexualized violence into post-conflict reparation programs may violate the rights to equality. Post-conflict States increasingly launch transitional justice programs that include administrative reparations. For various reasons, these programs are the most suitable way to repair the harm caused by conflict-related sexualized violence.[220] So far, however, these programs most often fail to include the needs of female victims. From a research undertaken by the Transitional Justice Institute at Ulster University 'not a single comprehensive administrative program encompassing substantive and adequate reparations for CRSV has been initiated in any conflict setting since the inception of UNSC resolution 1325'.[221] Such policies may violate the right to be free of discrimination. Despite a State having a margin of appreciation on the beneficiaries of positive measures, victim groups may, depending of the domestic legal system, successfully sue a State for discriminating against them.

C. Conclusion: Legal Framework Applicable to Violence Against Women

International humanitarian law addresses and prohibits only the cruelest forms of gender-based violence. Apart from the mere prohibition, it is with regard to sexualized violence committed in the context of an international armed conflict against specific persons that IHL foresees positive obligations under the grave breaches regime.

Human rights law, in turn, being applicable in peacetime and in conflict-related settings, encompasses any action or omission relating to gender-based violence, including acts committed against the State's own population and soldiers. It also covers gender-based violence that, while occurring in wartime, fails to fulfill the conflict nexus or threshold requirements, as established under humanitarian law.

On conflict-related sexualized violence where HRL provisions may conflict with IHL norms, the *extent* to which HRL applies depends on whether the state of emergency has been officially declared and on the rules of norm conflicts applicable.

[220] Rubio-Marín, 'Reparations for Conflict-Related Sexual and Reproductive Violence', (2012) 19 *William & Mary Journal of Women and the Law*, p. 79. These programs have a simplified procedure with a lower threshold of evidence. Additionally, they often spar cross-examination and avoid re-traumatization.

[221] Ní Aoláin/O'Rourke/Swaine, 'Transforming Reparations for Conflict-Related Sexual Violence', (2015) *Harv. Hum. Rts. J.*, p. 26.

The protecting human rights provisions may then be limited to the non-derogable ones and to CEDAW. Having analyzed frequent settings, it became apparent that most forms of gender-based violence occurring in wartimes are exclusively or predominantly covered by HRL. If both frameworks apply to a specific case, their legal assessments as to the prohibition of gender-based violence come to the same result.

Whereas it took a while until gender-based violence has been internationally acknowledged to constitute a human rights issue, today, it is internationally acknowledged that it can violate a series of rights such as the rights to life and integrity, as well as the prohibition of discrimination. In recent decades, the international *corpus iuris* has been complemented by various binding and non-binding instruments against gender-based violence. Most importantly, state parties to some regional conventions have acknowledged gender stereotypes and hierarchization as root causes of gender-based violence. Whether this acknowledgment is equipped with respective positive obligations will be analyzed in the next chapters.

Part II
State Responsibility for Violence Against Women: Transformative Potential of Primary and Secondary Human Rights Obligations

Chapter 4
Primary Obligations: Positive Human Rights Obligations in Context

Human rights theory distinguishes between negative and positive obligations. Negative obligations constitute the traditional form of human rights obligations. They essentially require a State to abstain from intrusions and abuse.[1] Hence, when a State commits an act from which it must abstain, this State violates negative obligations. This obligation is commonly known as the obligation to respect human rights.[2] A violation of negative obligations consists of actions committed by persons, whose acts are attributable to a State, that is, State organs or agents acting in an official capacity of that State, and, under restrictive circumstances, private parties.[3] On the issue at stake, one can think of *inter alia* gender-based violence committed by public officials, or custody rape or intentional terror spread among the population by members of the armed forces taking women as hostage, raping and maiming civilians as a military strategy.[4]

---

[1]Shelton/Gould, 'Positive and Negative Obligations', in Shelton, 2010, p. 563.

[2]Medina (ed.), *The American Convention on Human Rights*, 2014, p. 11.

[3]On the rules of attribution under the ILC Articles, see above Chap. 3 B. See also, Schutter, *International human rights law*, 2010, pp. 365; Mégret, 'Nature of Obligations', in Sivakumaran/Moeckli/Shah, p. 130; Akandji-Kombe, *Les obligations positives en vertu de la Convention européenne des Droits de l'Homme*, Council of Europe, 2006, p. 11; Shelton/Gould, 'Positive and Negative Obligations', in Shelton, 2010.

[4]E.g., ECtHR, *Aydin v. Turkey* [GC], Judgment, 25 September 1997; The IACtHR and the IAComHR have been confronted with countless cases on sexualized violence against women. For some, see IACtHR, *Plan de Sanchéz Massacre v. Guatemala (Reparations)*, Judgment (Reparations), 19 November 2004; IACtHR, *Case of Miguel Castro Castro Prison v. Peru*, Judgment (Merits, Reparations and Costs), 25 November 2006; IACtHR, *Rosendo Cantú y otra v. Mexico*, Judgment, 31 August 2010, paras 166; IACtHR, *Las Dos Erres Massacre v. Guatemala*, Judgment, 24 November 2009; IACtHR, *Fernández Ortega and others v. Mexico*, 30 August 2010; IACtHR, *Contreas and others v. El Salvador*, Judgment (Merits, Reparations and Costs), 31 August 2011.

E. V. Henn, *International Human Rights Law and Structural Discrimination*, Beiträge zum ausländischen öffentlichen Recht und Völkerrecht,
https://doi.org/10.1007/978-3-662-58677-8_4

In contrast, positive human rights obligations require from a State to actively take preventive and protective measures where a specific individual or group of individuals run the risk of being significantly harmed, or where an overall social setting is impairing the enjoyment of human rights. An act violating positive obligations thus consists of an omission. While from a legal philosophical standpoint positive State obligations are an old idea,[5] most human rights treaties do not explicitly mention such State obligations to take protective and preventive measures against human rights abuses. Nonetheless, human rights courts and treaty bodies have interpreted these conventions as to encompass positive duties.

Where historically grown structures within a society cause structural discrimination against specific social groups and where violence against them is prevalent, positive obligations are crucial. This chapter therefore draws on the theory and discourse of positive obligations in general concerning violence against women in particular. It first provides an overview on the normative basis (A.). It then explores the nature and content of and conceptual disagreement relating to positive human rights obligations and draws on the distinct terminology used in the context of positive obligations relating to violence against women. (B.) The chapter concludes with the basic categorical assumptions made and the terminology used throughout Part II (B).

A. Normative Basis

The recognition of positive obligations under human rights law is a comparatively new development. Historically, courts and human rights bodies developed positive obligations within the context of disappearance, where the establishment of a State's involvement is rarely possible,[6] and were typically seen to be embodied by social, cultural and economic rights only. Today, it is recognized that for the effectiveness of civil and political rights, States are required not only to respect but also to actively ensure such rights.[7] While general human rights treaties—in contrast to in thematic

[5]As Monika Hakimi recalls, it was *Thomas Hobbes* who first held that state protection is the condition for individuals to subject themselves to the state. Protection by the state is directly related to the justification of its existence. Where protection is neglected, the individual has the right to civil disobedience (Hobbes et al., *Man and citizen*, 1991). In the continuum of *Hobbes*, *John Locke* additionally discussed the danger emanating from state power itself. Besides protective duties, States should also have negative duties of non-intrusion (Locke, *Two treatises of government*, 1698). Simply put, historically, positive obligations were discussed as the very condition and justification for States to exist.

[6]IACtHR, *Velásquez-Rodriguez v. Honduras*, Judgment (Merits), 29 July 1988, para. 172; UNHRC, *General Comment No. 6, The Right to Life (Art. 6 ICCPR)*, 30 April 1982, para. 4; Schutter, *International human rights law*, 2010, p. 379.

[7]E.g., Reid (ed.), *A practitioner's guide to the European Convention on Human Rights*, 2011, p. 68; Shelton/Gould, 'Positive and Negative Obligations', in Shelton, 2010, p. 564; UN Human Rights Committee, *General Comment No. 31*, 26 May 2004, para. 9.

human rights treaties[8]—rarely mention positive duties explicitly, they have been interpreted as to contain positive obligations.

I. Thematic Human Rights Treaties

The first human rights conventions at both the global and regional levels, which explicitly established positive duties, were thematic conventions that aimed at protecting against particular severe harm. Subsequently, thematic conventions establishing positive duties have focused on structurally disadvantaged social groups such as children, racial minorities, migrant workers and women.

For example, under Article 5 of the Convention on the Prevention and Punishment of the Crime of Genocide (Genocide Convention), which was adopted in 1948 by the UNGA, the contracting parties agreed to prevent and to punish genocide, and for that purpose to 'undertake to enact, in accordance with their respective Constitutions, the necessary legislation to give effect to the provisions of the present Convention and, in particular, to provide effective penalties for persons guilty of genocide (. . .)'.

On group-specific conventions, attention should be drawn here to CERD, CEDAW and CRC.

CERD, which was adopted in 1965 by the UNGA, explicitly foresees a series of positive human rights obligations. To give but some examples, Article 2 (1) stipulates that

> State parties condemn racial discrimination and undertake to pursue by all appropriate means and without delay a policy of eliminating racial discrimination in all its forms and promoting understanding among all races, and, to this end: (a) Each State Party undertakes to engage in no act or practice of racial discrimination against persons, groups of persons or institutions and to ensure that all public authorities and public institutions, national and local, shall act in conformity with this obligation; (. . .) (d) Each State Party shall prohibit and bring to an end, by all appropriate means, including legislation as required by circumstances, racial discrimination by any persons, group or organization.

Moreover, according to Article 2 (2) CERD, state parties 'shall, when the circumstances so warrant, take, in the social, economic, cultural and other fields, special and concrete measures *to ensure the adequate development and protection* of certain racial groups or individuals belonging to them, for the purpose of guaranteeing them the full and equal enjoyment of human rights and fundamental freedoms'.[9]

Under Article 2 (c) CEDAW, state parties must undertake to ensure through competent public institutions effective protection of women against any act of

---

[8]Mowbray, *The development of positive obligations under the European Convention on Human Rights by the European Court of Human Rights*, 2004; Stahl, *Schutzpflichten im Völkerrecht*, 2012; Dröge, *Positive Verpflichtungen der Staaten in der Europäischen Menschenrechtskonvention*, 2003; Hakimi, 'State Bystander Responsibility', (2010) 21 *EJIL*.

[9]Emphasis added.

discrimination. As will be shown below,[10] CEDAW stipulates a series of positive obligations.

CRC, which was adopted in 1989, obliges in its Article 19 (1) state parties to 'take all appropriate (. . .) measures to protect the child from all forms of (. . .) violence (. . .), including sexual abuse, while in the care of parent(s), legal guardian(s) or any other person who has the care of the child'.

II. General Human Rights Treaties

Under general human rights treaties, various provisions have been held by their competent bodies and tribunals to encompass positive obligations. In this regard, the judicial interpretation of ECHR, ICCPR and IACHR are interesting to be looked at.

1. ACHR

The starting point of the development of positive human rights obligations in the Inter-American human rights system was the well-known *Velázquez-Rodrígues v. Honduras* case.[11] The human rights violations at issue before the IACtHR were crimes of systematic disappearance of political opponents that were not investigated and punished. Referring to the international responsibility of a State 'to ensure the free and full exercise of rights to every person subject to its jurisdiction' under Article 1 ACHR, the IACtHR held that a State must organize

> the governmental apparatus and, in general, all the structures through which public power is exercised, so that they are capable of juridically ensuring the free and full enjoyment of human rights. As a consequence of this obligation, the States must prevent, investigate and punish any violation of the rights recognized by the Convention and, moreover, if possible attempt to restore the right violated and provide compensation as warranted for damages resulting from the violation.[12]

The Court determined that the mere establishment of a legal system *de jure* designed to ensure compliance with the obligation would not fulfill this duty, but it would require 'the government to conduct itself so as to effectively ensure the exercise of human rights'.[13] This would entail, the Court further held, that a State could be held responsible if it fails to take

> reasonable steps to prevent human rights violations and to use the means at its disposal to carry out a serious investigation of violations committed within its jurisdiction, to identify

[10]Chapter 6.

[11]IACtHR, *Velásquez-Rodriguez v. Honduras*, Judgment (Merits), 29 July 1988.

[12]IACtHR, *Velásquez-Rodriguez v. Honduras*, Judgment (Merits), 29 July 1988, para. 166.

[13]Ibid., para. 167.

> those responsible, to impose the appropriate punishment and to ensure the victim adequate compensation.[14]

According to the Court, the duty to prevent also encompasses

> all those measures of a legal, political, administrative and cultural nature that promote the protection of human rights and ensure that any violations are considered and treated as illegal acts.[15]

Consequently, acts of private or unidentified persons may

> lead to the international responsibility of the State not because of the act itself, but because of the lack of due diligence to prevent the violation or to respond to it as required by the [American] Convention.[16]

2. ECHR

Under its Article 1, parties to the ECHR are obliged to '*secure* to everyone within their jurisdiction the rights and freedoms (. . .)' as defined under the Convention.[17] The Court has inferred from this provision different standards of positive obligations, depending on the right at risk/violated and the individual circumstances of each case.[18] It had first inferred a positive obligation from the necessity of an *effective respect*. It subsumed positive obligations to be encompassed by the 'obligation to respect human rights'.

On the right to respect for private and family life, for example, it held that 'the object of [Article 8] is "essentially" that of protecting the individual against arbitrary interference by the public authorities',[19] but that

> in addition to this primarily negative undertaking, there may be positive obligations inherent in an effective "respect" for family life. This means, amongst other things, that when the State determines in its domestic legal system the regime applicable to certain family ties (. . .), it must act in a manner calculated to allow those concerned to lead a normal family life. As envisaged by Article 8, respect for family life implies in particular, in the Court's view, the existence in domestic law of legal safeguards that render possible as from the moment of birth the child's integration in his family.[20]

---

[14]Ibid., para. 174.

[15]Ibid., para. 175; *cf.* also IACtHR, *Rodríguez Vera et al. (The disappeared from the palace of justice) v. Colombia*, Judgment (Preliminary Objections, Merits, Reparations and Costs), 14 November 2014, para. 519.

[16]IACtHR, *Velásquez-Rodriguez v. Honduras*, Judgment (Merits), 29 July 1988, para. 172. Emphasis added.

[17]Article 1 ECHR. Emphasis added.

[18]Mowbray, *The development of positive obligations under the European Convention on Human Rights by the European Court of Human Rights*, 2004, pp. 221.

[19]ECtHR, *Case 'relating to certain aspects of the laws on the use of languages in education in Belgium' v. Belgium*, Judgment (Merits), 23 July 1968, p. 33, para. 7.

[20]ECtHR, *Marckx v. Belgium*, Judgment (Merits and Just Satisfaction), 13 June 1979, para. 31 and ECtHR, *X and Y v. The Netherlands*, Judgment, 26 March 1985, paras 23, 27, 30.

In subsequent judgments, the ECtHR further specified positive obligations concerning acts committed by private or third actors.[21] In the well-known *Osman case*, the Court noted that the first sentence of Article 2 (1) (right to life)

> enjoins the State not only to refrain from the intentional and unlawful taking of life, but also to take appropriate steps to safeguard the lives of those within its jurisdiction (. . .). It is common ground that the State's obligation in this respect extends beyond its primary duty to secure the right to life by putting in place effective criminal-law provisions to deter the commission of offences against the person backed up by law-enforcement machinery for the prevention, suppression and sanctioning of breaches of such provisions. It is thus accepted by those appearing before the Court that Article 2 of the Convention may also imply in certain well-defined circumstances a positive obligation on the authorities to take preventive operational measures to protect an individual whose life is at risk from the criminal acts of another individual.[22]

3. ICCPR

Under the ICCPR, state parties undertake 'to respect and to *ensure* to all individuals within [their] territory and subject to its jurisdiction the rights recognized in the present Covenant, without distinction of any kind'.[23] In 2004, the Human Rights Committee held that under Article 2 (1) ICCPR

> obligations are binding on States and do not, as such, have direct horizontal effect as a matter of international law. The Covenant cannot be viewed as a substitute for domestic criminal or civil law. However the positive obligations on state parties to ensure Covenant rights will only be fully discharged if individuals are protected by the State, not just against violations of Covenant rights by its agents, but also against acts committed by private persons or entities that would impair the enjoyment of Covenant rights in so far as they are amenable to application between private persons or entities. There may be circumstances in which a failure to ensure Covenant rights as required by article 2 would give rise to violations by state parties of those rights, as a result of state parties' permitting or failing to take appropriate measures or to exercise due diligence to prevent, punish, investigate or redress the harm caused by such acts by private persons or entities. (Failure to investigate and to) bring to justice perpetrators of (. . .) violations could in and of itself give rise to a (. . .) breach of the Covenant.[24]

---

[21] E.g., for some ECtHR, *Aydin v. Turkey* [GC], Judgment, 25 September 1997; ECtHR, *Osman v. the United Kingdom*, Judgment, 28 October 1998, paras 115; ECtHR, *M.C. v. Bulgaria*, Judgment, 04 December 2003, para. 150; ECtHR, *Bevacqua and S. v. Bulgaria*, Judgment, 12 June 2008; ECtHR, *Opuz v. Turkey*, Judgment, 09 June 2009.

[22] Emphasis added, ECtHR, *Osman v. the United Kingdom*, Judgment, 28 October 1998, para. 115.

[23] Article 2 (1) ICCPR. Emphasis added.

[24] UN Human Rights Committee, *General Comment No. 31*, 26 May 2004, paras 8, 18.

B. Nature and Content of Positive Obligations

Positive obligations become virulent where individuals or legal and social structures impede, or even permanently unable groups or individuals, to exercise their human rights. In such settings a State, depending on the human rights treaty applicable, may have to take positive measures to ensure this exercise. On actors and discriminatory social structures involved in the context of violence against women, positive obligations are most crucial.

Positive obligations do however not formulate an obligation of result. Rather, as a proactive obligation of conduct and means,[25] positive obligations only require the responsible State *to attempt to achieve* the result determined in the primary norm.[26] It remains difficult, however, to define what positive human rights obligations do require exactly. In principle, they require a State to *actively* take administrative, legal and other measures. Thus and theoretically, a violation of positive obligations stems from a State's *omission* or failure in complying with this duty. In practice, however, international tribunals encounter significant challenges in qualifying a relevant State acts as actions or omissions.[27]

I. Measures Potentially Complying with Positive Obligations and the Right to an Effective Remedy

As to their content, positive measures may range from enabling individuals to avoid conflict with third actors, to prohibiting, criminalizing, investigating and prosecuting certain forms of behavior. Depending on the rights in need to be protected and promoted, different legislative and administrative measures come into question.[28] The type of measures taken depends on the respective State actor (legislative,

[25]E.g., IACtHR, *González v. Mexico (Cotton Field Case)*, Judgment (Preliminary Objection, Merits, Reparations, and Costs), 16 November 2009, para. 252; IACtHR, *Velásquez-Rodriguez v. Honduras*, Judgment (Merits), 29 July 1988, para. 166; Council of Europe, *Explanatory Report to the Council of Europe Convention on preventing and combating violence against women and domestic violence,* 2011, para. 59; Schutter, *International human rights law*, 2010, p. 414.

[26]Koivurova, 'Due diligence', in Wolfrum, 2012, para. 8.

[27]See, e.g., ECtHR, *McCann and others v. United Kingdom* [GC], Judgment (Merits and Just Satisfaction), 27 September 1995, paras 151, 212. While the Court does not explicitly determine whether a positive or a negative duty has been breached by the respondent state, it decisively relies on an organizational failure of the authorities. For the ECtHR, see Akandji-Kombe, *Les obligations positives en vertu de la Convention européenne des Droits de l'Homme*, Council of Europe, 2006, pp. 12; see also Dröge, *Positive Verpflichtungen der Staaten in der Europäischen Menschenrechtskonvention*, 2003 and Hakimi, 'State Bystander Responsibility', (2010) 21 *EJIL*.

[28]See below, Chap. 6.

administrative or judicative organ).[29] As a minimum standard, these measures need to be backed up by procedural remedies.

In this context, it is important to mention the primary right to an effective remedy which is encompassed in numerous human rights treaties.[30] The scope of this procedural right strongly intersects with positive obligations under substantive rights. Provisions encompassing the right to a remedy most often include both a procedural and a substantive dimension.[31]

The procedural dimension refers to the enactment of specific procedural legislation that enables the victim to have access to the judicial system and to safely participate in proceedings.[32] It also includes the establishment of complaint mechanisms, investigation bodies and other institutions.

The substantive dimension of the right to an effective remedy includes the establishment and enforcement at the domestic level of guarantees enabling victims to claim reparation from the offender and/or the State.[33]

Where provisions enshrining a right to an effective remedy do not include a substantive dimension (e.g. Art. 25 (1) and 8 (1) ACHR)), or take a limited approach protecting against human rights violations committed by State actors only (e.g. Art.

---

[29] *Cf.* Dröge, *Positive Verpflichtungen der Staaten in der Europäischen Menschenrechtskonvention*, 2003, *passim*. While Dröge suggested this categorization of positive obligations in view of the ECHR, this also applies to other treaties, be it on gender-based violence against women or otherwise.

[30] The right to an effective remedy and the state's obligation to procedurally protect substantive rights are encompassed by various HR treaties. To name but some human rights provisions encompassing the right to or an obligation to provide for an effective remedy: Applying a 'rights language', see Art. 8 UDHR, Art. 13 ECHR, Art. 7 African CPHR, Art. 24 (4) and (5) International Convention for the Protection of All Persons from Enforced Disappearances, Art. 25 (1) ACHR. Applying an 'obligation language': Art. 2 ICCPR, Art. 6 ICERD, Art. 14 CAT (see Committee against Torture, General Comment No. 3, Implementation of Article 14 by state parties, 19 November 2012, UN Doc. CAT/C/GC/3), Art. 25 ACHR, Arts 8 and 25 Protocol to the African Charter of Human and Peoples' Rights on the Rights of Women in Africa (Maputo Protocol); Art. 12 African Union Convention for the Protection and Assistance of Internally Displaced Persons in Africa. See also UNSG, *Reparations for Conflict-Related Sexual Violence*, 01 August 2014, p. 4; UNGA Res. 60/147, *Basic Principles and Guidelines on the Right to a Remedy and Reparation for Victims of Gross Violations of International Human Rights Law and Serious Violations of International Humanitarian Law*, 21 March 2006.

[31] In this context, one must mention the Basic Principles and Guidelines on the right to a remedy and reparation, which the UNGA adopted in 2006, UNGA Res. 60/147, *Basic Principles and Guidelines on the Right to a Remedy and Reparation for Victims of Gross Violations of International Human Rights Law and Serious Violations of International Humanitarian Law*, 21 March 2006.

[32] For the procedural dimension concerning victims of conflict-related sexualized violence, see UNSG, *Reparations for Conflict-Related Sexual Violence*, 01 August 2014, pp. 11–12.

[33] Shelton, *Remedies in international human rights law*, 2006, pp. 8.

13 ECHR), the respective Courts have tended to interpret *substantive* human rights provisions as to contain a procedural dimension, e.g. the obligation to provide for remedies, both against State and non-State actors.[34]

[34]Under the **ACHR,** the line drawn by the jurisprudence between procedural rights under Articles 25 (1), 8 (1) and the positive obligation to secure under Article 1 (1) appears random (Shelton, *Remedies in international human rights law*, 2006, pp. 137; Medina (ed.), *The American Convention on Human Rights*, 2014, p. 237; IACtHR, *Blake v. Guatemala (Reparations and Costs)*, Judgment (Reparations and Costs), 22 January 1999, paras 62). **Art. 25 (1) ACHR** enshrines the autonomous right to have access to domestic judicial authorities (Burgorgue-Larsen, 'The Right to Effective Remedy', in Burgorgue-Larsen/Úbeda de Torres/Greenstein, 2011, paras 26.10; Medina (ed.), *The American Convention on Human Rights*, 2014, p. 235) and Art. 8 (1) ACHR, 'sets forth the right of every person to a hearing, with due guarantees and within a reasonable time, by a competent, independent, and impartial judge or tribunal for his rights of any nature' (IACtHR, *Blake v. Guatemala (Reparations and Costs)*, Judgment (Reparations and Costs), 22 January 1999, paras 62–64). This right applies to conflicts between parties of all kinds (Medina (ed.), *The American Convention on Human Rights*, 2014, p. 174). The Court established that Art. 25 (1) 'is closely linked to the general obligation in Article 1.1 of the American Convention, in that it assigns duties of protection to the state parties through their domestic legislation [. . .] from which it is clear that the State has the obligation to design and embody in legislation an effective recourse, and also to ensure the due application of the said recourse by its judicial authorities'. IACtHR, *'Street Children' (Villagrán-Morales et al.) v. Guatemala*, Judgment (Merits), 19 November 1999, para. 237. **Article 8 (1) ACHR** too bears a 'direct relation to Art. 25 in conjunction with Art. 1 (1) of the Convention, which guarantees to all persons a simple and rapid recourse so that, among other things, those responsible for human rights violations will be tried and reparations may be obtained for the damages suffered' (IACtHR, *Blake v. Guatemala (Reparations and Costs)*, Judgment (Reparations and Costs), 22 January 1999, paras 62–64; Shelton, *Remedies in international human rights law*, 2006, p. 140). Hence, the three provisions taken together can be said to codify the right to an effective remedy (Shelton, *Remedies in international human rights law*, 2006, p. 140). However, the Inter-American Court also considers the duties to prevent as well as to investigate, trial and punish to be inherent to the substantive rights at stake in conjunction with the obligation to protect under Art. 1 (1), see Medina (ed.), *The American Convention on Human Rights*, 2014, pp. 58, 64, 122, 174. Finally, in some cases the Court even limited its findings on the obligation to protect without mentioning another provision, see Medina (ed.), *The American Convention on Human Rights*, 2014, p. 238. **Art. 13 ECHR** provides for an ancillary right of victims to an effective remedy under the chapter on 'rights and freedoms' (Grabenwarter (ed.), *European Convention on Human Rights*, 2014, Art. 13, para. 1). It is interpreted as to contain both a procedural and a substantive dimension of an accessory right to an effective remedy. Yet, it only applies to violations committed by state agents. Protection against private actors through procedural remedies, investigation and prosecution has been interpreted as to be encompassed by the procedural dimension of substantive rights guaranteed under the ECHR in conjunction with Art. 1 (1). (The disagreement on whether Art. 13 has a horizontal effect or not seems to be resolved (Con: Grabenwarter (ed.), *European Convention on Human Rights*, 2014, Art. 13, para. 10, referring to its accessory nature and the wording 'whose rights and freedoms. . .are violated' meaning that reference can only be made to violations of States because the Convention is only binding upon States; Pro: Clapham, *Human rights in the private sphere*, 1996, pp. 240–244). Legal protection against infringements of rights by private actors is encompassed by the positive obligations under substantive Convention rights, ECtHR, *S.Z. v. Bulgaria*, Judgment, 03 March 2015, para. 42; Dröge, *Positive Verpflichtungen der Staaten in der Europäischen Menschenrechtskonvention*, 2003, p. 60 wfr. See, e.g., ECtHR, *Opuz v. Turkey*, Judgment, 09 June 2009 and the commentary notes on the right to life and human treatment in Harris et al. (eds.), *Law of the European Convention on Human Rights*, 2014). A contracting party may have violated positive obligations under Article 1 (1) ECHR

II. Different Kinds of Positive Obligations

Whereas positive obligations can be reduced to require *positive actions* (whereas their breach come up to a legally relevant omissions), this classification has been further refined by legal doctrine.[35] Today, human rights theory generally distinguishes between *the obligations to protect* and the obligation *to fulfill* (also to aid/promote/facilitate). On gender-based violence, however, the international discourse has applied a different terminology.

1. Positive Obligations as Regards Third Actors: Obligation to Protect

Under international human rights doctrine, the obligation to protect requires a State to protect individuals and groups against private and third actors.[36] Measures complying with the obligation to protect may include *inter alia* the criminalization, investigations, prosecution of crimes and punishment of perpetrators. Measures of prevention and protection are required either where a specific act risks violating the rights of an individual or where, more generally, a situation entails such a risk for various individuals.[37] Thus, not only does the obligation to protect require States to take protective measures in a specific case, it also requires States to provide for legal remedies and for an effective legal and administrative framework.[38]

---

in conjunction with a substantive Convention right, if it failed to duly prevent the harm be it by taking legislative or administrative measures. However, if a State fails to duly investigate crimes and to afford compensation to the victim, it may also have violated the accessory right to an effective remedy under Art. 13 in conjunction with a substantive Convention right because 'the ineffectiveness of the criminal investigation undermined the effectiveness of any other remedy, including a civil action for damages'. (ECtHR, *El-Masri v. the Former Yugoslav Republic of Macedonia* [GC], Judgment, 13 December 2012, para. 261. See also ECtHR, *Al-Nashiri v. Poland*, Judgment, 24 July 2014; for further details, see Dröge, *Positive Verpflichtungen der Staaten in der Europäischen Menschenrechtskonvention*, 2003, pp. 62–70; Harris et al., 'Article13: The right to an effective national remedy', in Harris et al., 2014, p. 779. Consequently, under the ECHR too, the overlap of the right to an effective remedy and positive obligations, both in conjunction with substantive provisions is considerable.

[35]Laying the foundations, see Shue, *Basic rights*, 1996.

[36]Shelton/Gould, 'Positive and Negative Obligations', in Shelton, 2010, p. 566; Schutter, *International human rights law*, 2010, pp. 365; Hakimi, 'State Bystander Responsibility', (2010) 21 *EJIL*, p. 353.

[37]For case material, see Schutter, *International human rights law*, 2014, pp. 427.

[38]E.g., ECtHR, *O'Keeffe v. Ireland* [GC], Judgment, 28 January 2014; ECtHR, *Rantsev v. Cyprus and Russia*, Judgment, 07 January 2010; ECtHR, *Horváth and Kiss v. Hungary*, Judgment, 29 January 2013.

2. Positive Obligations as Regards the State Itself

Concerning its own organization, a State has also positive duties to ensure compliance with human rights obligations.[39] Accordingly, a State needs 'to organize the governmental apparatus and, in general, all the structures through which public power is exercised, so that they are capable of juridically ensuring the free and full enjoyment of human rights',[40] e.g. by providing for effective access to justice and human rights trainings to State officials or by maintaining an independent judiciary. Such obligations have also been said to be encompassed by the obligation to respect.[41] Hereinafter, because compliance with them requires State action, such State-related obligations will be treated as positive obligations.[42] As will be shown,[43] this does not imply a reduction of the liability standard or extent of such State-related obligations.

3. Obligation to Fulfill Human Rights

The obligation to fulfill human rights refers to a progressive and programmatic obligation to modify legal, administrative or societal structures, and to weaken the effect of disadvantaging societal institutions 'towards the full realization of human rights'.[44] In view of its programmatic nature, its fulfillment has often been dispelled to the political sphere. However, its programmatic character cannot deprive the obligation to fulfill from all meaningful content. As will be shown below, in the context of structural discrimination against women, it particularly requires the adoption of special measures and affirmative actions.[45]

---

[39]E.g., ECtHR, *Horváth and Kiss v. Hungary*, Judgment, 29 January 2013, para. 103, where 'the Court reiterates that the word "respect" in Article 2 of Protocol No. 1 means more than "acknowledge" or "take into account"; in addition to a primarily negative undertaking, it implies some positive obligation on the part of the State'.

[40]IACtHR, *Velásquez-Rodriguez v. Honduras*, Judgment (Merits), 29 July 1988, para. 166. See also Shelton/Gould, 'Positive and Negative Obligations', in Shelton, 2010, pp. 564.

[41]E.g., Dröge, *Positive Verpflichtungen der Staaten in der Europäischen Menschenrechtskonvention*, 2003, p. 6. Ambiguous, Shelton/Gould, 'Positive and Negative Obligations', in Shelton, 2010, p. 566 referring to Nowak (ed.), *U.N. Covenant on Civil and Political Rights*, 2005, p. xxi; Chinkin, 'Addressing violence against women in the Commonwealth within states' obligations under international law', (2014) 40 *Commonwealth Law Bulletin*, p. 489.

[42]For this approach, see also Shelton/Gould, 'Positive and Negative Obligations', in Shelton, 2010.

[43]See Chap. 5.

[44]Schutter, *International human rights law*, 2014, pp. 527, 562; Shelton/Gould, 'Positive and Negative Obligations', in Shelton, 2010, p. 565; Chinkin, 'Addressing violence against women in the Commonwealth within states' obligations under international law', (2014) 40 *Commonwealth Law Bulletin*, p. 479.

[45]See Chap. 6 A II.

4. Violence Against Women and the 'Due Diligence Standard'

On violence against women, international actors have frequently applied a distinct terminology of obligations, referring to a 'due diligence standard to prevent and protect against gender-based violence'. This terminology originally stems from the Inter-American human rights system, where it has first been applied in 1988[46] and is used to referring both case-specific and systemic obligations. However, this terminology does not entirely fit into the concept of obligations to protect and to fulfill human rights. It is rather a standard to measure the scope of positive obligations.

In fact, the IACtHR and the IAComHR have an extensive interpretation of positive obligations of States, distinguishing between the systemic obligation to generally prevent discriminatory settings and gender-based violence and the obligations arising concerning a specific case.[47] In *the Cotton field case*, for example, a leading case concerning the disappearance of three young women in the City of Juárez, a hotbed of organized crime with an extremely high rate of homicide against women (so-called femicide), the IACtHR found that

> States should adopt comprehensive measures to comply with due diligence in cases of violence against women. In particular, they should have an appropriate legal framework for protection that is enforced effectively, and prevention policies and practices that allow effective measures to be taken in response to the respective complaints. The prevention strategy should also be comprehensive; in other words, it should prevent the risk factors and, at the same time, strengthen the institutions that can provide an effective response in cases of violence against women. Furthermore, the State should adopt preventive measures in specific cases in which it is evident that certain women and girls may be victims of violence.[48]

The Inter-American approach has been incorporated by the above-mentioned CEDAW Committee's general recommendation No. 19 and the UNGA Declaration

[46]See Chaps. 4 A II and 5 B.

[47]E.g., in the *Maria da Penha v. Brazil case*, the IAComHR determined Ms *da Penha* to be a victim of domestic violence having suffered a violation of her rights to life and physical and psychological integrity as guaranteed by the ACHR and the Belém do Pará Convention. Apart from the case-specific failure to prosecute and convict the claimant's husband, Brazil was proven to have displayed a *general pattern* of negligence and lack of effectiveness when preventing 'these degrading practices'. (IAComHR, *Maria da Penha v. Brazil*, Case 12.051, Report No. 54/01, 16 April 2001, para. 56, emphasis added. The IAComHR further held that a 'general and *discriminatory* judicial ineffectiveness also creates a climate that is conducive to domestic violence, since society sees no evidence of willingness by the State, as the representative of the society, to take effective action to sanction such acts' (Para. 56). See also IACtHR, *Velásquez-Rodriguez v. Honduras*, Judgment (Merits), 29 July 1988, para. 172; IACtHR, *Case of Miguel Castro Castro Prison v. Peru*, Judgment (Merits, Reparations and Costs), 25 November 2006; IACtHR, *González v. Mexico (Cotton Field Case)*, Judgment (Preliminary Objection, Merits, Reparations, and Costs), 16 November 2009, paras 258, 281; IACtHR, *Las Dos Erres Massacre v. Guatemala*, Judgment, 24 November 2009; IAComHR, *Jessica Lenahan (Gonzales) et al. v. United States*, Case 12.626, Report No. 80/11, 21 July 2011; Schutter, *International human rights law*, 2010, pp. 389.

[48]IACtHR, *González v. Mexico (Cotton Field Case)*, Judgment (Preliminary Objection, Merits, Reparations, and Costs), 16 November 2009, para. 258; Emphasis added.

on Violence against Women which urge States to 'exercise due diligence to prevent, investigate and, (...) punish acts of violence against women, whether those acts are perpetrated by the State or private persons'.[49] In 2006, the UN Special Rapporteur on violence against women issued a document drawing on the 'due diligence standard as a tool for the elimination of violence against women'.[50] Ever since, in the context of gender-based violence, international jurisprudence and soft law instruments have frequently referred to the 'due diligence standard'.[51] However, the distinction between case-specific and systemic obligations as established by the IACtHR has not always been maintained.[52]

C. Conclusion: Basic Assumption and Terminology

International human rights theory distinguishes between two types of positive obligations, the obligations to protect and the obligation to fulfill human rights. However, there are also positive obligations concerning the State's own structures through which public power is exercised. Concerning positive human rights obligations relating to violence against women, international actors have applied a different terminology. They have applied the so-called 'due diligence standard' which originally stems from the Inter-American human rights system, distinguishing between case-specific and systemic obligations.

For the sake of clarity, no reference will be made to the 'due diligence standard'. Instead, the generally accepted terminologies (to protect and to fulfill) will be used were appropriate. Accordingly, the obligation to fulfill refers to programmatic measures that need to be taken progressively. The obligation to protect requires preventive and protective measures either where third-party acts risk to violate the rights of specific individuals or where, more generally, a situation entails such a risk for various individuals. However, positive duties to ensure compliance with human rights may also arise concerning the governmental apparatus or otherwise. Hence, on positive obligations that are no obligations to fulfill, it should be noted that general reference will be made *to obligations of prevention and protection.*

---

[49]CEDAW, *General Recommendation 19*, 1992, para. 9, UNGA Res. 48/104, *Declaration on the Elimination of Violence against Women*, 20 December 1993, Art. 4 (c).

[50]On the historical development of the 'due diligence standard' concerning violence against women, see UNCHR, *Integration of the human rights of women and the gender perspective*, 20 January 2006, paras 19.

[51]ECtHR, *Bevacqua and S. v. Bulgaria*, Judgment, 12 June 2008, paras 52, 53, 66–84; ECtHR, *Opuz v. Turkey*, Judgment, 09 June 2009, para. 131; UNGA Res. 64/137, *Intensification of efforts to eliminate all forms of violence against women*, 18 December 2009; UNHRC, *Report of the Special Rapporteur on violence against women, its causes and consequences*, 13 May 2013; UNGA Res. 69/147, *Intensification of efforts to eliminate all forms of violence against women and girls*, 18 December 2014.

[52]UNHRC, *Report of the Special Rapporteur on violence against women, its causes and consequences*, 13 May 2013, paras 70.

Chapter 5
Parameters to Establish the Existence and Extent of Positive Obligations

As shown in the preceding chapter, thematic conventions such as on gender-based or racial discrimination explicitly stipulate positive obligations on specific groups or situations. As to their thematic scope of application, these conventions often indicate *when* these obligations apply. However, some of them, such as CEDAW, do not necessarily specify the extent of positive obligations.[1] In turn, others, such as the Istanbul Convention, additionally spell out to *what extent* state parties have positive obligations.[2] In contrast, while being interpreted as to establishing positive obligations, general human rights treaties such as ECHR, ACHR and ICCPR neither indicate the conditions for the application of positive obligations nor do they name their extent and limits.

The questions thus arise *when* state parties to general human rights treaties have positive obligations and to *what extent* positive obligations more generally exist. While it would be too far reaching here to undertake an analysis of State practice concerning these two aspects, it can be assumed that State practice is widely inconsistent. Although international and regional human rights courts in particular have applied similar parameters to answer these questions, their practice on positive human rights obligations, too, is inconsistent. What appears to be generally accepted is that such obligations are not absolute and somewhat subject to a State's discretion. Hence, in the absence of parameters in positive law or coherent jurisprudence, legal

[1]See below, Chap. 6 A.

[2]See below, Chap. 6 A I.

E. V. Henn, *International Human Rights Law and Structural Discrimination*, Beiträge zum ausländischen öffentlichen Recht und Völkerrecht, https://doi.org/10.1007/978-3-662-58677-8_5

scholars have suggested different approaches concerning the conditions for the application and the extent of positive human rights obligations.[3]

Drawing on human rights theory and recent studies on positive human rights obligations,[4] this chapter analyzes international jurisprudence on positive obligations[5] and further develops criteria to establishing *when and to what extent* positive obligations apply. More precisely, this chapter first discusses parameters to establish the scope of application of positive obligations under those conventions whose wording does not provide for details as to when positive obligations apply. In this context, it is should be noted that the obligation to fulfill always applies to a State when this State ratified a treaty establishing such obligations. Consequently, there is no need for specific criteria of application. The chapter focuses on the jurisprudence of the European and Inter-American Human Rights Courts as well as the ICJ. As ECHR and ACHR do not establish obligations of a programmatic character but obligations and individual rights that are sufficiently precise to be justiciable, the first section focuses on obligations of protection and prevention (A.). The chapter then

---

[3]Stahl, *Schutzpflichten im Völkerrecht*, 2012; Hakimi, 'State Bystander Responsibility', (2010) 21 *EJIL*; Schutter, *International human rights law*, 2010, pp. 399; Mowbray, *The development of positive obligations under the European Convention on Human Rights by the European Court of Human Rights*, 2004; Conforti, 'Exploring the Strasbourg Case-Law', in Fitzmaurice/Sarooshi, 2004; Dröge, *Positive Verpflichtungen der Staaten in der Europäischen Menschenrechtskonvention*, 2003; Cook, 'State Responsibility for Violations of Women's Human Rights', (1994) 7 *Harv. Hum. Rts. J;* Clapham, *Human rights in the private sphere*, 1996.

[4]Hakimi, 'State Bystander Responsibility', (2010) 21 *EJIL*, scrutinizing the international (quasi-) judicial practice on the obligation to protect and draws conclusion thereof suggesting a framework on 'bystander responsibility'. Dröge, *Positive Verpflichtungen der Staaten in der Europäischen Menschenrechtskonvention*, 2003, analyzing the horizontal and social dimension of positive obligations under the ECHR. Stahl, *Schutzpflichten im Völkerrecht*, 2012, drawing from insights based on German constitutional, administrative and criminal law. *Stahl* suggests a general framework of protective duties (Schutzpflichten) that apply against private and third actors as well as in specific situations. These three studies differ inasmuch as they undertake different categorization concerning positive obligations (Dröge), protective duties (Stahl) and the obligation to protect (Hakimi). Additionally, they have different geographic foci (regional v. universal) and theoretical approaches, two authors largely drawing from a jurisprudential review (Hakimi and Dröge), the other developing a framework borrowing from various legal concepts to be found in the German doctrine on administrative and criminal law (Stahl).

[5]E.g., ICJ, *Case concerning application of the Convention of Prevention and Punishment of the Crime of Genocide (Bosnia and Herzegovina v. Serbia and Montenegro)*, Judgment, 26 February 2007; IACtHR, *González v. Mexico (Cotton Field Case)*, Judgment (Preliminary Objection, Merits, Reparations, and Costs), 16 November 2009; IACtHR, *Rosendo Cantú y otra v. Mexico*, Judgment, 31 August 2010; IACtHR, *Velásquez Paiz et al. v. Guatemala*, Judgment (Preliminary Objections, Merits, Reparations and Costs), 19 November 2015; ECtHR, *Osman v. the United Kingdom*, Judgment, 28 October 1998; ECtHR, *O'Keeffe v. Ireland* [GC], Judgment, 28 January 2014; ECtHR, *Horváth and Kiss v. Hungary*, Judgment, 29 January 2013; ECtHR, *Valiuliene v. Lithuania*, Judgment, 26 March 2013; ECtHR, *Opuz v. Turkey*, Judgment, 09 June 2009; ECtHR, *Bevacqua and S. v. Bulgaria*, Judgment, 12 June 2008; ECtHR, *M.C. v. Bulgaria*, Judgment, 04 December 2003; ECtHR, *DH v. Czech Republic* [GC], Judgment, 13 November 2007; ECtHR, *X and Y v. The Netherlands*, Judgment, 26 March 1985.

discusses the extent and limits of positive obligations more generally, including the obligation to fulfill (B.).

A. Parameters to Establish Whether Protective and Preventive Duties Apply

This section analyzes potential parameters to establish whether positive obligations of protection or prevention apply on a specific individual or group of individuals or a general situation. In light of the jurisprudence of the ICJ, the IACtHR and the ECtHR in particular, it is suggested that three criteria must be fulfilled cumulatively: first, a State must be informed or have constructive knowledge that there is a relevant danger to an individual right (I.)[6]; second, a State must have the capacity to influence the situation, be it through a *de jure* relationship with the abuser or through an influential *de facto* relationship (II.)[7]; and third, the harm in danger to occur must be severe (III.).[8] In this context, it will be shown that, while the alleged 'vulnerability' of persons (potentially) affected by severe harm has played a decisive role in judicial practice, this criterion is a misconception.

I. Danger of Harm and Knowledge About It

According to Article 14 (3) ILC Articles on State Responsibility, 'the breach of an international [primary] obligation requiring a State to prevent a given event occurs when the event occurs and extends over the entire period during which the event continues and remains not in conformity with that obligation'.[9] However, as the ICJ noted on the obligation to prevent genocide, this obviously does not mean that positive obligations only come into being when the event occurs. This

> would be absurd, since the whole point of the obligation is to prevent, or attempt to prevent, the occurrence of the act. In fact, a State's obligation to prevent, and the corresponding duty

[6] *Cf.* also Stahl, *Schutzpflichten im Völkerrecht*, 2012, pp. 137–169; Dröge, *Positive Verpflichtungen der Staaten in der Europäischen Menschenrechtskonvention*, 2003, pp. 298.

[7] *Cf.* also Hakimi, 'State Bystander Responsibility', (2010) 21 *EJIL*, pp. 355; Dröge, *Positive Verpflichtungen der Staaten in der Europäischen Menschenrechtskonvention*, 2003, pp. 294; Stahl, *Schutzpflichten im Völkerrecht*, 2012, pp. 182.

[8] *Cf.* also Hakimi, 'State Bystander Responsibility', (2010) 21 *EJIL*, pp. 367. According to Stahl, *Schutzpflichten im Völkerrecht*, 2012, pp. 188, this criterion should only influence the state's discretion.

[9] ICJ, *Case concerning application of the Convention of Prevention and Punishment of the Crime of Genocide (Bosnia and Herzegovina v. Serbia and Montenegro)*, Judgment, 26 February 2007, para. 431.

> to act, arise at the instant that the State learns of, or should normally have learned of, the existence of a serious risk that genocide will be committed.[10]

Unsurprisingly, human rights courts take this very same approach. To establish positive duties, they require that the State in question knows or should have known about a risk of harm.[11] (Constructive) knowledge as a subjective requirement for the existence of primary obligations is not in contradiction to the rules on international responsibility of States being guided by the principle of objective responsibility and not of fault or *culpa*.[12] Rather, it is a logical necessity, because influence can only be exercised or protective measures be taken if a State knows or should at least have known about the (danger of) harm.

In some contexts, a certain level of danger is necessary for positive, in particular preventive, obligations to apply. This is because, as the ECtHR put it, not every claimed risk to a right can entail for a State a 'requirement to take operational measures to prevent that risk from materialising'.[13] It appears that, as long as a risk has not materialized, the level of danger required differs, depending on whether a State allegedly violated its obligation to protect against a specific individual or to generally prevent human rights infringing settings or abuses.

1. Level of Danger Required for Positive Obligations to Arise in a Particular Case

For positive obligations to take operational measures to arise in a particular case, human rights courts have frequently required the establishment of circumstances giving rise to a credible suspicion that an identified individual or group of individuals had been, or was, at *real and imminent risk* of becoming a victim of a crime.[14]

In its well-known *Osman case*, the ECtHR established a standard for the obligation to protect against risks to life. The case concerned a former teacher who developed an unhealthy and obsessive attachment to one of his pupils, Ahmet Osman, while he taught him in school. The teacher's obsession, which triggered several incidents of stalking, harassment and intimidation, ultimately cumulated in the death of the father of Ahmet. The Court held, that

[10]ICJ, *Case concerning application of the Convention of Prevention and Punishment of the Crime of Genocide (Bosnia and Herzegovina v. Serbia and Montenegro)*, Judgment, 26 February 2007, para. 431, emphasis added; see also Stahl, *Schutzpflichten im Völkerrecht*, 2012, p. 154.

[11]E.g., ECtHR, *O'Keeffe v. Ireland* [GC], Judgment, 28 January 2014, para. 162; ECtHR, *E. and others v. The United Kingdom*, Judgment, 15 January 2003, para. 88; ECtHR, *Osman v. the United Kingdom*, Judgment, 28 October 1998, para. 116; IACtHR, *González v. Mexico (Cotton Field Case)*, Judgment (Preliminary Objection, Merits, Reparations, and Costs), 16 November 2009, para. 282.

[12]*Cf.* also Crawford, *Brownlie's Principles of public international law*, 2012, p. 558.

[13]ECtHR, *Osman v. the United Kingdom*, Judgment, 28 October 1998, para. 116.

[14]See, e.g., ECtHR, *Osman v. the United Kingdom*, Judgment, 28 October 1998, para. 116.

> where there is an allegation that the authorities have violated their positive obligation to protect the right to life in the context of their above-mentioned duty to prevent and suppress offences against the person (. . .), it must be established to its satisfaction that the authorities knew or ought to have known at the time of the existence of a real and immediate risk to the life of an identified individual or individuals from the criminal acts of a third party and that they failed to take measures within the scope of their powers which, judged reasonably, might have been expected to avoid that risk. The Court does not accept the Government's view that the failure to perceive the risk to life in the circumstances known at the time or to take preventive measures to avoid that risk must be tantamount to gross negligence or wilful disregard of the duty to protect life (. . .). Such a rigid standard must be considered to be incompatible with the requirements of Article 1 of the Convention and the obligations of Contracting States under that Article to secure the practical and effective protection of the rights and freedoms laid down therein, including Article 2 (. . .). For the Court, and having regard to the nature of the right protected by Article 2, a right fundamental in the scheme of the Convention, it is sufficient for an applicant to show that the authorities did not do all that could be reasonably expected of them to avoid a real and immediate risk to life of which they have or ought to have knowledge.[15]

While this standard had first been applied to the right to life (Article 2), the Court subsequently extended this standard to circumstances giving rise to a credible suspicion that an identified individual was at real and immediate risk of being trafficked, tortured, ill-treated or exploited (Article 3 and 4 ECHR).[16]

This very standard is also applied by the Inter-American Court. For example, in the above-mentioned *Cotton Field case,* the IACtHR held that

> the failure to prevent the disappearance does not per se result in the State's international responsibility because, even though the State was aware of the situation of risk for women in Ciudad Juárez, it has not been established that it knew of a real and imminent danger for the victims in this case.[17]

---

[15]ECtHR, *Osman v. the United Kingdom*, Judgment, 28 October 1998, para. 116, emphasis added. See also ECtHR, *Younger v. The United Kingdom* (dec.), 07 January 2003; ECtHR, *Opuz v. Turkey*, Judgment, 09 June 2009, paras 133; ECtHR, *Rantsev v. Cyprus and Russia*, Judgment, 07 January 2010, paras 220; ICJ, *Corfu Channel Case (UK v. Albania)*, Judgment (merits), 09 April 1949, pp. 4, 18, 22; Crawford, *Brownlie's Principles of public international law*, 2012, p. 558; IACtHR, *González v. Mexico (Cotton Field Case)*, Judgment (Preliminary Objection, Merits, Reparations, and Costs), 16 November 2009, para. 280; IACtHR, *Velásquez-Rodriguez v. Honduras*, Judgment (Merits), 29 July 1988; ICJ, *Case concerning application of the Convention of Prevention and Punishment of the Crime of Genocide (Bosnia and Herzegovina v. Serbia and Montenegro)*, Judgment, 26 February 2007, para. 431.

[16]ECtHR, *Rantsev v. Cyprus and Russia*, Judgment, 07 January 2010, para. 286.

[17]IACtHR, *González v. Mexico (Cotton Field Case)*, Judgment (Preliminary Objection, Merits, Reparations, and Costs), 16 November 2009, para. 282; IACtHR, *Rodríguez Vera et al. (The disappeared from the palace of justice) v. Colombia*, Judgment (Preliminary Objections, Merits, Reparations and Costs), 14 November 2014, para. 523; IACtHR, *Velásquez Paiz et al. v. Guatemala*, Judgment (Preliminary Objections, Merits, Reparations and Costs), 19 November 2015, para. 109 wfr.

2. Level of Danger Required for Obligations to Provide for a Legal and Administrative Framework

Relating to the obligation to generally prevent human rights abuses, which includes the obligation to put in place an appropriate legislative and administrative framework, both the ECtHR and the IACtHR require that a State has constructive knowledge about a sufficiently specified but not necessarily individualized risk (abstract danger) for the impairment of a right.

In the above-mentioned *Cotton field* case, the IACtHR established that 'the absence of a general policy which could have been initiated at least in 1998—*when the CNDH warned of the pattern of violence against women in Ciudad Juárez*—is a failure of the State to comply in general with its obligation of prevention'.[18] Thus, at the latest when public information was available, Mexico should have been aware of the general pattern of gender-based violence and should have taken general preventive policies.[19]

Along these lines, in *O'Keeffe v. Ireland*, a case of prevalent sexual child abuse in the mainly Church-run Irish educative system in the 1970s, the Grand Chamber of the ECtHR held Ireland responsible because it had failed to establish legal and administrative machinery containing sufficient mechanisms of child protection against inhuman treatment by sexualized abuse in primary schools.[20] At the time

---

[18]Emphasis added. IACtHR, *González v. Mexico (Cotton Field Case)*, Judgment (Preliminary Objection, Merits, Reparations, and Costs), 16 November 2009, para. 282.

[19]On trafficking in women, see also ECtHR, *Rantsev v. Cyprus and Russia*, Judgment, 07 January 2010, paras 290.

[20]ECtHR, *O'Keeffe v. Ireland* [GC], Judgment, 28 January 2014, paras 150, 159. At paras 168–169 the Court held that 'this is not a case which directly concerns the responsibility of LH [the perpetrator], of a clerical Manager or Patron, of a parent or, indeed, of any other individual for the sexual abuse of the applicant in 1973. Rather, the application concerns the responsibility of a State. More precisely, it examines whether the respondent State ought to have been aware of the risk of sexual abuse of minors such as the applicant in National Schools at the relevant time and *whether it adequately protected children, through its legal system,* from such treatment. The Court has found that it was an inherent positive obligation of government in the 1970s to protect children from ill-treatment. It was, moreover, an obligation of acute importance in a primary education context. That obligation was not fulfilled when the Irish State, which must be considered to have been aware of the sexual abuse of children by adults through, inter alia, its prosecution of such crimes at a significant rate, nevertheless continued to entrust the management of the primary education of the vast majority of young Irish children to non-State actors (National Schools), without putting in place any mechanism of effective State control against the risks of such abuse occurring. On the contrary, potential complainants were directed away from the State authorities and towards the non-State denominational Managers (paragraph 163 above). The consequences in the present case were the failure by the non-State Manager to act on prior complaints of sexual abuse by LH, the applicant's later abuse by LH and, more broadly, the prolonged and serious sexual misconduct by LH against numerous other students in that same National School. 169. In such circumstances, the State must be considered to have failed to fulfill its positive obligation to protect the present applicant from the sexual abuse to which she was subjected in 1973 whilst a pupil in Dunderrow National School. There has therefore been a violation of her rights under Article 3 of the Convention. Consequently, the Court dismisses the Government's preliminary objection to the effect that

of the applicant's abuse in 1973, it was because of the lack of adequate compliant mechanisms that the State 'neither knew nor ought to have known that this particular teacher, LH, posed a risk to this particular pupil, the applicant'.[21] However, from public reports the State had abstract knowledge about the frequent incidence of child abuse in its educative system and was thus legally responsible because of its inaction.[22]

On structures historically discriminatory against Roma, the ECtHR held in *Horváth and Kiss v. Hungary* 'that the State has specific positive obligations to avoid the perpetuation of past discrimination' against Roma children which had become manifest in its educative system.[23] Here again, as a consequence of a public report, the State should have been aware about the discriminatory structures in its educative system, which constituted, *per se*, an abstract danger to the enjoyment of human rights by members of the Roma community.[24]

II. State Capacity to Influence Effectively the Situation Impairing the Exercise of Human Rights

As stated above, a violation of positive obligations can consist of an omission or the failure to comply with the duty to appropriately protect individuals against criminal acts of others,[25] or to act appropriately to adopt its administrative and legal framework or even modify societal structures that are contrary to human rights. However, and evidently, a State cannot be responsible for every situation which jeopardizes the enjoyment of human rights and is known by the State. Instead, as the IACtHR held, there must be 'a reasonable possibility of preventing or avoiding that danger'.[26] To justify imposing positive obligations on a State, it thus appears useful to require an

this complaint was manifestly ill-founded.' Emphasis added. Note that these cases are the opposite of what *Stahl* claims. She argues that an abstract danger cannot establish a duty to protect against third actors and situations, see Stahl, *Schutzpflichten im Völkerrecht*, 2012, pp. 162.

[21] ECtHR, *O'Keeffe v. Ireland* [GC], Judgment, 28 January 2014, para. 148.

[22] ECtHR, *O'Keeffe v. Ireland* [GC], Judgment, 28 January 2014, para. 162.

[23] ECtHR, *Horváth and Kiss v. Hungary*, Judgment, 29 January 2013, para. 116. See also ECtHR, *DH v. Czech Republic* [GC], Judgment, 13 November 2007.

[24] The Court does not explicitly refer to the State's (constructive) knowledge, but refers to a public Report on Hungary of the European Commission against Racism and Intolerance and concludes that in light of the circumstances described in the report the State had positive obligations, ECtHR, *Horváth and Kiss v. Hungary*, Judgment, 29 January 2013, paras 114.

[25] Mégret, 'Nature of Obligations', in Sivakumaran/Moeckli/Shah, p. 130.

[26] IACtHR, *González v. Mexico (Cotton Field Case)*, Judgment (Preliminary Objection, Merits, Reparations, and Costs), 16 November 2009, para. 280; see also IACtHR, *Velásquez-Rodriguez v. Honduras*, Judgment (Merits), 29 July 1988.

influential link between the State and the abuser or the circumstances, be it through a de jure or a de facto relationship.[27]

1. De jure Relationship with the Abuser

An influential relationship is likely to exist, where a State has a legal relationship with the abuser.[28] According to the rules on attribution (ILC-Articles), such a legal relationship exists with State organs, with a person or entity empowered by internal law to exercise elements of the governmental authority acting in that capacity (actual agent) and even with abusers a State has substantial control over (de facto agent).[29] The very idea underlying the rules on attribution, that is, 'a State acts through its agents so should control them', plays a crucial role when establishing the existence of preventive and protective obligations.[30] For example, where sexist attitudes are a common problem among public officials, hindering the investigation and prosecution of gender-based crimes committed by private actors,[31] a State may have the obligation to prevent further harm from occurring by launching programs designed to create gender awareness among State officials.[32]

2. De facto Relationship with the Circumstances, the Abuser or the Victim

The capacity to influence effectively the general circumstances or actions of potential perpetrators may also be established by the existence of a *de facto* relationship with the abuser, the victim or the situation.[33] The State's ability to influence the course of the events may be determined by, for example, a previous human rights endangering activity, by a voluntary adoption of duties or by a particular relationship with the (potential) victim.[34] If such a previous activity can be established, subsequent omissions may legally be relevant. Interestingly, as *Dröge* and others

[27]ICJ, *Case concerning application of the Convention of Prevention and Punishment of the Crime of Genocide (Bosnia and Herzegovina v. Serbia and Montenegro)*, Judgment, 26 February 2007, para. 430; Hakimi, 'State Bystander Responsibility', (2010) 21 *EJIL*, wfr; Krähenmann, 'Positive obligations in human rights law during armed conflicts', in Kolb/Gaggioli, 2013, p. 175; Schutter et al., 'Commentary to the Maastricht Principles on extraterritorial obligations of states in the area of economic, social and cultural rights', (2012) 34 *Hum. Rts. Q.*, Principles No. 25, 26.

[28]Hakimi, 'State Bystander Responsibility', (2010) 21 *EJIL*, pp. 357.

[29]For details, see Chap. 3 B I. 3.

[30]Hakimi, 'State Bystander Responsibility', (2010) 21 *EJIL*, 356.

[31]IACtHR, *González v. Mexico (Cotton Field Case)*, Judgment (Preliminary Objection, Merits, Reparations, and Costs), 16 November 2009, paras 153, 198, 199, 202.

[32]E.g., IACtHR, *Rosendo Cantú y otra v. Mexico*, Judgment, 31 August 2010.

[33]Hakimi, 'State Bystander Responsibility', (2010) 21 *EJIL*, pp. 357.

[34]Stahl, *Schutzpflichten im Völkerrecht*, 2012, pp. 182–187; Dröge, *Positive Verpflichtungen der Staaten in der Europäischen Menschenrechtskonvention*, 2003, pp. 294, 300.

observed, under German and international criminal law doctrine, such settings are captured by the figures of the 'supervisor and protector guarantors'.[35] While this terminology can seldom be found in international human rights jurisprudence,[36] existing case law reflects the same idea.[37]

a. 'Supervisor Guarantor' Position

According to criminal law doctrine, the position of a 'supervisor guarantor' is 'imposed upon persons with a special responsibility over certain sources of danger, (...) which entail a duty to secure and supervise them (Überwachungs/ Sicherungspflicht)'.[38] Persons holding such a position have a duty to prevent harm from occurring. If they fail to do so, their criminal responsibility comes into question.[39]

When transferring this idea to human rights law, it can be held that a State holds such a position where it previously engaged in contractual, financial, military or political activities that endangered individual rights.[40] Along these lines, in the *Genocide case*, considering whether Serbia was obliged under Article 1 of the Genocide Convention to take preventive measures to protect the Bosnians against mass male executions and deportations, the ICJ found that Serbia maintained close *political, military* and *financial* links with the abusers.[41] While the massacre could not be attributed to Serbia, these links were deemed sufficient to hold Serbia responsible for having failed to protect Bosnians against genocide.[42] Similarly, the ECtHR established in *Ilascu v. Moldova and Russia*, that Russia had 'decisive

[35] *Cf.* also Stahl, *Schutzpflichten im Völkerrecht*, 2012, pp. 182–187; Dröge, *Positive Verpflichtungen der Staaten in der Europäischen Menschenrechtskonvention*, 2003, pp. 294, 300.

[36] But see IACtHR, *González v. Mexico (Cotton Field Case)*, Judgment (Preliminary Objection, Merits, Reparations, and Costs), 16 November 2009, Concurring Opinion of Judge *Diego Garcia-Sayan*, para. 3; and during the oral proceedings of *X and Y v. The Netherlands* before the ECtHR, Ser. B No. 74, p. 68.

[37] For details, see Ambos, *Treatise on international criminal law*, 2013, Chapter V, Omission, in particular command responsibility, pp. 184; Kühl, *Strafrecht. Allgemeiner Teil*, 2008, pp. 589.

[38] Ambos, *Treatise on international criminal law*, 2013, p. 184.

[39] Kühl, *Strafrecht. Allgemeiner Teil*, 2008, pp. 589.

[40] For details, see Stahl, *Schutzpflichten im Völkerrecht*, 2012, pp. 182–187; Dröge, *Positive Verpflichtungen der Staaten in der Europäischen Menschenrechtskonvention*, 2003, pp. 302.

[41] ICJ, *Case concerning application of the Convention of Prevention and Punishment of the Crime of Genocide (Bosnia and Herzegovina v. Serbia and Montenegro)*, Judgment, 26 February 2007, para. 430; see also ECtHR, *Ilaşcu v. Moldova and Russia* [GC], Judgment, 08 July 2004, para. 392, finding that Russia had 'decisive influence', and that the separatists 'survive[d] by virtue of [Russia's] military, economic, financial, and political support'.

[42] ICJ, *Case concerning application of the Convention of Prevention and Punishment of the Crime of Genocide (Bosnia and Herzegovina v. Serbia and Montenegro)*, Judgment, 26 February 2007, paras 434. But see Milanović, *Territorial Scope of Application of the Genocide Convention*, EJIL Talk!, December 2008.

influence', and that the separatists 'survive[d] by virtue of [Russia's] military, economic, financial, and political support'.[43] In this context, it should be recalled that absence of a territorial link might not automatically imply that the State concerned has no positive obligations to be taken from its *own* territory.[44]

To the same token, an influential relationship can also be established where a State delegates a public function to a private actor in a way that precludes attribution.[45] In such cases, it can be held that there is a normative expectation towards the delegating State to exercise influence upon the private actor.[46] A State should not be allowed to transfer its authority to another person circumventing its own responsibility.[47] Thus, the delegation of a public function is an adequate criterion that influences the scrutiny of whether the State had to take measures to prevent or protect against harm.

Along these lines, in *O'Keeffe v. Ireland*, the applicant held that

> [e]ven if the State outsourced [the obligation to provide education] to non-State entities, the National School model could and should have accommodated greater child protection regulations. One way or the other, a State could not avoid its Convention protective obligations by delegating primary education to a private entity.[48]

While the Court did not explicitly take up this argument, dissenting judges criticized that the majority attributed special importance to the fact that 'the respondent State had ceded its responsibility for the education of children to a private entity'.[49]

b. 'Protector Guarantor'

According to criminal law, the position of a 'protector guarantor' is imposed on a person 'who because of their special protective position with regard to certain legal

---

[43]ECtHR, *Ilaşcu v. Moldova and Russia* [GC], Judgment, 08 July 2004, para. 392.

[44]See above, Chap. 3 B.

[45]An act of a *de facto* organ is attributable to a State when it acted under the instructions, direction or control of the state to the extent that the delegate is dependent on the state (Article 8 ILC Articles; Milanović, *Extraterritorial application of human rights treaties*, 2011, p. 44; ICJ, *Military and paramilitary activities in and against Nicaragua (Nicaragua v. United States of America)*, Judgment (merits), 27 June 1986, para. 109 requiring complete dependence or control of the State over the armed groups to be considered *de facto* State organs) or where the state had effective control over the abuser, see ICJ, *Military and paramilitary activities in and against Nicaragua (Nicaragua v. United States of America)*, Judgment (merits), 27 June 1986, para. 115.

[46]Hakimi, 'State Bystander Responsibility', (2010) 21 *EJIL*, pp. 358, 377; Dröge, *Positive Verpflichtungen der Staaten in der Europäischen Menschenrechtskonvention*, 2003, p. 306.

[47]ECtHR, *O'Keeffe v. Ireland* [GC], Judgment, 28 January 2014, para. 150. On the 'non-circumvention principle', see also Halberstam/Stein, 'The United Nations, the European Union, and the King of Sweden', (2009) 46 *CMLRev*.

[48]ECtHR, *O'Keeffe v. Ireland* [GC], Judgment, 28 January 2014, paras 124, 145, 150.

[49]ECtHR, *O'Keeffe v. Ireland* [GC], Judgment, 28 January 2014, p. 60, para. 13 (ii).

interests (...) have a protective duty towards them (*Schutz/Obhutspflicht*)'.[50] This position may be because of a voluntary adoption of duties or to a particular relationship with the (potential) victim. Here again, persons holding such a position have a duty to prevent harm from occurring. If they fail to do so, their criminal responsibility comes into question.[51]

Transferring the criminal law concepts to States and to positive human rights obligations,[52] a State may hold the position of a 'protector guarantor' when having a capacity to influence the course of the event because of a particular relationship with the victim or the situation. For example, special responsibility exists vis-à-vis a State's own nationals or for persons being on its territory.[53] The ECtHR has indeed based its argument for positive obligations referring to the particular status the applicant had when the violations occurred.[54]

III. Severity of Harm and 'Vulnerability of Victims' Group'

When it has been established that the State has or ought to have knowledge about an abstract or individualized risk of harm and that this State is in a position to influence the situation or the abuser, this alone cannot establish the existence of positive obligations to generally prevent or protect against impairments of human rights. As the ECtHR held, it is because of 'the unpredictability of human conduct [that] not every claimed risk to [fundamental rights] can entail for the authorities (...) to take operational measures to prevent that risk from materialising'.[55] Moreover, concerning State-related positive obligations, it can be claimed that not every claimed malfunction of a State's structures can entail a legal duty to ensure a 'perfect' governmental system. This would amount to an exaggerated demand that risks undermining human rights obligations in their entirety. Hence, the *severity* of harm (potentially) caused appears to necessarily constitute an additional factor that influences the scrutiny whether a State has positive obligations.[56] This is widely

[50] Ambos, *Treatise on international criminal law*, 2013, p. 184.

[51] For details, see Kühl, *Strafrecht. Allgemeiner Teil*, 2008, pp. 589.

[52] *Cf.* also Stahl, *Schutzpflichten im Völkerrecht*, 2012, p. 185.

[53] Hakimi, 'State Bystander Responsibility', (2010) 21 *EJIL*, pp. 360.

[54] Referring to the status of prisoner, ECtHR, *Keenan v. The United Kingdom*, Judgment (Merits and Just Satisfaction), 03 April 2001, para. 91; Relying on the particular responsibility of public authorities to protect the well-being of pupils, ECtHR, *O'Keeffe v. Ireland* [GC], Judgment, 28 January 2014, paras 145, 150. For the protection against rebel and paramilitary groups, see Krähenmann, 'Positive obligations in human rights law during armed conflicts', in Kolb/Gaggioli, 2013, pp. 175.

[55] ECtHR, *Osman v. the United Kingdom*, Judgment, 28 October 1998, para. 116.

[56] Hakimi, 'State Bystander Responsibility', (2010) 21 *EJIL*, pp. 367. But see Stahl, she considers the intensity of possible harm to be a question that impacts the exercise of state discretion only, Stahl, *Schutzpflichten im Völkerrecht*, 2012, p. 188.

reflected both in specific human rights treaties and in international jurisprudence.[57] Moreover, international jurisprudence has referred to group-specific vulnerability as a further criterion. As will be shown, this second criterion is unnecessary, even conceptually misleading.

1. Severity of Harm

As *Hakimi* observed, the severity of harm as a criterion to establish positive duties may already be implied by the substantial scope of the right (at risk to be) impaired. This is true for rights pertaining to *jus cogens* (freedom from torture, genocide and racial discrimination).[58] Harm as a criterion to establish positive duties may also lie in the challenge to fundamental values of the legal community or the core rights such as the right to life or to be free of ill-treatment[59] or slavery.[60] Finally, the degree and scope of harm may also establish positive duties. This consideration applies particularly where crimes such as domestic violence[61] or discrimination against specific groups occur extensively.[62]

[57]See below, and Hakimi, 'State Bystander Responsibility', (2010) 21 *EJIL* wfr.

[58]As said, thematic conventions concerning these subjects (CAT, CERD and Genocide Convention) explicitly create positive obligations.

[59]On domestic violence, see ECtHR, *Valiuliene v. Lithuania*, Judgment, 26 March 2013, paras 73–78.

[60]On human trafficking as a form of forced labor or slavery under Art. 4 ECHR, see ECtHR, *Rantsev v. Cyprus and Russia*, Judgment, 07 January 2010.

[61]*Cf.* ECtHR, *Opuz v. Turkey*, Judgment, 09 June 2009, paras 132. The ECtHR held that 'the issue of domestic violence (. . .) cannot be confined to the circumstances of the present case. It is a general problem which concerns all member States and which does not always surface as it often takes place within personal relationships or closed circuits and it is not only women who are affected. The Court acknowledges that men may also be the victims of domestic violence and, indeed, that children, too, are often casualties of the phenomenon, whether directly or indirectly. Accordingly, the Court will bear in mind the gravity of the problem at issue when examining the present case.'

[62]E.g., ECtHR, *Horváth and Kiss v. Hungary*, Judgment, 29 January 2013.

2. Vulnerability as a Distinct Reason for Protection: A Critical Evaluation

Both, in international (quasi)judicial practice[63] and legal scholarship,[64] it has been suggested that positive obligations arise where people are affected by a harmful conduct *because* of their belonging to a *vulnerable* group.

To give but two examples, according to the UNHRC, for instance, women require more protection because of their particular vulnerability in wartime.[65] In the *Cotton field* case, the IACtHR acknowledged that the young women's 'humble background' and their (inner-Mexican) migrant worker status made them particularly vulnerable to sexualized violence.[66] The Court then held that the 'State must pay special attention to the needs and rights of the alleged victims owing to their condition as girls who, as women, belong to a *vulnerable* group'.[67]

While human rights treaties that explicitly require States to take protective and preventive measures do indeed relate to groups said to be vulnerable,[68] it is claimed here that the criterion of 'vulnerability' as a distinct reason for their protection is a misconception and unnecessary. This is because persons who are allegedly vulnerable are *made* vulnerable by societal circumstances, but are not by default more vulnerable than any other human being.[69] For example, a well-educated woman who is economically independent from her partner is less likely to accept domestic violence, as she is able to cover her living costs, than a woman with a weak socio-

---

[63]E.g., IACtHR, *González v. Mexico (Cotton Field Case)*, Judgment (Preliminary Objection, Merits, Reparations, and Costs), 16 November 2009, paras 282, 408; ECtHR, *Opuz v. Turkey*, Judgment, 09 June 2009, para. 159; ECtHR, *Bevacqua and S. v. Bulgaria*, Judgment, 12 June 2008; ECtHR, *M.C. v. Bulgaria*, Judgment, 04 December 2003; ECtHR, *O'Keeffe v. Ireland* [GC], Judgment, 28 January 2014, paras 144, 162; ECtHR, *DH v. Czech Republic* [GC], Judgment, 13 November 2007, paras 181–182; ECtHR, *Horváth and Kiss v. Hungary*, Judgment, 29 January 2013, para. 102; CEDAW, *General Recommendation No. 24 on article 12 of CEDAW*, 1999, para. 6, claiming that 'special attention should be given to the health needs and rights of women belonging to vulnerable and disadvantaged groups, such as migrant women, refugee and internally displaced women, the girl child and older women, women in prostitution, indigenous women and women with physical or mental disabilities'.

[64]Hakimi, 'State Bystander Responsibility', (2010) 21 *EJIL*, p. 368; Stahl, *Schutzpflichten im Völkerrecht*, 2012, p. 186; Dröge, *Positive Verpflichtungen der Staaten in der Europäischen Menschenrechtskonvention*, 2003, pp. 322.

[65]UN Human Rights Committee, *General Comment No. 28*, 29 March 2000, para. 8.

[66]IACtHR, *González v. Mexico (Cotton Field Case)*, Judgment (Preliminary Objection, Merits, Reparations, and Costs), 16 November 2009, para. 282.

[67]Emphasis added. CEDAW, *General Recommendation No. 24 on article 12 of CEDAW*, 1999, para. 6, claiming that 'special attention should be given to the health needs and rights of women belonging to vulnerable and disadvantaged groups, such as migrant women, refugee and internally displaced women, the girl child and older women, women in prostitution, indigenous women and women with physical or mental disabilities'.

[68]*Cf.* CEDAW, CRC, ICERD, CRMW, CRPD, Art. 9 Belém do Pará Convention.

[69]See also Article 46 (c) Istanbul Convention and ECtHR, *Valiuliene v. Lithuania*, Judgment, 26 March 2013, para. 69, where the Court rejects the argument that women are by default vulnerable.

economic or migrant status. A black person or Roma living in a predominantly white society, which structurally discriminates against people of color, is more likely to experience hate crimes and be less wealthy within that society than a white person. Hence, if one draws on the 'vulnerability' of a social group, one bolsters stereotypes concerning that group and conceals human-made root causes of circumstances that infringe human rights.[70]

Instead, the criterion of vulnerability comes down to the very same reason for protection, which is 'severe harm'. Harmful conduct directed against members of disadvantaged groups entails both an individual and a societal harm: at the individual level, it strengthens inequalities, undermines the victims' life capabilities[71] and may entail restricted agency.[72] On the societal and collective level, what makes certain kinds of harm indefensible for the legal and social community is the (risk of a) fundamental challenge to its grounding values. To take the European and Latin-American legal cultures for instance, one can think of values such as humanity, respect for the human person, democracy, cultural diversity[73] and the rule of law which includes equality and the protection of minorities[74] or other underprivileged groups, as well as private life as such fundamental bedrocks of legal and social communities. The severe harm ensuing from (potential) violations of fundamental rights and values will thus decide whether protection is required.

Hence, both types of cases, that is, where severe harm is inflicted upon a person through, for example, torture, or where members of allegedly vulnerable groups are discriminated against, trigger positive obligations *due to the harm* they potentially cause. It is the individual and/or collective harm at risk to occur what makes protection mandatory.

The following section first briefly lays the theoretical grounds on the different philosophical concepts of vulnerability. It then shows that cases, where courts have concluded that a State had positive duties because of the applicant's vulnerability, can also be analyzed through the criterion of 'severe harm'.

a. Philosophical Concepts of Vulnerability

At first glance, groups such as women, migrant workers, people of color and persons with disabilities seem to share the common denominator of being more *vulnerable* than people pertaining to more privileged groups. Stemming from philosophy, the

---

[70]But see ECtHR, *Valiuliene v. Lithuania*, Judgment, 26 March 2013, para. 69 where the Court rejects the argument that women are *by default* vulnerable. However, the Second Chamber of the Court fails to deal appropriately with the extensive prevalence of domestic violence against women in Lithuania, see also the dissenting opinion of Judge Pinto de Albuquerque.

[71]See also Hakimi, 'State Bystander Responsibility', (2010) 21 *EJIL*, p. 368.

[72]On the philosophical concept of 'agency', see Schlosser, 'Agency', in Zalta.

[73]E.g., ECtHR, *Chapman v. the United Kingdom* [GC], Judgment, 18 January 2001, paras 93–94.

[74]ECtHR, *Young, James u Webster v. the United Kingdom*, Judgment, 13 August 1981, para. 63.

concept of 'vulnerability' can, however, not be said to have one meaning only. Rather, three approaches influence international jurisprudence.

For some, vulnerability is an ontological condition of the embodied and social human existence that is universal to all of us. For others, it is the 'contingent susceptibility of particular persons or groups to specific kinds of harm or threat by others' because of 'inequalities of power, dependency, capacity, or need'.[75] Thus, according to the second approach, the alleged *vulnerability* itself gives rise to a moral duty to protect specific groups. This concept appears to be used by courts.

Whereas the first approach obscures social inequalities that generate specific needs and dispositions, the second approach, as applied by the human rights discourse, entails the risk of labeling particular subgroups and thus of triggering stereotypes and 'unwarranted and unjust paternalistic responses'.[76]

As *Mackenzie* and others observed, a third concept allows merging the two mentioned perspectives when

> acknowledg[ing] the ontological vulnerability that is inherent in the human condition while at the same time enabling the identification of context-specific forms of vulnerability. [Such an approach allows to] identify responsibilities owed to the "more than ordinarily" vulnerable and potential inventions to mitigate the effects of various forms of vulnerability.[77]

b. Severity of Harm as Unifying Criterion

Even if one viewed disadvantaged groups through the lens of the above-mentioned third concept of vulnerability, the group's or the individual's vulnerability should not be held to be the reason for positive obligations to apply. As said, the alleged vulnerability is *not* inherent in, *viz.* natural to, the individuals addressed by this concept, but rather the result of social structures disadvantaging the group the individual is a member of. When relying on the vulnerability instead of the harm caused by the relevant violations, the legal discourse conceals and perpetuates these social structures. Thus, focusing on their socially created vulnerability bears the risk of re-enforcing stereotypes.

The 'normative significance [of vulnerability rather] derives from its role in alerting us to the presence of other morally salient claims, such as those based on harm or need'.[78] Such an approach caters for the need of stringent parameters that measure whether positive obligations apply. The criterion of harm caused by an act infringing human rights can be measured based on facts. Both types of cases, that is, those where harm is caused by violations of *jus cogens* or against core values and rights, and those where harm particularly affects disadvantaged groups, can be subsumed under one parameter: it is the severity of individual and/or societal harm

[75] Mackenzie/Rogers/Dodds, 'Introduction', in Mackenzie, 2013, p. 6 wfr.

[76] Ibid.

[77] Ibid, p. 7.

[78] Emphasis added, ibid. p. 12.

to the legal and social community as a fundamental challenge of its grounding values and not the affiliation to a specific group that makes protection mandatory.

In this light, it is interesting to note that various judgments that concern 'vulnerable' individuals or groups/minorities not only refer to the alleged vulnerability but are also based on the particular harm to grounding values or to the individual applicant. To give but one example concerning the protection of Roma, in *Chapman v. UK* the ECtHR held that,

> the vulnerable position of Gypsies as a minority means that some special consideration should be given to their needs and their different lifestyle both in the relevant regulatory planning framework and in reaching decisions in particular cases (. . .). To this extent, there is thus a positive obligation imposed on the Contracting States by virtue of Article 8 to facilitate the Gypsy way of life (. . .).[79]

However, the Court also acknowledged that

> the special needs of minorities and an obligation to protect their security, identity and lifestyle (. . .), not only for the purpose of safeguarding the interests of the minorities themselves but to preserve a cultural diversity of value to the whole community.[80]

In a latter case concerning crimes against Roma, *Angelova and Iliev v. Bulgaria,* the ECtHR argued that

> when investigating violent incidents State authorities have the additional duty to take all reasonable steps to unmask any racist motive and to establish whether or not ethnic hatred or prejudice may have played a role in the events. Failing to do so and treating racially induced violence and brutality on an equal footing with cases that have no racist overtones would be to turn a blind eye to the specific nature of acts that are particularly destructive of fundamental rights.[81]

The Court further held that this would also be required to 'maintain the confidence of minorities in the ability of the authorities to protect them from the threat of racist violence'.[82]

In *Cotton Field,* the IACtHR found that the ECtHR's arguments as presented in *Angelova and Iliev v. Bulgaria* are 'wholly applicable when examining the scope of the obligation of due diligence in the investigation of cases of gender-based violence'.[83] Hence, protecting minorities or disadvantaged groups against excesses of

[79]ECtHR, *Chapman v. the United Kingdom* [GC], Judgment, 18 January 2001, para. 96.

[80]ECtHR, *Chapman v. the United Kingdom* [GC], Judgment, 18 January 2001, para. 93; see also ECtHR, *DH v. Czech Republic* [GC], Judgment, 13 November 2007, para. 181; ECtHR, *Oršuš and Others v. Croatia* [GC], Judgment, 16 March 2010, para. 148.

[81]Emphasis added. ECtHR, *Angelova and Iliev v. Bulgaria*, Judgment, 26 July 2007, para. 115. *Cf.* also ECtHR, *Chapman v. the United Kingdom* [GC], Judgment, 18 January 2001, paras 93–94; referring to the public interest in protecting minorities, see ECtHR, *DH v. Czech Republic* [GC], Judgment, 13 November 2007, para. 204.

[82]ECtHR, *Angelova and Iliev v. Bulgaria*, Judgment, 26 July 2007, para. 65.

[83]IACtHR, *González v. Mexico (Cotton Field Case)*, Judgment (Preliminary Objection, Merits, Reparations, and Costs), 16 November 2009, para. 293.

the majority constitutes a fundamental democratic value that is ultimately the ground for their protection; there is no need to fall back on the criterion of vulnerability.

c. Conclusion: Irrelevance of the 'Vulnerability' Criterion

To conclude, there is no need to maintain that vulnerability is one of the factors that establish positive obligations. From a theoretical viewpoint, it is even misleading and harmful. What is decisive is the severity of harm that can be caused on the societal, collective and individual level. Vulnerable conditions are the result of social structures and may only be *an indicator* for the danger of severe harm. Ultimately, such an approach avoids the perpetuation of stereotypes.

IV. Conclusion

1. Parameters to Establish the Existence of Positive Obligations of Protection and Prevention

It was the aim of this section to find parameters that allow conclusions to be drawn as to when positive obligations of protection and prevention apply. Drawing on previous and more comprehensive studies, the analysis has focused on a number of more recent judgments from the ECtHR, the IACtHR and the ICJ. In this light, it appears that there are three parameters to establish whether a State has positive obligations of prevention and protection. These parameters apply to the obligations to generally prevent abuses and to protect against them in a determined case.

Firstly, if there is a group or individual at risk to be harmed by whatever kind of actor or situation, the State needs to know or have constructive knowledge about that risk. For the obligation to protect in a specific case to apply, this risk must be *real and immediate*. Concerning the obligation to generally prevent, an *abstract danger* is sufficient.

Secondly, a State can only have positive obligations, if it has the capacity to exercise decisive influence on the abuser or the circumstances. It has been suggested that this influence can be established by a *de jure* relationship with the abuser to the extent that it could or should have exercised control over them. An exercise of influence on the abuser or the situation can also be expected where it is established that there is a *de facto* relationship with the abuser, the victim or the circumstances. Therefore, the concepts of a 'supervisor guarantor' or 'protector guarantor' position can be useful. The 'protector guarantor' position may play a role where a State has a special link with the victim (prisoner, pupil, resident). In turn, the transfer of public functions to private entities or other contractual, political, financial or territorial links between a State and the abuser are indicative of a 'supervisor guarantor' position.

Thirdly, and ultimately, if the severity and/or scope of the individual or collective harm (potentially) suffered is extensive, there is a normative expectation towards the

State to take preventive and protective measures. It is claimed here that a victim's (group) alleged vulnerability does not, of itself, have an impact on positive obligations. Rather, it is sufficient and more appropriate to rely on the harmful consequences at both the individual and societal/collective level.

2. Parameters Applied to Violence Against Women

The three criteria established are wholly applicable to violence against women. After two decades of UN focus on this subject, a State will hardly be able to claim not to have had (constructive) knowledge about this phenomenon. As the world's biggest-ever report on violence against women from the European Union Agency for Fundamental Rights (FRA) revealed, in EU member States 33% of all women experienced physical and/or sexualized violence which does not include harassment, stalking or similar assaults.[84] Regarding the level of danger for harm to realize, it seems that because of the statistical probability of violence against women, the danger to become a victim is permanent.[85] Depending on both, the statistical

---

[84]European Union Agency for Fundamental Rights, *Violence against women*, March 2014. See also European Agency for Fundamental Rights, Violence against Women: every day and everywhere, available at http://fra.europa.eu/en/press-release/2014/violence-against-women-every-day-and-everywhere, accessed 26 January 2016, where the key findings of this study are resumed as follows:

- 33% of women have experienced **physical and/or sexual violence** since the age of 15. That corresponds to 62 million women.
- 22% have experienced physical and/or sexual violence by a partner.
- 5% of all women have been **raped**. Almost one in 10 women who have experienced sexual violence by a non-partner, indicate that more than one perpetrator was involved in the most serious incident.
- 43% have experienced some form of **psychological violence** by either a current or a previous partner, such as public humiliation; forbidding a woman to leave the house or locking her up; forcing her to watch pornography; and threats of violence.
- 33% have **childhood experiences of physical or sexual violence** at the hands of an adult. 12% had childhood experiences of sexual violence, **of which half were from men they did not know**. These forms of abuse typically involve an adult exposing their genitals or touching the child's genitals or breasts.
- 18% of women have experienced **stalking** since the age of 15 and 5% in the 12 months prior to the interview. This corresponds to 9 million women. 21% of women who have experienced stalking said that it lasted for over 2 years.
- 11% of women have experienced inappropriate advances on social websites or have been subjected to sexually explicit emails or text (SMS) messages. 20% of young women (18–29) have been victims of such **cyber harassment**.
- 55% of women have experienced some form of **sexual harassment**. 32% of all victims of sexual harassment said the perpetrator was a boss, colleague or customer.
- 67% **did not report** the most serious incident of partner violence to the police or any other organization.

[85]Applying a structural view, it may also be claimed that the structural consequences and permanent daily-life restrictions on each woman's human rights flowing from the mere risk of gender-based

Negative obligation violated by state acts:	Parameters to establish the existence of **positive** obligations of prevention and protection, violated by state omissions:
de iure relationship (attribution)	1) obligation to generally prevent: (constructive) knowledge about *abstract* danger for a right; obligation to protect in a determined case: (constructive) knowledge about a real and *imminent* risk; 2) links that allow to exercise influence on the abuser/situation: *de jure* relationship or *de facto* relationship established by a 'guarantor position;' 3) (risk of) severe individual and/or societal harm.

Fig. 5.1 Three cumulative parameters to establish whether a State has positive obligations of protection and prevention

occurrence of violence against women in a region and the number of intersecting risk factors such as disability, skin color and socio-economic status (which, as said, increase the probability of being aggressed), the likelihood to become a victim may even be higher. Provided that these criteria apply cumulatively under a general or thematic human rights treaty a State is a party to, every State can be said to have positive obligations to prevent and, where a risk of harm is immediate, to protect against violence against women (Fig. 5.1).

---

violence not only constitutes a risk of harm, but a permanent harm. (On avoidance strategies employed by women fearing gender-based violence, see European Union Agency for Fundamental Rights, *Violence against women*, March 2014, pp. 139.) However, as long as this permanent danger is generally internalized as 'normal' or even declared as natural, it is most likely that law will not accept it as constituting (serious) harm or even a violation. As *Susanne Baer*, a judge at the German Constitutional Court, pointed out during the conference 'Autonomie im Recht – geschlechtertheoretisch vermessen' at Goethe University in Frankfurt (March 2016), law ends where internalization of oppression begins.

B. Scope of and Limits to Positive Obligations

The foregoing section has suggested three criteria that may trigger positive obligations of prevention and protection.[86] Accordingly, a State must, firstly, have knowledge about a relevant danger to an individual right. Secondly, a State must have the legal or factual capacity to influence the situation or abuser. Finally, the harm in danger to occur must be severe. Under these criteria, because of the endemic and structural occurrence of violence against women and its destructive impact on the individual and collective level, it has been concluded that all States can be said to have positive obligations to generally prevent and protect against it.

However, if a treaty explicitly establishes positive duties such as CEDAW and CERD[87] or where, according to the criteria developed above, a State has positive obligations of protection and prevention, nothing is said about the scope of and limits to positive obligations. As positive human rights obligations are obligations of means, *de facto* insufficient measures may legally be irrelevant. It may well be that a State acted within its discretion and the limits imposed by other obligations under international law.

This section therefore analyzes the scope of and limits to positive obligations. Thereby, it is suggested here that the considerations also apply, in principle, to obligations with a programmatic character (to fulfill) because their progressive character cannot imply 'a license to remain passive'.[88] It is clear though, that an individual claimant would in any event lack standing for claiming a violation of such obligations.[89] The section first discusses the standard used to measure compliance with positive human rights obligations (I.). As the standard allows for discretion to be exercised by a State, it then draws on the factors informing this discretion and the limits allowing for judicial scrutiny (II.). The section concludes with a discussion on additional parameters potentially required to establish a violation of positive obligations (III.).

I. Scope of Positive Obligations

Once it has been established that a State has positive obligations, the question arises what can legally and reasonably be expected from this State. As the ECtHR put it, it is because of limited resources and political priorities that a State cannot prevent every crime, detrimental conduct or circumstances.[90] It is therefore unanimous in

[86] On the notion of 'positive obligations of prevention and protection', see Chap. 3 C.

[87] See above, Chap. 4 A.

[88] Schutter, *International human rights law*, 2014, p. 564.

[89] On the procedural aspects of positive obligations, see Stahl, *Schutzpflichten im Völkerrecht*, 2012, pp. 358.

[90] ECtHR, *Osman v. the United Kingdom*, Judgment, 28 October 1998, para. 116.

practice that the scope of positive obligations is not absolute as to 'impose an impossible or disproportionate burden on the authorities'.[91] Rather, positive obligations constitute obligations of conduct and means[92] that do not require from States to succeed in their efforts by reaching the full realization of human rights enjoyment. They can be said to set a standard of reasonableness.

As it is generally assumed under international law, States are in the first place best situated to decide which kind of measures can terminate an infringement of human rights under their jurisdiction. Thus and in principle, human rights law leaves room for State's discretion. Instruments such as CEDAW have an open wording and accord to the state parties a broad degree of discretion.[93] However, some international instruments such as the Istanbul Convention provide clear guidance on the extent and limits of measures to be taken, so that States have little room for discretion.

The wording of conventions, non-binding documents and court decisions, which refer to the scope of positive duties, differs significantly. At times positive obligations are said to require from a State to take 'appropriate measures', 'reasonable or proper steps' or to 'exercise due diligence'. At first glance, a textual reading might suggest that there is a considerable difference between these standards. Therefrom, it is often—at least implicitly—assumed that the scope of these obligations differs.[94]

Furthermore, because due diligence is mostly mentioned in the context of gender-based violence, concerns have been raised that positive obligations relating to gender-based violence are 'reduced to a mere due diligence obligation' and that, apparently, this standard is weaker than the one required for a State to comply with other positive obligations.[95] For example, state parties to the Belém do Pará Conventions must act with '*due diligence* to prevent, prosecute and punish acts of violence against women'.[96] Under Article 5 (2) of the Istanbul Convention, States must 'take the necessary legislative and other measures *to exercise due diligence* to prevent, investigate, punish and provide reparation for acts of violence covered by the scope of this Convention that are perpetrated by non-State actors'. Finally, the UN Special Rapporteur on Violence against women, *Yakin Ertürk*, stated that 'under

[91]E.g., ECtHR, *Osman v. the United Kingdom*, Judgment, 28 October 1998, para. 116.

[92]IACtHR, *González v. Mexico (Cotton Field Case)*, Judgment (Preliminary Objection, Merits, Reparations, and Costs), 16 November 2009, para. 252; see also Council of Europe, *Explanatory Report to the Council of Europe Convention on preventing and combating violence against women and domestic violence,* 2011, para. 59; IACtHR, *Velásquez-Rodriguez v. Honduras*, Judgment (Merits), 29 July 1988, para. 166; *IACtHR, Perozo et al. v. Venezuela, Judgment (Preliminary Objections, Merits, Reparations, and Costs), 28 January 2009*, para. 149; *IACtHR, Anzualdo-Castro v. Peru, Judgment (Preliminary Objection, Merits, Reparations and Costs), 22 September 2009*, para. 30.

[93]*Cf.* also Hakimi, 'State Bystander Responsibility', (2010) 21 *EJIL*, pp. 371.

[94]E.g., Chinkin, 'Violence against Women', in Rudolf/Freeman/Chinkin, 2012, pp. 465–467.

[95]Kamminga, 'Due Diligence Mania', in Westendorp, 2012, pp. 411, 408; Hasselbacher, 'State Obligations Regarding Domestic Violence', (2010) 8 *Northwestern J. Int'l Hum. Rts.*

[96]Emphasis added. Article 7 b) of the Convention of Belém do Pará.

the *due diligence* obligation, States have a duty to take positive action to prevent and protect women from violence, punish perpetrators of violent acts and compensate victims of violence'.[97]

This section demonstrates that there is no difference—neither in meaning nor in content—between the different terms used to indicate the scope of positive obligations. Rather, it is for legal-historical and regional reasons that different terms have been employed concurrently.

1. Concept of 'Due Diligence' Under General International Law

Before analyzing the different terms used in practice to refer to the scope of positive obligations, we shall first explore the meaning of 'due diligence'. Due diligence is a principle of general international law. It originates in the obligation to protect aliens against the internationally illicit behavior of a State's own nationals that, in fact, implied a very low standard. In the *Neer Claim* (1926), for example, the General Claims Commission held that 'the treatment of an alien, in order to constitute an international delinquency [needed to] amount to an *outrage*, to *bad faith*, to *willful neglect of duty*, or to an insufficiency of governmental action so far short of international standards that every reasonable and impartial man (sic) would readily recognize its insufficiency'.[98]

Yet, this subjective understanding dramatically changed since the Second World War. Nowadays the general principle of due diligence is understood as to require from States to 'endeavour to reach the result set out in the obligation. A breach of [this obligation] consists not of failing to achieve the desired result but failing to *take the necessary, diligent steps* towards that end'.[99] Hence, the standard of responsibility is no more subjective but objective.

2. Standard Applied by International Courts and (Quasi-)Judicial Bodies

If today 'due diligence' is not subjective but objective, the question arises what a due diligence standard implies in the area of human rights. An analysis of the jurisprudence of the ICJ, IACtHR, ECtHR and CEDAW Committee reveals that in the context of human rights the 'due diligence' standard and the obligation to take 'appropriate measures/steps' require the very same efforts to be taken.

---

[97]UNCHR, *Integration of the human rights of women and the gender perspective*, 20 January 2006, Summery.

[98]Emphasis added. General Claims Commission, *L. F. H. Neer and Pauline Neer (U.S.A.) v. United Mexican States*, 15 October 1926. See also Shaw, *International law*, 2008, p. 825; Kamminga, 'Due Diligence Mania', in Westendorp, 2012, at p. 409.

[99]Koivurova, 'Due diligence', in Wolfrum, 2012, para. 3.

a. IACtHR

While being reluctant to refer to the margin of appreciation doctrine,[100] the IACtHR generally measures compliance with positive obligations with a due diligence standard.[101] The way it is used by the IACtHR, this standard comes down to a principle of effectiveness. The Court established this standard in its well-known *Velásquez-Rodriguez case*. It held that

> an illegal act which violates human rights and which is initially not directly imputable to a State (. . .) can lead to international responsibility of the State, not because of the act itself, but because of the lack of due diligence to prevent the violation or to respond to it as required by the Convention.[102]

Accordingly, the duty to protect with due diligence under the IACHR is not fulfilled by the mere establishment of a legal system *de jure* designed to ensure compliance with the obligation, but it requires 'the government to conduct itself as to *effectively* ensure the exercise of human rights'.[103] This approach was then taken as the Court's general standard.[104]

b. ECtHR

In contrast to the IACtHR, the ECtHR, when ruling on positive obligations, traditionally refers to the margin of appreciation doctrine.[105] This doctrine is a 'safeguard to reconcile the effective operation of the [ECHR] and the sovereign powers and responsibilities of governments in a democracy'.[106] Accordingly, a State is seen as the best qualified to 'appreciate the necessities of a particular situation' and thus to decide what is appropriate.[107] However, a State's margin of appreciation is restricted by the requirement of *effective* protection.[108]

---

[100] Crawford, *Brownlie's Principles of public international law*, 2012, p. 666.

[101] *Cf.* also Shelton/Gould, 'Positive and Negative Obligations', in Shelton, 2010, p. 579.

[102] IACtHR, *Velásquez-Rodriguez v. Honduras*, Judgment (Merits), 29 July 1988, para. 172.

[103] Emphasis added. IACtHR, *Velásquez-Rodriguez v. Honduras*, Judgment (Merits), 29 July 1988, para. 167.

[104] E.g., IACtHR, *González v. Mexico (Cotton Field Case)*, Judgment (Preliminary Objection, Merits, Reparations, and Costs), 16 November 2009, paras 250, 258; IACtHR, *Rodríguez Vera et al. (The disappeared from the palace of justice) v. Colombia*, Judgment (Preliminary Objections, Merits, Reparations and Costs), 14 November 2014, para. 480, *passim*; IACtHR, *Velásquez Paiz et al. v. Guatemala*, Judgment (Preliminary Objections, Merits, Reparations and Costs), 19 November 2015, para. 108.

[105] On the margin of appreciation doctrine, see Shany, 'Toward a general margin of appreciation doctrine in international law?' (2005) 16 *EJIL*.

[106] O'Donnell, 'The Margin of Appreciation Doctrine', (1982) 4 *Hum. Rts. Q.*, p. 476.

[107] Crawford, *Brownlie's Principles of public international law*, 2012, p. 666.

[108] See, e.g., ECtHR, *M.C. v. Bulgaria*, Judgment, 04 December 2003, para. 150, also referring to ECtHR, *X and Y v. The Netherlands*, Judgment, 26 March 1985. For an analysis of the Court's

In the well-known *Osman case,* for example, the legal defense of the respondent State had argued that the government's failure to act should amount to gross negligence or willful disregard to constitute a violation of the duty to protect. Remarkably, the wording employed recalls the historical understanding of 'due diligence' standard as applied in the *Neer Claim.*

However, the ECtHR rejected this claim and held that such

> a rigid standard must be considered to be incompatible with the requirements of Article 1 of the Convention and the obligations of Contracting States under that Article to secure the practical and effective protection of the rights and freedoms laid down therein, including Article 2 (. . .).[109]

The Court deemed it sufficient 'for an applicant to show that the authorities did not do all that could be reasonably expected of them to avoid a real and immediate risk (. . .)'.[110]

Interestingly, under the influence of the increasing *international corpus juris* on violence against women, the ECtHR changed the termini used to refer to the scope of positive obligations concerning violence against women. However, it did not change its approach. While in 2003 it had still relied on its traditional wording, in 2009 it adopted the wording used in international documents on gender-based violence. In *M.C. v. Bulgaria,* where public authorities had failed to effectively investigate the alleged rape of a girl, the Court still maintained its terminological tradition. It held that

> [p]ositive obligations on the State are inherent in the right to effective respect for private life under Article 8; these obligations may involve the adoption of measures even in the sphere of the relations of individuals between themselves. While the choice of the means to secure compliance with Article 8 in the sphere of protection against acts of individuals is in principle within the State's margin of appreciation, effective deterrence against grave acts such as rape, where fundamental values and essential aspects of private life are at stake, requires efficient criminal-law provisions.[111]

In cases concerning domestic violence, *Bevacqua and S. v. Bulgaria* (2008) and *Opuz v. Turkey* (2009), however, the Court explicitly referred to the need for the respondent State to exercise *due diligence* to protect women against violence. In *Bevacqua,* it first summarized existing international documents and instruments on gender-based violence in the judgment's section on 'relevant international and comparative-law materials'.[112] It then examined a violation of Article 8 ECHR

---

jurisprudence, see Mowbray, *The development of positive obligations under the European Convention on Human Rights by the European Court of Human Rights*, 2004.

[109]Emphasis added. ECtHR, *Osman v. the United Kingdom*, Judgment, 28 October 1998, para. 116. See also ECtHR, *McCann and others v. United Kingdom* [GC], Judgment (Merits and Just Satisfaction), 27 September 1995, para. 146.

[110]ECtHR, *Osman v. the United Kingdom*, Judgment, 28 October 1998, para. 116.

[111]Emphasis added. ECtHR, *M.C. v. Bulgaria*, Judgment, 04 December 2003, para. 150.

[112]ECtHR, *Bevacqua and S. v. Bulgaria*, Judgment, 12 June 2008, paras 52, 53. See also ECtHR, *Opuz v. Turkey*, Judgment, 09 June 2009, paras 72–90; Hasselbacher, 'State Obligations Regarding Domestic Violence', (2010) 8 *Northwestern J. Int'l Hum. Rts*, para. 34.

(family life). Although it did not include the due diligence standard into the section on 'relevant principles',[113] the ECtHR, for the very first time in this context, scrutinized whether on the interim measures taken (obligation to protect), the respondent State had exercised due diligence.[114] On the allegedly insufficient legal provisions, it referred to the State's margin of appreciation.[115] Most importantly, on both aspects, compliance with the obligation was submitted to an effectiveness-control.[116]

c. CEDAW Committee

The approach taken by the CEDAW Committee too reflects the merger of the two, allegedly different, standards to measure compliance with positive obligations. Although the wording of CEDAW requires appropriate measures to be taken, the Committee has referred to due diligence where the case was related to gender-based violence. The Committee then gave guidelines on the kind of measures to be taken.[117]

d. ICJ

The ICJ had various occasions to rule on the concept of due diligence in international environmental and general international law.[118] However, on its application within the context of human rights obligations, the Genocide case is of particular relevance. Concerning the obligation to prevent genocide under the Genocide Convention the Court held that

> the obligation of state parties is to employ all means reasonably available to them, so as to prevent genocide as far as possible. (...) responsibility is however incurred if the State manifestly failed to take all measures to prevent genocide which were within its power, and which might have contributed to preventing the genocide. In this area the notion of "due

---

[113]ECtHR, *Bevacqua and S. v. Bulgaria*, Judgment, 12 June 2008, paras 64–65; ECtHR, *Opuz v. Turkey*, Judgment, 09 June 2009, paras 128–130.

[114]ECtHR, *Bevacqua and S. v. Bulgaria*, Judgment, 12 June 2008, para. 73; see also ECtHR, *Opuz v. Turkey*, Judgment, 09 June 2009, paras 131, 146.

[115]ECtHR, *Bevacqua and S. v. Bulgaria*, Judgment, 12 June 2008, para. 82. In Opuz, there is no reference to the margin of appreciation doctrine.

[116]ECtHR, *Bevacqua and S. v. Bulgaria*, Judgment, 12 June 2008, para. 64; ECtHR, *Opuz v. Turkey*, Judgment, 09 June 2009, paras 128, 145.

[117]E.g., CEDAW, *Fatma Yildirim v. Austria*, Communication No. 6/2005, 01 October 2007; CEDAW, *A. T. v. Hungary*, Communication No. 2/2003, 26 January 2005.

[118]ICJ, *Military and paramilitary activities in and against Nicaragua (Nicaragua v. United States of America)*, Judgment (merits), 27 June 1986, para. 157; ICJ, *United States Diplomatic and Consular Staff in Teheran (United States of America v. Iran)*, Judgment, 24 May 1980, para. 63; ICJ, *Pulp Mills on the River Uruguay (Argentina v. Uruguay)*, 20 April 2010, para. 205; see also Koivurova, 'Due diligence', in Wolfrum, 2012, paras 36–43.

> diligence", which calls for an assessment in concreto, is of critical importance. Various parameters operate when assessing whether a State has duly discharged the obligation concerned.[119]

This statement reveals today's overlap of the allegedly different standards of 'due diligence' and 'appropriate/reasonable measures'.

3. Conclusion

Unlike the historical subjective understanding of due diligence, under today's human rights law the due diligence standard has nothing to do with bad faith or willful neglect. As a context-specific standard, it can be resumed to require reasonable measures 'that a well-administrated government could be expected to exercise under similar circumstances'.[120]

The development of the due diligence doctrine has been fuelled, particularly in the context of gender-based violence, by the jurisprudence of the IACtHR. On the global level, however, the term 'due diligence' creates confusions and may strengthen attempts to weaken the scope of positive obligations concerning violence against women. It can only be correctly understood before the backdrop of its originally Inter-American embedding. If the regional context remains unmentioned, many international lawyers may tend to think of a time when positive human rights obligations were in their infancy and due diligence a subjective standard.

The foregoing comparison has shown that the 'due diligence standard', often applied in the context of violence against women, does not differ from the general scope of positive obligations. Which term is applied mainly depends on the (quasi-) judicial body that uses it. The IACtHR generally applies the 'due diligence standard' when measuring compliance with positive obligations. In turn, the 'appropriate measures standard' is mostly applied by the ECtHR. Accordingly, it confers upon the State a margin of appreciation that allows the State to choose the measures that it considers appropriate. Yet, in the ECtHR's tradition, this discretion must be exercised in the light of the principle of effectiveness. What is effective ultimately depends on the very circumstances. Consequently, like under the due diligence standard applied by the IACtHR, the measures necessary to be taken will be context-specific.

Thus, both the 'due diligence standard' and the 'appropriate measures standard' allow for the respective State to exercise discretion regarding the measures to be taken to prevent and protect the rights at risk to be violated. Regardless of the room left for discretion, discretion can also be drastically limited where there is only one specific measure that is capable of being effective. In conclusion, the scope of

[119]ICJ, *Case concerning application of the Convention of Prevention and Punishment of the Crime of Genocide (Bosnia and Herzegovina v. Serbia and Montenegro)*, Judgment, 26 February 2007, para. 430. Emphasis added.

[120]Shelton/Gould, 'Positive and Negative Obligations', in Shelton, 2010, p. 577.

positive human rights obligations is the same, independently of whether protection is needed against gender-based violence or against other kinds of abuses and settings that infringe human rights.

II. Factors Informing and Limits to a State's Discretion

As shown, it depends on the circumstances which measure is 'due', 'reasonable' or 'appropriate'. It is thus at the discretion of the State to decide on the kind of measure to be taken. Nevertheless, this discretion cannot be exercised arbitrarily. As the CEDAW Committee noted

> failures [to take appropriate measures] may not be justified simply by averring powerlessness, or by explaining inaction through predominant market or political forces, such as those inherent in the private sector, private organization, or political parties.[121]

Instead, various parameters operate when assessing whether a State has duly discharged the obligation concerned. Therefore, this section first explores on parameters informing a State's discretion and then draws on the limits to discretion.

In this context, it should be noted that, for those being confronted with structural discrimination, judicial scrutiny of decisions based on discretion is most crucial. Otherwise, discretion may allow for a considerable dilution of positive obligations.[122] Within a democratic society, it may well be that the majority, when exercising its discretion, does not sufficiently consider the interests of those underrepresented in the political process. On gender-based violence, gender stereotypes, misogynist and other discriminatory assumptions, the main discourse of a society plays its part in the political appreciation on what kind of measures are 'reasonable'. Hence, it is important that this discretion is not exempt from judicial control. The protection of minorities and underprivileged parts of the population is part of a vital corpus of democratic but pluralistic societies. It is thus one of the key roles of the judiciary to re-integrate the marginalized, discriminated and underprivileged groups.[123] This integrative role of the judiciary comes into play when legislative and administrative decisions based on discretion are subject to judicial control.[124]

---

[121]CEDAW Committee, General Recommendation No. 25 on article 4, paragraph1 CEDAW (2004), para. 29.

[122]For a general critique of the weaker standard, see Shue, *Basic rights*, 1996.

[123]Benvenisti, 'Margin of appreciation, consensus, and universal standards', (1998) 31 *N.Y.U. J. Int'l L. & Pol.*, pp. 848.

[124]To guarantee that the discretion and its control are exercised while having the views and interests of underrepresented groups in mind, administrative personnel and judges need to be trained in gender and other anti-discrimination issues. For the sake of legitimacy judges must be themselves heterogenic. For detail, see Grossman, 'Sex on the bench: do women judges matter to the legitimacy of international courts', (2011) 12 *Chi. J. Int'l L;* Melville, 'Evaluating Judicial Performance and Addressing Gender Bias', (2014) 4 *Oñati Socio-legal Series.*

1. Factors That Inform a State's Discretion

Bearing in mind 'the difficulties involved in policing modern societies',[125] a State will necessarily need to consider rights of others as well as State interests and conflicting interests of the community.[126] Moreover, as reflected in international jurisprudence, a State's discretion must be exercised in light of the relationship with the abuser and the specific circumstances as well as the scale and intensity of harm at risk to occur.[127] Finally, the fact of limited financial resources being available to a State is, at first glance, susceptible of being a factor informing a State's discretion.[128]

a. Rights of Others

An important aspect that informs a State's discretion is that a State should restrain itself from (excessive) intrusion[129] and respect 'desired limits' on the rights of other individuals.[130] On gender-based violence, it is in the context of criminal investigations and prosecution that such considerations play a role. When preventing and prosecuting crimes, the authorities need to respect 'the due process and other guarantees which legitimately place restraints on the scope of their action to investigate crime and bring offenders to justice (. . .)'.[131] Yet, the rights and interests of potential offenders are again restricted by the need of an effective protection of the rights of the (potentially) aggressed. Otherwise, this private sphere of non-intrusion beyond the reach of States can 'turn out to be quite an unpleasant place to stay'.[132]

---

[125] ECtHR, *Osman v. the United Kingdom*, Judgment, 28 October 1998, para. 116.

[126] E.g., ECtHR, *Young, James u Webster v. the United Kingdom*, Judgment, 13 August 1981, para. 63. Stahl, *Schutzpflichten im Völkerrecht*, 2012, pp. 290.

[127] For details, see Hakimi, 'State Bystander Responsibility', (2010) 21 *EJIL*, pp. 371; Stahl, *Schutzpflichten im Völkerrecht*, 2012, pp. 284; Schutter, *International human rights law*, 2010, pp. 423.

[128] Schutter, *International human rights law*, 2010, pp. 423.

[129] Such assumptions, of course, maintain the power relations as historically instituted, Chinkin, 'A critique of the Public/Private Dimension', (1999) 10 *EJIL*. From an US-American perspective, Henry Shue criticized the divide of positive and negative obligations for implying that positive obligations are secondary, see Shue, *Basic rights*, 1996, pp. 35, 52.

[130] Schutter, *International human rights law*, 2014, pp. 511; Hakimi, 'State Bystander Responsibility', (2010) 21 *EJIL*, pp. 355–357; Stahl, *Schutzpflichten im Völkerrecht*, 2012, pp. 190.

[131] ECtHR, *Osman v. the United Kingdom*, Judgment, 28 October 1998, para. 116.

[132] Lawson, 'Out of Control: State Responsibility', in Baehr et al., 1998.

b. Interests of a State and the Community

More generally, interests of the State and of the community will also inform a State's discretion. Such limits to positive obligations are reflected in a number of restrictions inherent to human rights provisions.[133]

c. Relationship of a State with the Abuser/Situation

If a State has a legal relationship with the abuser, the discretion left to it will be quite limited. A State's proximity to the agents, the legal relationship between the parties and the normatively expected control of such agents ensuing therefrom imply that a State's discretion will be more restricted than concerning private actors.[134]

d. Scale and Intensity of Harm

The scale and intensity of individual and/or collective harm that already occurred or is still at risk to occur is an important factor which may significantly decrease a State's discretion.[135] The more a situation is likely to impair the exercise of fundamental human rights and freedoms, the more efforts are necessary and the discretion regarding the reasonableness of measures taken will be limited.[136] It is either the

---

[133] Stahl, *Schutzpflichten im Völkerrecht*, 2012, pp. 290; ECtHR, *Gaskin v. the United Kingdom*, Judgment, 07 July 1989, para. 42: 'In accordance with its established case-law, the Court, in determining whether such a positive obligation exists, will have regard to the fair balance that has to be struck between the general interest of the community and the interests of the individual (. . .). In striking this balance the aims mentioned in the second paragraph of Article 8 may be of a certain relevance, although this provision refers in terms only to 'interferences' with the right protected by the first paragraph – simply put, is concerned with the negative obligations flowing therefrom.' On the system of restrictions, see Arai, 'The system of restrictions', in van Dijk/ Arai, 2006.

[134] Hakimi, 'State Bystander Responsibility', (2010) 21 *EJIL*, *passim*; ECtHR, *Valiuliene v. Lithuania*, Judgment, 26 March 2013, para. 73. This stricter standard also becomes evident in Article 5 Istanbul Convention. According to the Explanatory Report to the Istanbul Convention 'Article 5, paragraph 1, addresses the State obligation *to ensure* that their authorities, officials, agents, institutions and other actors acting on behalf of the State refrain from acts of violence against women, whereas paragraph 2 sets out Parties' obligation *to exercise due diligence in relation* to acts covered by the scope of this Convention perpetrated by *non-State actors*. In both cases, failure to comply with the foregoing provisions will incur State responsibility.' Council of Europe, *Explanatory Report to the Council of Europe Convention on preventing and combating violence against women and domestic violence,* 2011, para. 57. Emphasis added.

[135] Hakimi, 'State Bystander Responsibility', (2010) 21 *EJIL*, pp. 372; Stahl, *Schutzpflichten im Völkerrecht*, 2012, pp. 188, 286, 337–339.

[136] See also for the ECHR, Dröge, *Positive Verpflichtungen der Staaten in der Europäischen Menschenrechtskonvention*, 2003, p. 56; Schutter, *International human rights law*, 2010, pp. 415.

nature of the right at risk to be impaired or violated,[137] or the scale and intensity of abuses that affects the reasonableness of State measures. An extensive occurrence of similar situations such as gender-based violence will thus significantly reduce the margin of appreciation.[138]

For example, in *Horváth and Kiss v. Hungary*, a case concerning the Hungarian educational system found to be discriminatory against Roma children, the ECtHR held that 'the State has specific positive obligations to avoid the perpetuation of past discrimination or discriminative practices disguised in allegedly neutral tests'[139] and that 'the State's margin of appreciation is substantially narrower and it must have very weighty reasons for the restrictions in question'.[140] While these considerations have been made in the context of discrimination against ethnic minorities, which is very close, if not equal to, to racial discrimination,[141] there is no reasonable argument why in light of structural discrimination of other groups such as women these arguments should not apply.

In *Maria da Penha vs. Brazil*, the IAComHR concluded that 'a general pattern of negligence and lack of effective action by the State' was evidence enough for insufficient State efforts.[142] In *Cotton field,* the IACtHR found that a generalized pattern of gender-based violence influences the scope of measures necessary to be taken.[143] The Court held that the investigation of gender-based crimes would need to be 'pursued with vigour and impartiality', having regard to the need to reassert continuously society's condemnation of misogynistic attitudes.[144] It held that 'the [procedural] obligation to investigate effectively has a wider scope when dealing with the case of a woman who is killed or, ill-treated or, whose personal liberty is affected'. Accordingly, the authorities' duty was of 'strict due diligence' to take prompt and immediate action without delay.[145]

---

[137]Along these lines, in Angelova and Iliev v. Bulgaria, the ECtHR ruled that when an 'attack is racially motivated, it is particularly important that the investigation is pursued with vigor and impartiality, having regard to need to reassert continuously society's condemnation of racism and to maintain the confidence of minorities in the ability of the authorities to protect them from the threat of racist violence', ECtHR, *Angelova and Iliev v. Bulgaria*, Judgment, 26 July 2007, para. 116.

[138]*Cf.* also Hakimi, 'State Bystander Responsibility', (2010) 21 *EJIL*, pp. 373.

[139]ECtHR, *Horváth and Kiss v. Hungary*, Judgment, 29 January 2013, para. 116.

[140]ECtHR, *Horváth and Kiss v. Hungary*, Judgment, 29 January 2013, paras 128, 104–129.

[141]On the ECtHR's specific prism on racial discrimination cases, see Rubio-Marín/Möschel, 'Anti-Discrimination Exceptionalism', (2015) 26 *EJIL*.

[142]IAComHR, *Maria da Penha v. Brazil*, Case 12.051, Report No. 54/01, 16 April 2001, para. 56.

[143]ECtHR, *Angelova and Iliev v. Bulgaria*, Judgment, 26 July 2007, para. 116.

[144]IACtHR, *González v. Mexico (Cotton Field Case)*, Judgment (Preliminary Objection, Merits, Reparations, and Costs), 16 November 2009, para. 293.

[145]IACtHR, *Velásquez-Rodriguez v. Honduras*, Judgment (Merits), 29 July 1988, para. 283. It is in this spirit too that the third-party intervener in the *Opuz* case, Interights, argued that the 'jus cogens nature of the right to freedom from torture and the right to life required exemplary diligence on the part of the State with respect to investigation and prosecution' of gender-based violence, see ECtHR, *Opuz v. Turkey*, Judgment, 09 June 2009, para. 127.

e. Compatibility of Measures with Other Obligations Under International Law

A State's discretion is also influenced by other obligations under international law. In view of the sovereignty of other States, this is particularly relevant where the measure aims to have an extraterritorial effect. If (potential) crimes occur extraterritorially, protective measures need to be restricted in their exercise. In a war-like scenario, a State may take preventive measures such as exercising diplomatic influence on the persons planning the crimes or stopping financial or military support even when these crimes are to be committed abroad.[146] A State may also be obliged to prosecute the perpetrators before its own courts or to provide for awareness-creating trainings to its agents before they are sent into conflict regions abroad.[147] In contrast, neither general preventive measures such as the adoption of appropriate criminal laws, nor investigation, prosecution and punishment of private actors can be expected from a State where it has no sufficient territorial control, as such measures would contravene the sovereignty of another State.

f. Financial Restrictions

Finally, what can reasonably be expected from States may be said to be subject to their financial resources and capacities.[148] Accordingly, if a State totally collapsed, is locally absent because of an armed conflict or otherwise, or has a very poor budget, measures taken concerning one social area may force a State to financially abandon other vital tasks. At first glance, one may thus conclude that financial restrictions are a factor that affect a State's discretion.[149] However, while it would be meaningless to burden a State with positive obligations if it cannot bear them,[150] the point of lacking financial resources is often made where political will is lacking.[151]

---

[146]See also ICJ, *Case concerning application of the Convention of Prevention and Punishment of the Crime of Genocide (Bosnia and Herzegovina v. Serbia and Montenegro)*, Judgment, 26 February 2007, para. 442.

[147]*Cf.* CEDAW, *Concluding Observation of the Committee on the Elimination of Discrimination against Women, Germany*, 10 February 2009, paras 51.

[148]Schutter, *International human rights law*, 2014, pp. 562.

[149]E.g., Art. 2 (1) CESCR.

[150]ICJ, *Military and paramilitary activities in and against Nicaragua (Nicaragua v. United States of America)*, Judgment (merits), 27 June 1986, para. 157; Nickel, 'How human rights generate duties to protect and provide', (1993) *Hum. Rts. Q.*, p. 81.

[151]UNCHR, *Integration of the human rights of women and the gender perspective*, 20 January 2006, para. 79. The necessity to allocate financial resources to improve the situation of underprivileged groups is often questioned even by rich countries. *Cf.* Chinkin, 'Article 3', in Rudolf/Freeman/Chinkin, 2012, p. 117. The *Maastricht Principles* suggest that, while cooperating when fulfilling human rights, States must prioritize the realization of the rights of disadvantaged and/or marginalized persons, Schutter et al., 'Commentary to the Maastricht Principles on extraterritorial obligations of states in the area of economic, social and cultural rights', (2012) 34 *Hum. Rts. Q.*, Principle 32, para. (2).

When taking a closer look, it appears that limited financial resources are not *per se* an admissible justification for not coming up with the needs of groups most likely to be exposed to severe harm. Rather, limited financial resources play a role when establishing whether a State can make use of the impossibility defense.[152] In this context it should be noted that, while judicial bodies have no competence to interfere in parliamentary decisions relating to the employment of resources, and while 'determinations of reasonableness may in fact have budgetary implications, [judicial scrutiny is not in itself] directed at rearranging budgets'.[153]

2. Limits to a State's Discretion: Fair-Balance Test

When considering the above-exposed factors informing a State's discretion, a State must strike a fair balance between the conflicting interests at stake.[154] To establish the legality of State acts, international judicial bodies frequently apply the so-called fair-balance test that reflects the customary law principle of proportionality.[155] Proportionality is a powerful tool which limits—and within the context of international proceedings enables courts to interfere in—a State's discretion. While the Inter-American Court appears to have no such explicit practice, the use of a fair-balance test is a settled case law in the European human rights system.[156]

The principle of proportionality requires that a State measure meets three elements.[157] First, it must be appropriate to the legal aim pursued (suitability); second, there must be no equally effective but less onerous measure (necessity); and third, the effects of the measure chosen must be balanced with the aim pursued, bearing in mind whether those effects are disproportionate as to the conflicting interests (proportionality *stricto sensu*).[158]

---

[152]Stahl, *Schutzpflichten im Völkerrecht*, 2012, pp. 322.

[153]Shelton, *Remedies in international human rights law*, 2006, pp. 46, referring to a judgment of the South African Constitutional Court, *Minister of Heath et al. Vs. Treatment Action Campaign*, 5th July 2002, para. 38.

[154]E.g., ECtHR, *Osman v. the United Kingdom*, Judgment, 28 October 1998, para. 116.

[155]Crawford, 'Proportionality', in Wolfrum, 2012, paras 13, 20; Dröge, *Positive Verpflichtungen der Staaten in der Europäischen Menschenrechtskonvention*, 2003, pp. 309; Stahl, *Schutzpflichten im Völkerrecht*, 2012, pp. 308.

[156]E.g., ECtHR, *Case 'relating to certain aspects of the laws on the use of languages in education in Belgium' v. Belgium*, Judgment (Merits), 23 July 1968, Considerations as to the first question, para. 7; ECtHR, *Gaskin v. the United Kingdom*, Judgment, 07 July 1989, para. 42; ECtHR, *Young, James u Webster v. the United Kingdom*, Judgment, 13 August 1981, para. 63; ECtHR, *McCann and others v. United Kingdom* [GC], Judgment (Merits and Just Satisfaction), 27 September 1995; Stahl, *Schutzpflichten im Völkerrecht*, 2012, pp. 308; *Cf.* also Crawford, 'Proportionality', in Wolfrum, 2012, paras 13, 20.

[157]Schutter, *International human rights law*, 2014, pp. 344.

[158]Crawford, 'Proportionality', in Wolfrum, 2012, para. 2; Arai-Takahashi, 'Proportionality', in Shelton, 2010.

While this principle has originally been conceptualized for violations of negative obligations, it can also apply to positive obligations, although to a modified extent.[159] It can be said that proportionality *stricto sensu* then comes up to a prohibition of insufficient action.[160] What is sufficient and necessary must be established in light of the circumstances of the case. As seen in the *O'Keeffe case*, as the non-existence of domestic legal provisions has had an impact on the impairment/violation of rights that occurred,[161] the omission of a legal reform may fail to pass the fair balance test and will consequently be contestable. Hence, where the exercise of discretion is limited by the prohibition of insufficient action, it may be that a State is held responsible for the omission of any measures.

III. Conclusion

In this section, it has been shown that the scope of positive obligations is in principle the same, independently of whether they relate to gender-based violence or other human rights infringing settings. Moreover, various parameters operate when assessing whether a State has duly discharged positive obligation concerned.

An analysis of different human rights instruments and relevant jurisprudence has revealed that independently of whether positive obligations relate to gender-based violence or against other settings that infringe human rights, their scope is in principle the same. While the wording of many provisions, jurisprudence and soft law instruments differs on the standard to measure compliance with positive obligations relating to gender-based violence and relating to other crimes, the 'due diligence standard' and the 'appropriate measures standard' do not differ in content. The European human rights system confers upon its contracting parties a margin of appreciation that allows a State to choose those measures that it considers appropriate. In the tradition of the ECtHR, this discretion must be exercised in light of the principle of effectiveness. What is effective ultimately depends on the very circumstances. Hence, like under the due diligence standard applied by the IACtHR, the measures necessary to be taken will be context-specific.

While the exercise of discretion risks to marginalize politically underrepresented groups, such negative effects are mitigated by the limits imposed on a State's discretion. When exercising its discretion, it appears that a State can or must consider the rights of others, the interests of the State and the community, its capacity to influence the abuser/the situation, the severity and scope of harm at risk to be

[159] See already ECtHR, *Marckx v. Belgium*, Judgment (Merits and Just Satisfaction), 13 June 1979, para. 31; ECtHR, *Rees v. The United Kingdom*, Judgment, 17 October 1986, para. 37; Stahl, *Schutzpflichten im Völkerrecht*, 2012, pp. 309 wfr.

[160] Stahl, *Schutzpflichten im Völkerrecht*, 2012, pp. 309 wfr, discussing the jurisprudence of the ECtHR more in detail.

[161] ECtHR, *O'Keeffe v. Ireland* [GC], Judgment, 28 January 2014, para. 187.

inflicted upon an individual and, finally, potentially conflicting obligations under international law. It has been claimed that, in principle, financial restrictions do not influence the extent of obligations. Moreover, the exercise of discretion is limited by the principle of proportionality and the fair-balance test that, in the case of positive obligations, may be reduced to a prohibition of insufficient action.

C. Factors Potentially Required to Establish a Violation of Preventive and Protective Obligations

While negative obligations are breached when the State interferes in rights without justification, establishing the violation of positive obligations may be more complex. Where it had been established that a State had positive obligation in a determined case or on a general situation, but that the measures taken were insufficient, international jurisprudence has occasionally required two additional aspects to establish a violation. First, it may be necessary that the event, which that State had to prevent, occurs for the individual to be able to successfully hold the State responsible (I.). Second, *causality* may be relevant to the breach of positive obligations (II.).

I. Occurrence of the Event Which the State Was Required to Prevent

Even if it has been established that a State had positive obligations in a specific case, there will be no breach, if an event, the obligations in question require that State to prevent, did not occur. Conversely, as codified in Article 14 (3) ILC Articles, a 'breach of an international obligation requiring a State to prevent a given event occurs when the event occurs (. . .)'. Along these lines, the ICJ held concerning the obligation of preventing genocide under Article 1 Genocide Convention that a State

> that omitted to act when it could have done so cannot be held responsible a posteriori, since the event did not happen which (. . .) must occur for there to be a violation of positive obligations to prevent.[162]

[162]Emphasis added. ICJ, *Case concerning application of the Convention of Prevention and Punishment of the Crime of Genocide (Bosnia and Herzegovina v. Serbia and Montenegro)*, Judgment, 26 February 2007, para. 431; *cf.* also IACtHR, *González v. Mexico (Cotton Field Case)*, Judgment (Preliminary Objection, Merits, Reparations, and Costs), 16 November 2009, para. 252; IACtHR, *Velásquez-Rodriguez v. Honduras*, Judgment (Merits), 29 July 1988, para. 166; IACtHR, IACtHR, *Rodríguez Vera et al. (The disappeared from the palace of justice) v. Colombia*, Judgment (Preliminary Objections, Merits, Reparations and Costs), 14 November 2014, para. 519.

Although the existence of a violation of an obligation largely depends on its content and on the particular facts of the case,[163] the rule as codified in Article 14 may play an important role in cases relating to alleged violations of the obligation to protect in a specific case. If, for example, the given event referred to is rape or another crime committed by a third actor, this crime needs to occur for the victim to be able to hold this State responsible. In a case of domestic violence, where the competent authorities omit to take any *protective* measures in relation to a complaint brought against a violent husband, the complainant will not be able to hold this State responsible for this very omission, if no more abuses occur. Yet, where a State must undertake investigations of domestic violence, murder or disappearance, but omits any action in this regard, a breach can be established, as the content of the obligation does not require preventing an event.

II. Relevance of Causality Between the Impairment of Rights and a State's Omission

The second aspect that may hinder the establishment of a violation of positive duties relates to the eventual lack of causality between the omission and the harmful event impairing the enjoyment of human rights. The requirement of causality generally also excludes remote consequences that allow for handling multiple causes.[164]

However, there is no uniform practice on the need of a causal nexus.[165] Both the IACtHR[166] and the ECtHR[167] have occasionally required a causal link between the

[163]Crawford (ed.), *The ILC Draft Articles on Responsibility of States for Internationally Wrongful Acts*, Art. 14, para. 1.

[164]Plakokefalos, 'Causation in the Law of State Responsibility and the Problem of Overdetermination', (2015) 26 *EJIL*.

[165]In her study on positive obligations, *Stahl* discusses such a requirement but claims that the causal nexus must be established between the impairment of the right (in her words 'Taterfolg') and the impairing act/situation which is not attributable to the state ('Übergriff'), see Stahl, *Schutzpflichten im Völkerrecht*, 2012, pp. 169–171. In my view, this approach does not reflect the jurisprudence she refers to.

[166]The IACtHR found in *Velásquez-Rodríguez v. Honduras* that it is its task 'to determine whether the violation *is the result* of a State's failure to fulfill its duty to respect and guarantee those rights, as required by Article 1 (1) of the Convention'. IACtHR, *Velásquez-Rodriguez v. Honduras*, Judgment (Merits), 29 July 1988, para. 173. Emphasis added.

[167]The ECtHR, e.g., has held that a State has positive obligations where it can be established that there is a direct and immediate link between the measures sought by an applicant and the latter's private and/or family life, see ECtHR, *Botta v. Italy*, Judgment, 24 February 1998, para. 34: 'Thus, in the case of Airey v. Ireland (judgment of 9 October 1979, Series A no. 32), the Court held that the applicant had been the victim of a violation of Article 8 because under domestic law there was no system of legal aid in separation proceedings, which by denying access to court *directly affected* her private and family life. In (...) X and Y v. the Netherlands case, which concerned the rape of a mentally handicapped person and accordingly related to her physical and psychological integrity, the Court found that because of its shortcomings the Netherlands Criminal Code had not provided

omission of measures and the impairment of rights inflicted by the non-attributable actions/circumstances. These cases concerned measures, such as legislative failures or lack of information by the State, that were omitted *prior to the harmful event.*

However, in *O'Keeffe v. Ireland*, where the respondent State was held responsible because its legal framework did not provide effective protection for children attending a national school against the risk of sexual abuse, the Grand Chamber majority opinion did not require a causal nexus. It held that

> it is not necessary to show that "but for" the State omission the ill-treatment would not have happened. A failure to take reasonably available measures which could have had a real prospect of altering the outcome or mitigating the harm is sufficient to engage the responsibility of the State.[168]

Had the ECtHR decided otherwise, it would have left room for hypothetical considerations and the obligation to provide for an effective protective legal framework would lack enforceability.

In *Opuz v. Turkey*, too, where the mother of the applicant was killed by the applicant's violent husband, the ECtHR was unable to 'conclude with certainty that matters would have turned out differently (. . .) if the authorities had acted otherwise'. However, the Court found that 'failure to take reasonable measures which could have had a real prospect of altering the outcome or mitigating the harm is sufficient to engage the responsibility of the State (. . .)'.[169]

In light of these cases, it appears that a causal nexus between an omission *prior to the harmful* event and the event itself is no mandatory condition to establishing a violation of positive obligations. If a causal nexus is required to establish that an omission prior to a harmful event constitutes a violation of positive duties, it can be

---

the person concerned with practical and effective protection (. . .). More recently, in the López Ostra v. Spain judgment (. . .), in connection with the harmful effects of pollution caused by the activity of a waste-water treatment plant situated near the applicant's home, the Court held that the respondent State had not succeeded in striking a fair balance between the interest of the town of Lorca's economic well-being—that of having a waste-treatment plant—and the applicant's effective enjoyment of her right to respect for her home and her private and family life (. . .). Lastly, in the Guerra and Others v. Italy judgment of 19 February 1998 (. . .), the Court held that the direct effect of the toxic emissions from the Enichem factory on the applicants' right to respect for their private and family life meant that Article 8 was applicable (. . .). It decided that Italy had breached that provision in that it had not communicated to the applicants essential information that would have enabled them to assess the risks they and their families might run if they continued to live in Manfredonia, a town particularly exposed to danger in the event of an accident within the confines of the factory (. . .).' See also Ugrekhelidze, 'Causation', in Caflisch/Wildhaber, 2007, p. 476.

[168]ECtHR, *O'Keeffe v. Ireland* [GC], Judgment, 28 January 2014, para. 149. Some dissenting judges criticized this decision, see the Joint Partly Dissenting Opinion of Judges Zupančič, Gyulumyan, Kalaydjieva, De Gaetano and Wojtyczek, para. 20. *Cf.* ECtHR, *E. and others v. The United Kingdom*, Judgment, 15 January 2003, para. 99.

[169]ECtHR, *Opuz v. Turkey*, Judgment, 09 June 2009, para. 136. *Cf.* also ICJ, *Case concerning application of the Convention of Prevention and Punishment of the Crime of Genocide (Bosnia and Herzegovina v. Serbia and Montenegro)*, Judgment, 26 February 2007, paras 430, 431.

said that the more remote the consequences of an omission, the less is a claimant likely to succeed.

At any rate, the requirement of a causal link is meaningless where it would totally undermine positive obligations. This is true for omissions (e.g. non-investigation and non-prosecution of a crime) occurring *after the harmful* event such as domestic violence, or where hypothetical considerations come into play. If a court accepted hypothetical considerations, a State would always be able to exculpate itself and would have no incentive at all to take preventive measures.

III. Conclusion

If a court concludes that a State had positive obligations on a given case and that this State failed to take reasonable steps, this does not necessarily imply the finding of a breach of its positive duties. First, obligations requiring to prevent a given event are only breached where this event occurs. Moreover, it may be that a causal nexus will still be required between a State's omission *prior to a harmful event* and the harmful event itself. While there is no consistent judicial practice concerning causality, such a requirement bears the potential to render the failure to take preventive measures irrelevant for constituting a violation. At any rate, where the requirement of a causal link undermines the very idea of positive obligations and thus their effectiveness, no such condition is likely to be required by the ECtHR. This is true for omissions occurring *after the harmful* event or where hypothetical considerations come into play.

Chapter 6
Measures Against Gender-Based Violence

It has been suggested in the previous chapter, that, where human rights treaties do not explicitly spell out when preventive and protective obligations apply, there are three criteria useful to establishing their existence. It therefore has been concluded that because of the endemic and structural occurrence of gender-based violence against women and its destructive impact on the individual and collective level, all States have positive obligations in this regard.[1]

As positive obligations confer upon a State discretion as to the means and measures of prevention and protection to be taken,[2] the question arises what kind of positive measures may be taken against gender-based violence. CEDAW, the Istanbul and the Belém do Pará Conventions foresee a series of measures, conferring upon contracting parties either a wide or a much-reduced margin of appreciation. Whereas at the time of writing the Istanbul and the Belém do Pará Conventions have only been ratified by 33 States respectively, provisions of CEDAW are binding on 189 state parties. For non-contracting States, measures against gender-based violence foreseen by these instruments can provide for a 'blueprint' of potential measures to be taken by non-contracting parties.[3]

Against the background of the 'iceberg model',[4] this chapter shows that a double approach that takes both a direct and a long-term strategy against gender-based violence, as encompassed by existing human rights treaties, is able to combat structural discrimination against women. Therefore, this chapter analyzes protective

[1]Chapter 5 A.

[2]Chapter 5 B.

[3]*Cf.* also Chinkin, 'Addressing violence against women in the Commonwealth within states' obligations under international law', (2014) 40 *Commonwealth Law Bulletin*.

[4]Chapter 2 B.

E. V. Henn, *International Human Rights Law and Structural Discrimination*, Beiträge zum ausländischen öffentlichen Recht und Völkerrecht,
https://doi.org/10.1007/978-3-662-58677-8_6

and preventive measures as explicitly foreseen in CEDAW, the Istanbul and the Belém Convention. The Belém do Pará Convention and the Istanbul Convention in particular foresee a detailed catalogue of preventive and protective measures that directly address gender-based violence. In turn, provisions addressing the other layers of the iceberg, that is discrimination, gender stereotypes and hierarchies as the root causes of gender-based violence, are particularly enshrined in CEDAW. The chapter considers, first, treaty provisions that apply a short-term strategy against gender-based violence (A. I) and, second, long-term measures that address its root causes (obligation to fulfill) (A. II). To conclude, the chapter discusses the content of positive obligations under customary international law (B.).

A. Measures Against Gender-Based Violence as Foreseen Under CEDAW, the Istanbul and the Belém do Pará Conventions

I. Short-Term Measures: Directly Addressing Gender-Based Violence

This section categorizes existing human rights obligations that directly address gender-based violence, be it committed in peacetime or in the context of an armed conflict.[5] Such measures, aiming at preventing and protecting gender-based violence, cover three temporal stages. First, they prevent violence from occurring; second, they respond to violence when it has occurred to limit its extent and consequences; and third, they provide long-term care and support for those who have suffered from violence.[6] These measures focus on the State level, the general public, the individual victim/perpetrator as well as on transnational cooperation between States.

1. State Level

Contracting parties to the Istanbul and Belém do Pará Conventions agreed to take a series of specific legislative and administrative measures to directly prevent and protect against gender-based violence. Moreover, in the absence of provisions explicitly foreseeing such obligations, the CEDAW Committee, the IACtHR and ECtHR have also established certain standards.

[5] Art. 2 (3) Istanbul Convention and Art. 9 Belém do Pará Convention.

[6] *Cf.* also UNSG, *In-Depth-Study on All Forms of Violence against Women*, 2006, para. 336; UN Women, Commission on the Status of Women, *Agreed Conclusions on the prevention and elimination of violence against women and girls 2013*, 15 March 2013.

a. Legislative Measures: Substantive and Procedural Provisions

While it can generally be held that substantive and procedural laws should be victim-friendly and allow for an effective prosecution of perpetrators, the detail and content of existing legal obligations under the respective treaties obviously differ. Although international (quasi)judicial bodies have found various failures of States concerning gender-based violence,[7] it should suffice here to take a closer look at the Istanbul and the Belém do Pará Conventions. They give detailed guidelines on how to criminalize, investigate, prosecute and punish effectively without putting at risk victims and witnesses.

1) Procedural Provisions

Under Article 7 (f) of Belém do Pará Convention, state parties agreed to 'establish fair and effective legal procedures for women who have been subjected to violence which include, among others, protective measures, a timely hearing and effective access to such procedures'. Contracting parties to the Belém do Pará Convention also agreed to 'adopt legal measures to require the perpetrator to refrain from harassing, intimidating or threatening the woman or using any method that harms or endangers her life or integrity, or damages her property'.

In contrast, Articles 49–58 Istanbul Convention foresee detailed legislative obligations concerning procedural provisions that effectively prevent and protect against gender-based violence. Article 49 (1) Istanbul Convention foresees that state parties 'shall take the necessary legislative or other measures to ensure that investigations and judicial proceedings in relation to all forms of violence covered by the scope of this Convention are carried out without undue delay while taking into consideration the rights of the victim during all stages of the criminal proceedings'. Accordingly, contracting parties must take legislative or other measures to ensure *inter alia* (1) that the responsible law enforcement agencies respond to all forms of gender-based and domestic violence promptly and appropriately by offering adequate and immediate protection to victims (Article 50); (2) that an assessment of the lethality risk, the seriousness of the situation and the risk of repeated violence is carried out by all relevant authorities to manage the risk and if necessary to provide co-ordinated safety and support (Article 51 (1)); (3) that the competent authorities are granted the power to order, in situations of immediate danger, a perpetrator of domestic violence to vacate the residence of the victim for a sufficient period of time and to prohibit the perpetrator from entering this residence (Article 52); (4) that appropriate restraining or protection orders are available to victims (Article 53); (5) that, in any civil or

---

[7]On procedural laws discriminatory against victims with disabilities, see ECtHR, *X and Y v. The Netherlands*, Judgment, 26 March 1985; regarding the prosecution of rape before military tribunals, see IACtHR, *Rosendo Cantú y otra v. Mexico*, Judgment, 31 August 2010. For an overview on the views and Concluding Observations adopted by the CEDAW Committee, Chinkin, 'Addressing violence against women in the Commonwealth within states' obligations under international law', (2014) 40 *Commonwealth Law Bulletin*, pp. 488.

criminal proceedings, evidence relating to the sexual history and conduct of the victim shall be permitted only when it is relevant and necessary (Article 54); (6) that investigations into or prosecution of grave offences shall not be wholly dependent upon a report or complaint filed by a victim if the offence was committed in whole or in part on its territory, and that the proceedings may continue even if the victim withdraws her or his statement or complaint (Article 55 (1)); (7) a series of specific measures to protect the rights and interests of victims, including their special needs as witnesses, at all stages of investigations and judicial proceedings (Article 56), legal assistance and free legal aid for victims (Article 57); and finally, (8) that the statute of limitation for initiating any legal proceedings of offences such as rape, forced marriage, forced sterilization, forced abortion and forced female mutilation shall continue for a period of time that is sufficient and commensurate with the gravity of the offence in question, to allow for the efficient initiation of proceedings after the victim has reached the age of majority (Article 58).[8]

2) Substantive Provisions

Under Article 7 (c) of Belém do Pará Convention, state parties agreed 'to undertake to include in their domestic legislation penal, civil, administrative and any other type of provisions that may be needed to prevent, punish and eradicate violence against women (...)'.[9] When it comes to substantive provisions, the Istanbul Convention is far more precise, foreseeing a detailed catalogue of obligations concerning the adoption of substantive provisions that improve the prevention and protection against gender-based violence.

This includes the obligation to adopt provisions codifying *inter alia* (1) that marriages concluded under force may be voidable, annulled or dissolved without undue financial or administrative burden placed on the victim (Article 32); (2) that stalking, psychological violence, forced marriage, female mutilation, forced abortion and forced sterilization are criminalized (Articles 33, 34, 37, 38, 39); (3) that rape constitutes a crime when committed without her or his explicit consent and also applies to acts committed against former or current spouses or partners (Article 36); (4) that any form of unwanted verbal, non-verbal or physical conduct of a sexual nature with the purpose or effect of violating the dignity of a person, in particular when creating an intimidating, hostile, degrading, humiliating or offensive environment (sexual harassment), is subject to criminal or other legal sanction (Article 40); and finally, (5) legislative measures to prohibit mandatory alternative dispute resolution processes, including mediation and conciliation, in relation to all forms of gender-based or domestic violence (Article 48).[10]

---

[8]For details, see Council of Europe, *Explanatory Report to the Council of Europe Convention on preventing and combating violence against women and domestic violence,* 2011.

[9]See also Art. 4 (2) (a) and (e) Maputo Protocol.

[10]For details, see Council of Europe, *Explanatory Report to the Council of Europe Convention on preventing and combating violence against women and domestic violence,* 2011.

3) Reparation Measures and Remedies

It is most likely that under domestic legal systems general civil law remedies allowing civil law courts to force (potential) perpetrator to take or omit a particular action as well as substantive provisions of tort law are already in place. States thereby comply with the obligations under the rights to a remedy.[11] However, it is because of the particularities of gender-based violence such as problems involving evidence and the burden of proof, cross-examinations,[12] potential intimidations by and socioeconomic dependence of the perpetrator, as well as the risk of re-traumatization, that these general remedies are unlikely to meet the requirements of a non-discriminatory and effective protection and reparation of victims. Therefore, the Belém and the Istanbul Convention enshrine special provisions on remedies against the perpetrator and reparation.

a) Belém do Pará Convention

State parties to the Belém do Pará Convention are required to ensure effective access to reparation for women who have been subjected to violence. Article 7 (g) enshrines the obligation to 'establish the necessary legal and administrative mechanisms to ensure that women subjected to violence have effective access to restitution, reparations or other just and effective remedies'.

As the wording of Article 7 (g) remains silent on the framing of such domestic legal remedies, States are given considerable discretion. The two so-called 'hemispheric reports' on the implementation of the Belém do Pará Convention issued by the 'Conference of States Party to the Follow-up Mechanism on Implementation of the Inter-American Convention on the Prevention, Punishment and Eradication of Violence against Women' (MESECVI) do not elucidate on how State practice interprets this provision because contracting parties omitted to provide information on reparation.[13]

Referring to the Inter-American human rights system and standards developed by the IACtHR,[14] the guide to the application of the Belém do Pará Convention issued by the MESECVI explains that satisfaction, rehabilitation, guarantees of non-repetition and compensation should be available[15] and have a *transformative* purpose tackling the root causes for violence against women and take a

[11] See Chap. 4 B I.

[12] *Cf.* ECtHR, *Y. v. Slovenia*, Judgment, 28 May 2015.

[13] MESECVI, *Second Hemispheric Report on the Implementation of the Belém do Pará Convention*, April 2012, p. 103; see also IAComHR, *Access to Justice for Women Victims of Violence in the Americas*, 20 January 2007, para. 219.

[14] IACtHR, *González v. Mexico (Cotton Field Case)*, Judgment (Preliminary Objection, Merits, Reparations, and Costs), 16 November 2009, paras 450, 495.

[15] MESECVI, *Guide to the Application of the Inter-American Convention on the Prevention, Punishment, Eradication of Violence against Women*, 2014, p. 48.

gender-perspective.[16] It remains unclear, though, whether the MESECVI guide points towards domestic reparation measures to be made by a State and/or the perpetrator only. Requiring that these measures aim at repairing structural discrimination and societal reasons for violence against women, such as gender-based hierarchies, structural subordination and structural inequalities,[17] it appears that the guide rather points towards reparation measures to be taken by a State.

b) Istanbul Convention

The Istanbul Convention is more precise. Its Article 5 establishes the general obligation of state parties to 'take the necessary legislative and other measures to (. . .) provide reparation for acts of violence covered by the scope of this Convention that are perpetrated by non-State actors'. Under the Explanatory Report, reparation refers to the generic understanding under international human rights law that includes restitution, compensation, rehabilitation, satisfaction and guarantees of non-repetition.[18]

This general obligation is further specified in Articles 29 (1) and (2), 30 (1) and (2). They foresee that States have, (1) to put in place a domestic legal framework of effective remedies that allows victims of gender-based violence to seek reparation from perpetrators; (2) to adopt laws providing for remedies against public authorities; and (3) a system of subsidiary State compensation for those cases where the perpetrator is not able or willing to pay compensation.

(1) Reparation Made by the Perpetrator

Under Article 29 (1), state parties must 'take the necessary legislative or other measures to provide victims with adequate civil remedies against the perpetrator'. As the Explanatory Report elucidates, this provision not only encompasses general

[16]MESECVI, *Guide to the Application of the Inter-American Convention on the Prevention, Punishment, Eradication of Violence against Women*, 2014, p. 48. See also *Nairobi Declaration on Women and Girls' Right to a Remedy and Reparation*, 21 March 2007, p. 2; IACtHR, *González v. Mexico (Cotton Field Case)*, Judgment (Preliminary Objection, Merits, Reparations, and Costs), 16 November 2009, paras 450, 495; UNHRC, *Report of the Special Rapporteur on violence against women, its causes and consequences, Rashida Manjoo*, 22 April 2010, para. 31; CEDAW Committee, *General Recommendation No. 30 on women in conflict prevention, conflict, and post conflict situations*, 18 October 2013, paras 77, 79; UNSG, *Reparations for Conflict-Related Sexual Violence*, 01 August 2014; Rashida Manjoo in her speech at IAComHR, *Mesa Redonda: Violencia de género y reparaciones*, 27 October 2014, at minute 17:20; ICC, *Prosecutor v. Thomas Lubanga Dyilo*, Appeals Chamber, Judgment on the Appeals against the 'Decision establishing the principles and procedures to be applied to reparations' of 7 August 2012 with amended order for reparations (Annex A) and public annexes 1 and 2, 03 March 2015, Annex A, paras 17, 18, 34. See Chap. 7.

[17]MESECVI, *Guide to the Application of the Inter-American Convention on the Prevention, Punishment, Eradication of Violence against Women*, 2014, p. 48.

[18]Council of Europe, *Explanatory Report to the Council of Europe Convention on preventing and combating violence against women and domestic violence*, 2011, para. 60.

civil law remedies allowing civil law courts to order a person to end or refrain from a conduct or to force (potential) perpetrator to take a particular action, but also more specifically barring orders, restraining orders, remedies against defamation and libel, and non-molestation orders.[19]

The obligation to provide for compensation is stated more precisely in Article 30 (1). Accordingly, States must take 'the necessary legislative or other measures to ensure that victims have the right to claim compensation from perpetrators for any of the offences established in accordance with this Convention'. These claims may not only be made in the context of civil but also criminal proceedings if victims get the status of '*partie civile*'. From a textual approach, Article 30 (1) does not exclude the personal liability of perpetrators who committed gender-based violence during the performance of an official duty. This provision thus enshrines a principle of primary liability of perpetrators.[20] It thereby expresses a general attitude among States according to which it is the perpetrator who must pay reparations, but not the State.[21]

(2) Reparation Provisions for State Failure

The Istanbul Convention also contains an obligation to set up a system of State liability. Under Article 29 (2), contracting parties must establish a mechanism of State liability under domestic law that applies if a State fails to 'diligently prevent, investigate and, punish acts of violence covered by the scope of this Convention'.[22] Accordingly, state parties 'shall take the necessary legislative or other measures to provide victims, in accordance with the general principles of international law, with adequate civil remedies against State authorities that have failed in their duty to take the necessary preventive or protective measures within the scope of their powers'. This also includes the restriction of governmental immunity of the forum state.[23]

---

[19] Council of Europe, *Explanatory Report to the Council of Europe Convention on preventing and combating violence against women and domestic violence,* 2011, para.157; Art. 29 (1), 52, 53 Istanbul Convention.

[20] Council of Europe, *Explanatory Report to the Council of Europe Convention on preventing and combating violence against women and domestic violence,* 2011, para. 165.

[21] Rashida Manjoo in her speech before the IAComHR, *Mesa Redonda: Violencia de género y reparaciones*, 27 October 2014, at minute 26:00.

[22] Council of Europe, *Explanatory Report to the Council of Europe Convention on preventing and combating violence against women and domestic violence,* 2011, para. 162. The commentary explains: '[Article 29 (2) reiterates the principle of liability of State authorities, who, in accordance with Article 5 of this Convention are under the obligation to diligently prevent, investigate and, punish acts of violence covered by the scope of this Convention. Failure to comply with this obligation can result in legal responsibility and civil law needs to offer remedies to address such failure (...).'

[23] Against the backdrop of the development of international human rights law, domestic courts developed doctrines such as the US-American 'political question doctrine' (this doctrine is extensively upheld, see initially US Supreme Court, Baker v. Carr, 369 U.S. 189, 217 (1992)), the British 'acts of state' or the French *actes de gouvernement,* excluding state liability for illegal acts and thus imposing a barrier to any action. The motif for such doctrines was to maintain the separation of

While awarding of such remedies corresponds to the compliance with a secondary obligation at the domestic level, from an international law perspective, both the establishment of such mechanisms and the award of reparation are primary duties. Article 29 (2) requires the enactment of remedies such as civil law action for damages for negligent and grossly negligent *omissions* and failures to act appropriately.[24]

As the Explanatory Report to the Convention clarifies, it remains within the discretion of a State to decide upon the extent of State authorities' civil liability.[25] While the Convention omits to explicitly mention an obligation on States to provide for reparation provisions for cases of illegal State *actions*, that is, when a State's own agents commit gender-based violence, such an obligation is encompassed by human rights provisions guaranteeing a right to a remedy.[26]

(3) Subsidiary State Compensation Schemes

Ultimately, the Istanbul Convention foresees a unique system of subsidiary State compensation. Under Article 30 (2), '[a]dequate State compensation shall be awarded to those who have sustained serious bodily injury or impairment of health, to the extent that the damage is not covered by other sources such as the perpetrator, insurance or State-funded health and social provisions'.

This compensation scheme may come into play when the perpetrator is unable or unwilling to pay compensation or if a victim is instantly in need of help and cannot wait until the end of the proceedings against the perpetrator.[27] Such a system may be said to reflect a liberal egalitarian principle of social justice aiming at compensating 'bad brute luck'.[28] However, any State party to the Istanbul Convention can make a reservation to be exempt from this obligation.[29]

---

powers in the domestic legal order. However, to counterbalance the necessities of sovereignty and democratic principles, on the one hand, and considerations of human rights and the rule of law, on the other hand, domestic courts recently tended to restrict governmental immunity of the forum state. This enables claims to be brought by individuals who suffered harm as a consequence of an internationally wrongful state act. For details, see Shelton, *Remedies in international human rights law*, 2006, pp. 28–30. For State practice, see Bagińska (ed.), *Damages for Violations of Human Rights*, 2015.

[24]Council of Europe, *Explanatory Report to the Council of Europe Convention on preventing and combating violence against women and domestic violence,* 2011, para. 162.

[25]Ibid.

[26]See above, Chap. 4 B.

[27]Council of Europe, *Explanatory Report to the Council of Europe Convention on preventing and combating violence against women and domestic violence,* 2011, paras 168–169.

[28]From a Luck-egalitarian perspective, *Ronald Dworkin* distinguishes two kinds of bad luck, i.e., brute luck and option luck: 'Option luck is a matter of how deliberate and calculated gambles turn out—whether someone gains or losses through accepting an isolated risk he or she should have anticipated and might have declined.' Brute luck is 'a matter of how risks fall out that are not in that sense deliberate gambles', see Dworkin, *Sovereign virtue: the theory and practice of equality*, 2002, p. 73.

[29]Cf. Art. 78 (2).

It should be noted that a similar subsidiary compensation scheme could only be found under the *European Convention on the Compensation of Victims of Violent Crimes* (ECV),[30] in three soft law instruments[31] and under Columbian law.[32] Nonetheless, it appears that, apart from the European context, an obligation under international law for a State to provide reparation for acts that are only attributable to private actors may be called, if at all, an 'emerging' customary norm or even a 'laudable aspiration'.[33]

c) Comparing Reparations Provisions Under the Belém do Pará and Istanbul Conventions

The provisions of the Istanbul Convention are quite precise, whereas those under the Belém do Pará Convention remain vague. Nonetheless, both Conventions give a considerable leeway to their contracting parties in implementing the obligations under the Conventions. Whereas the Belém do Pará Convention seems to focus on State liability and may be interpreted as to require a *transformative* approach, the Istanbul Convention stresses the liability of the perpetrator and leaves the extent of State liability within the discretion of a State. Given the necessity of an effective protection, each Convention is thus incomplete.[34]

---

[30]However, whereas discriminatory restrictions on any ground are prohibited under the Istanbul Convention (Article 4), the ECV limits the group of beneficiaries of subsidiary compensation to certain nationals (Article 3).

[31]UNGA Res. 40/34, *Declaration of Principles of Justice for Victims of Crimes and Abuses*, 29 November 1985, para. 12 which reads as follows: When compensation is not fully available from the offender or other sources, States *should* endeavor to provide financial compensation to: (a) Victims who have sustained significant bodily injury or impairment of physical or mental health from serious crimes; (b) The family, in particular dependants of persons who have died or become physically or mentally incapacitated because of such victimization. UNGA Res. 60/147, *Basic Principles and Guidelines on the Right to a Remedy and Reparation for Victims of Gross Violations of International Human Rights Law and Serious Violations of International Humanitarian Law*, 21 March 2006, para. 16. It reads as follows: 'States *should* endeavor to establish national programs for reparation and other assistance to victims in the event that the parties liable for the harm suffered are unable or unwilling to meet their obligations.' UNSG, *Reparations for Conflict-Related Sexual Violence*, 01 August 2014, p. 4, *passim*. It reads as follows: 'Reparations should be provided by a State for acts or omissions that can be attributed to it and that violate its obligations under international human rights law or international humanitarian law, or a person, a legal person, or other entity found liable for violations of international humanitarian law and making reparation. In the event that the parties liable for the harm suffered are unable or unwilling to meet their obligations, States should endeavor to establish programs for reparations and assistance to victims.'

[32]For details, see Ní Aoláin/O'Rourke/Swaine, 'Transforming Reparations for Conflict-Related Sexual Violence', (2015) *Harv. Hum. Rts. J.*, pp. 125.

[33]Bassiouni, 'International Recognition of Victims' Rights', (2006) 6 *Hum. Rts. L. Rev.*, p. 223. See also Rose, 'An Emerging Norm', (2010) 33 *Hastings Int'l & Comp. L. Rev.*

[34]Both conventions do not prejudice internal and other binding international law norms that may enshrine more comprehensive obligations and favorable rights to legal remedies, Art. 73 Istanbul Convention, Art. 14 Belém do Pará Convention.

To protect effectively, States should apply a twofold approach when dealing with, and ruling on, reparation for gender-based violence. Conversely, it is necessary to provide for remedies against both the State and the perpetrator. Civil remedies and reparation measures that enforce the victim's rights against offenders are important because of their deterrent, compensatory and restorative effect.[35] Missing rectification and compensation create a 'climate of impunity [leaving] serious negative consequences on the individual survivor and ultimately on society as a whole'.[36] Besides, holding a State accountable for human rights violations is crucial to ensuring the rule of law.[37] When focusing on the individual perpetrator's liability only, reparation measures may fail to come up to the structural nature of gender-based violence.

b. Administrative and Judicial Measures

1) Gender-Sensitive Investigation, Prosecution, Punishment

In peacetime settings, the investigation and prosecution of gender-based crimes has become a frequent State practice, when such crimes are reported to public authorities.[38] However, the majority of offenses are not reported to public authorities.[39] The risk of re-victimization, 'exposing women not only to psychological harm but also to reprisal, stigma and communal and family ostracism' is often tantamount as to hinder victims to come forward.[40] Gender-stereotyped beliefs significantly influence or even hinder effective investigations and prosecutions and thus infringe women's rights to a fair trial and to an effective remedy. For example, in some societies it is still quite frequent that women bringing a charge against a rapist or murder are not taken seriously because it is said to be their fault for deciding to go out.[41] Experts have therefore called for executive policies or plans of action that deal with the deeply rooted conviction of the inferiority of, and consequent disdain for,

---

[35]Shelton, *Remedies in international human rights law*, 2006, pp. 10 f.

[36]Ibid, p. 11.

[37]Ibid, p. 99.

[38]Ertürk, 'The Due Diligence Standards', in Benninger-Budel, 2008, p. 37.

[39]For EU member States, see European Union Agency for Fundamental Rights, *Violence against women*, March 2014.

[40]UNHRC, *Report of the Special Rapporteur on violence against women, its causes and consequences, Rashida Manjoo*, 22 April 2010, para. 35; European Union Agency for Fundamental Rights, *Violence against women*, March 2014.

[41]For some misogynist responses given by the officials, see IACtHR, *González v. Mexico (Cotton Field Case)*, Judgment (Preliminary Objection, Merits, Reparations, and Costs), 16 November 2009, paras 153, 198, 199, 202. On gender-sensitive investigation and prosecution, see UN Department of Social and Economic Affairs - Division for the Advancement of Women, *Handbook for legislation on violence against women*, 2010; IAComHR, *Verdad, justicia y reparación*, 31 December 2013, p. 366.

women within the criminal justice system and the police[42] and for the installation of a gender-ombudsperson and health personal to assist the proceedings.[43]

Along these lines, Article 7 (c) Belém do Pará Convention not only foresees the obligation of contracting parties to investigate and prosecute gender-based violence effectively, as well as to punish perpetrators.[44] Contracting parties also agreed to undertake progressively programs to promote the education and training of all those involved in the administration of justice, police and other law enforcement officers responsible for implementing policies for the prevention, punishment and eradication of violence against women (Article 8 (c)).[45]

Similarly, parties to the Istanbul Convention must 'provide or strengthen appropriate training for the relevant professionals dealing with victims or perpetrators of all acts of gender-based or domestic violence, on the prevention and detection of such violence, equality between women and men, the needs and rights of victims, as well as on how to prevent secondary victimization' (Article 15 (1)).

2) Support Services for (Potential) Victims

State parties to the Belém do Pará Convention agreed to undertake progressively programs to provide appropriate specialized services for women who have been subjected to violence, through public and private sector agencies, including shelters, counseling services for all family members where appropriate, and care and custody of the affected children (Article 8 (d)).

In contrast, the Istanbul Convention codifies detailed obligations according to which contracting parties must ensure a series of support services facilitating the recovery from violence. This includes legal and psychological counseling, financial assistance, housing, education, training and assistance in finding employment (Article 20). Contracting parties also must ensure that victims have information on and access to applicable regional and international individual/collective complaints mechanisms (Article 21). They also must provide or arrange for, in an adequate geographical distribution, immediate, short- and long-term specialist support services to any victim subjected to any of the acts of violence covered by the scope of this Convention (Article 22). This includes telephone help lines, shelter, medical and trauma support, counseling centers, and special protection and support

[42]UNCHR, *Integration of the human rights of women and the gender perspective*, 20 January 2006. An excellent example for misogynist attitudes among judges can be found in the joint dissenting opinion of Gölcüklü, Matscher, Pettiti, De Meyer, Lopes Rocha, Makarczyk and Gotchev in ECtHR, *Aydin v. Turkey* [GC], Judgment, 25 September 1997.

[43]Chinkin, 'Addressing violence against women in the Commonwealth within states' obligations under international law', (2014) 40 *Commonwealth Law Bulletin*, p. 496.

[44]See also Art. 4 (2) (a) and (e) Maputo Protocol.

[45]For details, see MESECVI, *Guide to the Application of the Inter-American Convention on the Prevention, Punishment, Eradication of Violence against Women*, 2014, p. 45. See also IACtHR, *Las Dos Erres Massacre v. Guatemala*, Judgment, 24 November 2009, paras. 250–251; IAComHR, *Maria da Penha v. Brazil*, Case 12.051, Report No. 54/01, 16 April 2001, para. 61(4).

for child witnesses (Articles 23–26). Ultimately, a State must ensure that victims receive adequate and timely information on available support services and legal measures in a language they understand (Article 19).[46]

2. Addressing the Public

Contracting parties to the Belém do Pará Convention agreed to undertake progressively programs to promote awareness and observance of the right of women to be free from violence, and the right of women to have their human rights respected and protected (Article 8 (a)) and to promote and support governmental and private sector education designed to raise the awareness of the public with respect to the problems of and remedies for violence against women (Article 8 (e)).

In contrast, state parties to the Istanbul Convention Parties must promote or conduct, on a regular basis and at all levels, awareness-raising campaigns or programs, including in co-operation with national human rights institutions and equality bodies, civil society and non-governmental organizations, especially women's organizations, where appropriate, to increase awareness and understanding among the general public of the different manifestations of all forms of violence covered by the scope of this Convention, their consequences on children and the need to prevent such violence (Article 13 (1)). Moreover, contracting parties must ensure the wide dissemination among the general public of information on measures available to prevent acts of violence (Article 13 (2)).[47]

3. Addressing the Individual

At the individual level, measures need to address both (potential) victims of violence and perpetrators. Women victims need empowerment. Engaging in empowerment discourse means educating women on their rights and possibilities under domestic law, as well as to impart skills that make them independent to break cycles of accepting subordination and thus violence.

Individual empowerment is therefore one of the crucial principles and methods of the Istanbul Convention.[48] Similarly, parties to the Belém do Pará Convention more vaguely agreed to undertake progressively measures to provide women who are

---

[46]For details, see Council of Europe, *Explanatory Report to the Council of Europe Convention on preventing and combating violence against women and domestic violence,* 2011.

[47]Awareness-raising campaigns, including large-scale media campaigns, 'zero tolerance' campaigns and national action days on violence against women have become a frequent state practice UNCHR, *Integration of the human rights of women and the gender perspective*, 20 January 2006. See also IAComHR, *Maria da Penha v. Brazil*, Case 12.051, Report No. 54/01, 16 April 2001; Bandeira/Mara Campos de Almeida, Tania, 'Vinte anos da convencao de belem do para e a Lei Maria da Penha', (2015) *Revista Estudo Feministas.*

[48]See Arts. 1 (1) b, 6, 12 (6), 18 (3).

subjected to violence access to effective readjustment and training programs to enable them to fully participate in public, private and social life (Article 8 f)).

While the Belém do Pará Convention does not focus on the treatment of perpetrators, state parties to the Istanbul Convention are obliged to set up or support programs aimed at teaching perpetrators of domestic violence to adopt non-violent behavior in interpersonal relationships with a view to preventing further violence and changing violent behavioral patterns; contracting parties also must provide for treatment programs aimed at preventing perpetrators, in particular sex offenders, from re-offending (Article 16).[49]

4. Interstate Cooperation

As perpetrators may take advantages from going abroad to commit a crime or to escape criminal sanctions, interstate cooperation is crucial. For that purpose, the Istanbul Convention establishes a series of obligations of interstate cooperation in the area of victim assistance, investigations, enforcement of relevant civil and criminal judgments, including protection orders.[50] In contrast, duties of transnational cooperation are less developed under the Bélem do Pará Convention. Therein, States agreed to progressively undertake measures 'for the exchange of ideas and experiences and the execution of programs aimed at protecting women who are subjected to violence'.[51]

5. Conclusion

The Istanbul and Belém do Pará Conventions stipulate a number of positive obligations that require States to *directly* prevent and protect against gender-based violence. While the Istanbul Convention enshrines a series of very precise obligations, parties to the Belém do Pará Convention have a greater margin of appreciation on both the measures and the time of their adoption.

At the State level, contracting parties must take a series of substantive, procedural as well as administrative measures to prevent and protect against gender-based violence. They need to investigate crimes, prosecute and punish perpetrators in a gender-sensitive manner. Public awareness for violence against women and gender equality needs to be promoted, and victims need to be empowered and supported. state parties to the Istanbul Convention must provide for treatment and support programs aimed at preventing perpetrators from re-offending and are also encouraged to cooperate with other States to effectively prevent transnational crimes.

---

[49] *Cf.* also ECtHR, *Branko Tomašić and others v. Croatia*, Judgment, 15 January 2015, para. 61.
[50] Arts 62–65.
[51] Art. 8 (i) Belém do Pará Convention.

II. Long-Term Prevention: Towards Transformation[52]

In fact, violence against women being entangled with a larger net of various forms of discrimination against women, short-term measures directly addressing violence against women will not suffice to sustainably end it.[53] As shown by the 'iceberg model',[54] the occurrence and acceptance of violence against women is fuelled and perpetuated by various forms of gender-based discrimination in the social, religious, economic and cultural fields (structural discrimination).[55] To address the interdependency between gender-based violence, discrimination, gender hierarchies and stereotypes, and to sustainably lessen the incidence of gender-based violence against women in the long run, policies, laws and programs need to be comprehensive, including all stages and fields of life, and embrace the underlying causes for violence against women.[56]

Mostly CEDAW[57] but also the Istanbul and the Belém do Pará Conventions require a long-term strategy that addresses the ground level and second layer of the 'iceberg'[58] and have thus an enormous transformative potential. They take a threefold approach to combat discrimination, gender stereotypes and hierarchies. Accordingly, and first, existing laws, regulations, penal laws, customs and practices that constitute or enable direct or indirect discrimination against women by both public

---

[52]An earlier version of this section has been published in Henn, 'Gender injustice, discrimination, and the CEDAW: A women's life course perspective', in Jänterä-Jareborg/Tigroudja, 2016.

[53]See also, UN Women, Commission on the Status of Women, *Elimination and prevention of all forms of violence against women and girls*, 15 March 2013, para. 22.

[54]Chapter 2 B.

[55]UNHRC, *Report of the Special Rapporteur on violence against women, its causes and consequences, Rashida Manjoo*, 02 May 2011, paras 35, 40, 50; UNHRC, *Report of the Special Rapporteur on violence against women, its causes and consequences*, 13 May 2013; UNGA, *Advancement of Women*, 01 August 2011; UNSG, *In-Depth-Study on All Forms of Violence Against Women*, 2006; UNSG, *Reparations for Conflict-Related Sexual Violence*, 01 August 2014, p. 8.

[56]UNCHR, *Integration of the human rights of women and the gender perspective*, 20 January 2006, paras 16, 79; UNHRC, *Report of the Special Rapporteur on violence against women, its causes and consequences, Rashida Manjoo*, 02 May 2011, para. 57; UNHRC, *Report of the Special Rapporteur on violence against women, its causes and consequences*, 13 May 2013, para. 20. CEDAW, *General Recommendation No. 25 on article 4, paragraph 1, of the Convention on the Elimination of All Forms of Discrimination against Women, on temporary special measures*, 2004, para. 7; CESCR, *General Comment 16*; see also UNSG, *Report of the Secretary-General on the review of the implementation of the Beijing Declaration and Platform for Action and the outcome of the twenty-third special session and its contribution to shaping a gender perspective in the realization of the Millennium Development Goals*, 08 February 2010; Holtmaat, 'CEDAW: A holistic approach to women's equality and freedom', in Hellum/Aasen, 2013, p. 111.

[57]Extensive reservations have been declared. They are, however, only valid if they do not contradict the very purpose of a treaty, see Article 28 (2) CEDAW. Regarding the family rights under Art. 16, for instance, the Committee has considered reservations incompatible and thus invalid, as they contradict the very purpose of the Convention, see CEDAW, *General Recommendation No. 29 on article 16 of CEDAW*, 26 February 2013, para. 3.

[58]See Chap. 2 B IV.

and private actors must be *modified or abolished* (I.).[59] Second, the *de facto* position of women needs to be *improved* through concrete and effective programs and policies to reach *de facto* equality (II.).[60] Finally, States need to address the persistence of gender hierarchies and harmful 'stereotypes that affect women not only through individual acts by individuals, but also through legal and societal structures and institutions' (III.).[61] Unlike the provisions of the Istanbul and Belém do Pará Conventions, the long-term strategy of CEDAW is binding upon almost all States given the quasi-universal ratification of this convention.

1. Combating *de jure* and *de facto* Discrimination Against Women by Public and Private Actors

While ending *de jure* discrimination appears to be the most obvious and simplest way to promote women's status, equality in law does not safeguard equality in practice. Policies that are limited to end *de jure* discrimination and to stop at this very point will not be able to end discrimination.[62] Because of historically developed unjust structures, achieving factual equality requires greater efforts in respect of the disadvantaged groups compared to the advantaged groups.[63] To counteract *de facto* discrimination by public acts and corresponding structural disadvantages, a 'gender audit of all legislation'[64] and gender mainstreaming[65] are useful tools if carried out and used properly.[66] Allegedly sex-neutral laws, policies and programs should be

---

[59] Arts 2 (e), (f), (g) CEDAW; Arts 6 (a), 7 (e) Belém do Pará Convention; Arts 1 (1) b, 4 (2) Istanbul Convention.

[60] Art. 3 CEDAW; Arts 7, 8 Belém do Pará Convention; Arts. 1, 4 (2), 4 (4), 6, 14 (1), 15 (1) Istanbul Convention.

[61] CEDAW, *General Recommendation No. 25 on Article 4, paragraph 1, of the Convention on the Elimination of All Forms of Discrimination against Women, on temporary special measures*, 2004, para. 7 referring to the obligations under Arts 4 and 5 CEDAW; Arts 6 (a), 7 (e) Belém do Pará Convention; Arts. 12 (1), 14 (1) Istanbul Convention.

[62] For an introduction to the growing body of critical academic writing on the discontent with existing equal treatment legislation, see Holtmaat, *Towards Different Law and Public Policy: The significance of Article 5a CEDAW for the elimination of structural gender discrimination*, 2004, pp. 17.

[63] Schutter, *International human rights law*, 2014, pp. 732.

[64] Parties to the Istanbul Convention must undertake to include a gender perspective in the implementation and evaluation of the impact of the provisions of this Convention (Article 6).

[65] Under the general definition by the Council of Europe, gender mainstreaming 'is the (re) organisation, improvement, development and evaluation of policy processes, so that a gender equality perspective is incorporated in all policies at all levels and at all stages, by the actors normally involved in policy-making'. Council of Europe, http://www.coe.int/t/dghl/standardsetting/equality/03themes/gender-mainstreaming/index_en.asp, accessed 28 January 2016.

[66] Chinkin, 'Addressing violence against women in the Commonwealth within states' obligations under international law', (2014) 40 *Commonwealth Law Bulletin*, p. 478; Beveridge/Nott, 'Mainstreaming', (2002) 10 *Feminist Legal Studies*.

monitored as to their gender impact not only before their adoption, but also after their implementation, by collecting and analyzing statistical data. To include overlapping and multiple forms of discrimination, data must be disaggregated by sex, age and other relevant factors such as ethnicity.[67] If accordingly a measure places women at a disadvantage, it needs to be adjusted by the competent public authority.

Along these lines, state parties to CEDAW agreed to pursue by all appropriate means and without delay a policy of eliminating *de jure* and *de facto* discrimination and to adopt, on the constitutional level and elsewhere, the principle of equality between women and men (Article 2). States must prevent *de facto* discrimination by means other than legislation. To protect women against all kinds of gender-based discrimination by private actors, such as intimate partners, family and community members, religious institutions, companies, employers and unknown individuals, in all areas of life, state parties to CEDAW agreed to undertake to prohibit actions that constitute discrimination, through sanctions if appropriate, and by providing effective judicial protection (Article 2 (b), (c) CEDAW).[68]

While under Article 5 Belém do Pará Convention, state parties recognize that the 'right of every woman to be free from violence includes [the] right of women to be free from all forms of discrimination', this wording does not imply a binding obligation.

State parties to the Istanbul Convention recognize 'that the realization of *de jure* and *de facto* equality between women and men is a key element in the prevention of violence against women'[69] and condemn by Article 4 (2)

> all forms of discrimination against women and take, without delay, the necessary legislative and other measures to prevent it, in particular by embodying in their national constitutions or other appropriate legislation the principle of equality between women and men and ensuring the practical realisation of this principle; prohibiting discrimination against women, including through the use of sanctions, where appropriate; abolishing laws and practices which discriminate against women.

As the Explanatory Report to the Istanbul Convention clarifies, state parties thereby

> recognized that the enjoyment of the right to be free from violence is interconnected with the Parties' obligation to secure equality between women and men to exercise and enjoy all (. . .) rights as set out in the human rights instruments of the Council of Europe (. . .) and other international instruments, particularly CEDAW.[70]

[67]CESCR, *General Comment 16*, para. 18; Council of Europe, *Gender Mainstreaming*, 2004.

[68]For details, see Byrnes, 'Article 2', in Rudolf/Freeman/Chinkin, 2012, pp. 83–85.

[69]Preamble.

[70]For details, see Council of Europe, *Explanatory Report to the Council of Europe Convention on preventing and combating violence against women and domestic violence*, 2011, Article 4, at para. 50.

2. Improving the Position of Women by Special Measures

When aiming at improving *de facto* equality of structurally disadvantaged groups, the adoption of positive actions, *viz.* general and temporary special measures, plays a crucial role.[71] On women's *de facto* equality, temporary special measures can range from quotas, allocation of resources, preferential treatment, to numerical goals connected with timetables and benchmarks.[72] In turn, general measures may encompass gender budgeting, the establishment of institutions aimed at the advancement of women, action plans aimed at removing social obstacles, educational and empowerment programs, and the integration of a gender perspective in all decision-making processes.[73]

Along these lines, Article 3 CEDAW holds that state parties 'shall take in all fields, in particular in the political, social, economic and cultural fields, all appropriate measures, including legislation, to ensure the full development and advancement of women'. As to the wording of this norm, being typical for positive obligations, this provision can be interpreted as to establish a binding obligation, which, however, confers upon a State a wide margin of appreciation that is only limited by the prohibition of insufficient action.[74] Read in conjunction with Article 4, which allows for temporary special measures,[75] the CEDAW Committee

---

[71] Schutter, *International human rights law*, 2014, pp. 732.

[72] For details see, Raday, 'Systematizing the Application of Different Types of Temporary Special Measures under Article 4 of CEDAW', in Boerefijn, 2003, pp. 38; On benchmarks and indicators, see Schutter, *International human rights law*, 2014, pp. 544.

[73] UNCHR, *Integration of the human rights of women and the gender perspective*, 20 January 2006, paras 78. Integrating a gender perspective in all decision-making processes has internationally been acknowledged to constitute a tool for the sustainable development of a society, UNSG, *Report of the Secretary-General on the review of the implementation of the Beijing Declaration and Platform for Action and the outcome of the twenty-third special session and its contribution to shaping a gender perspective in the realization of the Millennium Development Goals*, 08 February 2010, para. 486; The World Bank (ed.), *Engendering development through gender equality in rights, resources, and voice*, 2001; Fourth World Conference on Women, *Beijing Declaration and Platform for Action*, 1995, para. 56.

[74] On the prohibition of insufficient action, see Chap. 5 B.

[75] Special measures that enhance the position of members of disadvantaged groups do not constitute discrimination, Schutter, *International human rights law*, 2014, pp. 740; Council of Europe, *Explanatory Report to the Council of Europe Convention on preventing and combating violence against women and domestic violence,* 2011, Art. 4, para. 55. The Commentary explains that this approach 'is in line with the concept of discrimination as interpreted by the European Court of Human Rights in its case law concerning Article 14 ECHR. In particular, this case law has made clear that not every distinction or difference of treatment amounts to discrimination. As the Court has stated, for example in the *Abdulaziz, Cabales and Balkandali v. the United Kingdom* judgment, "a difference of treatment is discriminatory if it has no objective and reasonable justification, that is, if it does not pursue a legitimate aim or if there is not a reasonable relationship of proportionality between the means employed and the aim sought to be realised". The fact that women experience gender-based violence, including domestic violence, to a significantly larger extent than men can be considered an objective and reasonable justification to employ resources and take special measures for the benefit of women victims only.'

considers that States need to apply a twofold approach when improving women's *de facto* equality. Accordingly, CEDAW requires to adopt both temporary special measures to achieve specific goals and general mechanisms to enhance the development and advancement of women.[76]

3. Addressing Harmful Gender Stereotypes and Hierarchies

As shown above,[77] detrimental gender stereotyping and gender hierarchies prevent the achievement of full equality between women and men and enable violence against women to occur. Hence, transforming concepts of gender stereotypes, gender-biased customs and fixed parental gender roles is crucial to achieving full equality. Therefore, Article 5 CEDAW establishes that state parties must

> take all appropriate measures
>
> (a) to modify the social and cultural patterns of conduct of men and women, with a view to achieving the elimination of prejudices and customary and all other practices which are based on the idea of the inferiority or the superiority of either of the sexes or on stereotyped roles for men and women;
>
> (b) to ensure that family education includes a proper understanding of maternity as a social function and the recognition of the common responsibility of men and women in the upbringing and development of their children, it being understood that the interest of the children is the primordial consideration in all cases.[78]

This provision comprises an enormous transformative potential on structural discriminatory settings.[79]

Similarly, the Belém do Pará Convention calls for the transformation of gender stereotypes and the eradication of misogynist prejudices.[80] Article 12 (1) Istanbul Convention requires that contracting parties

---

[76]CEDAW, *General Recommendation No. 25 on article 4, paragraph 1, of the Convention on the Elimination of All Forms of Discrimination against Women, on temporary special measures*, 2004; Boerefijn (ed.), *Temporary Special Measures: Accelerating de facto equality of women under article 4 (1) UN Convention on the Elimination of All Forms of Discrimination Against Women*, 2003.

[77]Chapter 2 B.

[78]See also the Preamble, para. 14, Arts 2 to 4 and 24 CEDAW. These provisions function as a general *clausula* and need consequently to be applied in relation to articles 6 to 16 of the Cedaw, see CEDAW, *General Recommendation No. 25 on article 4, paragraph 1, of the Convention on the Elimination of All Forms of Discrimination against Women, on temporary special measures*, 2004, para. 24.

[79]On the far reaching effect of Art. 5, see Holtmaat, 'CEDAW: A holistic approach to women's equality and freedom', in Hellum/Aasen, 2013, pp. 108.

[80]Under Article 8 (b) state parties agreed to undertake 'to modify social and cultural patterns of conduct of men and women, including the development of formal and informal educational programs appropriate to every level of the educational process, to counteract prejudices, customs and all other practices which are based on the idea of the inferiority or superiority of either of the

> take the necessary measures to promote changes in the social and cultural patterns of behaviour of women and men with a view to eradicating prejudices, customs, traditions and all other practices which are based on the idea of the inferiority of women or on stereotyped roles for women and men.

As gender stereotypes and hierarchies are perpetuated by the educational system, publicity and (mass) media, they can be modified through these very institutions.[81] It is for that reason that CEDAW,[82] the Belém do Pará[83] and the Istanbul Conventions[84] call on state parties to address the educational sector, the media and private actors.

For example, state parties to the Istanbul Convention need to include teaching material on non-stereotyped gender roles at all levels of education, but also in 'informal educational facilities, as well as in sports, cultural and leisure facilities and the media'.[85] This can include measures in the field of primary and secondary education, such as gender-sensitive schoolbooks,[86] and a dialogue with cultural stakeholders,[87] which are crucial to raise awareness for gender equality and strengthen the rejection of misogyny and end detrimental practice.[88] State parties to the Belém do Pará and the Istanbul Convention must encourage the media and private actors such as advertising companies 'to participate in the elaboration and implementation of policies and to set guidelines and self-regulatory standards to prevent violence against women and to enhance respect for their dignity'.[89]

---

sexes or on the stereotyped roles for men and women which legitimize or exacerbate violence against women'.

[81] Holtmaat, 'Article 5', in Rudolf/Freeman/Chinkin, 2012, p. 161; UN Women, Commission on the Status of Women, *Elimination and prevention of all forms of violence against women and girls*, 15 March 2013, para. 29.

[82] Art. 10 (c) CEDAW.

[83] Art. 8 (e), (g) Belém do Pará Convention.

[84] Art. 14, 17 Istanbul Convention.

[85] Art. 14 Istanbul Convention. See also Article 8 (e) Belém Convention, which reads as follows: The state parties agree to undertake progressively specific measures, including programs: to promote and support governmental and private sector education designed to raise the awareness of the public with respect to the problems of and remedies for violence against women. See Art. 4 (2) (d) Maputo Protocol and IAComHR, *Maria da Penha v. Brazil*, Case 12.051, Report No. 54/01, 16 April 2001, para. 61(4).

[86] See Article 10 (c) CEDAW.

[87] Holtmaat, 'CEDAW: A holistic approach to women's equality and freedom', in Hellum/Aasen, 2013, p. 120.

[88] Holtmaat, 'Article 5', in Rudolf/Freeman/Chinkin, 2012, p. 162.

[89] Art. 17 Istanbul Convention; Art. 8 (g) Belém do Pará Convention. See also CEDAW Committee, CO New Zealand, A/49/38, 13th Session (1994), para. 641. Holtmaat, 'Article 5', in Rudolf/Freeman/Chinkin, 2012, p. 162; On the influence of media on gender stereotyping, see Collins, 'Content Analysis of Gender Roles in Media', (2011) 64 *Sex Roles*.

4. Conclusion: Towards Transformation

State parties to CEDAW, the Istanbul and the Belém do Pará Conventions recognize the need for a threefold approach, which under CEDAW is obligatory unless permissible reservations have been declared.[90] Accordingly, contracting parties to CEDAW have, first, to abolish direct and indirect discrimination by public and private actors, second, to improve the *de facto* position of women by general and specific programs and, third, to combat gender stereotypes and hierarchization in media, education and publicity and to end gender hierarchies. State parties to the Istanbul Convention have also to combat gender stereotypes and hierarchies. This threefold approach allows for taking a transformative approach, combating structural discrimination as illustrated by an 'iceberg-model'.

Still, provisions under CEDAW leave much room for State discretion. As this room of discretion may only be limited by the prohibition of insufficient action,[91] there is no obligation to take a *specific* measure aiming at complying with the obligations to improve the *de facto* position of women and to combat stereotypes and hierarchies.[92] However, either within the context of a communication[93] or a State reporting procedure may the CEDAW Committee recall a State's obligation by recommending the State to take special measures addressing gender stereotypes and improving the position of women in that country.

III. Conclusion

The Istanbul and the Belém do Pará Conventions foresee a variety of measures the adoption of which is either at a State's discretion or obligatory. Detailed provisions under the Istanbul Convention and the Belém do Pará Convention provide guidance on short-term measures (obligations of protection and to protect and State-related duties) to be taken when gender-based crimes are about to occur or have already been committed. Independently from any specific case, parties to these Conventions need to take legislative and administrative measures providing for a procedural and substantial legal framework that effectively prevents and protects against (further) violence. States have also to provide for programs creating gender sensitivity among public officials and other State agents.

---

[90]Nevertheless it appears that until 2013 only one federal State, Victoria (Australia), has taken 'a long-term, multi-sectoral and holistic approach to prevention' of violence against women, UN Women, Commission on the Status of Women, *Elimination and prevention of all forms of violence against women and girls*, 15 March 2013, para. 61.

[91]Chapter 5 B.

[92]For details, Stahl, *Schutzpflichten im Völkerrecht*, 2012, pp. 364, 368.

[93]E.g., CEDAW, *Medvedeva v. Russian Federation*, Communication No. 60/2013, 25 February 2016, para. 13 (b).

Additionally, CEDAW, the Belém do Pará and the Istanbul Conventions either require or encourage state parties to adopt long-term policies combating structural discrimination against women. While the wording of the Belém do Pará Convention concerning this threefold approach is rather programmatic, parties to the Istanbul Convention must take a transformative approach on gender stereotypes and hierarchies and are encouraged to abolish *de facto* discrimination and improve the *de facto* position of women. Regarding CEDAW, Articles 2–5 clearly require contracting parties to, first, address *de jure* and *de facto* discrimination in all fields of life, second, improve women's *de facto* position and, third, transform gender stereotypes and hierarchies as root causes of gender-based violence.

B. Content of Positive Obligations Under Customary International Law

As to the variety of binding and non-binding legal sources on positive obligations relating to gender-based violence against women,[94] the question arises whether there is a rule under customary international law obliging States to actively take short-term or even long-term measures against gender-based violence.

Based on a review of State practice and *opinio juris,* the UN Special Rapporteur on Violence against women, *Yakin Ertürk,* concludes that 'there is a rule of customary international law that obliges States to prevent and respond to acts of violence against women'.[95] She admitted though that the

> application of due diligence standard [whereby she refers to positive obligations relating to gender-based violence against women], to date, has tended to be State-centric and limited to responding to violence when it occurs, largely neglecting the obligation to prevent and compensate.[96]

However, according to a latter study undertaken by the succeeding Special Rapporteur, *Rashida Manjoo*, State practice is fragmentary and less 'than 10 per cent of States articulate their responsibility to act with due diligence as emanating from legally binding international human rights law'.[97]

---

[94]Chapters 6 and 3 B.

[95]UNCHR, *Integration of the human rights of women and the gender perspective*, 20 January 2006, para. 29.

[96]UNCHR, *Integration of the human rights of women and the gender perspective*, 20 January 2006, Summery. See also UNCHR, *Integration of the human rights of women and the gender perspective*, 20 January 2006, para. 46; UN Department of Social and Economic Affairs - Division for the Advancement of Women, *Handbook for legislation on violence against women*, 2010. Regretting the lack of practice regarding remedies for women, see also Ní Aoláin/O'Rourke/Swaine, 'Transforming Reparations for Conflict-Related Sexual Violence', (2015) *Harv. Hum. Rts. J.*, p. 102.

[97]UNHRC, *Report of the Special Rapporteur on violence against women, its causes and consequences*, 13 May 2013, paras 41.

Thus, when considering the rules on how customary law traditionally comes into being, the first mentioned Rapporteur's conclusions appear premature. Traditionally, the formation of customary international law requires two elements. As the ICJ has repeatedly held, '[n]ot only must the acts concerned amount to a settled practice, but they must also be such, or be carried out in such a way, as to be evidence of a belief that this practice is rendered obligatory by the existence of a rule requiring it'.[98] Hence, it requires, firstly, an extensive and uniform State practice which is, secondly, coupled with the respective acceptance of this practice as binding international law (*opinio juris*).[99]

Against this backdrop, it must be concluded that gender-based violence committed by State actors is prohibited by customary law (and when constituting torture even as *jus cogens*).[100] Moreover, it may be concluded that penalizing and prosecuting gender-based crimes, in particular sexualized violence, has become an obligation under customary law. However, even if one advocated for emphasizing *opinio juris* over practice,[101] it can hardly be concluded that other positive obligations on violence against women have reached customary law status. Moreover, it may generally be claimed that, compared to the obligation to respect, positive human rights obligations are rather a recent development and far from recognized by States beyond their treaty obligations. Hence, it seems rather too optimistic to claim that

---

[98]E.g., ICJ, *North Sea Continental Shelf Case (Federal Republic of Germany v. Denmark; Federal Republic of Germany v. Netherlands)*, Dissenting Opinion Judge Sørensen, 20 February 1969, para. 74; ICJ, *Military and paramilitary activities in and against Nicaragua (Nicaragua v. United States of America)*, Judgment (merits), 27 June 1986, pp. 14, 109; ICJ, *Jurisdictional Immunity of States (Germany v. Italy: Greece intervening)*, Judgment, 03 February 2012, pp. 99, 122, para. 55.

[99]ILC, *Third Report on Identification of customary international law*, 27 March 2015, paras 12; Crawford, *Brownlie's Principles of public international law*, 2012, p. 24.

[100]Since UNSC Resolution 1325 (2000), and the 'women, Peace and Security' agenda, different actors have increased their calls for the elimination of sexualized violence against women. Ever since, member States to the Africa Union ratified the Maputo Protocol, member States to the Council of Europe have ratified the Istanbul Convention, countless soft law instruments, that, as such may have a role in the formation of customary law (ILC, *Third Report on Identification of customary international law*, 27 March 2015, para. 45), have been adopted by UN organs. These actors all have acknowledged the disastrous effects of gender-based violence and the will and need for its elimination.

[101]Sometimes international practice has emphasized *opinio juris* over practice to establish a rule of customary law. This is particularly true for international criminal law, see ILC, *Second Report on identification of customary international law*, 22 May 2014, para. 28, wfr at fn. 48. For an overview on practice and scholarship, see ILC, *Second Report on identification of customary international law*, 22 May 2014; ILC, *Third Report on Identification of customary international law*, 27 March 2015. Some scholars have suggested different approaches that come down to favoring *opinio juris* over practice under certain circumstances, see Tomuschat, *Obligations arising for States without or against their will*, 1993, p. 303; Schachter, *International law in theory and practice*, 1991, pp. 334. It has also been suggested that 'the more destabilizing or more distasteful the activity (. . .,) the more readily international decision-makers will substitute one element by the other', Kirgis, 'Custom on a sliding scale', (1987) 81 *AJIL*, p. 149; this suggestion appears to refer to State actions. Arguing in favor of an emphasis of practice over *opinio juris*, see, e.g., Lepard, *Customary international law*, 2010 and Akehurst, 'The hierarchy of the sources of international law', (1976) 47 *BYIL*.

more precise positive obligations, even relating to a systemic prevention and reparation of gender-based violence as encompassed by CEDAW, the Istanbul and the Belém do Pará Conventions, have reached customary law status. For non-contracting parties and other actors, these instruments read in conjunction with the views issued by the CEDAW Committee and the UN Special Rapporteurs on Violence against Women may only 'provide a blueprint of recommended actions and strategies for governments'.[102]

[102]Chinkin, 'Addressing violence against women in the Commonwealth within states' obligations under international law', (2014) 40 *Commonwealth Law Bulletin*, p. 471.

Chapter 7
Secondary Obligations: Individual Reparation and Beyond

It has been shown in the foregoing chapters under which conditions States may have positive human rights obligations to actively take reasonable measures of protection and prevention. Certain human rights treaties even explicitly foresee primary obligations that require to address the root causes of gender-based violence, that are gender stereotypes, hierarchies and discrimination in all fields of life. Particularly, CEDAW establishes transformative obligations to improve the *de facto* position of women and to combat stereotypes and hierarchies. Measures aiming at complying with these obligations to fulfill are able to address structural discrimination. However, it is at the discretion of the State to choose the kind of measures to be taken, as long as the measures chosen serve the goal prescribed by the obligation. As State discretion is limited by the principle of proportionality, more precisely by the prohibition of insufficient action,[1] failure to take *any* measure is likely to establish a violation of positive duties.[2]

However, individuals need to have a standing to invoke primary obligations.[3] More generally, treaties allowing an individual to file a claim or communication against a contracting State require—as a rule—that this individual claims to be the victim of a violation of a right established under the respective treaty.[4] Whether the primary right claimed to be violated can be invoked by an individual depends on

[1]Chapter 5 B.

[2]But see additional factors potentially required to establish a violation (harm and causality), Chap. 5 C.

[3]For procedural aspects, see Stahl, *Schutzpflichten im Völkerrecht*, 2012, pp. 364.

[4]E.g., Art. 34 ECHR, Art. 2 OP-ICESCR, Art. 2 Optional Protocol-CEDAW. See in this chapter Section B II.

E. V. Henn, *International Human Rights Law and Structural Discrimination*, Beiträge zum ausländischen öffentlichen Recht und Völkerrecht,
https://doi.org/10.1007/978-3-662-58677-8_7

the respective provision and type of obligation allegedly violated.[5] On programmatic obligations (to fulfill human rights), a standing in this regard is unlikely. Hence, an individual is unable to claim a violation of primary obligations to address structural discrimination. It follows therefrom that, at first glance, such obligations are, if at all, only enforceable within the context of State reporting procedures and similar monitoring mechanisms, but not by individual claimants.

What thus needs to be explored is the transformative potential of secondary obligations. Conversely, the question arises whether an individual claim based on a violation of positive obligations can, in one way or another, trigger systemic change that combats structural discrimination.

Tellingly, the IACtHR and other international actors have ordered or called for *transformative reparation.*[6] Accordingly, reparation should include a society-transforming and rectifying element of change. This approach should not only be applied to the individual victim through the principle of non-discrimination, but also to the societal level when awarding reparation measures having a collective repercussion.

Against this backdrop, the question arises whether the idea of transformative reparation can indeed be meaningfully translated to existing concepts of secondary obligations under human rights law. *A priori*, as reparation measures need to be intrinsically linked with both the violation and the victim, and be proportionate to the harm caused by the specific violation, major obstacles appear to prevent such a transformative approach from being successful. There may, however, be other means such as the obligation to comply with a treaty that allow a complaint brought before an international human rights body or court to have a systemic impact. In fact, there is an increasing practice of international human rights bodies and courts to indicate or recommend general measures.[7]

As to their extensive practice and comparatively strong enforcement mechanisms, this chapter explores the approaches taken by the IACtHR and the ECtHR. It draws on the possibilities and limits of transformative reparation and other means that may have the potential to address the root causes of human rights obligations, structural discrimination and gender-based violence in particular.

[5]Applying the German theory of '*Drittschutz*', it can be said that this provision should not only protect individuals reflexively but must aim at providing protection for individuals, see Stahl, *Schutzpflichten im Völkerrecht*, 2012, pp. 365. Whether this is the case must be interpreted in light of objective criteria, the object and purpose of the treaty as well as the principle of effectiveness, Art. 31 (1) VCLT, Çali, 'Specialized Rules of Treaty Interpretation', in Hollis, 2014.

[6]IACtHR, *González v. Mexico (Cotton Field Case)*, Judgment (Preliminary Objection, Merits, Reparations, and Costs), 16 November 2009, para. 450. For further references, see in this chapter Section A.

[7]To give but some examples, UN Human Rights Committee, *General Comment No. 31*, 26 May 2004; CERD, *Dragan Durmic v. Serbia and Montenegro*, Communication No. 29/2003, 06 March 2006, para. 11; CEDAW, *Goekce v. Austria*, Communication No. 5/2005, 06 August 2007, para. 12.3; CEDAW, *Medvedeva v. Russian Federation*, Communication No. 60/2013, 25 February 2016, para. 13(b).

The chapter proceeds as follows: section A outlines the notion of reparation under human rights law and traces the development of the international plea for transformative reparation. Section B draws on the different concepts of victims as beneficiaries of reparative measures under international soft law, the ACHR and the ECHR. Focusing on the reparation and compensation practice of the ECtHR and the IACtHR, section C shows that the competence of both courts in awarding transformative reparation is somewhat limited, but less than one may generally expect.

A. Notion of Reparation

I. Notion of 'Reparation' in Human Rights Law

Under human rights law, the term 'reparation' is usually used in two contexts. At times, it is used to refer to the substantial aspect of the primary right to a remedy, at times, as hereinafter, it is used to refer to the legal consequences of human rights violations.[8]

Although the existence of the individual's secondary rights to reparation under customary international law is disputed and traditionally neglected,[9] State-created

[8]Quite often, however, many authors ignore the distinct nature of these two levels of obligations: e.g., Saris/Lofts, 'Reparation Programmes: A Gender Perspective', in Stephens/Ferstman/Goetz, 2009, p. 84; Evans, *The right to reparation in international law for victims of armed conflict*, 2012, pp. 33; Echeverria, 'Do victims of torture and other serious human rights violations have an independent and enforceable right to reparation?', (2012) 16 *The International Journal of Human Rights*, pp. 698. Article 2 (3) ICCPR appears to be an exception, providing both for primary and secondary obligations. In its General comment No. 31 (29 March 2004), the HRC stated: 'Article 2, paragraph 3, requires that state parties make reparation to individuals whose Covenant rights have been violated. Without reparation to individuals whose Covenant rights have been violated, the obligation to provide an effective remedy, which is central to the efficacy of article 2, paragraph 3, is not discharged. In addition to the explicit reparation required by articles 9, paragraph 5, and 14, paragraph 6, the Committee considers that the Covenant generally entails appropriate compensation. The Committee notes that, where appropriate, reparation can involve restitution, rehabilitation and measures of satisfaction, such as public apologies, public memorials, guarantees of non-repetition and changes in relevant laws and practices, as well as bringing to justice the perpetrators of human rights violations.' The Committee bases its recommendations to award reparation on this very same provision. For an overview of the HRC's practice, see Evans, *The right to reparation in international law for victims of armed conflict*, 2012, pp. 45; UN Human Rights Committee, *General Comment No. 31*, 26 May 2004, para. 16. See also Klein, 'Individual Reparation Claims under the International Convent of Civil and Political Rights', in Randelzhofer/Tomuschat, 1999; Tomuschat, 'La Protection Internationale des Droits des Victims', in Flauss, 2009, p. 12.

[9]But see, Evans, *The right to reparation in international law for victims of armed conflict*, 2012, pp. 39. She claims that the right to reparation has acquired a degree of recognition as forming part of customary law. For a comprehensive overview on that debate, see Echeverria, 'Do victims of torture and other serious human rights violations have an independent and enforceable right to reparation?', (2012) 16 *The International Journal of Human Rights*; Mazzeschi, 'Reparation Claims by

enforcement mechanisms entail[10] or presuppose[11] secondary obligations allowing the respective monitoring body to order different kinds of reparation measures to be awarded to victims. While the ECtHR has limited its orders of 'just satisfaction' under Article 41 ECHR to monetary compensation based on equity, the IACtHR has regularly ordered compensation as well as non-monetary reparation measures such as restitution and satisfaction. In cases of serious human rights violations, this Court has also ordered measures of rehabilitation and guarantees of non-repetition, which it has framed as reparation measures.[12]

II. International Plea for Transformative Reparation

As stated in the introduction of this chapter, some international actors have called for transformative reparation. Before analyzing the European and Inter-American practice of reparation, it is necessary to draw on the background and evolution of this call. As will be shown, the idea of transformative reparation first referred to the individual and then to the societal level. It is the second aspect which is interesting in the context of structural discrimination. However, from an international legal perspective, where State sovereignty is one of the core principles, reparation measures that aim at transforming the societal root causes sound, to say the least, surprising, because they are suspicious of interfering in the State's discretion.

It was within the context of administrative reparation programs carried out in post-conflict and transitional societies that the discriminatory effect of the preferred and long-standing form of reparation,[13] *restitutio in integrum,* was

---

Individuals for State Breaches of Humanitarian Law and Human Rights', (2003) 1 *J. Int'l Crim. Just;* Nowak, 'The Right of Victims of Gross Human Rights Violations to Reparation', in Boven/Coomans, 2000; Stephens/Ferstman/Goetz (eds.), *Reparations for victims of genocide, war crimes and crimes against humanity*, 2009.

[10]E.g., Art. 63 ACHR.

[11]E.g., Art. 41 ECHR. Although Article 41 ECHR is a jurisdictional norm applicable to the Court and not a substantive duty imposed on state parties, it assumed to presuppose a secondary right to reparation, see Peukert, 'Artikel 41', in Frowein/Peukert, 2009, para. 3; Ossenbühl/Cornils, *Staatshaftungsrecht*, 2013, p. 633.

[12]*Cf.* IACtHR, *Las Dos Erres Massacre v. Guatemala*, Judgment, 24 November 2009; see also Evans, *The right to reparation in international law for victims of armed conflict*, 2012, pp. 57, 66; Shelton, 'The jurisprudence of human rights tribunals on remedies for human rights violations', in Flauss, 2009; IACtHR, *Annual Report 2012*, 2012, pp. 17.

[13]Already in 1928, the PCIJ stated that 'reparation must, as far as possible, wipe out all the consequences of the illegal act and re-establish the situation which would, in all probability, have existed if that act had not been committed. Restitution in kind, or, if this is not possible, payment of a sum corresponding to this value which a restitution in kind would bear; the award, if need be, of damages for loss sustained which would not be covered by restitution in kind or payment in place of it—such are the principles which should serve to determine the amount of compensation due for an act contrary to international law.' PCIJ, *Factory of Chorzów (Germany v. Poland)*, Judgment,

criticized.[14] As it aims at returning the victim to where she was before the harmful event occurred, restitution is meaningful where property has been illegally sized, where children have been kidnapped from oppositionists or where liberty has been restricted by custody.[15] Yet, within the context of structural discrimination, setting back the victim in the situation she was in before can in itself be discriminatory,[16] if the 'goal is simply to put you back to a point where pervasive and systematic harms can once again be used as the non-harm standard'.[17] Therefore, it was claimed that reparation measures should transform the root causes of armed conflicts and not simply put the victims back in the situation they were in before the relevant conflict occurred.

This idea of transformative reparation has then been increasingly discussed in the context of judicial proceedings and been applied to non-conflict settings.[18] In the above analyzed case concerning the femicide of three women in Mexico (*Cotton field* case), the IACtHR held that

> the concept of "integral reparation" (restitutio in integrum) entails the re-establishment of the previous situation and the elimination of the effects produced by the violation, as well as the payment of compensation for the damage caused. However, bearing in mind the context of structural discrimination in which the facts of this case occurred, which was acknowledged by the State (...), the reparations must be designed to change this situation, so that their effect is not only of restitution, but also of rectification. In this regard, reestablishment of the same structural context of violence and discrimination is not acceptable.[19]

According to the Court, transformative reparation should therefore 'restore the victims to their situation prior to the violation insofar as possible to the extent that this does not interfere with the obligation not to discriminate'. They also should be 'designed to identify and eliminate the factors that cause discrimination'. Finally, the

---

13 September 1928, p. 47. *Cf.* also ICJ, *Legal Consequences of the Construction of a Wall in the Occupied Palestinian Territory*, Advisory Opinion, 09 July 2004, para. 152.

[14]For detail, see Gready/Robins, 'From Transitional to Transformative Justice', (2014) 8 *Int. J. Transit. Just.*

[15]*Cf.*, e.g., PCIJ, *Factory of Chorzów (Germany v. Poland)*, Judgment, 13 September 1928.

[16]Saris/Lofts, 'Reparation Programmes: A Gender Perspective', in Stephens/Ferstman/Goetz, 2009, p. 90, referring to an unpublished Conference paper of *Geneviève Painter* (Paris 2006); Rubio-Marin/Sandoval, 'Engendering the reparations jurisprudence of the Inter-American court of human rights', (2011) 33 *Hum. Rts. Q.*, p. 1070; Ní Aoláin/Haynes/Cahn, *On the Frontlines: Gender, War, and the Post-conflict Process*, 2011, pp. 187–191; Gready/Robins, 'From Transitional to Transformative Justice', (2014) 8 *Int. J. Transit. Just.*, p. 347. The first, though, who seems to have taken this approach, is *Suzanne Levitt*, see Levitt, 'Rethinking Harm', (1994) 34 *Washburn L.J.*, p. 358.

[17]Footnotes omitted, Levitt, 'Rethinking Harm', (1994) 34 *Washburn L.J.*, pp. 537–538.

[18]ICC, *Prosecutor v. Thomas Lubanga Dyilo*, Appeals Chamber, Judgment on the Appeals against the 'Decision establishing the principles and procedures to be applied to reparations' of 7 August 2012 with amended order for reparations (Annex A) and public annexes 1 and 2, 03 March 2015, Annex, para. 16, 17, 18, 34, 67.

[19]IACtHR, *González v. Mexico (Cotton Field Case)*, Judgment (Preliminary Objection, Merits, Reparations, and Costs), 16 November 2009, para. 450.

Court held that reparation orders should avoid to be gender biased, bearing in mind 'the different impact that violence has on men and women'.[20]

The idea was then taken up by the UN Special Rapporteur on violence against women, *Rashida Manjoo*, who held that

> [e]ven in non-conflict scenarios, acts of violence against women are part of a larger system of gender hierarchy that can only be fully grasped when seen in the broader structural context. [Reparation measures] should aspire, to the extent possible, to subvert, instead of reinforce, pre-existing structural inequality that may be at the root causes of the violence the women experience before, during and after the conflict.[21]

Moreover, as crosscutting patterns of discrimination (namely, structural discrimination) enable violence against women to occur, transformative measures of redress should be linked to the individual, institutional and structural level.[22]

Subsequently, the CEDAW Committee,[23] the Follow-Up Mechanism on the Implementation of the Convention of Belém do Pará (MESECVI)[24] and the UNSG took up the idea of giving reparation a transformative effect.[25] In his 2014 Guidance Note, the UNSG, too, referred to pre-existing inequalities and structures such as gender stereotypes of subordination, sexual entitlement, 'masculinity and constructions of gender and sexual identity around power and domination', to explain the need of a transformative approach.[26] Consequently, both administrative and judicial reparations should not 'reinstate or reinforce the structural conditions within society that uphold such practices and beliefs and that inform the perpetration of sexual violence'.[27]

---

[20]IACtHR, *González v. Mexico (Cotton Field Case)*, Judgment (Preliminary Objection, Merits, Reparations, and Costs), 16 November 2009, para. 451; see also CEDAW Committee, *General Recommendation No. 30 on women in conflict prevention, conflict, and post conflict situations*, 18 October 2013, para. 74.

[21]Emphasis added. UNHRC, *Report of the Special Rapporteur on violence against women, its causes and consequences, Rashida Manjoo*, 22 April 2010, para. 31.

[22]Rashida Manjoo in her speech at IAComHR, *Mesa Redonda: Violencia de género y reparaciones*, 27 October 2014, at minute 27:00, see also 17:20.

[23]In its General Recommendation No. 30, it held that '[r]ather than re-establishing the situation that existed before the violations of women's rights, reparation measures should seek to transform the structural inequalities which led to the violations of women's rights, respond to women's specific needs and prevent their re-occurrence'. CEDAW Committee, *General Recommendation No. 30 on women in conflict prevention, conflict, and post conflict situations*, 18 October 2013, paras 77, 79. The GR 30 refers to both judicial and administrative mechanisms providing for reparation in post-conflict settings.

[24]MESECVI, *Guide to the Application of the Inter-American Convention on the Prevention, Punishment, Eradication of Violence against Women*, 2014, p. 48, see also Chap. 5 A.

[25]UNSG, *Reparations for Conflict-Related Sexual Violence*, 01 August 2014. The Guidance Note 'aims to provide policy and operational guidance for United Nations engagement in the area of [judicial and administrative] reparations for victims of conflict-related sexual violence', see p.1.

[26]UNSG, *Reparations for Conflict-Related Sexual Violence*, 01 August 2014, pp. 1, 6.

[27]UNSG, *Reparations for Conflict-Related Sexual Violence*, 01 August 2014, p. 8.

Finally, when establishing principles of reparation to be applied by Trial Chambers in 2015, the ICC Appeals Chamber extended the idea of transforming gender injustice through reparation to other forms of structural discrimination and injustice. Accordingly, reparations

> need to address any underlying injustices and in their implementation the Court should avoid replicating discriminatory practices or structures that predated the commission of the crime. (. . .) [O]rdered modalities of reparations [therefore] include restitution, compensation and rehabilitation, as well as other types of reparations such as those with a symbolic, preventative or transformative value.[28]

Whereas it remains to be seen how these principles will be implemented in the ICC's practice, it is evident that an individual offender cannot be held responsible for structural reasons of gender-based violence that predated the commission of the crime for which he or she has been found guilty.[29]

B. Status of Victim

As seen, the idea of transformative reparation is no more a peripheral phenomenon. Regarding the individual level of the victim, it appears more than meaningful, even mandatory of the principle of non-discrimination. However, on reparation measures that aim at transforming the societal root causes concerns may arise. Clearly, from an international law perspective, no concerns arise where a State itself conceptualizes or controls the conceptualization of transformative reparation, which is typically the

---

[28]Emphasis added. ICC, *Prosecutor v. Thomas Lubanga Dyilo*, Appeals Chamber, Judgment on the Appeals against the 'Decision establishing the principles and procedures to be applied to reparations' of 7 August 2012 with amended order for reparations (Annex A) and public annexes 1 and 2, 03 March 2015, Annex A, paras 17, 18, 34, 67.

[29]*Cf.* also UNHRC, *Report of the Special Rapporteur on violence against women, its causes and consequences, Rashida Manjoo*, 22 April 2010, para. 36. As the ICC put it, '[r]eparation orders are intrinsically linked to the individual whose criminal liability is established in a conviction and whose culpability for the criminal acts is determined in a sentence' (ICC, *Prosecutor v. Thomas Lubanga Dyilo*, Appeals Chamber, Judgment on the Appeals against the 'Decision establishing the principles and procedures to be applied to reparations' of 7 August 2012 with amended order for reparations (Annex A) and public annexes 1 and 2, 03 March 2015, Annex A, para. 20). Consequently, the individual's responsibility for reparations must be proportional to the harm caused and to the participation in the crime. (ICC, *Prosecutor v. Thomas Lubanga Dyilo*, Appeals Chamber, Judgment on the Appeals against the 'Decision establishing the principles and procedures to be applied to reparations' of 7 August 2012 with amended order for reparations (Annex A) and public annexes 1 and 2, 03 March 2015, paras 118, 237.) The transformative potential will be limited to the individual level in so far as it can 'avoid replicating discriminatory practices'. (ICC, *Prosecutor v. Thomas Lubanga Dyilo*, Appeals Chamber, Judgment on the Appeals against the 'Decision establishing the principles and procedures to be applied to reparations' of 7 August 2012 with amended order for reparations (Annex A) and public annexes 1 and 2, 03 March 2015, Annex A, para. 17.) Yet, the limited financial resources notwithstanding, measures taken by the Trust Fund for Victims under Art. 79 ICC may have a transformative effect.

case within the context of transitional justice programs—where the idea has first been applied.[30] However, in proceedings before international courts, a judicial conceptualization of reparative measures that go beyond the specific case is suspicious of interfering in a State's sovereignty. Therefore, it is argued here, reparation measures owed by a State need to be intrinsically linked to the victim and the harmful event he or she has suffered. It follows therefrom that the transformative potential of reparations will necessarily be limited to the victim. As will be shown below, there are nonetheless pathways allowing for harmonizing the need for transformation with State sovereignty.

Before analyzing the reparation practice of the IACtHR and the ECtHR, we shall explore who is considered a victim under international human rights law. As most human rights provisions foreseeing the competence of an international court to order reparations remain silent as to the definition of 'victim',[31] international courts and quasi-judicial bodies have developed their own concept.[32] However, it appears that they have been influenced by two UN soft law instruments that—being based on domestic and international practice—provide for a definition of direct and indirect victims.[33] This section first outlines the approaches taken by these two soft law instruments (I.). It then focuses on the notions of victim applied by the IACtHR and the ECtHR. Thereby, it also considers the Courts' approaches taken on aspects related to the concept of victim, namely, the kinds of harm considered, the requirement of causality between the violation and the harm caused and, finally, the standard of proof as applied by the Courts (II.).[34]

I. Definition of Victim in International Soft Law

The *UN Declaration of Principles of Justice for Victims of Crimes and Abuse of Power* (hereafter Victims Declaration of 1985) was the first international instrument to provide a definition of 'victim'.[35] Adopted in 1985 by the UN General Assembly, it defines *direct victims* as

> persons who, individually or collectively, have suffered harm, including physical or mental injury, emotional suffering, economic loss or substantial impairment of their fundamental rights, through acts or omissions that are in violation of criminal laws (...), including those

[30]Walker, 'Transformative Reparations?', (2016) 10 *Int. J. Transit. Just. 108.*

[31]But see Art. 24 (1) of the Convention on disappearance (ICCPPED) which reads as follows: For the purposes of this Convention, 'victim' means the disappeared person and any individual who has suffered harm as the direct result of an enforced disappearance. (Emphasis added). See also below.

[32]E.g., CAT, *General Comment No. 3*, para. 3. For the ECtHR and the IACtHR see below.

[33]Contreras-Garduno/Fraser, 'The Identification of Victims before the Inter-American Court of Human Rights and the International Criminal Court and its Impact on Participation and Reparations', (2015) *Int. Am. & Eur. Hum. Rts. J.*, pp. 177.

[34]For a similar approach on the definition of victim before the ICC and the IACtHR, see ibid.

[35]Ibid., p. 176.

laws proscribing criminal abuse of power (or) that do not yet constitute violations of national criminal laws but of internationally recognized norms relating to human rights.[36]

Besides containing a definition of direct victims, the Victims Declaration also offers a definition of *indirect victims*. Accordingly, immediate family members or dependants of direct victims and persons who have suffered harm in intervening to assist victims in distress or to prevent harm may have a victim status.[37] Hence, direct victims suffer harm because of a violation of their own rights, whereas indirect victims suffer harm from violation of rights of direct victims. The Declaration's concept was picked up and specified by the 2006 Basic Principles and Guidelines on the Right to a Remedy and Reparation for Victims of Gross Violations of International Human Rights Law and Serious Violations of International Humanitarian Law (hereafter Basic Principles).[38]

II. Regional Concepts of Victim

It is central to the understandings of victim whether a person directly or indirectly suffered harm from the violation under review. The following considerations therefore focus on the concepts of direct and indirect victims as well as on the requirement of harm, causality and standard of proof as applied by the European and Inter-American Courts of human rights.

1. Concept of Victim According to the ECtHR

a. Direct and Indirect Victims

In the context of proceedings before the ECtHR, those who may be the beneficiaries of reparative measures ordered by the Court are necessarily the applicants, having a *ius standi*. Given that Article 34 ECHR restricts individual applications to the ECtHR to any 'person, non-governmental organization or group of individuals claiming to be

[36]UNGA Res. 40/34, *Declaration of Principles of Justice for Victims of Crimes and Abuses*, 29 November 1985, paras. 1 and 18.

[37]UNGA Res. 40/34, *Declaration of Principles of Justice for Victims of Crimes and Abuses*, 29 November 1985, para. 2.

[38]The Basic Principles are the result of more than 15 years of research and consultancy undertaken by the UN Commission of Human Rights and the special Rapporteurs *Theo van Boven* and *Mahmoud Cherif Bassiouni*. For details, see Boven, 'Victims Rights to a Remedy and Reparation', in Stephens/Ferstman/Goetz, 2009, pp. 28; Tomuschat, 'Reparation In Favour of Individual Victims of Gross Violations of Human Rights and International Humanitarian Law', in Kohen/Kohen/Caflisch, 2007.

the victim of a violation'[39] and given that Article 41 allows 'just satisfaction' to be ordered by the Court only in favor of the *injured party*,[40] that is, the victim(s),[41] those potentially eligible for reparative measures ordered by the Court are, in principle, limited from the very outset of the proceedings. Consequently, unlike the Inter-American system, the European human rights system does not allow for complaints lodged to defending other than the applicant's interests.[42]

The Court has in principle accepted both direct and indirect victims. As the Court put it, besides direct victims, persons 'to whom the violation would cause harm or who would have a valid and personal interest in seeing it brought to an end'[43] may introduce an application and eventually be eligible for just satisfaction.

A closer look at the jurisprudence shows though that the Court has a very restrictive concept of indirect victims.[44] It is the 'nature of the violation alleged and considerations of the effective implementation of (...) the most fundamental provisions in the Convention system' that has led the Court to accept indirect victims.[45] Apart from cases where the alleged violations were linked to the death or disappearance of the direct victim involving *substantive* violations of the rights to life, liberty and security and freedom of torture and ill-treatment under Articles 2, 3, 5 ECHR,[46] the Court has only exceptionally granted standing and satisfaction to persons who could demonstrate a moral or material interest of their own.[47]

One can, in principle,[48] distinguish two groups of indirect victims, namely, successors of direct victims (a) or close family members who have been violated

[39] Art. 34 reads as follows: 'The Court may receive applications from any person, non-governmental organisation or group of individuals claiming to be the victim of a violation by one of the High Contracting Parties of the rights set forth in the Convention or the protocols thereto. The High Contracting Parties undertake not to hinder in any way the effective exercise of this right.'

[40] Art. 41 reads as follows: 'If the Court finds that there has been a violation of the Convention or the protocols thereto, and if the internal law of the High Contracting Party concerned allows only partial reparation to be made, the Court shall, if necessary, afford just satisfaction to the injured party.

[41] The meaning of the terms 'victim' in Art. 34 and 'injured party' are identical, Peukert, 'Artikel 41', in Frowein/Peukert, 2009, p. 539 wfr.

[42] For a non-governmental organization to be able to introduce an application (and thus to be a victim), the Court requires 'a sufficiently direct link between the applicant and the damages which he or she claims to have sustained as a result of the alleged violation for an applicant to be able to claim that he or she is the victim of a violation (...).' ECtHR, *Stiching mothers of Srebrenica and others v. The Netherlands* (dec.), 13 June 2013, para. 114.

[43] ECtHR, *Vallianatos and Others v. Greece* [GC], Judgment (Merits and Just Satisfaction), 07 November 2013, para. 47.

[44] Council of Europe/ECtHR, *Practical Guide On Admissibility Criteria*, Third Edition, 2014, p. 14.

[45] ECtHR, *Fairfield v. the United Kingdom* (dec.), 08 March 2005, last para.

[46] E.g., ECtHR, *Varnava and Others v. Turkey* [GC], Judgment, 18 September 2009, paras 111-113.

[47] Council of Europe/ECtHR, *Practical Guide On Admissibility Criteria*, Third Edition, 2014, para. 22.

[48] These successor cases need to be distinguished from proceedings where the applicant deceased *during* the proceedings. In such cases, the Court may award compensation if close family members or the legal successor claim and prove to have suffered damages from the alleged violation. The

in their own rights because of death or disappearance of the direct victim (b).[49] The second group thus does not constitute indirect victims *stricto sensu*.

1) Heirs as Indirect Victims

Where the alleged direct victim had disappeared or died in circumstances giving rise to a violation of the right to life in its *substantive* dimension, the Court has granted standing and eventually awarded just satisfaction to heirs on behalf of the direct victim.[50] In this context, the Court has distinguished between moral and pecuniary damages.

Concerning *moral* damages for successors, the Court has awarded compensation to heirs on behalf of the victim if it has been proven that the direct victim was tortured or arbitrarily detained before being killed.[51]

As there must be a 'causal link between the damage claimed by the applicant and the violation' of a right guaranteed by the ECHR,[52] *pecuniary* damages such as loss of earnings or earning potential can only be claimed by successors on behalf of a direct victim where the respondent State violated the substantive aspect of the right to life.[53] Conversely, it must be proven that State agents killed the direct victim or failed to protect her before she died and that because of the death the applicant suffered harm. It follows therefrom that, in the absence of a causal link between the violation and the harm claimed, heirs are not accepted as indirect victims, where a violation of procedural rights occurred after a harmful event caused by third parties.

2) Close Family Members as Victims in Their Own Rights

In the context of disappearances and extrajudicial executions and death, close family members of direct victims may have access to reparative measures for damages because of a violation of *their own rights*.[54] As said, they thus do not constitute indirect victims *stricto sensu*.

Court has ordered respondent States to pay compensation where the proven violation caused an immaterial damage to the deceased (ECtHR, *Baragan v. Romania*, Judgment, 01 October 2002, para. 49) and where the violation prejudiced the inheritance causing a material damage or where it affected the family members/successors at least indirectly (ECtHR, *Colozza v. Italy*, Judgment (Merits and Just Satisfaction), 12 February 1985; see also Peukert, 'Artikel 41', in Frowein/Peukert, 2009, p. 539).

[49]Rubio-Marín/Sandoval-Villalba/Días, 'Repairing Family Members', in Rubio-Marín, 2009.

[50]Rubio-Marín/Sandoval-Villalba/Días, 'Repairing Family Members', in Rubio-Marín, 2009, p. 225; Council of Europe/ECtHR, *Practical Guide On Admissibility Criteria*, Third Edition, 2014, p. 14.

[51]Rubio-Marín/Sandoval-Villalba/Días, 'Repairing Family Members', in Rubio-Marín, 2009, p. 227.

[52]ECtHR, *Çakıcı v. Turkey* [GC], Judgment (Merits and Just Satisfaction), 08 July 1999, para. 127.

[53]ECtHR, *Çakıcı v. Turkey* [GC], Judgment (Merits and Just Satisfaction), 08 July 1999, para. 127.

[54]ECtHR, *Varnava and Others v. Turkey* [GC], Judgment, 18 September 2009, paras 224, 225; ECtHR, *Opuz v. Turkey*, Judgment, 09 June 2009, para. 210.

Close family members may claim compensation for having suffered moral damages through inhuman treatment (Article 3) because of the disappearance and/or death of their next of kin if the public authorities failed to react appropriately.[55] However, unlike the IACtHR,[56] the Court has rejected the 'emotional distress which may be regarded as inevitably caused to relatives of a victim of a serious human rights violation'[57] to be sufficient for family members to constitute victims in their own rights. Rather, the moral harm suffered must be distinct from that 'expectable' suffering.[58] Applicants who were not able to prove a violation of Article 3 were often found to be victims of a violation of the right to an effective remedy under Article 13 (in conjunction with the right to life) and were awarded compensation for moral damages.[59]

b. Harm, Causality and Standard of Proof

It is central to the understandings of victim whether a person directly or indirectly suffered harm from the violation under review. This section therefore draws on the requirements of harm and causality between the claimed damage and the alleged violation as applied by the ECtHR.

In general terms, the ECtHR hardly differentiates between direct, indirect and consequential damages. In light of the guiding principle of 'equity, which, above all, involves flexibility and an objective consideration of what is just, fair and reasonable in all the circumstances of the case',[60] any kind of material damages for loss of earnings (*damnun emergens*) and earnings potential (*lucrum cesans*), as well as non-pecuniary harm, are, in principle, liable for compensation.[61]

[55]ECtHR, *Varnava and Others v. Turkey* [GC], Judgment, 18 September 2009, para. 200.

[56]Pasqualucci, *The practice and procedure of the Inter-American Court of Human Rights*, 2013, p. 194.

[57]ECtHR, *Çakıcı v. Turkey* [GC], Judgment (Merits and Just Satisfaction), 08 July 1999, para. 98.

[58]In the *Çakıcı* case, the Court established further elements that need to be fulfilled for a family member to constitute a victim of inhuman treatment. Accordingly, relevant factors 'include the proximity of the family tie (. . .), the particular circumstances of the relationship, the extent to which the family member witnessed the events in question, the involvement of the family member in the attempts to obtain information about the disappeared person and the way in which the authorities responded to those enquiries'. ECtHR, *Çakıcı v. Turkey* [GC], Judgment (Merits and Just Satisfaction), 08 July 1999, para. 98.

[59]Rubio-Marín/Sandoval-Villalba/Días, 'Repairing Family Members', in Rubio-Marín, 2009, p. 232–237 wfr.

[60]ECtHR, *Al-Skeini and others v. the UK* [GC], Judgment, 07 July 2011, para. 182.

[61]Ossenbühl/Cornils, *Staatshaftungsrecht*, 2013, p. 647.

However, as 'regards pecuniary loss, there must be a causal nexus between the damage claimed and the violation of the Convention established'[62] unless the President of the competent chamber directs otherwise.[63]

When the Court finds serious violations which led to significant suffering, it may award a sum in non-pecuniary damages.[64] On 'real/lost opportunities'[65] and other non-pecuniary damages, the ECtHR has randomly applied a weaker standard of both causality and proof than it normally requires (namely 'beyond reasonable doubts').[66] While this uncertain practice is critical as it provides no legal certainty, it is not surprising that causality oftentimes carries no decisive weight concerning immaterial damages if the decision on satisfaction is based on equity.

2. Concept of Victim According to the IACtHR

Under the rules of procedure of the IACtHR, the victim does not need to be identical with the applicant, as others may have standing before the Court.[67] The ACHR provides no definition of those eligible for reparations. Article 63 (1) simply refers to the 'injured party'[68] which is identical to the term 'victim'.[69] As will be shown, in

[62]ECtHR, *O'Keeffe v. Ireland* [GC], Judgment, 28 January 2014, para. 201.

[63]*Cf.* Art. 60 (1) and (2) Rules of the Court which read as follows: '1. An applicant who wishes to obtain an award of just satisfaction under Article 41 of the Convention in the event of the Court finding a violation of his or her Convention rights must make a specific claim to that effect. 2. The applicant must submit itemized particulars of all claims, together with any relevant supporting documents, within the time-limit fixed for the submission of the applicant's observations on the merits unless the President of the Chamber directs otherwise.' See also Ugrekhelidze, 'Causation', in Caflisch/Wildhaber, 2007, p. 477.

[64]ECtHR, *El-Masri v. the Former Yugoslav Republic of Macedonia* [GC], Judgment, 13 December 2012, para. 269.

[65]Peukert, 'Artikel 41', in Frowein/Peukert, 2009, para. 9; Ossenbühl/Cornils, *Staatshaftungsrecht*, 2013, p. 649; Garin, 'La perte de chance, un préjudice indemnisable', in Flauss/Lambert-Abdelgawad, 2011.

[66]Ossenbühl/Cornils, *Staatshaftungsrecht*, 2013, pp. 649–654.

[67]The IACtHR developed specific procedures for the identification of victims and beneficiaries of reparations, see Úbeda de Torres, 'Determination of victims', in Burgorgue-Larsen/Úbeda de Torres/Greenstein, 2011, paras 5.20; Pasqualucci, *The practice and procedure of the Inter-American Court of Human Rights*, 2013, pp. 193.

[68]Art. 63 (1) ACHR reads as follows: 'If the Court finds that there has been a violation of a right or freedom protected by this Convention, the Court shall rule that the injured party be ensured the enjoyment of his right or freedom that was violated. It shall also rule, if appropriate, that the consequences of the measure or situation that constituted the breach of such right or freedom be remedied and that fair compensation be paid to the injured party.'

[69]Whereas the Court previously applied the terms 'victim' and 'injured party' to have diverging meanings (injured party being the broader term), it now considers them to be synonymous; Pasqualucci, *The practice and procedure of the Inter-American Court of Human Rights*, 2013, p. 193; Contreras-Garduno/Fraser, 'The Identification of Victims Before the Inter-American Court of Human Rights and the International Criminal Court and its Impact on Participation and

contrast to the ECtHR, the IACtHR has taken a very flexible approach to the concept of victim and applied a flexible standard of causation and proof regarding the harm caused from the violation.

a. Direct and Indirect Victims Before the IACtHR

Article 2 (33) of the IACtHR's Rules of Procedure of 2009 define 'victim' as a 'person whose rights have been violated, according to a judgment pronounced by the Court'.[70] In fact, this definition is narrower than the definition applied in the practice of the Court. Accordingly, the Court has held that 'under Article 63 (1) of the Convention, the injured party is considered to be the persons declared a victim of the violation of any right recognized in the Convention'.[71]

A direct victim can be resumed to be an 'individual against whom the illegal conduct of a State agent is directed immediately, explicitly and deliberately'.[72] The term 'individual' has a broader meaning, referring to natural persons,[73] as well as to groups of persons.[74]

Reparations', (2015) *Int. Am. & Eur. Hum. Rts. J.*, p. 177, Carrillo, 'Justice in Context', in Greiff, 2006, p. 514.

[70]For details see also Contreras-Garduno/Fraser, 'The Identification of Victims before the Inter-American Court of Human Rights and the International Criminal Court and its Impact on Participation and Reparations', (2015) *Int. Am. & Eur. Hum. Rts. J;* Pasqualucci, *The practice and procedure of the Inter-American Court of Human Rights*, 2013, pp. 193.

[71]IACtHR, *Véliz Franco et al. v. Guatemala*, Judgment (Preliminary Objections, Merits, Reparations and Costs), 19 May 2014, para. 246.

[72]IACtHR, *Ituango Massacres v. Columbia*, Judgment (Preliminary Objections, Merits, Reparations and Costs), 29 June 2006, Concurring Opinion of Judge S. García Ramírez, para. 11.

[73]*Cf.* Art. 1 (2) ACHR which makes clear that person means every human being.

[74]The IACtHR accepts the concept of victim groups that are composed of several, identified or identifiable victims listed by the Commission before and, exceptionally, during the proceedings (see Art. 35 (2) Rules of Procedure 2009). In contrast to what has been claimed or discussed (Burgorgue-Larsen, 'The Right to Determine Reparations', in Burgorgue-Larsen/Úbeda de Torres/Greenstein, 2011, paras. 10.08.), it seems that communities or even abstract groups are not considered by the Court as beneficiaries of reparation. Most of the cases concerning communities or abstract groups related to indigenous communities and mass crimes such as massacres or enforced disappearance. In Plan de Sanchez Massacre v. Guatemala, for instance, the Court ordered reparations to be made not only in favor of the village community the claimants were members of but also of various other Mayan Achí communities (IACtHR, *Plan de Sanchéz Massacre v. Guatemala (Reparations)*, Judgment (Reparations), 19 November 2004, paras 93, 110). The Court though made no reference to these communities as 'victims' *stricto sensu*. Rather, it claimed that the non-pecuniary damages needed to have public repercussions owing to the extreme gravity of the facts and, most importantly, to the collective nature of the damage caused to the Mayan Achí community. In Yakye Axa Indigenous Community v. Paraguay, the Court referred to the cultural ties and the social organization of the community to justify additional measures which were to be granted collectively. However, the Court explicitly rejected the Community itself to be a beneficiary of the reparation ordered and thus to be a victim. The IAComHR alleged that both the Yakye Axa Community and the listed victims, members of that community, should be entitled to reparations

When referring to 'indirect victim', the Court alludes to individuals who see their

> own rights [that is, interests] affected or violated, from the impact on the so-called direct victim. The damage suffered by the indirect victim is an effect of the damage suffered by the direct victim, but when the violation affects him, he becomes an injured party (...).[75]

In principle, indirect victims are close family members. However, applying an inclusive and flexible approach unbound by the definitions given by domestic family law, the Court has also considered the closeness of the relationship with the victim,[76] whether the person was involved in seeking justice against the abuse[77] and, where applicable, indigenous customary law.[78] In principle, harm must not be proven where parents, children, siblings, spouses or permanent partners, that is, indirect victims, allege to have suffered harm from the direct victim's suffering.[79]

Remarkably, as long as the direct victim is alive, it is only under exceptional circumstances that the Court has accepted family members to consider victims, too.[80] However, in *Fernández Ortega*, where military officials raped a woman at home in front of her children to receive information from her, the Court considered

---

and considered to be victims. While the Court agreed that the individuals of the community had to be considered from a collective and individual perspective (IACtHR, *Yakye Axa Indigenous Community v. Paraguay*, Judgment (Merits, Reparations and Costs), 17 June 2005, paras 185, 188), it adhered to an individualized concept of victim. In another case, where NGOs represented and gathered all the victims, some of them had not been identified (Úbeda de Torres, 'Determination of victims', in Burgorgue-Larsen/Úbeda de Torres/Greenstein, 2011, paras 5.08, 5.23), the Court ordered collective reparation to unidentified beneficiaries as 'members of the communities' (e.g. IACtHR, *The Mayagna (Sumo) Awas Tingni Community v. Nicaragua*, Judgment (Merits, Reparations and Costs), 31 August 2001, paras 164, where the Court constantly refers to the 'members of the community' who are neither listed nor identified in the judgment. In his separate opinion to this judgment, Judge Sergio Garcia-Ramirez argues in favor of collective rights and rightholdership, however he bases his argument on the importance of the collective in the indigenous culture, especially concerning property).

[75]IACtHR, *Ituango Massacres v. Columbia*, Judgment (Preliminary Objections, Merits, Reparations and Costs), 29 June 2006, Concurring Opinion of Judge S. García Ramírez, para. 11. On the development of the jurisprudence, see Sandoval-Villalba, 'The Concept of "Injured Party" and "Victim" of Gross Human Rights Violations in the Jurisprudence of the Inter-American Court of Human Rights', in Stephens/Ferstman/Goetz, 2009, p. 262.

[76]IACtHR, *Kawas Fernández v. Honduras*, Judgment (Merits, Reparations and Costs), 03 April 2009, para. 128.

[77]IACtHR, *Valle Jaramillo et al. v. Colombia*, Judgment (Merits, Reparations and Costs), 27 November 2008, para. 119.

[78]Contreras-Garduno/Fraser, 'The Identification of Victims Before the Inter-American Court of Human Rights and the International Criminal Court and its Impact on Participation and Reparations', (2015) *Int. Am. & Eur. Hum. Rts. J.*, p. 178.

[79]Burgorgue-Larsen, 'The Right to Determine Reparations', in Burgorgue-Larsen/Úbeda de Torres/Greenstein, 2011, para. 10.14; Pasqualucci, *The practice and procedure of the Inter-American Court of Human Rights*, 2013, p. 194.

[80]Pasqualucci, *The practice and procedure of the Inter-American Court of Human Rights*, 2013, p. 193.

her children as victims, although she survived the attack.[81] While it is not astonishing that her children were held to have been psychologically tortured when forced to watch their mother's rape, it was rather an exceptional move to consider her husband as victim, too, because he had not been at home when she had been raped. The Court (rightly) rejected his loss of reputation for not having been able to protect his wife 'appropriately' to be a considerable harm. The Court, however, acknowledged that he had suffered a violation of his personal integrity because of his fear and anguish experienced when seeking justice before domestic authorities.[82]

b. Harm, Causality and Standard of Proof

For a victim to be eligible for reparations before the IACtHR, she must have suffered harm from the violation which, in principle, unless presumed by the Court, needs to be proven by the potential beneficiary or the Commission.[83] In its case law, the Court has developed the concepts of both pecuniary and non-pecuniary damage.

According to the Court, the existence of pecuniary 'damage supposes the loss of or detriment to the income of the victims, the expenses incurred because of the facts, and the consequences of a pecuniary nature that have a causal nexus with the facts of the case'.[84] While the Court had first considered the victim's salary, it has later chosen to assess the damage based on equity and fairness.[85] Non-pecuniary damage includes 'both the suffering and affliction caused to the direct victim and next of kin, the harm to values that are very significant to the individual, as well as the alterations, of a non-pecuniary nature, in the living conditions of the victim or family'.[86] Finally, the Court has also accepted a new category of damage which affects the 'life project' of a victim.[87]

---

[81]IACtHR, *Fernández Ortega and others v. Mexico*, 30 August 2010, para. 224.

[82]IACtHR, *Fernández Ortega and others v. Mexico*, 30 August 2010, paras 144, 145-146.

[83]Pasqualucci, *The practice and procedure of the Inter-American Court of Human Rights*, 2013, p. 171.

[84]IACtHR, *Case of the Massacres of El Mozote and nearby places v. El Salvador*, Judgment (Merits, Reparations and Costs), 25 October 2012, para. 382 wfr.

[85]Burgorgue-Larsen, 'The Right to Determine Reparations', in Burgorgue-Larsen/Úbeda de Torres/Greenstein, 2011, para. 10.13 wfr.

[86]IACtHR, *Case of the Massacres of El Mozote and nearby places v. El Salvador*, Judgment (Merits, Reparations and Costs), 25 October 2012, para. 382; IACtHR, *Case of the 'Street Children' (Villagrán-Morales et al.) v. Guatemala*, Judgment (Reparations and Costs), 26 May 2001, para. 84; IACtHR, *Case of the Río Negro Massacres v. Guatemala*, Judgment (Preliminary Objection, Merits, Reparations, and Costs), 04 September 2012, para. 307.

[87]For details, see Burgorgue-Larsen, 'The Right to Determine Reparations', in Burgorgue-Larsen/Úbeda de Torres/Greenstein, 2011, paras 10.15; Pasqualucci, *The practice and procedure of the Inter-American Court of Human Rights*, 2013, pp. 245.

The Court requires a causal link between the facts of the case, the violation, the damage and the measures requested to repair the resulting damages.[88] While in earlier judgments the Court required a direct link,[89] it has also accepted consequential damages such as cancer.[90]

Furthermore, in the absence of procedural rules establishing a certain standard of proof, the Court has applied a flexible approach based on judicial discretion. The Court held that proceedings before international court are less formal[91]; they 'recognize different burdens of proof, depending upon the nature, character and seriousness of the case'.[92]

3. Conclusion

The concepts of direct and indirect victims are well established in the European and Inter-American human rights systems. Nonetheless, the concepts developed by the IACtHR and the ECtHR differ significantly. The reasons may partly be found in the social, political and legal contexts the courts are embedded. The Inter-American Court has usually been confronted with gross human rights violations that amounted to genocidal settings or general policies of disappearance particularly applied by oppressive military regimes. Its role may be described as to fulfilling a system-correcting function. The European Court, in turn, has taken a strictly individual approach to victims because of its procedural framework.

a. Direct and Indirect Victims

The ECtHR has taken a rigid and individualistic approach to the extent that, as compared to the IACtHR, one may claim that the Court largely rejects indirect victims. Only when a direct victim died during the event giving rise to a substantive violation has the ECtHR accepted heirs or close family members as indirect victims.

---

[88]E.g., IACtHR, *Ticona Estrada et al. v. Bolivia*, Judgment (Merits, Reparations and Costs), 27 November 2008, para. 110.

[89]IACtHR, *Aloeboetoe et al. v. Suriname*, Judgment (Reparations and Costs), 10 September 1993, para. 63.

[90]IACtHR, *Bulacio v. Argentina*, Judgment (Merits, Reparations and Costs), 18 September 2003, para. 99. Contreras-Garduno/Fraser, 'The Identification of Victims Before the Inter-American Court of Human Rights and the International Criminal Court and its Impact on Participation and Reparations', (2015) *Int. Am. & Eur. Hum. Rts. J.*, p. 195.

[91]IACtHR, *Velásquez-Rodriguez v. Honduras*, Judgment (Merits), 29 July 1988, paras 127, referring to ICJ, *Corfu Channel Case (UK v. Albania)*, Judgment (merits), 09 April 1949, p. 248 and ICJ, *Military and paramilitary activities in and against Nicaragua (Nicaragua v. United States of America)*, Judgment (merits), 27 June 1986, paras. 29-30, 59-60.

[92]IACtHR, *Velásquez-Rodriguez v. Honduras*, Judgment (Merits), 29 July 1988, paras 127; Pasqualucci, *The practice and procedure of the Inter-American Court of Human Rights*, 2013, p. 173.

Heirs as indirect victims only come into play where a State actively violates the obligation to respect or where preventive measures are omitted before the harmful event occurs. In contrast, procedural violations occurring after the victim's death cannot entail the obligation to pay compensation to heirs. However, in such cases, close family members may claim compensation as a violation in their own rights.

In contrast, the IACtHR applies an inclusive and flexible approach to indirect victims, being unbound by definitions given by domestic family law. It has considered *inter alia* the closeness of the relationship in each case, whether the person was involved in seeking justice against the abuse and indigenous customary law.[93] While this appears still to be an exception, the Court has accepted indirect victims even where the direct victim did not die.

b. Approaches Taken Regarding Harm, Causality and Standard of Proof

In principle, both the ECtHR and the IACtHR apply a broad notion of harm; they have accepted direct, indirect and consequential damages. It is the potential beneficiary who generally carries the burden of proof. To establish the status of victims and thus beneficiaries of reparation measures, the IACtHR has applied context-specific standards of both proof and causality between the violation and the harm caused that, accordingly, 'depend upon the circumstances of the specific case'.[94] Consequently, evidentiary weaknesses relating to harm suffered from sexualized crimes and State omissions related therewith may be overcome. In contrast, the ECtHR has applied a more rigid standard of causality and proof (beyond reasonable doubt) from which it has only deviated occasionally on non-pecuniary damages.

C. Practice of the IACtHR and the ECtHR: Individual Reparation and Beyond

Having analyzed the different concepts of the injured parties before the ECtHR and the IACtHR, we shall now consider the practice of the ECtHR and IACtHR to address the consequences of violations of primary human rights obligations. Because

---

[93] Úbeda de Torres, 'Determination of victims', in Burgorgue-Larsen/Úbeda de Torres/Greenstein, 2011, para. 5.13; Contreras-Garduno/Fraser, 'The Identification of Victims Before the Inter-American Court of Human Rights and the International Criminal Court and its Impact on Participation and Reparations', (2015) *Int. Am. & Eur. Hum. Rts. J.*, p. 178.

[94] ICC, *Prosecutor v. Thomas Lubanga Dyilo*, Appeals Chamber, Judgment on the Appeals against the 'Decision establishing the principles and procedures to be applied to reparations' of 7 August 2012 with amended order for reparations (Annex A) and public annexes 1 and 2, 03 March 2015, para. 81 and Annex A, para. 11. Such a standard has already been applied in the past when the circumstances inhibited a strict standard of proof, see Stephens/Ferstman/Goetz (eds.), *Reparations for victims of genocide, war crimes and crimes against humanity*, 2009, pp. 155.

of a State-centric understanding of the role of international courts, both courts have initially been reluctant on the award of reparation measures to a victim/the injured party or the indication of general measures to be taken by the respondent State. Declaratory judgments were considered the least intrusive remedy sufficient to satisfy the victim.[95] The only thing a State had to do was thus to openly admit the violation. Consequently, reparations were limited to a mere declaration of illegality. This judicial practice, however, has dramatically changed.

The following section draws on the legal possibilities and limits of an individual complaint brought before the Inter-American or the European Court of Human Rights to have a systemic impact which may transform structurally discriminatory settings. While the international discourse on transformative reparation[96] refers to both, the individual and the societal level, the following section particularly focuses on measures that aim at having a societal-transformative or at least systemic impact.

I. Practice of the IACtHR Under Article 63 (1) ACHR

1. A Broad Definition of Reparation

The IACtHR has taken a very far-reaching approach to reparations awarded to victims. Article 63 ACHR requires the Court to

> rule that the injured party be ensured the enjoyment of his right or freedom that was violated. It shall also rule, if appropriate, that the consequences of the measure or situation that constituted the breach of such right or freedom be remedied and that fair compensation be paid to the injured party.[97]

This provision has been interpreted by the Court as to incorporate 'the principle of international law that any violation of an international obligation which results in harm entails the obligation to make adequate reparation'.[98] The Court has repeatedly held that

> reparation of the damage flowing from a breach of an international obligation calls for, if practicable, full restitution (restitutio in integrum), which consists in restoring a previously-existing situation. If not feasible, the international court will then be required to define a set of measures such that, in addition to ensuring the enjoyment of the rights that were violated, the consequences of those breaches may be remedied and compensation provided for the damage thereby caused. In addition, there is also the State's obligation to adopt affirmative

[95]Shelton, *Remedies in international human rights law*, 2006, pp. 255; see also Pasqualucci, *The practice and procedure of the Inter-American Court of Human Rights*, 2013, pp. 228.

[96]Chapter 6 A.

[97]Emphasis added.

[98]*Cf.*, e.g., IACtHR, *González v. Mexico (Cotton Field Case)*, Judgment (Preliminary Objection, Merits, Reparations, and Costs), 16 November 2009, para. 446.

measures to guarantee that no injurious occurrences such as those analysed in the case at hand will take place in the future.[99]

Under the header of reparation, the Court has thus awarded measures of restitution, compensation for pecuniary and moral damages, satisfaction, rehabilitation and guarantees of non-repetition.[100]

Moreover, the Court has found that—at the secondary level—a State has the 'obligation to investigate the facts and identify, prosecute and punish'. The Court has argued that this obligation 'constitute[s] a part of the reparation of the consequences of the violations of rights and freedoms'.[101] As will be discussed later,[102] this obligation is nothing else but the obligation to cease the violation of the primary positive obligation.[103]

2. Transformative Potential of Non-monetary Measures Ordered in Gender-Based Violence Cases

As mentioned above, it was in the *Cotton Field case* concerning systemic gender-based violence and murder in a Mexican city that the IACtHR first referred to transformative reparations having a systemic repercussion. Ever since, other cases concerning gender-based violence followed. The following subsection focuses on reparation measures awarded in these judgments, including satisfaction (a.) and guarantees of non-repetition (b.) as non-monetary forms of reparation.

a. Satisfaction: Recognizing the Wrong Done by Gender-Based Violence

In the Court's practice, measures of satisfaction are aimed at repairing the non-pecuniary damage. They include, 'acts or objects of public scope or impact, such as acts to acknowledge responsibility, public apologies to the victims, and acts

---

[99]Footnotes omitted, IACtHR, *La Cantuta v. Peru*, Judgment (Merits, Reparations and Costs), 29 November 2006, at para. 201.

[100]Fortas, *La surveillance de l'exécution des arrêts et décisions des Cours européenne et interaméricaine des droits de l'Homme*, 2015, pp. 87; Pasqualucci, *The practice and procedure of the Inter-American Court of Human Rights*, 2013, pp. 188. *Cf.* also UNGA Res. 60/147, *Basic Principles and Guidelines on the Right to a Remedy and Reparation for Victims of Gross Violations of International Human Rights Law and Serious Violations of International Humanitarian Law*, 21 March 2006.

[101]IACtHR, *Velásquez-Rodríguez v. Honduras*, Judgment (Reparations and Costs), 21 July 1989, para. 33; IACtHR, *Las Dos Erres Massacre v. Guatemala*, Judgment, 24 November 2009, paras 229; Pasqualucci, *The practice and procedure of the Inter-American Court of Human Rights*, 2013, pp. 223; Fortas, *La surveillance de l'exécution des arrêts et décisions des Cours européenne et interaméricaine des droits de l'Homme*, 2015, pp. 92.

[102]Chapter 6 C III 1.

[103]For a critique of this secondary 'obligation to investigate the facts and identify, prosecute and punish', see in this chapter Section C III.

to commemorate the victims, with the aim of recovering the memory of the victims, recognizing their dignity and consoling their next of kin'.[104]

In the *Cotton Field* case, the IACtHR ordered the publication of its judgment by the respondent State (which the Court frequently does), the erection of a memorial to commemorate the women victims of gender-based violence in the city concerned, including the three victims of the case under review, and the State's public acknowledgment of its responsibility.[105] The Court was of the view that these measures were

> sufficient for the purposes of the satisfaction of the victims. Consequently, it [did] not find it necessary [as required by the victims' representative] to grant the request that November 6 each year should be commemorated as the "National Day in memory of the victims of femicide," even though a measure of this type can be discussed by the pertinent domestic bodies.[106]

Hence, while somewhat leaving a margin of appreciation as to the extent of satisfactory measures, the mandatory measures awarded have a strong focus on recognizing the wrong done to *all* victims of gender-based violence in the city of Juaréz. This is important, for recognition is intrinsically linked to equality. As *Nikolaidis* put it, '[r]ecognition of everyone's equal worth [and consequently of wrong done to this worth by denigrating practices] is often perceived as necessary in order to form one's identity unhindered by the demeaning behaviour of other people, thereby realising one's full potential'.[107] Symbolic forms of recognition can thus set the proper interpretative framework for other reparation measures.[108] The measures ordered by the Court may therefore contribute to the public recognition of women in Mexico and the dispraise of violence against them.

b. Guarantees of Non-repetition

According to the IACtHR's constant jurisprudence, guarantees of non-repetition aim at ensuring the

> non-recurrence of human rights violations such as those that occurred in the case examined by the Court. These guarantees are of public scope or impact and, in many cases, resolve structural problems, so that not only the victim in the case benefits but also other groups or

[104] IACtHR, *Annual Report 2012*, 2012, p. 18.

[105] IACtHR, *González v. Mexico (Cotton Field Case)*, Judgment (Preliminary Objection, Merits, Reparations, and Costs), 16 November 2009, paras 468-471.

[106] IACtHR, *González v. Mexico (Cotton Field Case)*, Judgment (Preliminary Objection, Merits, Reparations, and Costs), 16 November 2009, paras 471.

[107] Nikolaidis, *The right to equality in European human rights law*, 2015, p. 13. *Cf.* also Fraser, 'From redistribution to recognition? Dilemmas of justice in a "post-socialist" age', (1995) *NLR*; Young, 'Unruly categories', (1997) *NLR;* Fraser/Honneth/Golb, *Redistribution or recognition?*, 2003.

[108] Rubio-Marín, 'Reparations for Conflict-Related Sexual and Reproductive Violence', (2012) 19 *William & Mary Journal of Women and the Law*, pp. 94.

> members of society. The guarantees of non-repetition can be divided into three groups, according to their nature and purpose, namely: (a) measures to adapt domestic law to the parameters of the Convention; (b) human rights training for public officials, and (c) adoption of other measures to guarantee the non-repetition of violations.[109]

Along these lines, in the *Cotton Field case*, the Court ordered to Mexico to take a series of guarantees of non-repetition relating to the effective investigation of gender-based crimes and disappearance in general.[110] These measures largely correspond to what has been characterized above as 'short-term prevention measures'. They mainly include the harmonization of its investigation tools with international standards,[111] but also the education of public officials. More precisely, Mexico was ordered to provide

> permanent education and training programs and courses in:
>
> (i) human rights and gender;
> (ii) a gender perspective for due diligence in conducting preliminary investigations and judicial proceedings in relation to the discrimination, abuse and murder of women based on their gender, and
> (iii) elimination of stereotypes of women's role in society.[112]

These courses should be given to public officials and, in view of the situation of discrimination against women, be offered to the general public.[113] While eliminating stereotyped ideas concerning women is only half the way and might be less effective if stereotyped ideas about male (sexual) entitlement, power and performance prevail, the last aspect (iii) is clearly an attempt to point towards long-term prevention.[114]

On more far-reaching measures, a procedural obstacle prevented the Court from examining whether they would be appropriate to be ordered. The Commission and the victims' representatives had required an integral, coordinated and long-term policy to ensure that cases of violence against women are prevented. While such a request being framed as a guarantee of non-repetition is, in principle, admissible within the Inter-American human rights system, neither the Commission nor the

[109] IACtHR, IACtHR, *Annual Report 2012*, 2012, p. 18.

[110] For an analysis, see also Rubio-Marin/Sandoval, 'Engendering the reparations jurisprudence of the Inter-American court of human rights: The promise of the cotton field judgment', (2011) 33 HRQ, pp. 1087.

[111] IACtHR, *González v. Mexico (Cotton Field Case)*, Judgment (Preliminary Objection, Merits, Reparations, and Costs), 16 November 2009, para. 502.

[112] IACtHR, *González v. Mexico (Cotton Field Case)*, Judgment (Preliminary Objection, Merits, Reparations, and Costs), 16 November 2009, para. 541.

[113] The Court recalled that 'under Article 34 (1) of the Rules of Procedure [RoP], the Commission must indicate its claims for reparations and costs in the application, together with the justification and the pertinent conclusions. This obligation to provide the rationale and the justification is not fulfilled by general requests with no factual or legal arguments or evidence that would allow the Tribunal to examine their purpose, reasonableness and scope'. IACtHR, *González v. Mexico (Cotton Field Case)*, Judgment (Preliminary Objection, Merits, Reparations, and Costs), 16 November 2009, para. 543.

[114] On long-term measures of prevention under CEDAW, see Chap. 6 A II.

representatives complied with their procedural obligation to substantiate their request. The Court held that they should have 'provided sufficient arguments on practical problems encountered with the actions implemented by the State to date, or clarified why the series of measures adopted by the State cannot be considered an "integral, coordinated policy"'.[115]

The Court however established a general standard which may function both as a recommendation to a State on how its policies should be conceptualized and as an indication to the Commission and victim representatives in future cases on how to proceed to succeed regarding guarantees of non-repetition that have a transformative effect at the societal level. The Court held that it

> does not have result indicators in relation to how the policies implemented by the State could constitute reparations with a gender perspective to the extent that they:
>
> (i) question and, by means of special measures, are able to modify, the status quo that causes and maintains violence against women and gender-based murders;
> (ii) have clearly led to progress in overcoming the unjustified legal, political, social, formal and factual inequalities that cause, promote or reproduce the factors of gender-based discrimination, and
> (iii) raise the awareness of public officials and society on the impact of the issue of discrimination against women in the public and private spheres.[116]

In a subsequent case concerning gender-based violence, *Véliz Franco et al. v. Guatemala*, the Court again referred to the lack of information to explain why it did not order the 'adoption of integrated public policies and institutional programs aimed at eliminating discriminatory stereotypes regarding the role of women and promoting the eradication of discriminatory socio-cultural patterns that prevent their full access to justice'.[117]

---

[115] IACtHR, *González v. Mexico (Cotton Field Case)*, Judgment (Preliminary Objection, Merits, Reparations, and Costs), 16 November 2009, paras 493. For a critique of such an approach, see Rubio-Marin/Sandoval, Engendering the reparations jurisprudence of the Inter-American court of human rights: The promise of the cotton field judgment, (2011) 33 HRQ, pp. 1088.

[116] Ibid, para. 495.

[117] E.g., IACtHR, *Véliz Franco et al. v. Guatemala*, Judgment (Preliminary Objections, Merits, Reparations and Costs), 19 May 2014, paras 265, 275-277. The Commission and representative in particular had required such measures. The Court ordered 'the implementation of education and training programs for State officials, the Court establishes that the State must, within a reasonable time, implement programs and courses for public officials who are members of the Judiciary, the Public Prosecution Service, and the National Civil Police, and who are involved in the investigation of the murder of women, on standards with regard to prevention, and the eventual punishment and eradication of the murder of women, and provide them with training on the proper application of the relevant laws and regulations'. However, 'with regard to the other measures of reparation that have been requested, the Court consider[ed] that the measures granted are sufficient; accordingly it does not find it necessary to order the adoption of other measures. In relation to the Commission's request that the State be ordered "[t]o introduce reforms in the State's education programs, starting with the early, formative years, so as to promote respect for women as equals, and observance of their rights to non-violence and non-discrimination" and to "take measures and launch campaigns designed to make the general public aware of the duty to respect and ensure the human rights of children," it has not been demonstrated to the Court that the obligation to respect and ensure the human rights of

However, in *Velásquez Paiz et al. v. Guatemala*, a case concerning gender-based violence and State failure to effectively investigate such crimes, the Court ordered the respondent State to incorporate a permanent education program in its national education system, at all levels of education, on the need to eliminate discrimination against women, gender stereotyping and violence against women.[118] Although this measure is limited to the education sector, and does not promote the *de facto* position of women more generally, it partly addresses the three layers of the 'iceberg model', namely, stereotypes, discrimination and violence.

Having in mind the 'iceberg model' and long-term measures required to combat the root causes of gender-based violence,[119] it thus can be concluded that through its measures of non-repetition, the Court applies, in fact, a transformative approach which addresses the root causes, leaving to the State a certain margin of discretion as to the exact framing of such programs.

II. Practice Within the European Human Rights System: Individual Compensation and Beyond

1. Limited Competence Under Article 41 ECHR

According to Article 41 ECHR, if the ECtHR finds 'that there has been a violation of the Convention or the Protocols thereto, and if the internal law of the High Contracting Party concerned allows only partial reparation to be made', it shall, if

---

women and children cannot be guaranteed by the continuation of the existing programs and the diffusion of measures that, as indicated by the State, are already included among its activities. Moreover, the Court does not find it pertinent to order such measures for the reasons stated previously.'

[118]IACtHR, *Velásquez Paiz et al. v. Guatemala*, Judgment (Preliminary Objections, Merits, Reparations and Costs), 19 November 2015, it held (only available in Spanish): '248. Si bien Guatemala ha indicado que ya cuenta con programas educativos dirigidos a promover el respeto de los derechos de las mujeres, la Corte nota que, de los programas descritos por Guatemala, solo uno estaría dirigido a la prevención de la violencia contra la mujer: la "estrategia" de "Prevención de la Violencia" presuntamente realizado por las Direcciones Generales y Departamentales con apoyo y acompañamiento de la Unidad de Equidad de Género con Pertinencia Étnica adscrita a la Dirección de Planificación Educativa. Sin embargo, el Estado no proporcionó información alguna respecto del contenido, alcance o implementación de dicha "estrategia". En consecuencia, teniendo en cuenta la situación de discriminación y violencia en contra de la mujer constatada, **la Corte ordena al Estado, en un plazo razonable, incorporar al currículo del Sistema Educativo Nacional, en todos los niveles educativos, un programa de educación permanente sobre la necesidad de erradicar la discriminación de género, los estereotipos de género y la violencia contra la mujer en Guatemala, a la luz de la normativa internacional en la materia y la jurisprudencia de este Tribunal.** A tal efecto, el Estado deberá presentar un informe anual por tres años, en el que indique las acciones que se han realizado para tal fin. La Corte no considera necesario ordenar, adicionalmente, la cátedra sobre derechos de las mujeres solicitada por los representantes.'

[119]See Chaps. 2 B IV and 6 B II.

necessary, afford to the injured party just satisfaction for moral and pecuniary damages. Since 1972, the Court has increasingly made use of this competence.[120]

Nonetheless, the Court has repeatedly recalled

> that it is not its role under Article 41 to function akin to a domestic tort mechanism court in apportioning fault and compensatory damages between civil parties. Its guiding principle is equity, which above all involves flexibility and an objective consideration of what is just, fair and reasonable in all the circumstances of the case, including not only the position of the applicant but the overall context in which the breach occurred. Its non-pecuniary awards serve to give recognition to the fact that moral damage occurred as a result of a breach of a fundamental human right and reflect in the broadest of terms the severity of the damage (. . .).[121]

While Article 41 presupposes an individual right to reparation,[122] the limited mandate given to the Court entails that it is unable to take a transformative approach to secondary obligations owed to the individual victim. At most, when assessing in light of equity loss of income, the Court may calculate the amount in light of the principle of non-discrimination by considering loss of non-paid work capacity, such as household chores, child rearing and caretaking of other dependent members of the family.

2. The Practice Under Article 46 ECHR

In contrast to the IACtHR, the ECtHR does not order other measures than compensation to be taken by the respondent State. However, according to Article 46 (1), where the ECtHR finds a violation of the Convention, the respondent State is obliged to abide by the final judgment of the Court. This provision has been interpreted by the Court to imply a threefold obligation on the respondent State, namely, to cease the violation, make reparation and to guarantee compliance in the future.[123] Thus, the execution of the judgment may necessitate the adoption of further measures which, in principle, are at the respondent State's discretion. However, Article 46 ECHR allows for both the ECtHR and the Committee of Ministers of the Council of Europe to play a crucial role in the adoption by the respondent State of further

[120]*Cf.* the leading case *ECtHR, De Wilde, Ooms and Versyp (Vagrancy) v. Belgium, Judgment (Art. 50), 10 March 1972.*

[121]E.g., ECtHR, *Al-Skeini and others v. the UK* [GC], Judgment, 07 July 2011, para. 182. For details, see Harris et al., 'The European Court of Human Rights: Organization, Practice, and Procedure', in Harris et al., 2014, pp.155; Ossenbühl/Cornils, *Staatshaftungsrecht*, 2013, pp. 630; Peukert, 'Artikel 41', in Frowein/Peukert, 2009.

[122]Ossenbühl/Cornils, *Staatshaftungsrecht*, 2013, pp. 633, 637 wfr; Peukert, 'Artikel 41', in Frowein/Peukert, 2009, p. 540.

[123]Keller/Marti, 'Reconceptualizing Implementation', (2015) 26 *EJIL*, p. 832; ECtHR, *Papamichalopoulos et al. v. Greece*, Judgment (Art. 50), 31 October 1995, para. 34; Fortas, *La surveillance de l'exécution des arrêts et décisions des Cours européenne et interaméricaine des droits de l'Homme*, 2015, pp. 77.

measures which, while being independent from the individual victim, allow for systemic change.

a. Supervision of the Execution and Implementation of Judgments by the Committee of Ministers

In principle, respondent States 'have freedom of choice as regards the means to be employed in order to meet their obligations under the ECHR'.[124] However, according to Article 46 (2), the execution and implementation of judgments is subject to supervision by the Committee of Ministers.[125] While this organ of the Council of Europe is primarily a political one, the supervision procedure is increasingly judicialized.[126]

When supervising the execution of a judgment, the Committee of Ministers examines whether compensation has been paid and, most importantly, whether 'individual measures have been taken to ensure that the violation has ceased and that the injured party is put, as far as possible, in the same situation as that party enjoyed prior to the violation of the Convention' (*restitutio in integrum*) and whether 'general measures have been adopted, preventing new violations similar to that or those found or putting an end to continuing violations'.[127] Thus, general measures include guarantees of non-repetition aiming at preventing similar violations in future and cessation of continuing violations.[128] Such general measures can consist of *inter*

[124] Article 46 (2) reads as follows: 'The final judgment of the Court shall be transmitted to the Committee of Ministers, which shall supervise its execution.' Council of Europe, Committee of Ministers, *Supervision of the Execution of Judgments, 3rd Annual report, 2009*, April 2010, p. 19, para. 19.

[125] Harris et al., 'The European Court of Human Rights: Organization, Practice, and Procedure', in Harris et al., 2014, pp. 164. E.g., ECtHR, *Gülay Çetin c. Turquie*, Judgment, 05 March 2013, at para. 143. The judgment reads as follows: L' Etat 'reste libre cependant, sous le contrôle du Comité des Ministres, de choisir les moyens de s'acquitter de son obligation juridique au regard de l'article 46 de la Convention pour autant que ces moyens soient compatibles avec les conclusions contenues dans l'arrêt de la Cour'. See also Keller/Marti, 'Reconceptualizing Implementation', (2015) 26 *EJIL*, pp. 834.

[126] For details, see Keller/Marti, 'Reconceptualizing Implementation', (2015) 26 *EJIL*, pp. 831; Fortas, *La surveillance de l'exécution des arrêts et décisions des Cours européenne et interaméricaine des droits de l'Homme*, 2015, pp. 185.

[127] Art. 6 (2) b Rules of the Committee of Ministers for the supervision of the execution of judgments and of the terms of friendly settlements (adopted by the Committee of Ministers on 10 May 2006 at the 964th meeting of the Ministers' Deputies and amended on 18 January 2017 at the 1275th meeting of the Ministers' Deputies).

[128] Fortas, *La surveillance de l'exécution des arrêts et décisions des Cours européenne et interaméricaine des droits de l'Homme*, 2015, pp. 77.

alia legislative reforms, the modification of an administrative or judicial practice or even constitutional amendments.[129]

The supervision of the execution of judgments entails a particular potential for systemic change where the Court finds the respondent State's practice to come up to indirect discrimination against specific groups.[130] For example, within the context of the still pending enhanced supervision of the execution of the *Opuz* case group *v. Turkey*, relating to authorities' failure to provide for protection against domestic violence, the respondent State has already taken a series of measures that can mainly be characterized as short-term measures[131]: Turkey has adapted its legislation in line with the Istanbul Convention, vesting 'administrative and judicial authorities, as well as law enforcement officials in urgent cases, the power to take preventive/protective measures'; it has increased the number of women guest houses and provided capacity building programs and awareness-raising measures. It has also ratified the Istanbul Convention.[132] However, in the Committee's view, the continuous generalized and discriminatory pattern of judicial passivity in response to domestic violence and impunity enjoyed by aggressors as found by the Court[133] indicate that there had been insufficient commitment to taking appropriate action to combat domestic violence. In the opinion of the Committee, further measures have thus to be taken.[134]

---

[129]Ibid, pp. 78.

[130]On the execution procedure of DH v. Czech Republic, where the Court had established an indirect discrimination of Roma children in the educative system of the respondent state, see Smekal/Sipulova, 'DH v. Czech Republic Six Years Later', (2014) 32 *Neth. Q. Hum. Rts*, pp. 288.

[131]On short-term and long-term measures under CEDAW and Istanbul Convention, see Chap. 6 A.

[132]Council of Europe, HUDOC EXCE, Opuz case group, <http://hudoc.exec.coe.int/eng#{%22fulltext%22:[%22opuz%22],%22EXECDocumentTypeCollection%22:[%22CEC%22],%22EXECIdentifier%22:[%22004-37222%22]}>, accessed 29 March 2017. Accordingly, while not being sufficient, these measures have already shown an impact: 'The number of protective/preventive measures applied between 2012 and 2016 increased from 5303 to 14,332 for protective measures and from 175,290 to 302,831 for preventive measures. Likewise the number of women supported by the Violence Protection and Monitoring Centres increased from 14,853 to 31,298 between 2013 and 2016. There are 137 guesthouses for 3443 persons. "Research on Domestic Violence against Women in Turkey" was published in December 2014. The report compares the percentage of women in Turkey subjected to domestic violence in 2008 and 2014 and indicates that physical violence inflicted by partners fell from 39% to 36%; sexual violence from 15% to 12%; both physical and sexual violence from 41.9% to 38%; physical violence in cities from 38% to 35% and in rural areas from 43% to 37.5%; physical violence inflicted by people other than spouses from 17.8% to 14%. The rate of women who remained silent about the violence to which they were subjected decreased from 48.5% to 44% whereas the rate of women who sought official help increased from 8% to 11%.'

[133]ECtHR, *Opuz v. Turkey*, Judgment, 09 June 2009, paras 198.

[134]Council of Europe, HUDOC EXCE, Opuz case group, <http://hudoc.exec.coe.int/eng#{%22fulltext%22:[%22opuz%22],%22EXECDocumentTypeCollection%22:[%22CEC%22],%22EXECIdentifier%22:[%22004-37222%22]}>, accessed 29 March 2017.

b. Practice of the Court to Indicate Measures and to Initiate Pilot Judgment Procedures

While the majority of judgments remain silent as to the nature and scope of measures to be taken by the respondent State, the Court has exceptionally provided guidance on specific execution measures, either within the context of pilot-judgment procedures, or to put an end to a systemic problem or to discontinue a continuous situation.

It was in *Papamichalopoulos v. Greece* that the Court first considered that 'a judgment in which the Court finds a breach imposes on the respondent State a legal obligation to put an end to the breach', that is, to cease the violation.[135] Ever since, and in view of the general obligation of contracting parties to ensure that their acts conform to the Convention (*pacta sunt servanda*), the Court has, in certain circumstances,[136] indicated either in the operative part of the judgment or in the section of the judgment dealing with Article 46 (1) measures to be taken by the respondent State.[137]

Since 2004, the Court has also indicated specific measures to be taken by respondent States, where a systemic problem had been revealed by a number of repetitive cases brought against them.[138] Within the context of these so-called pilot procedures, the Court gives priority treatment to one or more of these repetitive cases, while the other cases are adjourned. The Court then not only decides whether a violation occurred in the pilot case, but also identifies the root cause of the systemic problem. It then indicates to the State concerned which type of measure is needed to resolve all cases.[139] While most of the pilot judgment procedures were so far concerned with property rights, the non-enforcement of domestic decisions,

[135]ECtHR, *Papamichalopoulos et al. v. Greece*, Judgment (Art. 50), 31 October 1995, para. 34; Fortas, *La surveillance de l'exécution des arrêts et décisions des Cours européenne et interaméricaine des droits de l'Homme*, 2015, pp. 77.

[136]In ECtHR, *Khodorkovskiy v. Russia*, Judgment, 31 May 2011, para. 270, the Court held that it 'will seek to indicate the type of measure that might be taken only exceptionally, for example to put an end to a systemic problem, as in Broniowski v. Poland (. . .), or to discontinue a continuous situation, as in Hasan and Eylem Zengin v. Turkey (. . .). In other exceptional cases, the nature of the violation found may be such as to leave no real choice as to the measures required to remedy it and the Court may decide to indicate only one such measure (. . .). Finally, in some situations the Court indicated to the respondent Government how to remedy a violation found in the applicant's case, for example, by way of reopening of the proceedings which had been fundamentally unfair (. . .), or by transferring the applicant's pension rights to a specific pension fund (. . .).'

[137]Fortas, *La surveillance de l'exécution des arrêts et décisions des Cours européenne et interaméricaine des droits de l'Homme*, 2015, pp. 70.

[138]The pilot judgment procedure was first suggested by the Court as a consequence of its increasing caseload of 'clone cases' that 'originated in a systemic problem connected with the malfunctioning of domestic legislation and practice', see ECtHR, ECtHR, *Broniowski v. Poland* [GC], Judgment, 22 June 2004, operative part, point 3, see also in the reasons given for the judgment, paras 188.

[139]Art. 61 Rules of Court, ECHR (1 June, 2015), available at www.echr.coe.int/Documents/Rules_Court_ENG.pdf accessed 22 February 2016. The procedure was generally accepted at the High Level Conference on the Future of the European Court of Human Rights, 'Brighton Declaration', (19 April 2012), http://www.echr.coe.int/Documents/2012_Brighton_FinalDeclaration_ENG.pdf.

inhuman conditions of detention and the excessive length of domestic proceedings,[140] it is—in principle—conceivable that such a procedure may also be initiated where a number of repetitive cases reveals systemic authorities' failure to provide for protection against gender-based violence.

III. Comparing the Approaches of the IACtHR and the ECtHR

As has been shown, the Inter-American and European Courts differ as to their theoretical, procedural and textual approaches taken towards reparation and other legal consequences of a violation of primary obligations. As has already been said, the different approaches taken may be because of the distinct social and political contexts in which the two Courts are embedded. At any rate, both approaches bear the potential to address systemic failure and root causes. However, on structural discrimination of specific social groups, in particular women, both human rights systems only provide for a limited set of solutions. According to the above-suggested taxonomy of short-term and long-term measures,[141] guarantees of non-repetition, ordered by the IACtHR or taken by respondent States under the supervision of the Committee of Ministers, largely encompass short-term measures only. However, regarding the Inter-American jurisprudence, there is a certain tendency towards ordering long-term measures that address the root causes of gender-based violence.

1. Differences Regarding Their Theoretical and Procedural Approaches

Article 63 ACHR enables the Court to 'rule that the injured party be ensured the enjoyment of his right or freedom that was violated' and to 'rule, if appropriate, that the consequences of the measure or situation that constituted the breach of such right or freedom be remedied and that fair compensation be paid to *the injured party*'.[142] In the Court's understanding, reparation measures under Article 63 encompass not only restitution, compensation, satisfaction and rehabilitation but also guarantees of non-repetition and cessation. Moreover, the Court has established 'that reparations should have a causal nexus to the facts of the case, the violations declared, the harm proved, and the measures requested to repair the respective harm'.[143]

---

[140] Leach et al., *Responding to Systemic Human Rights Violations*, 2010, p. 177; Harris et al., 'The European Court of Human Rights: Organization, Practice, and Procedure', in Harris et al., 2014, pp. 164, 149; Garlicki, 'Broniowski and after', in Caflisch/Wildhaber, 2007; Schutter, *International human rights law*, 2014, pp. 993.

[141] Chapter 5 A.

[142] Emphasis added.

[143] Cf. IACtHR, *Ticona Estrada et al. v. Bolivia*, Judgment (Merits, Reparations and Costs), 27 November 2008, para. 110 and IACtHR, *Liakat Ali Alibux v. Suriname*, Judgment (Preliminary Objections, Merits, Reparations and Costs), 30 January 2014, para. 139.

From a theoretical viewpoint, the Court's classification of guarantees of non-repetition and cessation as reparation is questionable. In fact, the Inter-American Court's approach to characterize guarantees of non-repetition and the 'obligation to investigate the facts and identify, prosecute and punish' as forms of reparation is misleading because guarantees of non-repetition and cessation[144] are best qualified as to belong to the obligation to comply with a treaty which is owed to the contracting parties.

As the former President of the IAComHR, *Dinah Shelton*, put it, cessation

> is not part of reparation, but is part of the general obligation to conform to the norms of international law. In the case of a treaty, it is inherent in the notion of pacta sunt servanda. To include cessation within the notion of reparation seems to imply that in the absence of a victim there is no duty of cessation. It undermines the rule of law which is the basis of the obligation to cease any conduct that is not in conformity with an international duty.[145]

The same is true for guarantees of non-repetition, because 'the continuation in force of the underlying obligation is a necessary assumption of both [cessation and guarantees of non-repetition], since if the obligation has ceased following its breach, the question of cessation does not arise and no assurances and guarantees can be relevant'.[146] Cessation and guarantees of non-repetition are therefore better situated in between the primary and secondary level of obligations.[147] Ultimately, cessation and guarantees of non-repetition are not linked to the individual claimant as an individual right at the secondary level, but rather to the obligations to comply with the Convention which is owed to all state parties. Moreover, the wording of Article 63 enables the court to rule on remedies and on fair compensation to be paid to *the injured party*. This personal nexus to the injured party is significantly weakened when the Court orders a State to take guarantees of non-repetition that have a public scope and impact 'so that not only the victim in the case benefits but also other groups or members of society'.[148]

---

[144]The order to comply with a primary obligation is an order of cessation. As James Crawford put it, the 'function of cessation is to put an end to a violation of international law and to safeguard the continuing validity and effectiveness of the underlying primary rule'. Crawford (ed.), *The ILC Draft Articles on Responsibility of States for Internationally Wrongful Acts*, Art. 30, para. 5.

[145]Shelton, *Remedies in international human rights law*, 2006, p. 75.

[146]Crawford (ed.), *The ILC Draft Articles on Responsibility of States for Internationally Wrongful Acts*, Art. 30, para. 1.

[147]As the ILC held, '[i]n terms of legal theory, cessation may be ascribed either to the continued normal operation of the "primary" rule of which the previous wrongful conduct constitutes a violation or to the operation of the "secondary" rule coming into play as an effect of the occurrence of the wrongful act. The Commission is of the view that the very distinction between primary and secondary rules is a relative one and that cessation is situated, so to speak, in between the two categories of rules. With regard to the former, it operates in the sense of concretizing the primary obligation, the infringement of which by the wrongdoing State is in progress. With regard to the latter, it operates in the sense of affecting—without providing directly for reparation—the quality and quantity of reparation itself and the modalities and conditions of the measures to which the injured State or States, or an international institution, may resort in order to secure reparation.' ILC, *Report of the Commission to the General Assembly on the work of its forty-fifth session*, p. 55.

[148]IACtHR, IACtHR, *Annual Report 2012*, 2012, p. 18.

Hence, from a theoretical perspective, the approach taken under the ECHR is more stringent. Accordingly, guarantees of non-repetition and cessation stem from the obligation under Article 46 (1) ECHR to comply with the judgment and thus with the ECHR. Moreover, it is a requirement of the principle of subsidiarity to leave, in principle, at the discretion of the State the choice of measures appropriate to end violations and to guarantee future compliance.[149] Moreover, it may be claimed that the supervised and partly judicialized process of implementing a judgment bears a higher potential of ownership on measures taken by the State than whatever kind of reparation measures ordered by an international court which is expected to exercise judicial restraint and show deference *vis-à-vis* the domestic level. However, as gender stereotypes and hierarchies are in fact deeply rooted—also in the heads of state officials setting the Committee of Ministers—it is questionable whether this process of implementing a judgment will in fact tackle structural discrimination. Civil society participation is therefore crucial.

2. Content of Guarantees of Non-repetition

On the content of guarantees of non-repetition, it appears that measures ordered by the IACtHR, on the one hand, and the European practice to supervise the execution and implement a judgment by a respondent State, one the other hand, are quite similar.

The IACtHR has ordered guarantees of non-repetition such as legal reforms and awareness-raising programs for State officials. When adopted by the respondent State, such measures are likely to have a systemic impact, preventing in the short term further abuses. In *Velásquez Paiz et al. v. Guatemala,* the Court even ordered educative programs on human rights, gender stereotypes and discrimination against women, which were ordered to be implemented at all levels of the national education system in Guatemala. Such measures address the root causes of gender-based violence and are able to contribute to the prevention of violence against women in the long run.

In turn, as exemplified by the still pending implementation process of the *Opuz* case group, respondent States have adopted similar short-term measures where room for discretion was left to them. Regarding Turkey, this encompassed the adjustment of its legislative framework to the standards as established under the Istanbul Convention, the increase of women guesthouses as well as awareness-raising programs for public officials.

[149] Council of Europe, Committee of Ministers, *Supervision of the Execution of Judgments, 3rd Annual report, 2009*, April 2010, p. 19, para. 19; Neumann, 'Subsidiarity', in Shelton, 2010.

3. Transformative Potential on Structurally Discriminatory Settings

The above analysis has demonstrated that an individual complaint before the ECtHR or the IACtHR can indeed have a systemic impact and improve the human rights situation in the respondent State. However, as seen, apart from the educative program ordered to Guatemala, guarantees of non-repetition—whether ordered by the IACtHR and taken by Turkey on the *Opuz* case group under the supervision of the Committee of Ministers—hardly address the larger context of gender-based violence as illustrated in the 'iceberg model' and thus fail to be transformative indeed. If they were to address the structural context, they would need to additionally encompass general and special measures aiming at the improvement of women's *de facto* position in all fields of life.

While an individual claimant/victim will have no standing for such a complaint, it is because of the seriousness of structural discrimination and the principle of effectiveness that the obligation to comply with a human rights treaty might be interpreted as to require a wider range of transformative measures (obligation to fulfill). This of course depends on each treaty and would require a closer analysis. At any rate, the obligation to comply with a treaty can legally require no more efforts than the primary norms already require. For example, while CEDAW entails programmatic obligations, such a broad interpretation of ECHR has clearly to be dismissed. Neither ECHR nor its Protocol No. 12, stipulating a self-standing general prohibition of discrimination, provide for obligations of a programmatic character. The wording of Article 14 ECHR, establishing the prohibition of discrimination, does not explicitly foresee such a wide-ranging obligation.[150] Article 14 must be applied in combination with another right foreseen by the Convention.[151] These provisions, following the individualistic conception of the ECHR, guarantee rights sufficiently precise to be invoked by individual rights holders.[152]

---

[150]For an analysis of the ECtHR's jurisprudence on positive obligations under Article14, see Nikolaidis, *The right to equality in European human rights law*, 2015, pp. 72.

[151]Art. 14 ECHR reads as follows: The enjoyment of the rights and freedoms set forth in this Convention shall be secured without discrimination on any ground (. . .).

[152]As the Council of Europe's Steering Committee for Human Rights held concerning primary obligations to take special measures to reach full and effective equality (affirmative actions) under Protocol No. 12 to the ECHR, stipulating a self-standing general prohibition of discrimination, such a 'programmatic obligation would sit ill with the whole nature of the Convention and its control system which are based on the collective guarantee of individual rights which are formulated in terms sufficiently specific to be justiciable'. (Council of Europe, *Explanatory Report to the Protocol No. 12 to the Convention for the Protection of Human Rights and Fundamental Freedoms*, 04 November 2000, para. 16.) A fortiori, this also holds true for the obligation to comply with the treaty.

D. Conclusion

The preferred and long-standing form of reparation *restitutio in integrum* aims at putting back the victim in the situation she was in before the violation causing harm occurred. Restitution is therefore inadequate where the circumstances before the violation were structurally discriminatory against a victim. Against this background, *transformative* reparations have first been discussed within the context of administrative and political reparation programs carried out in post-conflict societies. Subsequently, various international actors such as the CEDAW Committee, the IACtHR and the ICC have applied this concept to non-conflict settings. Accordingly, transformative reparation should 'restore the victims to their situation prior to the violation insofar as possible to the extent that this does not interfere with the obligation not to discriminate'. Most importantly, they should also be 'designed to identify and eliminate the factors that cause discrimination'.[153]

Against this backdrop, this chapter has drawn on the legal possibilities and limits of a complaint based on a violation of positive obligations of prevention and protection brought before the IACtHR or the ECtHR to have a systemic impact that may transform structurally discriminatory settings in which the violation was embedded. As to the restrictive concepts of victims, the circle of those entitled to reparation measures or compensation for harm suffered from violence against women is very limited.

Before the ECtHR, beneficiaries of reparative measures ordered by the Court are necessarily the applicants having a *ius standi*. They are, primarily, direct victims whose rights under the Convention have been violated. Regarding indirect victims, the ECtHR has taken a rigid approach, to the extent that it has largely rejected them. Where direct victims died under circumstances given rise to a violation of the obligation to respect, or where preventive measures were omitted before the harmful event occurred, heirs have been accepted as indirect victims and have been awarded compensation on behalf of the direct victim. Close family members may claim compensation in their own rights for violations of procedural obligations occurring after a victim's death.

In contrast, before the IACtHR, those being potentially eligible for reparation do not need to be identical with the applicants. Moreover, the Inter-American Court has applied a flexible approach when identifying indirect victims. It has considered *inter alia* the closeness of the personal relationship in each case and whether the person was involved in seeking justice against the abuse. Under exceptional circumstances, the Court has accepted indirect victims even where the direct victim did not die.

Where a systemic problem is revealed by a case, a complaint brought before the Inter-American and European Courts can indeed have a systemic impact and

---

[153] IACtHR, *González v. Mexico (Cotton Field Case)*, Judgment (Preliminary Objection, Merits, Reparations, and Costs), 16 November 2009, para. 451; see also CEDAW Committee, *General Recommendation No. 30 on women in conflict prevention, conflict, and post conflict situations*, 18 October 2013, para. 74.

improve the human rights situation in the respective State. This is particularly true regarding guarantees of non-repetition. While the European and the Inter-American human rights systems have taken significantly different theoretical and procedural approaches, both of them address systemic failure and, on the IACtHR at least to some extent, the root causes of gender-based violence.

It has been revealed from a theoretical viewpoint that the concept of *transformative reparation* as applied by the IACtHR is a misconception *as far as,* within the context of proceedings before human rights courts, it aims at addressing and rectifying the structural context in which the violation was embedded. Applying the perspective of the law of state responsibility, this may be explained by, first, reparations that need to be linked to the individual victim and the violation that occurred. Second, guarantees of non-repetition, which are those measures that can have a systemic impact, stem from the primary obligation to comply with a treaty. However, this obligation continues in force independently of whether there is a victim or not. They are thus no secondary obligations owed to the victim. Instead, they are owed to all contracting parties and better situated between the primary and the secondary level of obligations. Consequently, linking guarantees of non-repetition with the individual victim undermines the rule of law. It has therefore been concluded that, from a theoretical perspective, the European practice to conceptualize guarantees of non-repetition as to result from the obligation to comply with the judgment and the treaty is more consistent. Ultimately, when leaving freedom of choice to the respondent State as to the measures to be taken, the execution process is more likely to generate ownership at the domestic level and allows for civil society intervention. Nonetheless, the different practices may be because of the different context in which both Courts are embedded and must respond to.

As compared to the content and outcome of guarantees of non-repetition, it appears that measures—whether ordered by the IACtHR or indicated by the ECtHR and/or taken by a respondent State under the supervision of the Committee of Ministers—are quite similar.

However, regarding structural discrimination of specific social groups, in particular women, both human rights systems only provide for a limited set of solutions. According to the taxonomy of short-term and long-term measures,[154] guarantees of non-repetition, ordered by the IACtHR as reparation measures or taken by respondent States under the supervision of the Committee of Ministers, are largely limited to short-term prevention. Regarding ECHR, it appears that long-term measures could not be legally expected from a contracting party because the obligation to comply with the Convention is not programmatic in character. However, at least in one judgment, the IACtHR ordered educative programs that may enable to modify beliefs on the inferiority of women compared to men and gender stereotypes. Nonetheless, the larger context of gender-based violence as illustrated in the 'iceberg model' remains largely unaddressed. A transformative approach which addresses the structurally discriminatory context would additionally require special measures aiming at the improvement of the *de facto* position of women in all fields of life.

[154]Chapter 5 A.

Chapter 8
Findings

International actors and courts have increasingly drawn attention to structural discrimination against women, Roma and other disadvantaged social groups. Structural discrimination is characterized by its omnipresence in all spheres of life, 'resulting in a situation where the prohibition of discrimination in any one of these spheres or, indeed in all of them, will not suffice to ensure effective equality'.[1] It is rooted in historically grown, unequal power relations between members of different social groups and unintentionally perpetuated by symbols, customs, sublimed assumptions of subordination and dominance, stereotypes and socio-political as well as economic structures. While it is no legal concept, structural discrimination allows for broadening the perspective for past and present social structures the disadvantageous effect of which may be revealed where indirect discrimination occurs. This additional perspective may render anti-discrimination policies more effective.

Against this backdrop, it was the aim of this study to analyze whether and to what extent the different international and regional human rights frameworks require from state parties to take a root cause-sensitive and transformative approach to violence against women as an expression and result of structural discrimination against them. Based on the assumption that violence against women is by and large a result of gender hierarchies, stereotypes and gender-based discrimination in all fields of life ('iceberg-model'), the study has focused on violence against women. In contrast to a general international trend to separately address and combat conflict-related sexualized violence (against women) and violence against women in peacetime, the study has analyzed both phenomena, assuming that conflict-related sexualized violence against women is the '*continuum*' of 'ordinary' gender-based violence of all kinds. As positive human rights obligations bear an important potential on structurally

[1] Schutter, *International human rights law*, 2014, p. 732.

E. V. Henn, *International Human Rights Law and Structural Discrimination*, Beiträge zum ausländischen öffentlichen Recht und Völkerrecht,
https://doi.org/10.1007/978-3-662-58677-8_8

human rights infringing settings and third actors, the study has focused on such obligations.

It can generally be concluded that human rights law is not entirely blind for structural discrimination against women and even provides for some promising avenues. Thematic conventions on discrimination and violence against women foresee obligations to address the root causes. Individual cases before human rights courts that reveal a systemic problem or historically grown inequalities can trigger systemic change and—to some extent—also initiate societal transformation.

The following sections summarize the findings of this study with a particular focus on the transformative potential regarding structurally discriminatory settings as revealed by violence against women. Section A resumes the findings concerning *thematic* conventions on discrimination against women (CEDAW, the Istanbul and the Belém do Para Conventions). Distinguishing between positive obligations at the primary level and secondary obligations, section B sums up the transformative potential and limits under *general* human rights treaties, in particular under ACHR and ECHR.

A. Thematic Human Rights Conventions Address Violence Against Women and Structural Discrimination

Provisions under CEDAW, the Istanbul and the Belém do Pará Conventions stipulate, to a more or less detailed extent, positive obligations that can be categorized into short-term measures against gender-based violence and long-term measures against structural discrimination. These conventions do not allow for derogation during armed conflicts.

The Istanbul and Belém do Pará Conventions stipulate a number of positive obligations that entail a short-term strategy on the elimination of gender-based violence. These obligations require States to directly prevent and protect against gender-based violence. While the Istanbul Convention enshrines a series of very precise obligations, parties to the Belém do Pará Convention have a greater margin of appreciation regarding both the measures and the time of their adoption. Contracting parties must take a series of substantive and procedural as well as administrative measures to prevent and protect against gender-based violence. These measures address the individual level by providing for both support and empowerment to victims, and treatment and support programs aimed at preventing perpetrators from re-offending. State parties have also to take measures with a systemic impact on legal and administrative structures. Accordingly, state parties need to criminalize certain discriminatory conduct, investigate crimes, prosecute and punish perpetrators in a gender-sensitive manner and promote public awareness for violence against women and gender equality.

Regarding a long-term strategy combating structural discrimination against women CEDAW, the Belém do Pará and the Istanbul Conventions either require or encourage state parties to take a threefold approach that addresses the three layers of the 'iceberg-model'. While the wording of the Belém do Pará Convention on this threefold approach rather implies a non-binding character, parties to the Istanbul Convention are obliged to take a transformative approach on gender stereotypes and hierarchies. Parties to the Istanbul Convention are also encouraged to abolish *de facto* discrimination and improve the *de facto* position of women. Under Articles 2–5 CEDAW, state parties are required to, first, end *de jure* and *de facto* discrimination in all fields of life, second, improve women's *de facto* position through general and special measures and, third, transform gender stereotypes and hierarchies as root causes of gender-based violence. This transformative approach notwithstanding, the scope of these programmatic obligations is imprecise, leaving much room for discretion. As this room may only be limited by the prohibition of insufficient action, no specific measure can be required. Moreover, the enforceability of this threefold approach is limited to the context of State reporting procedures or individual communication where the CEDAW Committee may recall a State's obligations by recommending special measures.

B. Addressing Structural Discrimination Under General Human Rights Treaties

In contrast to thematic human rights conventions, general conventions do not explicitly foresee positive obligations. Nonetheless, the competent courts and monitoring bodies have interpreted these treaties as to encompass positive obligations at the primary level. They may not only imply an obligation to take protective measures regarding a specific individual but also systemic obligations that require a modification of the legal and administrative framework.

In search of transformative potentials concerning primary obligations, the study has therefore explored, first, possible parameters to establish when positive obligations apply; second, the extent of positive obligations, drawing on criteria that are likely to inform the States discretion; and third, potential factors that hinder the finding of a violation of positive obligations.

Moreover, on the European and Inter-American human rights systems, this study has shown that consequential obligations ensuing from a violation of primary obligations may have a systemic and partly transformative impact, independently of whether they are ordered by the IACtHR as secondary level reparation or taken by a respondent State as a consequence of a proceeding before the ECtHR under the *pacta sunt servanda* principle.

I. Primary Obligations

Where human rights treaties only stipulate that state parties must 'ensure'/'secure' human rights, the question arises whether and to what extent positive obligations do exist. Based on human rights theory, an analysis of international jurisprudence and preceding research, this study has therefore further developed criteria to establish *when* state parties to general human rights treaties have positive obligations of prevention and protection, and to *what extent* positive obligations exist. Drawing from general international law, it has also analyzed potential factors impeding the finding of a violation of positive obligations.

1. Conditions for Positive Obligations of Protection and Prevention to Apply

Based on human rights theory and jurisprudence of the ECtHR, the IACtHR and the ICJ, it can be concluded that three cumulative parameters allow conclusions to be drawn as to when positive obligations of protection and prevention apply. These three parameters are applicable to violence against women but also apply to other forms of structural discrimination such as against Roma.

First, if there is a group or individual at risk to be harmed by whatever kind of actor or situation, a State needs to know or have constructive knowledge about that risk. For protective case-specific obligations to apply, this risk must be *real and immediate*. On more general preventive obligations such as to provide for an effective administrative and legal framework, an *abstract danger* is sufficient. While on domestic violence the requirement of an immediate risk may be too severe to provide for an effective protection, the requirement of an abstract danger is particularly important in the context of structurally discriminatory settings.

Second, a State can only have positive obligations if it has the capacity to exercise decisive influence on the abuser or the circumstances. This influence can be established by a legal relationship with the abuser to the extent that a State could or should have exercised control over them. An exercise of influence on the abuser or the situation can also be expected where it is established that there is a *de facto* relationship with the abuser, the victim or the circumstances. In this context, the criminal law concepts of 'supervisor guarantor' or 'protector guarantor' held responsible for failure to prevent the occurrence of a specific event can be useful. When transferring this concept to human rights law and positive obligations, the position of 'protector guarantor' may play a role where a State has a special link with the victim (e.g. prisoner, public school pupil, resident or national of that State). Moreover, the transfer of public functions to private entities or other contractual, political, financial or territorial links between a State and the abuser are indicative of a 'supervisor guarantor' position.

Third, and ultimately, if the severity and/or scope of the individual or collective harm (potentially) suffered is extensive, there is a normative expectation towards the

State to take preventive and protective measures. This criterion not only applies to an individual case of gender-based violence but also to its widespread occurrence, and other situations revealing a history of past and present discrimination and inequalities.

In contrast to international jurisprudence, it has been claimed here that a victim's alleged vulnerability should not, of itself, have an impact on the applicability of positive obligations. This is because persons who are allegedly vulnerable are made vulnerable by societal circumstances but are not by default more vulnerable than any other human being. If one draws on the 'vulnerability' of a social group, one bolsters stereotypes on that group and conceals human-made root causes of circumstances that infringe human rights. It is sufficient and more appropriate, instead, to rely on the harmful consequences at the individual and/or societal/collective level which are particularly far-reaching in settings that are structurally discriminatory against the group an individual is a member of.

2. Scope of Positive Obligations

Regarding the extent of positive obligations, it has been suggested that the same considerations apply, independently of whether obligations of protection and prevention or obligations with a programmatic character (to fulfill) are concerned.

While the wording of many provisions, jurisprudence and soft law instruments differs, the 'appropriate measures standard' and the 'due diligence standard', which has particularly been used in the context of gender-based violence, do not differ in content. Both standards confer upon a State room for discretion which must be exercised in light of the respective circumstances and the principle of effectiveness.

When exercising its discretion, it appears that a State can or must consider rights of others, the interests of the State and the community, its capacity to influence the abuser/the situation and potentially conflicting obligations under international law. In principle, financial restrictions do not influence the extent of obligations. Most importantly, the State's discretion (margin of appreciation) will be significantly reduced by the severity and scope of harm at risk to be inflicted upon an individual or group of individuals. Particularly in cases that reveal historically grown structures of discrimination and inequalities, this criterion will play an important role. Ultimately, while the exercise of discretion risks to marginalize politically underrepresented groups, such negative effects are mitigated by the limits imposed by the principle of proportionality which, in the case of positive obligations, may be reduced to a prohibition of insufficient action.

3. Factors Impeding the Finding of a Violation of Positive Obligations

If a court concludes that a State had positive obligations concerning a given case or circumstances and that this State failed to take reasonable steps, this does not necessarily imply the finding of a breach of its positive duties.

As regards obligations requiring to prevent a given event such as to protect against violence in a specific case, Article 14 ILC Articles on State Responsibility codifies a customary rule according to which such preventive obligations are only breached when the event occurs. It may thus be that no violation can be found. However, as the application of this rule depends on the content of the primary norm and the specific circumstances of the case, no general conclusions can be drawn as to what it may imply for gender-based violence or structural discrimination.

Moreover, it may be that a causal nexus will still be required between a State's omission *prior to a harmful event* and the harmful event itself. While there is no consistent judicial practice on causality, such a requirement bears the potential to render the failure to take preventive measures irrelevant for constituting a violation. For example, it may be that no sufficiently direct nexus can be established between the non-establishment of a legal framework and a specific sexual abuse. However, it has been claimed here that where the requirement of a causal link undermines the very idea of positive obligations and thus their effectiveness, no such condition can be required. This is particularly true for omissions occurring *after the harmful* event, or where hypothetical considerations come into play.

II. Secondary Obligations and Beyond: An Individual Complaint Concerning Gender-Based Violence Brought Before the ECtHR or the IACtHR Can Have a Systemic and Partly Transformative Impact

Where an international human rights court concludes that a respondent State violated its primary obligations of protection and prevention, secondary obligations may arise. Against the backdrop of an international plea for transformative reparation that should not only have a transformative impact on the individual victim but also modify pre-existing inequalities that enabled the violation to occur, the study has scrutinized the transformative potential of secondary obligations which may either be owed to the victim or to all contracting parties. Having focused on societal-transformative guarantees of non-repetition, it has been revealed that, although the conceptual and theoretical approaches taken towards the consequences ensuing from a violation of primary obligations differ significantly, an individual complaint before the IACtHR or the ECtHR can indeed have a systemic impact, implying the modification of legal and administrative practices in a country. Nonetheless, the transformative potential on gender stereotypes and hierarchies, and thus structural discrimination, is limited.

1. Legal Framework and Practice

According to Article 63 ACHR, the IACtHR has the competence to order reparation measures which the Court interpreted to include restitution, compensation, satisfaction, rehabilitation, cessation and guarantees of non-repetition. In the interpretation of the Court, these measures are owed to the victim.

In contrast, according to Article 41 ECHR, the ECtHR has only the competence to order compensation to be paid to the victim. Besides, it is a requirement of the principle of subsidiarity under ECHR to leave, in principle, at the discretion of the respondent State the choice of measures appropriate to be taken to comply with the judgment (Article 46) and, thus, with the treaty. This obligation is owed to all contracting parties and not to the claimant. Hence, although the implementation of judgments is supervised by the Council of Europe's Committee of Ministers, it is to the respondent State to decide on the measures taken to end violations and to guarantee future compliance. Only under exceptional circumstances or within the context of pilot judgment procedures has the ECtHR indicated the type of measures to be taken to ensure compliance with the judgment.

2. Comparing the Transformative Potential of Guarantees of Non-Repetition

Individual complaints brought before the IACtHR and the ECtHR can have a *systemic* impact and improve the human rights situation in the respondent State. As compared to the content and outcome of guarantees of non-repetition, measures—whether ordered by the IACtHR or indicated by the ECtHR and/or taken by a respondent State under the supervision of the Committee of Ministers—are quite similar. However, regarding structural discrimination of specific social groups, in particular women, both human rights systems only provide for a limited set of solutions. According to the taxonomy of short-term and long-term measures, guarantees of non-repetition are largely limited to short-term prevention such as the adoption of the legislative and administrative framework and training of gender trainings of public officials. However, at least in one case, the IACtHR ordered public educative programs that may enable to modify socially prevalent beliefs on the inferiority of women compared to men and gender stereotypes. Nonetheless, the larger context of gender-based violence as illustrated in the 'iceberg model' remains largely unaddressed. This can be explained by the fact that guarantees of non-repetition, when misleadingly conceptualized as reparation measures at the secondary level, need to be linked to the specific violation and, when conceptualized as pertaining to the obligation to comply with the treaty, can legally require no more efforts than the primary norms of the treaty already do.

3. Transformative Reparation: A Theoretically Flawed Concept

The international plea for transformative reparation has significantly been pushed by the Inter-American Court. While this idea has revealed the discriminatory element inherent in the traditional concept of restitution, it has been shown by this study that the concept of transformative reparation is a theoretically flawed concept in so far as, within the context of proceedings before human rights courts, it not only aims at addressing and rectifying the individual discrimination the victim has suffered but also the structurally discriminatory context in which the violation was embedded.

This is because, first, reparations need to be linked to the individual victim and the violation that occurred. Second, from a theoretical perspective, guarantees of non-repetition stem from the primary obligation to comply with a treaty. This obligation continues in force independently of whether there is a victim claiming reparation. Thus, guarantees of non-repetition are no secondary obligations owed to the victim. Instead, they are owed to all contracting parties and better situated between the primary and the secondary level of obligations. Consequently, linking guarantees of non-repetition with the individual victim risks to undermine the rule of law. Finally, the idea of transformative reparations ordered by an international human rights court is in conflict with the principle of State sovereignty and subsidiarity of international courts.

Hence, while the different approaches taken by the IACtHR and the ECtHR may be explained by the distinct social and political contexts in which they are embedded, it has been concluded that, from a theoretical perspective, the European practice to conceptualize guarantees of non-repetition as to result from the obligation to comply with the judgment and the treaty is more consistent. Moreover, an execution process as under the European system allows for continuous civil society intervention. Ultimately, a supervised and partly judicialized process of implementing a judgment bears a higher potential of ownership on the measures taken by the State than whatever kind of reparation measures ordered by international human rights courts that are generally expected to exercise judicial restraint and demonstrate deference *vis-à-vis* the domestic level.

A. Table of Cases, Documents and Reports

I. International and Regional Jurisprudence

1. International Jurisprudence

a. Permanent Court of International Justice

- *Factory of Chorzów (Germany v. Poland),* Judgment, 13 September 1928, PCIJ Rep Series A - No. 17.

b. International Court of Justice

- *Corfu Channel Case (UK v. Albania),* Judgment (merits), 09 April 1949, ICJ Reports 1949, p. 4.
- *North Sea Continental Shelf Case (Federal Republic of Germany v. Denmark; Federal Republic of Germany v. Netherlands),* Dissenting Opinion Judge Sørensen, 20 February 1969, ICJ Reports 1969, p. 242.
- *United States Diplomatic and Consular Staff in Teheran (United States of America v. Iran),* Judgment, 24 May 1980, ICJ Reports 1980, p. 3.
- *Military and paramilitary activities in and against Nicaragua (Nicaragua v. United States of America),* Judgment (merits), 27 June 1986, ICJ Reports 1986, p. 14.
- *Legality of the Threat or Use of Nuclear Weapons,* Advisory Opinion, 08 July 1996, ICJ Reports 1996, p. 226.
- *Legal Consequences of the Construction of a Wall in the Occupied Palestinian Territory,* Advisory Opinion, 09 July 2004, ICJ Reports 2004, p. 136.

E. V. Henn, *International Human Rights Law and Structural Discrimination*, Beiträge zum ausländischen öffentlichen Recht und Völkerrecht, https://doi.org/10.1007/978-3-662-58677-8

- *Armed Activities on the territory of the Congo (DRC v. Uganda),* Judgment, 19 December 2005, ICJ Reports 2005, p. 168.
- *Case concerning application of the Convention of Prevention and Punishment of the Crime of Genocide (Bosnia and Herzegovina v. Serbia and Montenegro),* Judgment, 26 February 2007, ICJ Reports 2007, p. 43.
- *Case concerning Application of the International Convention on the Elimination of all Forms of Racial Discrimination (Georgia v. Russian Federation),* Order on the Indication of Provisional Measures, 15 October 2008, ICJ Reports 2008, p. 353.
- *Pulp Mills on the River Uruguay (Argentina v. Uruguay)*, 20 April 2010, ICJ Reports 2010, p. 14.
- *Ahmadou Sadio Diallo (Republic of Genuia v. Democratic Republic of Congo),* Judgment (merits), 30 November 2010.
- *Jurisdictional Immunity of States (Germany v. Italy: Greece intervening),* Judgment, 03 February 2012, ICJ Reports 2012, p. 99.

c. International Criminal Court

- *Prosecutor v. Thomas Lubanga Dyilo*, ICC-01/04-01/06 A A 2 A 3, Appeals Chamber, Judgment on the Appeals against the 'Decision establishing the principles and procedures to be applied to reparations' of 7 August 2012 with amended order for reparations (Annex A) and public annexes 1 and 2, 03 March 2015.

d. International Criminal Tribunal for the Former Yugoslavia

- *Prosecutor v. Furundžija,* IT-95-17/1-T, Trial Chamber, Judgment, 10 December 1998.
- *Kunarac, Kovač and Vuković,* IT-96-23 and IT-96-23/1-A, Appeals Chamber, Judgment, 12 June 2002.

e. Human Rights Committee

- *Delia Saldias de Lopez Burgos v. Uruguay,* Communication No. 52/1979, 29 July 1981, UN Doc. CCPR/C/13/D/52/1979.
- *Lilian Celiberti de Casariego v. Uruguay,* Communication No. 56/1979, 29 July 1981, UN Doc. CCPR/C/OP/1 at 92 (1985).
- *Mabel Pereira Montero v. Uruguay,* Communication No. 106/1981, 31 March 1983, UN Doc. CCPR/C/OP/2 at 136 (1990).

f. CEDAW Committee

- *T. v. Hungary,* Communication No. 2/2003, 26 January 2005, UN Doc. CEDAW/C/36/D/2003.
- *Dragan Durmic v. Serbia and Montenegro,* Communication No. 29/2003, 06 March 2006, UN Doc. CERD/C/68/D/29/2003 (2006).
- *Goekce v. Austria,* Communication No. 5/2005, 06 August 2007, UN Doc. CEDAW/C/39/D/5/2005.
- *Fatma Yildirim v. Austria,* Communication No. 6/2005, 01 October 2007, UN Doc. CEDAW/C/39/D/6/2005.
- *Medvedeva v. Russian Federation,* Communication No. 60/2013, 25 February 2016, UN Doc. CEDAW/C/63/D/60/2013.

g. International Arbitration

- *L. F. H. Neer and Pauline Neer (U.S.A.) v. United Mexican States*, 15 October 1926, Reports of International Arbitral Awards, Vol. IV, pp. 60–66.
- *Partial Award, Civilians Claims Ethiopia's Claim Nr. 5, between The Federal Democratic Republic of Ethiopia and The State of Eritrea*, 17 December 2004, (2005) 44 ILM 630.

2. *Regional Jurisprudence*

a. Inter-American Commission of Human Rights

- *Alejandre v. Cuba,* Case 11.589, Report No. 86/99, 29 September 1999, Annual Report of the IAComHR 1999, OEA/Ser.L/V/II.106.
- *Maria da Penha v. Brazil,* Case 12.051, Report No. 54/01, 16 April 2001, OEA/Ser.L/V/II.111 Doc. 20 rev. at 704 (2000).
- *Jessica Lenahan (Gonzales) et al. v. United States,* 12.626, Case 12.626, Report No. 80/11, 21 July 2011.

b. Inter-American Court of Human Rights

- *Velásquez-Rodriguez v. Honduras,* Judgment (Merits), 29 July 1988, Inter-Am. Ct.H.R. (Ser. C) No. 4.
- *Velásquez-Rodríguez v. Honduras,* Judgment (Reparations and Costs), 21 July 1989, Inter-Am.Ct.H.R. (Ser. C) No. 7.
- *Aloeboetoe et al. v. Suriname,* Judgment (Reparations and Costs), 10 September 1993, Inter-Am. Ct. H.R. (Ser. C) No. 15.

- *Blake v. Guatemala (Reparations and Costs),* Judgment (Reparations and Costs), 22 January 1999, Inter-Am. Ct. H.R. (Ser. C) No. 48.
- *'Street Children' (Villagrán-Morales et al.) v. Guatemala,* Judgment (Merits), 19 November 1999, Inter-Am. Ct. H.R. (Ser. C) No. 63.
- *Case of the "Street Children" (Villagrán-Morales et al.) v. Guatemala,* Judgment (Reparations and Costs), 26 May 2001, Inter-Am. Ct. H.R. (Ser. C) No. 77.
- *The Mayagna (Sumo) Awas Tingni Community v. Nicaragua,* Judgment (Merits, Reparations and Costs), 31 August 2001, Inter-Am. Ct. H.R., (Ser. C) No. 79.
- *Bulacio v. Argentina,* Judgment (Merits, Reparations and Costs), 18 September 2003, Inter-Am. Ct. H.R. (Ser. C) No. 100.
- *Gómez-Paquiyauri Brothers v. Peru,* Judgment (Merits, Reparations and Costs), 08 July 2004, Inter-Am. Ct. H.R., (Ser. C) No. 110.
- *Tibi v. Ecuador,* Judgment (Preliminary Objections, Merits, Reparations and Costs), 07 September 2004, Inter-Am. Ct. H.R., (Ser. C) No. 114.
- *Plan de Sanchéz Massacre v. Guatemala (Reparations),* Judgment (Reparations), 19 November 2004, Inter-Am. Ct. H.R., (Ser. C) No. 116.
- *Yakye Axa Indigenous Community v. Paraguay,* Judgment (Merits, Reparations and Costs), 17 June 2005, Inter-Am. Ct. H.R., (Ser. C) No. 125.
- *Ituango Massacres v. Columbia,* Judgment (Preliminary Objections, Merits, Reparations and Costs), 29 June 2006, Inter-Am. Ct. H.R., (Ser. C) No. 148.
- *Case of Miguel Castro Castro Prison v. Peru,* Judgment (Merits, Reparations and Costs), 25 November 2006, Inter-Am. Ct. H.R., (Ser. C) No. 160.
- *La Cantuta v. Peru,* Judgment (Merits, Reparations and Costs), 29 November 2006, Inter-Am. Ct. H.R. (Ser. C) No. 162.
- *Valle Jaramillo et al. v. Colombia,* Judgment (Merits, Reparations and Costs), 27 November 2008, Inter-Am. Ct. H.R. (Ser. C) No. 192.
- *Ticona Estrada et al. v. Bolivia,* Judgment (Merits, Reparations and Costs), 27 November 2008, Inter-Am. Ct. H.R. (Ser. C) No. 191.
- *Perozo et al. v. Venezuela,* Judgment (Preliminary Objections, Merits, Reparations, and Costs), 28 January 2009, Inter-Am. Ct. H.R., (Ser. C) No. 195.
- *Kawas Fernández v. Honduras,* Judgment (Merits, Reparations and Costs), 03 April 2009, Inter-Am. Ct. H.R. (Ser. C) No. 196.
- *Anzualdo-Castro v. Peru,* Judgment (Preliminary Objection, Merits, Reparations and Costs), 22 September 2009, Inter-Am. Ct. H.R., (Ser. C) No. 202.
- *González v. Mexico (Cotton Field Case),* Judgment (Preliminary Objection, Merits, Reparations, and Costs), 16 November 2009, Inter-Am. Ct. H.R., (Ser. C) No. 205.
- *Las Dos Erres Massacre v. Guatemala,* Judgment, 24 November 2009, Inter-Am. Ct. H.R., (Ser. C) No. 211.
- *Fernández Ortega and others v. Mexico*, 30 August 2010, Inter-Am. Ct. H.R. (Ser. C) No. 215.
- *Rosendo Cantú y otra v. Mexico,* Judgment, 31 August 2010, Inter-Am. Ct. H.R., (Ser. C) No. 216.
- *Contreas and others v. El Salvador,* Judgment (Merits, Reparations and Costs), 31 August 2011, Inter-Am. Ct. H.R., (Ser. C) No. 232.

- Reparations and Costs), 19 May 2014, Inter-Am. Ct. H.R., (Ser. C) No. 277.
- *Case of the Río Negro Massacres v. Guatemala,* Judgment (Preliminary Objection, Merits, Reparations, and Costs), 04 September 2012, Inter-Am. Ct. H.-R. (Ser. C) No. 250.
- *Case of the Massacres of El Mozote and nearby places v. El Salvador,* Judgment (Merits, Reparations and Costs), 25 October 2012, Inter-Am. Ct. H.R., (Ser. C) No. 252.
- *Liakat Ali Alibux v. Suriname,* Judgment (Preliminary Objections, Merits, Reparations and Costs), 30 January 2014, Inter-Am. Ct. H.R. (Ser. C) No. 276.
- *Véliz Franco et al. v. Guatemala,* Judgment (Preliminary objections, merits, reparations and costs), 19 May 2014, Inter-Am. Ct. H.R. (Ser. C) No. 277.
- *Rodríguez Vera et al. (The disappeared from the palace of justice) v. Colombia,* Judgment (Preliminary Objections, Merits, Reparations and Costs), 14 November 2014, Inter-Am. Ct. H.R. (Ser. C) No. 287.
- *Velásquez Paiz et al. v. Guatemala,* Judgment (Preliminary Objections, Merits, Reparations and Costs), 19 November 2015, Inter-Am. Ct. H.R., (Ser. C) No. 307.

c. European Court of Human Rights

- *Case "relating to certain aspects of the laws on the use of languages in education in Belgium" v. Belgium,* App. No. 1474/62, 1677/62, 1691/62, 1769/63, 1994/63 & 2126/64, Judgment (Merits), 23 July 1968.
- *De Wilde, Ooms and Versyp (Vagrancy) v. Belgium,* App. No. 2832/66; 2835/66; 2899/66, Judgment (Art. 50), 10 March 1972.
- *Marckx v. Belgium,* App. No. 6833/74, Judgment (Merits and Just Satisfaction), 13 June 1979.
- *Young, James u Webster v. the United Kingdom,* App. No. 7601/76 & 7806/77, Judgment, 13 August 1981.
- *Colozza v. Italy,* App. No. 9024/80, Judgment (Merits and Just Satisfaction), 12 February 1985.
- *X and Y v. The Netherlands,* App. No. 8978/80, Judgment, 26 March 1985.
- *Rees v. The United Kingdom,* App. No. 9532/81, Judgment, 17 October 1986.
- *Gaskin v. the United Kingdom,* App. No. 10454/83, Judgment, 07 July 1989.
- *McCann and others v. United Kingdom* [GC], App. No. 18984/91, Judgment (Merits and Just Satisfaction), 27 September 1995.
- *Papamichalopoulos et al. v. Greece,* App. No. 14556/89, Judgment (Art. 50), 31 October 1995.
- *Aydin v. Turkey* [GC], App. No. 57/1996/676/866, Judgment, 25 September 1997.
- *Botta v. Italy,* App. No. 21439/93, Judgment, 24 February 1998.
- *Osman v. the United Kingdom,* App. No. 87/1997/871/1083, Judgment, 28 October 1998.
- *Çakıcı v. Turkey* [GC], App. No. 23657/94, Judgment (Merits and Just Satisfaction), 08 July 1999.

- *Mazurek v. France,* App. No. 34406/97, Judgment, 01 February 2000.
- *Thlimmenos v. Greece* [GC], App. No. 34369/97, Judgment, 06 April 2000.
- *Chapman v. the United Kingdom* [GC], App. No. 27238/95, Judgment, 18 January 2001.
- *Keenan v. The United Kingdom,* App. No. 27229/95, Judgment (Merits and Just Satisfaction), 03 April 2001.
- *Bankovic and others v. Belguim and others* [GC] (dec.), App. No. 52207/99, 12 December 2001.
- *Baragan v. Romania,* App. No. 33627/96, Judgment, 01 October 2002.
- *Younger v. The United Kingdom* (dec.), App. No. 57420/00, 07 January 2003.
- *E. and others v. The United Kingdom,* App. No. 33218/96, Judgment, 15 January 2003.
- *M.C. v. Bulgaria,* App. No. 39272/98, Judgment, 04 December 2003.
- *Broniowski v. Poland* [GC], App. No. 31443/96, Judgment, 22 June 2004.
- *Ilaşcu v. Moldova and Russia* [GC], App. No. 48787/99, Judgment, 08 July 2004.
- *Fairfield v. the United Kingdom* (dec.), App. No. 24790/04, 08 March 2005.
- *Angelova and Iliev v. Bulgaria,* App. No. 55523/00, Judgment, 26 July 2007.
- *DH v. Czech Republic* [GC], App. No. 47325/00, Judgment, 13 November 2007.
- *Bevacqua and S. v. Bulgaria,* App. No. 71127/01, Judgment, 12 June 2008.
- *Glor v. Switzerland,* App. No. 13444/04, Judgment, 30 April 2009.
- *Opuz v. Turkey,* App. No. 33401/02, Judgment, 09 June 2009.
- *Varnava and Others v. Turkey* [GC], App. No. 16064/90, 16065/90, 16066/90, 16068/90, 16069/90, 16070/90, 16071/90, 16072/90 & 16073/90, Judgment, 18 September 2009.
- *Rantsev v. Cyprus and Russia,* App. No. 25965/04, Judgment, 07 January 2010.
- *Oršuš and Others v. Croatia* [GC], App. No. 15766/03, Judgment, 16 March 2010.
- *Khodorkovskiy v. Russia,* App. No. 5829/04, Judgment, 31 May 2011.
- *Al-Skeini and others v. the UK* [GC], App. No. 55721/07, Judgment, 07 July 2011.
- *Hirisi Jaama er all v. Italy* [GC], App. No. 27765/09, Judgment, 23 February 2012.
- *El-Masri v. the former Yugoslav Republic of Macedonia* [GC], App. No. 39630/09, Judgment, 13 December 2012.
- *Gülay Çetin c. Turquie,* App. No. 44084/10, Judgment, 05 March 2013.
- *Horváth and Kiss v. Hungary,* App. No. 11146/11, Judgment, 29 January 2013.
- *Valiuliene v. Lithuania,* App. No. 33234/07, Judgment, 26 March 2013.
- *Stiching mothers of Srebrenica and others v. The Netherlands* (dec.), App. No. 65542/12, 13 June 2013.
- *Vallianatos and Others v. Greece* [GC], App. No. 29381/09 & 32684/09, Judgment (Merits and Just Satisfaction), 07 November 2013.
- *O'Keeffe v. Ireland* [GC], App. No. 35810/09, Judgment, 28 January 2014.
- *T.M. and C.M. v. The Republic of Moldova,* App. No. 26608/11, Judgment, 28 January 2014.
- *Al-Nashiri v. Poland,* App. No. 28761/11, Judgment, 24 July 2014.

- *Hassan vs. UK* [GC], App. No. 29750/09, Judgment, 16 September 2014.
- *Jaloud v. The Netherlands* [GC], App. No. 47708/08, Judgment, 20 November 2014.
- *Branko Tomašić and others v. Croatia,* App. No. 46598/06, Judgment, 15 January 2015.
- *S.Z. v. Bulgaria,* App. No. 29263/12, Judgment, 03 March 2015.
- *Y. v. Slovenia,* App. No. 41107/10, Judgment, 28 May 2015.

d. European Court of Justice

- Association Belge des Consommateurs Test-Achats and Others v. Conseil des ministres (Grand Chamber), C-236/09, Judgment, 01 March 2011.

II. International and Regional Documents

1. International Documents

a. UN General Assembly

- UNGA Res. 40/34, *Declaration of Principles of Justice for Victims of Crimes and Abuses*, 29 November 1985, UN Doc. A/Res/40/34.
- UNGA Res. 48/104, *Declaration on the Elimination of Violence against Women*, 20 December 1993, UN Doc. A/Res/48/104.
- UNGA Res. 57/181, *Elimination of all forms of violence against women*, 04 February 2003, UN Doc. A/RES/57/181.
- UNGA Res. 60/1, *2005 World Summit Outcome*, 24 October 2005, UN Doc. A/RES/60/1.
- UNGA Res. 60/147, *Basic Principles and Guidelines on the Right to a Remedy and Reparation for Victims of Gross Violations of International Human Rights Law and Serious Violations of International Humanitarian Law*, 21 March 2006, UN Doc. A/RES/60/147.
- UNGA Res. 64/137, *Intensification of efforts to eliminate all forms of violence against women*, 18 December 2009, UN Doc. A/RES/64/137.
- UNGA Res. 69/147, *Intensification of efforts to eliminate all forms of violence against women and girls*, 18 December 2014, UN Doc. A/RES/69/147.

b. UN Security Council

- UNSC Res. 1325 (2000), 31 October 2000, UN Doc. S/Res/1325 (2000).
- UNSC Res. 1674 (2006), 28 April 2006, UN Doc. S/Res/1674 (2006).
- UNSC Res. 1889 (2009), 5 October 2009, UN Doc. S/RES/1889 (2009).

- UNSC Res. 1820 (2008), *On Acts of Sexual Violence against Civilians in Armed Conflicts,* 19 June 2008, UN Doc. S/Res/1820 (2008).

c. UN Secretary General

- UNSG, *In-Depth-Study on All Forms of Violence Against Women*, Report of the Secretary-General, 2006, UN Doc. A/61/122/Add.1.
- UNSG, *Report of the Secretary-General on the review of the implementation of the Beijing Declaration and Platform for Action and the outcome of the twenty-third special session and its contribution to shaping a gender perspective in the realization of the Millennium Development Goals*, 08 February 2010, UN Doc. E/2010/4 - E/CN.6/2010/2.
- UNSG, *Reparations for Conflict-Related Sexual Violence*, Guidance Note of the Secretary-General, 01 August 2014, <http://www.unwomen.org/en/docs/2014/6/reparations-for-conflict-related-sexual-violence> accessed 11 April 2017.

d. World Health Organization

- WHO, *World Report on Violence and Health*, 2002, <http://www.who.int/violence_injury_prevention/violence/world_report/en/> accessed 11 April 2017.
- WHO, *Preventing intimate partner and sexual violence against women: Taking action and generating evidence and sexual violence*, 2010, <http://www.who.int/reproductivehealth/publications/violence/9789241564007/en/> accessed 11 April 2017.
- WHO et al., *Global and regional estimates of violence against women: Prevalence and health effects of intimate partner violence and non-partner sexual violence*, 2013, <http://www.who.int/reproductivehealth/publications/violence/9789241564625/en/> accessed 11 April 2017.

e. UN Women

- UN Women, Commission on the Status of Women, *Agreed Conclusions on the prevention and elimination of violence against women and girls 2013*, 15 March 2013, UN Doc. E/CN/6/2013/11.
- UN Women, Commission on the Status of Women, *Elimination and prevention of all forms of violence against women and girls: Report of the Expert Group Meeting on Prevention of Violence against Women and Girls*, 15 March 2013, UN Doc. EGM/PP/2012/Report.

f. International Law Commission

- ILC, *Report of the Commission to the General Assembly on the work of its forty-fifth session,* Yearbook of the International Law Commission 1993, Vol. II (Part Two), UN Doc. A/CN.4/SER.4/1993/Add.1 (Part 2).
- ILC, *Draft articles on Responsibility of States for Internationally Wrongful Acts with commentaries*, 2001, UN Doc. A/56/10.
- ILC, *Fragmentation of International Law: Difficulties arising from the diversification and expansion of international law*, Report of the study group of the International Law Commission, 13 April 2006, UN Doc. A/CN.4/L.682.
- ILC, *Fragmentation of International Law: Difficulties arising from the diversification and expansion of international law*, Report of the Study Group of the International Law Commission, 18 July 2006, UN Doc. A/CN.4/L.702.
- ILC, *Effects of Armed Conflicts on Treaties, with commentaries*, 2011, UN Doc. A/Cn.4/L.777.
- ILC, *Second Report on identification of customary international law*, 22 May 2014, UN Doc. A/CN.4/672.
- ILC, *Third Report on Identification of customary international law*, 27 March 2015, UN Doc. A/CN.4/682.

g. Human Rights Committee

- *General Comment No. 6, The Right to Life (Art. 6 ICCPR)*, 30 April 1982, UN Doc. Doc. HRI\GEN\1\Rev.1 at 6 (1994).
- *General Comment No. 28: Equality of rights between men and women (article 3)*,, 29 March 2000, UN Doc. CCPR/C/21/Rev.1/Add.10 (2000).
- *General Comment No. 31: The Nature of the General Legal Obligation imposed on state parties to the Covenant*, 26 May 2004, UN Doc. CCPR/C/21/Rev.1/Add.13.
- *Accelerating efforts to eliminate all forms of violence against women: violence against women as a barrier to women's political and economic empowerment*, 25 June 2014, UN Doc. A/HRC/26/L.26/Rev.1.

h. CAT

- CAT, General Comment No. 3: Implementation of article 14 by state parties, UN Doc. CAT/C/GC/3.

i. CEDAW

- CEDAW, *General Recommendation No. 17: Measurement and quantification of the unremunerated domestic activities of women and their recognition in the gross national product,* UN Doc. A/46/38 (1991).
- CEDAW, *General Recommendation No. 18: Disabled Women,* UN Doc. A/46/38 (1991).
- CEDAW, *General Recommendation 19: Violence Against Women*, 1992, UN Doc. HRI/GEN/1/Rev.9 (Vol. II).
- CEDAW, *General Recommendation No. 21: Equality in marriage and family relations*, 1994, UN Doc. A/49/38.
- CEDAW, *General recommendation No. 23 on women in political and public life,* UN Doc. A/52/38 (1997).
- CEDAW, *General Recommendation No. 24 on article 12 of CEDAW: Women and Health*, 1999, UN Doc. A/54/38 (Part I).
- CEDAW, *General Recommendation No. 25 on article 4, paragraph 1, of the Convention on the Elimination of All Forms of Discrimination against Women, on temporary special measures*, 2004, UN Doc. HRI/GEN/1/Rev.9 (Vol. II).
- CEDAW, *General Recommendation No. 28 on the core obligations of State parties under article 2 of the CEDAW*, 2010, UN Doc. CEDAW/C/GC/28.
- CEDAW, *General Recommendation No. 29 on article 16 of CEDAW: Economic consequences of marriage, family relations and their dissolution*, 26 February 2013, UN Doc. CEDAW/C/GC/29.
- CEDAW, *General Recommendation No. 30 on women in conflict prevention, conflict, and post conflict situations*, 18 October 2013, UN Doc. CEDAW/C/GC/30.
- CEDAW, *Report on Mexico produced by the Committee on the Elimination of Discrimination against Women under article 8 of the Optional Protocol to the Convention, and reply from the Government of Mexico*, 27 January 2005, UN Doc. CEDAW/C/2005/OP.8/MEXICO.
- CEDAW, *Consideration of reports submitted by state parties under article 18 of the Convention on the Elimination of All Forms of Discrimination against Women: Combined third and fourth periodic report of state parties*, Morocco, 18 September 2006, UN Doc. CEDAW/C/MAR/4.
- CEDAW, *Concluding Observation of the Committee on the Elimination of Discrimination against Women, Germany*, 10 February 2009, UN Doc. CEDAW/C/DEU/CO/6.
- CEDAW, *Consideration of reports submitted by state parties under article 18 of the Convention: Fourth and fifth periodic reports of state parties due in 2014, Lebanon*, 15 May 2014, UN Doc. CEDAW/C/LBN/4-5.
- CEDAW, *List of issues and questions in relation to the combined seventh and eighth periodic reports of Spain*, 17 November 2014, UN Doc. CEDAW/C/ESP/Q/7-8.

j. CERD

- CERD, *General recommendation No. 34: Racial discrimination against people of African descent*, 11 October 2011, UN Doc. CERD/C/GC/34.
- CERD Committee, *Consideration of reports submitted by state parties under article 9 of the Convention, Concluding observations Israel*, 09 March 2012, UN Doc. CERD/C/ISR/CO.14-16.

k. CESC

- CESCR, *General Comment 16: Article 3: the equal right of men and women to the enjoyment of social, economic and cultural rights,* UN Doc. E/C.12/2005/3.
- CESCR, *General Comment No. 20: Non-discrimination in economic, social and cultural rights (art. 2, para. 2, of the International Covenant on Economic, Social and Cultural Rights)*, 02 July 2009, UN Doc. E/C.12/GC/20.
- UNCESCR, *Consideration of reports submitted by state parties under articles 16 and 17 of the Covenant, Concluding observations Israel*, 16 December 2011.

l. Reports of Special Rapporteurs

- The United Nations Special Rapporteur on Violence against Women, *15 Years of the United Nations Special Rapporteur on Violence against Women, its causes and consequences*, 2009.
- UNCHR, *Torture and other cruel, inhuman or degrading treatment or punishment*, Report by the Special Rapporteur, Mr. P. Kooijmans, appointed pursuant to Commission on Human Rights resolution 1985/33, 19 February 1986, UN Doc. E/CN.4/1986/15.
- UNCHR, *Action visant à encourager et developper davantage le respect des droits de l'homme et des libertés fondamentales et, notamment, question du programme et des méthodes de travail de la Commission: Autres méthodes et moyens qui s'offrent dans le cadre des organismes des Nations Unies pour mieux asssurer la jouissance effective des droits de l'homme et des libertés fondamtenales*, Rapport de la rapporteuse spéciale chargée de la question de la violence contre les femmes, y compris ses causes et ses conséquences, Mme Radhika Coomaraswamy, presenté conformément à la resolution 1997/44 de la commission, 26 January 1998, UN Doc. E/CN.4/1998/54.
- UNCHR, *Contemporary Forms of Slavery: Systematic Rape, Sexual Slavery, and slavery-like practices during armed conflicts*, Final Report submitted by the Ms. Gay McDougall, Special Rapporteur, 22 June 1998, UN Doc. E/CN.4/Sub. 2/1998/13.
- UNCHR, *Contemporary Forms of Slavery: Systematic Rape, Sexual Slavery and Slavery-like Practices During Armed Conflict*, Update to the final report

submitted by Ms. Gay J. McDougall, Special Rapporteur, 06 June 2000, UN Doc. E/CN.4/Sub. 2/2000/21.

- UNCHR, *Integration of the human rights of women and the gender perspective: The due diligence standard as a tool for the elimination of violence against women*, Report of the Special Rapporteur on violence against women, its causes and consequences, Yakin Ertürk, 20 January 2006, UN Doc. E/CN.4/2006/61.
- UNGA, *Advancement of Women: Note of the Secretary General*, Report of the Special Rapporteur on violence against women, its causes and consequences, 01 August 2011, UN Doc. A/66/215.
- UNGA, *Violence against women, its causes and consequences: Note of the Secretary General*, Report of the Special Rapporteur on violence against women, its causes and consequences, 07 August 2014, UN Doc. A/69/368.
- UNHRC, *Report of the Special Rapporteur on Torture, and other cruel, inhuman or degrading treatment or punishment, Manfred Nowak*, 15 January 2008, UN Doc. A/HRC/7/3.
- UNHRC, *Report of the Special Rapporteur on violence against women, its causes and consequences, Rashida Manjoo*, 22 April 2010, UN Doc. A/HRC/14/22.
- UNHRC, *Report of the Special Rapporteur on violence against women, its causes and consequences, Rashida Manjoo*, 02 May 2011, UN Doc. A/HRC/17/26.
- UNHRC, *Report of the Special Rapporteur on violence against women, its causes and consequences*, 13 May 2013, A/HRC/23/49.

m. Other UN Documents and Reports

- Fourth World Conference on Women, *Beijing Declaration and Platform for Action*, 1995, <http://www.un.org/womenwatch/daw/beijing/platform/> accessed 14 April 2017.
- ILO, *Gender equality at the heart of decent work*, International Labour Conference Report VI, 98th session, Sixth item on the agenda, 2009, <http://www.ilo.org/wcmsp5/groups/public/@ed_norm/@relconf/documents/meetingdocument/wcms_105119.pdf> accessed 13 April 2017.
- OHCHR, *Report of the Panel on Remedies and Reparation for Victims of Sexual Violence in the Democratic Republic of Congo to the High Commissioner for Human Rights*, March 2011.
- Rehn, E. and Sirleaf, E. J., *Women, war and peace: The independent expert assessment on the impact of armed conflict on women and women's role in peace-building* (United Nations Development Fund for Women, 2002).
- Stop rape now—UN Action against Sexual Violence in Conflict, *Analytical and Conceptual Framing of Conflict-related Sexual Violence*, June 2011, <http://stoprapenow.org/uploads/files/63711.pdf> accessed 11 April 2017.
- United Nations Statistics Division, *The World's Women 2015, Trends and Statistics: Chapter 6, Violence against Women*, <http://unstats.un.org/unsd/gender/chapter6/chapter6.html> accessed 11 April 2017.

2. *Regional Documents*

a. Council of Europe

- Council of Europe, *Convention on preventing and combating violence against women and domestic violence (Istanbul Convention): Historical Background,* 2014, <http://www.coe.int/en/web/istanbul-convention/historical-background> accessed 22 October 2015.
- Council of Europe, *Explanatory Report to the Council of Europe Convention on preventing and combating violence against women and domestic violence,* 2011, <http://rm.coe.int/CoERMPublicCommonSearchServices/DisplayDCTMContent?documentId=09000016800d383a> accessed 28 January 2015.
- Council of Europe, *Explanatory Report to the Protocol No. 12 to the Convention for the Protection of Human Rights and Fundamental Freedoms*, 04 November 2000, ETS 177.
- Council of Europe, *Gender Mainstreaming: Conceptual Framework, Methodology and Presentation of Good Practices*, Final report of activities of the Group of Specialists on Mainstreaming, 2004, EG-S-MS (98) 2 rev, <https://rm.coe.int/CoERMPublicCommonSearchServices/DisplayDCTMContent?documentId=0900001680596135> accessed 23 April 2017.
- Council of Europe and ECtHR, *Practical Guide On Admissibility Criteria*, Third Edition, 2014.
- Council of Europe, Committee of Ministers, *Recommendation Rec(2002)5 of the Committee of Ministers to member states on the protection of women against violence*, 30 April 2002.
- Council of Europe, Committee of Ministers, *Supervision of the Execution of Judgments, 3rd Annual report, 2009*, April 2010, <http://www.coe.int/en/web/execution/annual-reports> accessed 14 April 2017.

b. Organization of American States

- IAComHR, *Report on the Situation of Human Rights in Chile*, 25 October 1974, OEA/Ser.L/V/II.34 doc. 21 corr.1.
- IAComHR, *Report on the Situation of Human Rights in Paraguay*, 31 January 1978, OEA/Ser.L/V/II.43 doc. 13 corr. 1.
- IAComHR, *Access to Justice for Women Victims of Violence in the Americas*, 20 January 2007, OEA/Ser.L/V/II. Doc. 68.
- IAComHR, *Verdad, justicia y reparación: Cuarto informe sobre la situación de derechos humanos en Colombia*, 31 December 2013, OEA/Ser.L/V/II. Doc. 49/13.
- IAComHR, *Mesa Redonda: Violencia de género y reparaciones*, 27 October 2014, <http://www.oas.org/en/iachr/women/activities/activities.asp> <http://

www.youtube.com/watch?v=GeWwENjMRk4&feature=youtu.be> accessed 11 April 2017.
- IACtHR, *Annual Report 2012*, 2012, <http://www.corteidh.or.cr/sitios/informes/docs/ENG/eng_2012.pdf> accessed 14 April 2017.
- MESECVI, *Second Hemispheric Report on the Implementation of the Belém do Pará Convention*, April 2012, OEA/Ser.L/II.6.10.
- MESECVI, *Guide to the Application of the Inter-American Convention on the Prevention, Punishment, Eradication of Violence against Women*, 2014, OEA/Ser.L/II.6.14.

3. Other Documents and Reports

- African Commission on Human and Peoples' Rights Res. 111, *Resolution on the Right to a Remedy and Reparation for Women and Girls Victims of Sexual Violence*, 28 November 2007, ACHPR/Res. 111 (XXXXII) 07.
- Bundesministerium für Familie Senioren Frauen und Jugend, *Neue Wege - Gleiche Chancen: Gleichstellung von Frauen und Männern im Lebensverlauf*, Erster Gleichstellungsbericht, 16 June 2011, BT Drs. 17/6240.
- European Union Agency for Fundamental Rights, *Violence against women: An EU-wide survey*, Results at a glance, March 2014, <http://fra.europa.eu/en/publication/2014/violence-against-women-eu-wide-survey-results-glance> accessed 13 April 2015.
- Global Summit to End Sexual Violence in Conflict, *International Protocol on the Documentation and Investigation of Sexual Violence in Armed Conflicts: Basic Standards of best Practice on the Documentation of Sexual Violence as a Crime under International Law*, June 2014, <https://www.gov.uk/government/publications/international-protocol-on-the-documentation-and-investigation-of-sexual-violence-in-conflict> accessed 11 April 2017.
- *Nairobi Declaration on Women and Girls' Right to a Remedy and Reparation*, 21 March 2007, <https://www.fidh.org/IMG/pdf/NAIROBI_DECLARATIONeng.pdf> accessed 11 April 2017.
- World Bank (ed.), *Engendering development through gender equality in rights, resources, and voice: A World Bank Policy Research Report* (Oxford University Press, 2001).
- World Bank, *World Development Report 2011: Conflict, Security, and Development*, 2011, <https://siteresources.worldbank.org/INTWDRS/Resources/WDR2011_Full_Text.pdf> accessed 11 April 2017.

Bibliography

Abresch, W., 'A Human Rights Law of Internal Armed Conflict: The European Court of Human Rights in Chechnya', (2005) 16 *EJIL* 741.

Adams, A., *Der Tatbestand der Vergewaltigung im Völkerstrafrecht* (Duncker & Humblot, 2013).

Akandji-Kombe J.-F., *Les obligations positives en vertu de la Convention européenne des Droits de l'Homme,* 2006, <https://rm.coe.int/CoERMPublicCommonSearchServices/DisplayDCTMContent?documentId=090000168007ff61> accessed 13 April 2017.

Akehurst, M., 'The hierarchy of the sources of international law', (1976) 47 *BYIL* 273.

Altman, A., 'Discrimination', in E. N. Zalta (ed.), *The Stanford Encyclopedia of Philosophy* (Spring 2011), <http://plato.stanford.edu/archives/spr2011/entries/discrimination/>.

Alvarez, J., 'Legal Perspective', in T. G. Weiss and S. Daws (eds.), *The Oxford handbook on the United Nations* (Oxford University Press, 2008) 58.

Ambos, K., *Treatise on international criminal law: Volume I: Foundations and general part* (Oxford University Press, 2013).

Anderson, L., 'Politics by Other Means: When does Sexual Violence Threaten International Peace and Security?', (2010) 17 *International Peacekeeping* 244.

Antrobus, P., *The Global Women's Movement: Origins, Issues and Strategies* (Fern wood Publishing, 2004).

Arai, Y., 'The system of restrictions', in P. van Disk and Y. Arai (eds.), *Theory and practice of the European Convention on Human Rights* (Intersentia; Gaunt, 4th ed., 2006) 333.

Arai-Takahashi, Y., 'Proportionality', in D. Shelton (ed.), *The Oxford Handbook of International Human Rights Law* (Oxford University Press, 2010) 446.

Arnardóttir, O. M., *Equality and non-discrimination under the European Convention on Human Rights* (Martinus Nijhoff Publishers, 2003).

Arostegui, J., 'Gender, conflict, and peace-building: how conflict can catalyse positive change for women', (2013) 21 *Gender & Development* 533.

Askin, K. D., 'Treatment of Sexual Violence in Armed Conflicts: A Historical Perspective and the Way Forward', in A.-M. d. Brouwer, C. Ku; Römkens, R. and L. van den Herik (eds.), *Sexual Violence as an International Crime: Interdisciplinary Approaches* (Intensia, 2013) 19.

Askin, K. D., *War crimes against women: Prosecution in international war crimes tribunals* (Martinus Nijhoff Publishers, 1997).

Attia, I., Köbsell, S. and Prasad, N. (eds.), *Dominanzkultur reloaded: Neue Texte zu gesellschaftlichen Machtverhältnissen und ihren Wechselwirkungen*, Sozialtheorie (transcript, 2015).

E. V. Henn, *International Human Rights Law and Structural Discrimination*, Beiträge zum ausländischen öffentlichen Recht und Völkerrecht, https://doi.org/10.1007/978-3-662-58677-8

Baer, S., *Würde oder Gleichheit?: Zur angemessenen grundrechtlichen Konzeption von Recht gegen Diskriminierung am Beispiel sexueller Belästigung am Arbeitsplatz in der Bundesrepublik Deutschland und den USA* (Nomos, 1995).

Bagińska, E. (ed.), *Damages for Violations of Human Rights: A Comparative Study of Domestic Legal Systems* (Springer International Publishing, 2015).

Banda, F., 'Article 10', in B. Rudolf, M. A. Freeman and C. Chinkin (eds.), *The UN Convention on the Elimination of all Forms of Discrimination against Women: A commentary* (Oxford University Press, 2012a) 253.

Banda, F., 'Article 14', in B. Rudolf, M. A. Freeman and C. Chinkin (eds.), *The UN Convention on the Elimination of all Forms of Discrimination against Women: A commentary* (Oxford University Press, 2012b) 358.

Bandeira, L. M. and Mara Campos de Almeida, T., 'Vinte anos da Convencao de Belem do para e a Lei Maria da Penha', (2015) *Revista Estudo Feministas* 501.

Barrow, A., 'UN Security Council Resolutions 1325 and 1820: constructing gender in armed conflict and international humanitarian law', (2010) 92 *IRRC* 221.

Bassiouni, M. C., 'International Recognition of Victims' Rights', (2006) 6 *Hum. Rts. L. Rev.* 203.

Bedford, K., 'Gender and institutional strengthening: the World Bank's policy record in Latin America', (2009) 15 *Contemporary Politics* 197.

Bellinger, J. and Haynes, W. J., 'A US Government Response to the Study of the International Committee of the Red Cross Study Customary International Law', (2007) 40 *IRRC* 443.

Ben Naftali, O. (ed.), *International humanitarian law and international human rights law: Pas de deux* (Oxford University Press, 2011).

Benvenisti, E., 'Margin of appreciation, consensus, and universal standards', (1998) 31 *N.Y.U. J. Int'l L. & Pol.* 843.

Bergsmo, M. (ed.), *Thematic prosecution of international sex crimes*, FICHL publication series no. 13 (Torkel Opsahl Academic EPublisher, 2012).

Bergsmo, M., Skre, A. B. and Wood, E. J. (eds.), *Understanding and proving international sex crimes*, FICHL publication series No. 12 (Torkel Opsahl Academic EPublisher, 2012).

Beveridge, F. and Nott, S., 'Mainstreaming: A case for optimism and cynicism', (2002) 10 *Feminist Legal Studies* 299.

Boerefijn, I. (ed.), *Temporary Special Measures: Accelerating de facto equality of women under article 4 (1) UN Convention on the Elimination of All Forms of Discrimination Against Women* (Intersentia, 2003).

Bogdandy, A. v. and Venzke, I., *In wessen Namen?: Internationale Gerichte in Zeiten globalen Regierens* (Suhrkamp, 2014).

Bourdieu, P., *La domination masculine, suivi de 'Quelques questions sur le mouvement gay et lesbien'* (Éd. Points, 2002).

Boven, T. C. v., 'Victims' Rights to a Remedy and Reparation: The New United Nations Principles and Guidelines', in A. Stephens, C. Ferstman and M. Goetz (eds.), *Reparations for victims of genocide, war crimes and crimes against humanity: Systems in place and systems in the making* (Martinus Nijhoff Publishers, 2009) 19.

Boyle, A. E. and Chinkin, C., *The making of international law* (Oxford University Press, 2007).

Brown, W., '"We are all democrats now..."', in G. Agamben, A. Badiou, D. Bensaid et al. (eds.), *Democracy in what state?* (Columbia University Press, 2012) 44-59//55-71.

Brownmiller, S., *Against our will: Men, Women and Rape* (1975).

Burgorgue-Larsen, L., 'The Right to Determine Reparations', in L. Burgorgue-Larsen, A. Úbeda de Torres and R. Greenstein (eds.), *The Inter-American Court of Human Rights: Case-law and commentary* (Oxford University Press, 2011a) 217.

Burgorgue-Larsen, L., 'The Right to an Effective Remedy', in L. Burgorgue-Larsen, A. Úbeda de Torres and R. Greenstein (eds.), *The Inter-American Court of Human Rights: Case-law and commentary* (Oxford University Press, 2011b) 673.

Burgorgue-Larsen, L., Úbeda de Torres, A. and Greenstein, R. (eds.), *The Inter-American Court of Human Rights: Case-law and commentary* (Oxford University Press, 2011).

Buss, D. E., 'Rethinking 'Rape as a Weapon of War', (2009) 17 *Feminist Legal Studies* 145.
Byrnes, A., 'Article 1', in B. Rudolf, M. A. Freeman and C. Chinkin (eds.), *The UN Convention on the Elimination of all Forms of Discrimination against Women: A commentary* (Oxford University Press, 2012a) 51.
Byrnes, A., 'Article 2', in B. Rudolf, M. A. Freeman and C. Chinkin (eds.), *The UN Convention on the Elimination of all Forms of Discrimination against Women: A commentary* (Oxford University Press, 2012b) 71.
Cahill, A. J., *Rethinking rape* (Cornell University Press, 2001).
Çali, B., 'Specialized Rules of Treaty Interpretation: Human Rights', in D. B. Hollis (ed.), *The Oxford guide to treaties* (Oxford University Press, 2014) 525.
Carrillo, A. J., 'Justice in Context: The Relevance of Inter-American Human Rights Law and Practice to Repairing the Past', in P. de Greiff (ed.), *The Handbook of reparations* (Oxford University Press, 2006) 504.
Chamblee, L. E., 'Rhetoric or Rights: When Culture and Religion Bar Girls' Right to Education', (2003) 44 *Virginia Journal of International Law* 1073.
Charlesworth, H., 'Concepts of Equality in International Law', in G. Huscroft and P. Rishworth (eds.), *Litigating rights: Perspectives from domestic and international law* (Hart, 2002) 137.
Charlesworth, H. and Chinkin, C., *The Boundaries of International Law: A Feminist Analysis* (Manchester University Press, 2000).
Charlesworth, H. and Chinkin, C., 'The Gender of Jus Cogens', (1993) 15 *Hum. Rts. Q.* 63.
Chinkin, C., 'A critique of the Public/Private Dimension', (1999) 10 *EJIL* 387.
Chinkin, C., 'Addressing violence against women in the Commonwealth within states' obligations under international law', (2014) 40 *Commonwealth Law Bulletin* 471.
Chinkin, C., 'Article 3', in B. Rudolf, M. A. Freeman and C. Chinkin (eds.), *The UN Convention on the Elimination of all Forms of Discrimination against Women: A commentary* (Oxford University Press, 2012a).
Chinkin, C. and Freeman, M. A., 'Introduction', in B. Rudolf, M. A. Freeman and C. Chinkin (eds.), *The UN Convention on the Elimination of all Forms of Discrimination against Women: A commentary* (Oxford University Press, 2012) 1.
Chinkin, C., 'Normative Development in the International Legal System', in D. Shelton (ed.), *Commitment and compliance: The role of non-binding norms in the international legal system* (Oxford University Press, 2003) 21.
Chinkin, C., 'Violence Against Women', in B. Rudolf, M. A. Freeman and C. Chinkin (eds.), *The UN Convention on the Elimination of all Forms of Discrimination against Women: A commentary* (Oxford University Press, 2012b) 443.
Christian, M., et al., 'Sexual and gender based violence against men in the Democratic Republic of Congo: effects on survivors, their families and the community', (2011) 27 *Medicine, conflict and survival* 227.
Clapham, A., *Human rights in the private sphere* (Clarendon Press, Paperback ed., 1996).
Cockburn, C., 'The continuum of violence: a gender perspective on war and peace', in W. M. Giles and J. Hyndman (eds.), *Sites of violence: Gender and conflict zones* (University of California Press, 2004) 24.
Collins, R., 'Content Analysis of Gender Roles in Media: Where Are We Now and Where Should We Go?', (2011) 64 *Sex Roles* 290.
Conforti, B., 'Exploring the Strasbourg Case-Law: Reflections on State Responsibility for the Breach of Positive Obligations', in M. A. Fitzmaurice and D. Sarooshi (eds.), *Issues of state responsibility before international judicial institutions* (Hart, 2004) 129.
Contreras-Garduno, D. and Fraser, J., 'The Identification of Victims Before the Inter-American Court of Human Rights and the International Criminal Court and its Impact on Participation and Reparations: A Domino Effect?', (2015) *Int. Am. & Eur. Hum. Rts. J* 174.
Cook, R. J., 'State Responsibility for Violations of Women's Human Rights', (1994) 7 *Harv. Hum. Rts. J.* 125.

Cook, R. J. and Undurraga, V., 'Article 12', in B. Rudolf, M. A. Freeman and C. Chinkin (eds.), *The UN Convention on the Elimination of all Forms of Discrimination against Women: A commentary* (Oxford University Press, 2012) 311.

Crawford, J., *Brownlie' s Principles of public international law* (Clarendon Press; Oxford University Press, 8th edn, 2012a).

Crawford, E., 'Proportionality', in R. Wolfrum (ed.), *The Max Planck Encyclopedia of International Public Law* (Oxford University Press, 2012b).

Crawford, J., *State responsibility: The general part* (Cambridge Univ. Press, 2013).

Crawford, J., 'State Responsibility', in R. Wolfrum (ed.), *The Max Planck Encyclopedia of International Public Law* (Oxford University Press, 2012c).

Crawford, J. (ed.), *The ILC Draft Articles on Responsibility of States for Internationally Wrongful Acts: Commentary* Yearbook of the International Law Commission 2001, Vol. II, Part Two.

Crenshaw, K., 'Demarginalizing the intersection of race and sex: A black feminist critique of antidiscrimination doctrine, feminist theory and antiracist politics', (1989) *Univ. Chicago Legal Forum* 139.

Crenshaw, K., 'Mapping the margins: Intersectionality, identity politics, and violence against women of color', (1991) 43 *Stan. L. Rev.* 1241.

Cronin, B. and Hurd, I. (eds.), *The UN Security Council and the politics of international authority*, Security and governance series (Routledge, 2008).

Cusack, S. and Pusey, L., 'CEDAW and the Rights to Non-Discrimination and Equality', (2013) 14 *Melb. J. Int'l L.* 1.

David, E., *Principes de droit des conflits armés* (Bruylant, 5th, 2012).

Davis, A., 'Intersectionality and International Law: Recognizing Complex Identities on the Global Stage', (2015) 28 *Harv. Hum. Rts. J.* 205.

Doswald-Beck, L. and Henckaerts, J.-M. (eds.), *Customary international humanitarian law: Volume I: Rules* (Cambridge Univ. Press, 2005a).

Doswald-Beck, L. and Henckaerts, J.-M. (eds.), *Customary International Humanitarian Law: Volume II: Practice* (2005b).

Dröge, C., 'Elective Affinities?: Human rights and humanitarian law', (2008) 90 *IRRC* 501.

Dröge, C., 'The Interplay Between International Humanitarian Law And International Human Rights Law In Situations Of Armed Conflict', (2007) 40 *Isr. L. Rev.* 310.

Dröge, C., *Positive Verpflichtungen der Staaten in der Europäischen Menschenrechtskonvention* (Springer, 2003).

Duggan, C. and Jacobson, R., 'Reparation of Sexual Violence and Reproductive Violence: Moving from Codification to Implementation', in R. Rubio-Marín (ed.), *The gender of reparations: Unsettling sexual hierarchies while redressing human rights violations* (Cambridge University Press, 2009) 121.

Dworkin, R., *Sovereign virtue: the theory and practice of equality* (Harvard University Press, 2002).

Echeverria, G., 'Do victims of torture and other serious human rights violations have an independent and enforceable right to reparation?', (2012) 16 *The International Journal of Human Rights* 698.

Edwards, A., 'The 'Feminizing' of Torture under International Human Rights Law', (2006) 19 *Leiden JIL* 349.

Elshtain, J., *Women and War* (University of Chicago Press, 1987).

Elsuni, S., *Geschlechtsbezogene Gewalt und Menschenrechte: Eine geschlechtertheoretische Untersuchung der Konzepte Geschlecht, Gleichheit und Diskriminierung im Menschenrechtssystem der Vereinten Nationen* (Nomos, 2011).

Engle, K., 'The force of shame', in C. McGlynn and V. Munro (eds.), *Rethinking rape law: International and comparative perspectives* (Routledge, 2010) 76.

Eriksson, M., *Defining rape: Emerging obligations for states under international law?*, Doctoral Thesis (Örebro University, 2010).

Eriksson, M., *Defining rape: Emerging obligations for states under international law?* (Martinus Nijhoff Publishers, 2011).

Eriksson Baaz, M. and Stern, M., *Sexual violence as a weapon of war?: Perceptions, prescriptions, problems in the Congo and beyond* (Zed Books [etc.], 2013).

Ertürk, Y., 'The Due Diligence Standards: What does it entail for Women's Rights?', in C. Benninger-Budel (ed.), *Due diligence and its application to protect women from violence* (Martinus Nijhoff Publishers, 2008) 27.

European Union Agency for Fundamental Rights, *Handbook on European non-discrimination law* (Publ. Office of the Europ. Union, 2011).

Evans, C., *The right to reparation in international law for victims of armed conflict* (Cambridge University Press, 2012).

Evans, M., 'State Responsibility and the European Convention on Human Rights: role and realm', in M. A. Fitzmaurice and D. Sarooshi (eds.), *Issues of state responsibility before international judicial institutions* (Hart, 2004).

Fortas, A.-C., *La surveillance de l'exécution des arrêts et décisions des Cours européenne et interaméricaine des droits de l'Homme: Contribution à l'étude du droit du contentieux international* (A. Pedone, 2015).

Fraser, N., 'From redistribution to recognition? Dilemmas of justice in a 'post-socialist' age', (1995) *NLR* 68.

Fraser, N., Honneth, A. and Golb, J., *Redistribution or recognition?: A political-philosophical exchange* (Verso, 2003).

Fredman, S., 'Beyond the Dichotomy of Formal and Substantial Equality: Towards a New Definition of Equal Rights', in I. Boerefijn (ed.), *Temporary Special Measures: Accelerating de facto equality of women under article 4 (1) UN Convention on the Elimination of All Forms of Discrimination Against Women* (Intersentia, 2003).

Freeman, M. A., 'Article 16', in B. Rudolf, M. A. Freeman and C. Chinkin (eds.), *The UN Convention on the Elimination of all Forms of Discrimination against Women: A commentary* (Oxford University Press, 2012) 409.

Frowein, J., 'Ius cogens', in R. Wolfrum (ed.), *The Max Planck Encyclopedia of International Public Law* (Oxford University Press, 2012).

Gaggioli, G., 'Sexual violence in armed conflicts: A violation of international humanitarian law and human rights law', (2014) 96 *IRRC* 503.

Galtung, J., 'Violence, peace and peace research', (1969) 6 *Journal of Peace Research* 167.

Gardam, J. and Jarvis, M., *Women, armed conflict, and international law* (Kluwer Law International, 2001).

Garin, A., 'La perte de chance, un préjudice indemnisable', in J.-F. Flauss and É. Lambert-Abdelgawad (eds.), *La pratique d'indemnisation par la Cour européenne des droits de l'homme* (Bruylant, 2011) 155.

Garlicki, L., 'Broniowski and After: On the Dual Nature of 'Pilot Judgments'', in L. Caflisch and L. Wildhaber (eds.), *Liber amicorum Luzius Wildhaber: Human rights - Strasbourg views = Droits de l'homme - Regards de Strasbourg* (Engel, 2007).

Gebhardt, M., *Als die Soldaten kamen: Die Vergewaltigung deutscher Frauen am Ende des Zweiten Weltkriegs* (DVA, 2015).

Gioia, A., 'The Role of the European Court of Human Rights in Monitoring Compliance with Humanitarian Law in Armed Conflict', in O. Ben Naftali (ed.), *International humanitarian law and international human rights law: Pas de deux* (Oxford University Press, 2011) 201.

Goonesekere, S., 'Article 15', in B. Rudolf, M. A. Freeman and C. Chinkin (eds.), *The UN Convention on the Elimination of all Forms of Discrimination against Women: A commentary* (Oxford University Press, 2012).

Gosepath, S., 'Equality', in E. N. Zalta (ed.), *The Stanford Encyclopedia of Philosophy* (Spring 2011), <http://plato.stanford.edu/entries/equality/>.

Grabenwarter, C. (ed.), *European Convention on Human Rights: A Commentary* (Beck, Hart, Nomos, 2014).

Grabham, E., Cooper, D., Jrishnadas, J. et al. (eds.), *Intersectionality and beyond: Law, power and the politics of location* (Routledge, 2008).

Gready, P. and Robins, S., 'From Transitional to Transformative Justice: A New Agenda for Practice', (2014) 8 *Int. J. Transit. Just.* 339.

Grossman, N., 'Sex on the bench: do women judges matter to the legitimacy of international courts', (2011) 12 *Chi. J. Int'l L.* 647.

Grossmann, A., 'The "Big Rape": Sex and Sexual Violence, War and Occupation in Post-World-War II Memory and Imagination', in E. D. Heineman (ed.), *Sexual violence in conflict zones: From the ancient world to the era of human rights* (University of Pennsylvania Press, 2011) 137.

Hakimi, M., 'State Bystander Responsibility', (2010) 21 *EJIL* 341.

Halberstam, D. and Stein, E., 'The United Nations, the European Union, and the King of Sweden: Economic sanctions and individual rights in a plural world order', (2009) 46 *CMLRev* 13.

Harris, D., et al., 'Article13: The right to an effective national remedy', in D. Harris, M. O'Boyle, E. Bates et al. (eds.), *Law of the European Convention on Human Rights* (Oxford Univ. Press, 3rd edn., 2014a) 764.

Harris, D., et al., 'The European Convention on Human Rights in Context', in D. Harris, M. O'Boyle, E. Bates et al. (eds.), *Law of the European Convention on Human Rights* (Oxford Univ. Press, 3rd edn., 2014b) 3.

Harris, D., et al., 'The European Court of Human Rights: Organization, Practice, and Procedure', in D. Harris, M. O'Boyle, E. Bates et al. (eds.), *Law of the European Convention on Human Rights* (Oxford Univ. Press, 3rd edn., 2014c) 103.

Harris, D., O'Boyle, M., Bates, E. et al. (eds.), *Law of the European Convention on Human Rights* (Oxford Univ. Press, 3rd edn, 2014).

Hart, H. L. A., *The concept of law* (Oxford University Press, 3rd edn, 2012).

Hasselbacher, L., 'State Obligations Regarding Domestic Violence: The European Court of Human Rights, Due Diligence, and International Legal Minimums of Protection', (2010) 8 *Northwestern J. Int'l Hum. Rts.* 190.

Heijer, M. d. and Lawson, R., 'Extraterritorial human rights and the concept of 'jurisdiction'', in M. Langford (ed.), *Global justice, state duties: The extraterritorial scope of economic, social, and cultural rights in international law* (Cambridge University Press, 2013).

Henckaerts, J.-M., 'Concurrent Application of Humanitarian Law and Human Rights Law: A Victim Perspective', in R. Arnold and N. N. R. Quénivet (eds.), *International humanitarian law and human rights law: Towards a new merger in international law* (Martinus Nijhoff Publishers, 2008) 237.

Henn, E. V., 'Gender injustice, discrimination, and the CEDAW: A women's life course perspective', in M. Jänterä-Jareborg and H. Tigroudja (eds.), *Women's Right and the Elimination of Discrimination* (Brill; Martinus Nijhoff Publishers, 2016) 183.

Hirschl, R., 'The Judicialization of Politics', in K. E. Whittington, R. D. Kelemen and G. A. Caldeira (eds.), *The Oxford handbook of law and politics* (Oxford University Press, 2008).

Hobbes, T., et al., *Man and citizen: De homine and De cive* (Hackett Pub. Co, 1991).

Holtmaat, R., 'Article 5', in B. Rudolf, M. A. Freeman and C. Chinkin (eds.), *The UN Convention on the Elimination of all Forms of Discrimination against Women: A commentary* (Oxford University Press, 2012) 141.

Holtmaat, R., 'CEDAW: A holistic approach to women's equality and freedom', in A. Hellum and H. S. Aasen (eds.), *Women's Human Rights: CEDAW in International, Regional and National Law* (Cambridge University Press, 2013) 95.

Holtmaat, R., *Towards Different Law and Public Policy: The significance of Article 5a CEDAW for the elimination of structural gender discrimination* (Ministry of Social Affairs and Employment, 2004).

Inal T., *"So what?" The Impact of Legalization on Change on the Ground: Pillage and Rape on the Ground*, APSA 2010 Annual Meeting Paper, available at SSRN: http://papers.ssrn.com/sol3/papers.cfm?abstract_id=1641616, 2010.

Inal, T., *Looting and rape in wartime: Law and change in international relations* (University of Pennsylvania Press, 2013).
Inglis, S. C., 'Expanding International and National Protections Against Trafficking for Forced Labour Using a Human Rights Framework', (2001) 7 *Buff. Hum. Rts. L. Rev.* 55.
Jankowska-Gilberg, M., 'Das Al-Skeini-Urteil des Europäischen Gerichtshofs für Menschenrechte – eine Abkehr von Bankovic′?', Bericht, (2012) 50 *AVR* 61.
Joseph, S., Schultz, J. and Castan, M. (eds.), *The international covenant on civil and political rights: Cases, materials, and commentary* (Oxford University Press, 2nd edn, 2004).
Kamminga, M. T., 'Due Diligence Mania: Chapter 19', in I. Westendorp (ed.), *The Women's Convention turned 30: Achievements, setbacks, and progress* (Intersentia, 2012) 407.
Kapur, R., 'Tragedy of Victimization Rhetoric: Resurrecting the "Native" Subject in International/ Post-Colonial Feminist Legal Politics', (2002) 15 *Harv. Hum. Rts. J.* 1.
Keller, H. and Marti, C., 'Reconceptualizing Implementation: The Judicialization of the Execution of the European Court of Human Rights' Judgments', (2015) 26 *EJIL* 829.
Kelly, J. and Azuero Quijano, A., 'A Tale of Two Conflicts: an Unexpected Reading of Sexual Violence in Conflict through the Case of Colombia and the Democratic Republic of the Congo', in M. Bergsmo, A. B. Skre and E. J. Wood (eds.), *Understanding and proving international sex crimes* (Torkel Opsahl Academic EPublisher, 2012) 437.
Kirgis, F. L., 'Custom on a sliding scale', (1987) 81 *AJIL* 146.
Klein, E., 'Individual Reparation Claims under the International Convent of Civil and Political Rights: The Practice of the Human Rights Committee', in A. Randelzhofer and C. Tomuschat (eds.), *State responsibility and the individual: Reparation in instances of grave violations of human rights* (M. Nijhoff Publishers, 1999) 27.
Koivurova, T., 'Due diligence', in R. Wolfrum (ed.), *The Max Planck Encyclopedia of International Public Law* (Oxford University Press, 2012).
Kolb, R., 'The relationship between international humanitarian law and human rights law: A brief history of the 1948 Universal Declaration of Human Rights and the 1949 Geneva Conventions', (1998) 38 *IRRC* 409.
Krähenmann, S., 'Positive obligations in human rights law during armed conflicts', in R. Kolb and G. Gaggioli (eds.), *Research Handbook on Human Rights and Humanitarian Law* (Edward Elgar Publishing, 2013) 170.
Kühl, K., *Strafrecht. Allgemeiner Teil* (Franz Vahlen, 6th edn, 2008).
Lawson, R., 'Out of Control: State Responsibility', in P. R. Baehr, M. C. Castermans-Holleman, G. J. H. van Hoof et al. (eds.), *The role of the nation-state in the 21st century: Human rights, international organisations, and foreign policy: essays in honour of Peter Baehr* (Kluwer Law International, 1998).
Leach, P., et al., *Responding to Systemic Human Rights Violations: An Analysis of 'Pilot Judgments' of the European Court of Human Rights and their Impact at National Level* (Intersentia, 2010).
Leatherman, J., *Sexual violence and armed conflict* (Polity, 2011).
Lepard, B. D., *Customary international law: A new theory with practical applications* (Cambridge University Press, 2010).
Levitt, S. J., 'Rethinking Harm: A Feminist Essay', (1994) 34 *Washburn L.J.* 531.
Lewis, D. A., 'Unrecognized victims: Sexual violence against men in conflict settings under international law', (2009) 27 *Wis. Int'l L.J.* 1.
Lewis N., et al., *Making the normative case: Implementing Security Council resolution 1325 as part of a legal framework on women, peace and security*, April 2015.
Liebling-Kalifani, H., et al., 'Experiences of Women War-Torture Survivors in Uganda: Implications for Health and Human Rights', (2007) 8 *Journal of International Women's Studies* 1.
Locke, J., *Two treatises of government* (London, 1698).
Mackenzie, C., Rogers, W. and Dodds, S., 'Introduction', in C. Mackenzie (ed.), *Vulnerability: New essays in ethics and feminist philosophy* (Oxford University Press, 2013).
MacKinnon, C. A., 'Auf dem Weg zu einer neuen Theorie der Gleichheit', (1994) *KritV* 363.

MacKinnon, C. A., *Women's lives, men's laws* (Belknap, 2007).
Manji, A., 'Eliminating Poverty? 'Financial Inclusion', Access to Land, and Gender Equality in International Development', (2010) 73 *The Modern Law Review* 985.
Manjoo, R., 'Violence against women as a barrier to the realisation of human rights and the effective exercise of citizenship', (2016) 112 *Feminist Review* 11.
Marks, S., 'Human rights and root causes', (2011) 74 *The Modern Law Review* 57.
Marshall, J., 'Positive Obligations and Gender-based Violence: Judicial Developments', (2008) 10 *Int'l Comm. L. Rev.* 143.
Martin, F., 'Application du droit international humanitaire par la Cour interaméricaine des droits de l'homme', (2001) 83 *IRRC* 1037.
Mazzeschi, R. P., 'Reparation Claims by Individuals for State Breaches of Humanitarian Law and Human Rights: An Overview', (2003) 1 *J. Int'l Crim. Just.* 339.
McQuigg, R. J., 'Domestic Violence as a Human Rights Issue: Rumor v. Italy', (2015) 26 *EJIL* 1009.
McWilliams, M. and Ni Aolain, F. D., "There is a War Going on You Know': Addressing the Complexity of Violence against Women in Conflicted and Post Conflict Societies', (2013) 1 *Transitional Justice Review*.
Medina, C. (ed.), *The American Convention on Human Rights* (Intersentia, 2014).
Mégret, F., 'Nature of Obligations', in S. Sivakumaran, D. Moeckli and S. Shah (eds.), *International Human Rights Law* 124.
Melville, A., 'Evaluating Judicial Performance and Addressing Gender Bias', (2014) 4 *Oñati Socio-legal Series* 880–897, available at SSRN: http://ssrn.com/abstract=2533912.
Meron, T., 'Rape as a Crime under International Humanitarian Law', (1993) 87 *AJIL* 424.
Milanovic, M., 'A Norm Conflict Perspective on the Relationship between International Humanitarian Law and Human Rights Law', (2010) 14 *JCSL* 459.
Milanovic, M., *Extraterritorial application of human rights treaties: law, principles, and policy* (Oxford University Press, 2011a).
Milanovic, M., 'Norm Conflicts, International Humanitarian Law, and Human Rights Law', in O. Ben Naftali (ed.), *International humanitarian law and international human rights law: Pas de deux* (Oxford University Press, 2011b) 95.
Milanović M., *Territorial Scope of Application of the Genocide Convention,* December 2008, <http://www.ejiltalk.org/territorial-scope-of-application-of-the-genocide-convention/> accessed 26 April 2015.
Miller, B. D., 'Female-Selective Abortion in Asia: Patterns, Policies, and Debates', (2001) 103 *American Anthropologist* 1083.
Mortimer, J. T. and Shanahan, M. J. (eds.), *Handbook of the life course* (Springer, 2006).
Mouthaan, S., 'Sexual Violence against Men and International Law: Criminalising the Unmentionable', (2013) 13 *Int'l Crim. L. Rev.* 665.
Mowbray, A. R., *The development of positive obligations under the European Convention on Human Rights by the European Court of Human Rights* (Hart Pub., 2004).
Naert, F., 'The European Court of Human Rights' Al-Jedda and Al-Skeini Judgments: an Introduction and Some Reflections', (2011) 50 *Military Law Review* 315.
Neumann, G., 'Subsidiarity', in D. Shelton (ed.), *The Oxford Handbook of International Human Rights Law* (Oxford University Press, 2010) 360.
Neumayer, E. and Plümper, T., 'The gendered nature of natural disasters: The impact of catastrophic events on the gender gap in life expectancy, 1981-2002', (2007) 97 *Annals of the Association of American Geographers* 551.
Ní Aoláin, F. D., Haynes, D. F. and Cahn, N., *On the Frontlines: Gender, War, and the Post-conflict Process* (Oxford University Press, 2011).
Ní Aoláin, F. D., O'Rourke, C. and Swaine, A., 'Transforming Reparations for Conflict-Related Sexual Violence: Principles and Practice', (2015) *Harv. Hum. Rts. J.* 97.
Nickel, J. W., 'How human rights generate duties to protect and provide', (1993) *Hum. Rts. Q.* 77.

Nikolaidis, C., *The right to equality in European human rights law: The quest for substance in the jurisprudence of the European courts* (Routledge, 2015).

Norris, A. and Watkin, K., *Non-International Armed Conflict in the Twenty-first Century* (2012).

Nowak, M., 'The Right of Victims of Gross Human Rights Violations to Reparation', in T. C. v. Boven and F. Coomans (eds.), *Rendering justice to the vulnerable: Liber amicorum in honour of Theo van Boven* (Kluwer Law International, 2000) 203.

Nowak, M. (ed.), *U.N. Covenant on Civil and Political Rights: ICCPR commentary* (N.P. Engel, 2nd edn, 2005).

Nussbaum, M. and Sen, A., *The quality of life* (Oxford University Press, 1993).

Nussbaum, M. C., *Women and human development: The capabilities approach* (Cambridge University Press, 2000).

O'Donnell, T. A., 'The Margin of Appreciation Doctrine: Standards in the Jurisprudence of the European Court of Human Rights', (1982) 4 *Hum. Rts. Q.* 474.

Olugbuo, B. C., 'Thematic Prosecution of International Sex Crimes and Stigmatisation of Victim and Survivors: Two Sides of the Same Coin?', in M. Bergsmo (ed.), *Thematic prosecution of international sex crimes* (Torkel Opsahl Academic EPublisher, 2012) 109.

Onyango, M. A. and Hampanda, K., 'Social constructions of masculinity and male survivors of wartime sexual violence: An analytical review', (2011) 23 *International Journal of Sexual Health* 237.

Ossenbühl, F. and Cornils, M., *Staatshaftungsrecht* (Beck, 6th edn, 2013).

Owen, M., 'Human rights of widows in developing countries', in K. Askin and D. Koenig (eds.), *Women and International Human Rights Law: Introduction to women's human rights issues* (Transitional Publishers, Incorporated, 1999-2001) p. 241-266.

Pahuja, S., 'Trading Spaces: Locating Sites for Challenge within International Trade Law', (2000) 14 *Australian Feminist Law Journal* 38.

Pasqualucci, J. M., *The practice and procedure of the Inter-American Court of Human Rights* (Cambridge Univ. Press, 2nd edn, 2013).

Peukert, W., 'Artikel 41', in J. Frowein and W. Peukert (eds.), *Europäische Menschenrechtskonvention: EMRK-Kommentar* (Engel, 3rd edn., 2009).

Pictet, J. (ed.), *The Geneva Conventions of 12 August 1949 - Commentary: Geneva Convention Relative to the Protection of Civilian Persons in the Time of War* IV (ICRC, 1958).

Pictet, J., Gasser, H.-P., Junod, S. S. et al. (eds.), *Commentary on the Additional Protocols of June 8 1977 to the Geneva Conventions of 12 August 1949* (Martinus Nijhoff Publishers, 1987).

Pilch, F. T., 'The Crime of Rape in International Humanitarian Law', (1998) 9 *USAF Acad. J. Legal Stud.* 99.

Plakokefalos, I., 'Causation in the Law of State Responsibility and the Problem of Over-determination: In Search of Clarity', (2015) 26 *EJIL* 471.

Provost, R., *International human rights and humanitarian law* (Cambridge University Press, 2002).

Raday, F., 'Article 11', in B. Rudolf, M. A. Freeman and C. Chinkin (eds.), *The UN Convention on the Elimination of all Forms of Discrimination against Women: A commentary* (Oxford University Press, 2012) 279.

Raday, F., 'Systematizing the Application of Different Types of Temporary Special Measures under Article 4 of CEDAW', in I. Boerefijn (ed.), *Temporary Special Measures: Accelerating de facto equality of women under article 4 (1) UN Convention on the Elimination of All Forms of Discrimination Against Women* (Intersentia, 2003) 35.

Reid, K. (ed.), *A practitioner's guide to the European Convention on Human Rights* (Sweet & Maxwell, 4th edn, 2011).

Riddle, J., 'Making CEDAW Universal: A Critique of CEDAW's Reservation Regime Under Article 28 and the Effectiveness of the Reporting Process', (2002) 34 *Geo. Wash. Int'l L. Rev.* 605.

Ronzitti, N., 'Access to Justice and Compensation for Violations of the Law of War', in F. Francioni (ed.), *Access to justice as a human right* (Oxford University Press, 2007) 97.

Rose, C., 'An Emerging Norm: The Duty of States to Provide Reparations for Human Rights Violations by Non-State Actors', (2010) 33 *Hastings Int'l & Comp. L. Rev.* 307.

Ross, A., *On law and justice* (Lawbook Exchange, 4th edn, 2009).

Roxstrom, E. M. T., 'The NATO Bombing Case (Bancovic et al. v. Belgium at al.) and the limits of western human rights protection', (2005) 23 *B.U. Int'l L.J.* 55.

Rubio-Marin, R. and Sandoval, C., 'Engendering the reparations jurisprudence of the Inter-American court of human rights: The promise of the cotton field judgment', (2011) 33 *Hum. Rts. Q.* 1062.

Rubio-Marín, R., 'Gender and Collective Reparation in the Aftermath of Conflict and Political Repression', in R. Rubio-Marín (ed.), *The gender of reparations: Unsettling sexual hierarchies while redressing human rights violations* (Cambridge University Press, 2009) 381.

Rubio-Marín, R., 'Reparations for Conflict-Related Sexual and Reproductive Violence: A Decalogue', (2012) 19 *William & Mary Journal of Women and the Law* 69.

Rubio-Marín, R. and Möschel, M., 'Anti-Discrimination Exceptionalism: Racist Violence before the ECtHR and the Holocaust Prism', (2015) 26 *EJIL* 881.

Rubio-Marín, R., Sandoval-Villalba, C. and Días, C., 'Repairing Family Members: Gross Human Rights Violations and Communities of Harm', in R. Rubio-Marín (ed.), *The gender of reparations: Unsettling sexual hierarchies while redressing human rights violations* (Cambridge University Press, 2009) 215.

Rudolf, B., 'Article 13', in B. Rudolf, M. A. Freeman and C. Chinkin (eds.), *The UN Convention on the Elimination of all Forms of Discrimination against Women: A commentary* (Oxford University Press, 2012).

Rudolf, B., 'Menschenrechte und Geschlecht - eine Diskursgeschichte', in U. Lembke (ed.), *Menschenrechte und Geschlecht* (Nomos, 2014) 24.

Ryngaert, C., 'Jurisdiction: Towards a reasonable test', in M. Langford (ed.), *Global justice, state duties: The extraterritorial scope of economic, social, and cultural rights in international law* (Cambridge University Press, 2013) 192.

Sacksofsky, U., *Das Grundrecht auf Gleichberechtigung: Eine rechtsdogmatische Untersuchung zu Artikel 3 Absatz 2 des Grundgesetzes* (Nomos, 2nd edn, 1996).

Saltzman L. E. and Basile K. C., *Sexual Violence Surveillance: Uniformed Definition and Recommended Data Elements,* 2009, <https://www.cdc.gov/violenceprevention/pdf/sv_surveillance_definitionsl-2009-a.pdf> accessed 13 April 2017.

Sandoval-Villalba, C., 'The Concept of 'Injured Party' and 'Victim' of Gross Human Rights Violations in the Jurisprudence of the Inter-American Court of Human Rights: A Commentary on their Implications on Reparations', in A. Stephens, C. Ferstman and M. Goetz (eds.), *Reparations for victims of genocide, war crimes and crimes against humanity: Systems in place and systems in the making* (Martinus Nijhoff Publishers, 2009) 243.

Saris, A. and Lofts, K., 'Reparation Programmes: A Gender Perspective', in A. Stephens, C. Ferstman and M. Goetz (eds.), *Reparations for victims of genocide, war crimes and crimes against humanity: Systems in place and systems in the making* (Martinus Nijhoff Publishers, 2009) 79.

Sassòli, M., 'State Responsibility for violation of international humanitarian law', (2002) 84 *IRRC* 401.

Sassòli, M., 'The Role of Human Rights and International Humanitarian Law in New Types of Armed Conflicts', in O. Ben Naftali (ed.), *International humanitarian law and international human rights law: Pas de deux* (Oxford University Press, 2011) 34.

Schachter, O., *International law in theory and practice* (Martinus Nijhoff Publishers, 1991).

Schlosser, M., 'Agency', in E. N. Zalta (ed.), *The Stanford Encyclopedia of Philosophy* (Fall 2015), <https://plato.stanford.edu/archives/fall2015/entries/agency/>.

Schöpp-Schilling, H.-B., 'Impediments to Progress: The Formal Labor Market', in H.-B. Schöpp-Schilling and C. Flinterman (eds.), *The circle of empowerment: Twenty-five years of the UN Committee on the Elimination of Discrimination against Women* (Feminist Press at the City University of New York, 2007) 159.

Schutter, O. de, et al., 'Commentary to the Maastricht Principles on extraterritorial obligations of states in the area of economic, social and cultural rights', (2012) 34 *Hum. Rts. Q.* 1084.

Schutter, O. de, *International human rights law: Cases, materials, commentary* (Cambridge University Press, 2010).

Schutter, O. de, *International human rights law: Cases, materials, commentary* (Cambridge Univ. Press, 2nd edn, 2014).

Scott, J. B. (ed.), *The Proceedings of the Hague Peace Conferences: The Conference of 1907*, Translation of the Official Texts (Oxford University Press, 1920).

Seyler M. M., *Rape in Conflict: Battling the Impunity that Stifles its Recognition as a Jus Cogens Human Right,* 2011, available at <https://works.bepress.com/michelle_seyler/1/> accessed 13 April 2017.

Shany, Y., 'Toward a general margin of appreciation doctrine in international law?', (2005) 16 *EJIL* 907.

Shaw, M. N., *International law* (Cambridge University Press, 6th ed., 2008).

Shelton, D., *Remedies in international human rights law* (Oxford University Press, 2nd edn, 2006).

Shelton, D., 'The jurisprudence of human rights tribunals on remedies for human rights violations', in J. F. Flauss (ed.), *La protection internationale des droits de l'homme et les droits des victimes: International protection of human rights and victims' rights* (Bruylant, 2009) 57.

Shelton, D. and Gould, A., 'Positive and Negative Obligations: Chapter 24', in D. Shelton (ed.), *The Oxford Handbook of International Human Rights Law* (Oxford University Press, 2010) 562.

Shue, H., *Basic rights: Subsistence, affluence, and U.S. foreign policy* (Princeton University Press, 2nd edn, 1996).

Silverstein, G., *Law's allure: How law shapes, constrains, saves, and kills politics* (Cambridge University Press, 2009).

Simma, B., 'Universality of International Law from the Perspective of a Practitioner', (2009) 20 *EJIL* 265.

Sivakumaran, S., 'Prosecuting Sexual Violence against Men and Boys', in A.-M. d. Brouwer, C. R. R. Ku and L. d. van Herik (eds.), *Sexual Violence as an International Crime: Interdisciplinary Approaches* (Intensia, 2013) 79.

Sivakumaran, S., 'Sexual Violence Against Men in Armed Conflict', (2007) 18 *EJIL* 253.

Slaughter A.-M., *Why Women can't still have it all,* 2012, <http://www.theatlantic.com/magazine/archive/2012/07/why-women-still-cant-have-it-all/309020/?single_page=true> accessed 13 April 2017

Smekal, H. and Sipulova, K., 'DH v. Czech Republic Six Years Later: On the Power of an International Human Rights Court to Push through Systemic Change', (2014) 32 *Neth. Q. Hum. Rts.* 288.

Stahl, S., *Schutzpflichten im Völkerrecht - Ansatz einer Dogmatik: Ein Beitrag zu Grund, Inhalt und Grenzen der völkerrechtlichen Schutzpflichtendogmatik im Bereich konventionell geschützter Menschenrechte* (Springer, 2012).

Stark, L. and Ager, A., 'A systematic review of prevalence studies of gender-based violence in complex emergencies', (2011) 12 *Trauma, Violence, & Abuse* 127.

Staton, J. K. and Moore, W. H., 'Judicial power in domestic and international politics', (2011) 65 *International Organization* 553.

Stephens, A., Ferstman, C. and Goetz, M. (eds.), *Reparations for victims of genocide, war crimes and crimes against humanity: Systems in place and systems in the making* (Martinus Nijhoff Publishers, 2009).

Stewart, A., 'Who Do We Care About? Reflections on Gender Justice in a Global Market', (2007) 58 *Northern Ireland Legal Quarterly* 358.

Tachou-Sipowo, A.-G., 'The Security Council on women in war: between peacebuilding and humanitarian protection', (2010) 92 *IRRC* 197.

Talmon, S., 'The Security Council as world legislature', (2005) *AJIL* 175.

Thornberry, P., *The International Convention on the Elimination of All Forms of Racial Discrimination: A commentary* (Oxford University Press, 2016).

Ticehurst, R., 'The Martens Clause and the laws of armed conflict', (1997) *IRRC* 125.
Tiefenbrun, S. W., *Women's international and comparative human rights* (Carolina Academic Press, 2012).
Tigroudja, H., 'The Inter-American Court of Human Rights and international humanitarian law', in R. Kolb and G. Gaggioli (eds.), *Research Handbook on Human Rights and Humanitarian Law* (Edward Elgar Publishing, 2013) 466.
Tiroch, K., 'Violence against Women by Private Actors: The Inter-American Court's Judgment in the Case of Gonzalez et al. ("Cotton Field") v. Mexico', (2010) 14 *Max Planck UNYB* 371.
Tomuschat, C., 'La Protection Internationale des Droits des Victims', in J. F. Flauss (ed.), *La protection internationale des droits de l'homme et les droits des victimes: International protection of human rights and victims' rights* (Bruylant, 2009) 1.
Tomuschat, C., *Obligations arising for States without or against their will* (Martinus Nijhoff, 1993).
Tomuschat, C., 'Reparation In Favour of Individual Victims of Gross Violations of Human Rights and International Humanitarian Law', in M. G. Kohen and L. Caflisch (eds.), *Promoting justice, human rights and conflict resolution through international law: Liber amicorum Lucius Caflisch = La promotion de la justice, des droits de l'homme et du règlement des conflits par le droit international* (Martinus Nijhoff Publishers, 2007) 569.
Totsuka, E., 'Commentary on a Victory for "Comfort Women": Japan's Judicial Recognition of Military Sexual Slavery', (1999) 8 *Pacific Rim Law and Policies Journal* 47.
Tryggestad, T. L., 'Trick or Treat? The UN and Implementation of Security Council Resolution 1325 on Women, Peace, and Security', (2009) 15 *Global Governance: a review of multilateralism and international organizations* 539.
Úbeda de Torres, A., 'Determination of victims', in L. Burgorgue-Larsen, A. Úbeda de Torres and R. Greenstein (eds.), *The Inter-American Court of Human Rights: Case-law and commentary* (Oxford University Press, 2011) 108.
Ugrekhelidze, M., 'Causation: Reflections in the mirror of the European Convention of Human Rights', in L. Caflisch and L. Wildhaber (eds.), *Liber amicorum Luzius Wildhaber: Human rights - Strasbourg views = Droits de l'homme - Regards de Strasbourg* (Engel, 2007) 469.
UN Department of Social and Economic Affairs - Division for the Advancement of Women, *Handbook for legislation on violence against women* (United Nations, 2010).
Vöneky, S., 'Der Lieber's Code und die Wurzeln des modernen Kriegsvölkerrechts', (2002) 62 *ZaöRV* 423.
Vöneky, S., *Die Fortgeltung des Umweltvölkerrechts in internationalen bewaffneten Konflikten* (Springer, 2012).
Walker, L. E., *The battered woman syndrome* (Springer, 3rd ed., 2009a).
Walker, M. U., 'Gender and Violence in Focus: A Background for Gender Justice in Reparations', in R. Rubio-Marín (ed.), *The gender of reparations: Unsettling sexual hierarchies while redressing human rights violations* (Cambridge University Press, 2009b) 18.
Walker, M. U., 'Transformative Reparations? A Critical Look at a Current Trend in Thinking about Gender-Just Reparations', (2016) 10 *Int. J. Transit. Just.* 108.
Ward, T., Polaschek, D. and Beech, A., *Theories of Sexual Offending* (Wiley, 2006).
Watkin, K., 'Controlling the use of force: a role for human rights norms in contemporary armed conflict', (2004) *AJIL* 1.
Wenzel, N., 'Human Rights, Treaties, Extraterritorial Application and Effects', in R. Wolfrum (ed.), *The Max Planck Encyclopedia of International Public Law* (Oxford University Press, 2012).
Wersig, M., *Der lange Schatten der Hausfrauenehe: Zur Reformresistenz des Ehegattensplittings* (Budrich, 2013).
Whittington, K. E., Kelemen, R. D. and Caldeira, G. A. (eds.), *The Oxford handbook of law and politics*, The Oxford handbooks of political science (Oxford University Press, 2008).
Wolff, J. and De-Shalit, A., *Disadvantage* (Oxford University Press, 2007).

Wood, E. J., 'Rape During War is Not Inevitable: Variations in Wartime Sexual Violence', in M. Bergsmo, A. B. Skre and E. J. Wood (eds.), *Understanding and proving international sex crimes* (Torkel Opsahl Academic EPublisher, 2012) 389.

Woodward, A. E., 'From equal treatment to gender mainstreaming and diversity management', in G. Abels and J. M. Mushaben (eds.), *Gendering the European Union: New approaches to old democratic deficits* (Palgrave Macmillan, 2012) 85.

Wright, S., 'Women and the Global Economic Order: A Feminist Perspective', (1994) 10 *Am. U.J. Int'l L. & Pol'y* 861.

Young, I. M., *Justice and the politics of difference* (Princeton University Press, 1990 (2011)).

Young, I. M., 'Unruly categories: A critique of Nancy Fraser's dual systems theory', (1997) *NLR* 147.

Zegveld, L., 'The Inter-American Commission on Human Rights and International Humanitarian Law: A Comment on the Tablada Case', (1998) 38 *IRRC* 505.

Max-Planck-Institut für ausländisches öffentliches Recht und Völkerrecht

Beiträge zum ausländischen öffentlichen Recht und Völkerrecht

Hrsg.: A. von Bogdandy, A. Peters

Bde. 27–59 erschienen im Carl Heymanns Verlag KG Köln, Berlin (Bestellung an: Max-Planck-Institut für Völkerrecht, Im Neuenheimer Feld 535, 69120 Heidelberg); ab Band 60 im Springer-Verlag GmbH

---

280 Elisabeth Veronika *Henn*: **International Human Rights Law and Structural Discrimination**. 2019. X 221 Seiten. € 93,59

279 Eike *Blitza*: **Auswirkungen des Meeresspiegelanstiegs auf maritime Grenzen**. 2019. XV 292 Seiten. € 87,46

278 Anna Katharina *Struth*: **Hassrede und Freiheit der Meinungsäußerung**. 2019. XV, 472 Seiten. Geb. € 109,99

277 Franziska *Sucker*: **Der Schutz und die Förderung kultureller Vielfalt im Welthandelsrecht.** 2018. XXIV, 635 Seiten. Geb. € 109,99

276 Clemens *Mattheis*: **Die Konstitutionalisierung des Völkerrechts aus systemtheoretischer Sichtweise.** 2018. XXIV, 557 Seiten. Geb. € 109,99

275 Aydin *Atilgan*: **Global Constitutionalism.** 2018. X, 312 Seiten. Geb. € 114,99 zzgl. landesüblicher MwSt.

274 Andreas *Kolb*: **The UN Security Council Members' Responsibility to Protect**. 2018. XXI 624 Seiten. Geb. € 199,99 zzgl. landesüblicher MwSt.

273 Matthias *Goldmann*, Silvia *Steininger* (eds.): **Democracy and Financial Order: Legal Perspectives**. 2018. V, 228 Seiten. Geb. € 114,99 zzgl. landesüblicher MwSt.

272 Jochen *Rauber*: **Strukturwandel als Prinzipienwandel.** 2018. XXXIV, 970 Seiten. Geb. € 159,99

271 Anja *Höfelmeier*: **Die Vollstreckungsimmunität der Staaten im Wandel des Völkerrechts.** 2018. XX, 356 Seiten. Geb. € 89,99

270 Rudolf *Bernhardt*, Karin *Oellers-Frahm*: **Das Max-Planck-Institut für ausländisches öffentliches Recht und Völkerrecht.** 2018. XII, 344 Seiten. Geb. € 89,99

269 Philine *Wehling*: **Wasserrechte am Nil.** 2018. XVI, 351 Seiten. Geb. € 84,99

268 Katharina *Berner*: **Subsequent Agreements and Subsequent Practice in Domestic Courts.** 2018. XLV, 298 Seiten. Geb. € 114,99 zzgl. landesüblicher MwSt.

267 Josephine *Asche*: **Die Margin of Appreciation.** 2018. XII, 255 Seiten. Geb. € 84,99

266 Nele *Yang*: **Die Leitentscheidung.** 2018. XI, 362 Seiten. Geb. € 84,99

265 Roya *Sangi*: **Die auswärtige Gewalt des Europäischen Parlaments.** 2018. XV, 179 Seiten. Geb. € 69,99

264 Anna *Krueger*: **Die Bindung der Dritten Welt an das postkoloniale Völkerrecht.** 2018. XII, 434 Seiten. Geb. € 89,99

263 Björnstjern *Baade*: **Der Europäische Gerichtshof für Menschenrechte als Diskurswächter.** 2017. XVIII, 543 Seiten. Geb. € 99,99

262 Felix *Lange*: **Praxisorientierung und Gemeinschaftskonzeption.** 2017. XIV, 403 Seiten. Geb. € 94,99

261 Johanna Elisabeth *Dickschen*: **Empfehlungen und Leitlinien als Handlungsform der Europäischen Finanzaufsichtsbehörden.** 2017. XIX, 277 Seiten. Geb. € 84,99

260 Mohamed *Assakkali*: **Europäische Union und Internationaler Währungsfonds.** 2017. XV, 516 Seiten. Geb. € 99,99

259 Franziska *Paefgen*: **Der von Art. 8 EMRK gewährleistete Schutz vor staatlichen Eingriffen in die Persönlichkeitsrechte im Internet.** 2017. XV, 220 Seiten. Geb. € 69,99

258 Tim René *Salomon*: **Die internationale Strafverfolgungsstrategie gegenüber somalischen Piraten.** 2017. XXXII, 743 Seiten. Geb. € 129,99

257 Jelena *Bäumler*: **Das Schädigungsverbot im Völkerrecht.** 2017. XIX, 379 Seiten. Geb. € 89,99

256 Christopher *Peters*: **Praxis Internationaler Organisationen - Vertragswandel und völkerrechtlicher Ordnungsrahmen.** 2016. XXVIII, 498 Seiten. Geb. € 99,99

255 Nicole *Appel*: **Das internationale Kooperationsrecht der Europäischen Union.** 2016. XVIII, 608 Seiten. Geb. € 109,99

254 Christian *Wohlfahrt*: **Die Vermutung unmittelbarer Wirkung des Unionsrechts.** 2016. XIX, 300 Seiten. Geb. € 84,99

253 Katja *Göcke*: **Indigene Landrechte im internationalen Vergleich.** 2016. XVII, 818 Seiten. Geb. € 139,99

252 Julia *Heesen*: **Interne Abkommen.** 2015. XXI, 473 Seiten. Geb. € 94,99

251 Matthias *Goldmann*: **Internationale öffentliche Gewalt.** 2015. XXIX, 636 Seiten. Geb. € 109,99

250 Isabelle *Ley*: **Opposition im Völkerrecht.** 2014. XXIII, 452 Seiten. Geb. € 94,99

249 Matthias *Kottmann*: **Introvertierte Rechtsgemeinschaft.** 2014. XII, 352 Seiten. Geb. € 84,99

247 Jürgen *Friedrich*: **International Environmental "soft law".** 2014. XXI, 503 Seiten. Geb. € 94,99 zzgl. landesüblicher MwSt.

246 Anuscheh *Farahat*: **Progressive Inklusion.** 2014. XXIV, 429 Seiten. Geb. € 94,99

245 Christina *Binder*: **Die Grenzen der Vertragstreue im Völkerrecht.** 2013. XL, 770 Seiten. Geb. € 119,99

244 Cornelia *Hagedorn*: **Legitime Strategien der Dissensbewältigung in demokratischen Staaten.** 2013. XX, 551 Seiten. Geb. € 99,99

243 Marianne *Klumpp*: **Schiedsgerichtsbarkeit und Ständiges Revisionsgericht des Mercosur.** 2013. XX, 512 Seiten. Geb. € 94,99

242 Karen *Kaiser* (Hrsg.): **Der Vertrag von Lissabon vor dem Bundesverfassungsgericht.** 2013. XX, 1635 Seiten. Geb. € 199,99

241 Dominik *Steiger*: **Das völkerrechtliche Folterverbot und der "Krieg gegen den Terror".** 2013. XXX, 821 Seiten. Geb. € 139,99

240 Silja *Vöneky*, Britta *Beylage-Haarmann*, Anja *Höfelmeier*, Anna-Katharina *Hübler* (Hrsg.): **Ethik und Recht - Die Ethisierung des Rechts/Ethics and Law - The Ethicalization of Law.** 2013. XVIII, 456 Seiten. Geb. € 94,99

239 Rüdiger *Wolfrum*, Ina *Gätzschmann* (eds.): **International Dispute Settlement: Room for Innovations?** 2013. XIV, 445 Seiten. Geb. € 94,95 zzgl. landesüblicher MwSt.

238 Isabel *Röcker*: **Die Pflicht zur rahmenbeschlusskonformen Auslegung nationalen Rechts.** 2013. XXIII, 410 Seiten. Geb. € 89,95

237 Maike *Kuhn*: **Die Europäische Sicherheits- und Verteidigungspolitik im Mehrebenensystem.** 2012. XIII, 325 Seiten. Geb. € 79,95

236 Armin *von Bogdandy*, Ingo *Venzke* (eds.): **International Judicial Lawmaking.** 2012. XVII, 509 Seiten. Geb. € 94,95 zzgl. landesüblicher MwSt.

235 Susanne *Wasum-Rainer*, Ingo *Winkelmann*, Katrin *Tiroch* (eds.): **Arctic Science, International Law and Climate Change.** 2012. XIX, 374 Seiten. Geb. € 84,95 zzgl. landesüblicher MwSt.

234 Mirja A. *Trilsch*: **Die Justiziabilität wirtschaftlicher, sozialer und kultureller Rechte im innerstaatlichen Recht.** 2012. XIX, 559 Seiten. Geb. € 99,95

233 Anja *Seibert-Fohr* (ed.): **Judicial Independence in Transition.** 2012. XIII, 1378 Seiten. Geb. € 169,95 zzgl. landesüblicher MwSt.

232 Sandra *Stahl*: **Schutzpflichten im Völkerrecht - Ansatz einer Dogmatik.** 2012. XXX, 505 Seiten. Geb. € 94,95

231 Thomas *Kleinlein*: **Konstitutionalisierung im Völkerrecht.** 2012. XLII, 940 Seiten. Geb. € 149,95

230 Roland *Otto*: **Targeted Killings and International Law.** 2012. XVIII, 661 Seiten. Geb. € 109,95 zzgl. landesüblicher MwSt.

229 Nele *Matz-Lück*, Mathias *Hong* (Hrsg.): **Grundrechte und Grundfreiheiten im Mehrebenensystem - Konkurrenzen und Interferenzen.** 2012. VIII, 394 Seiten. Geb. € 89,95

228 Matthias *Ruffert*, Sebastian *Steinecke:* **The Global Administrative Law of Science,** 2011. IX, 140 Seiten. Geb. € 59,95 zzgl. landesüblicher MwSt.

227 Sebastian *Pritzkow*: **Das völkerrechtliche Verhältnis zwischen der EU und Russland im Energiesektor.** 2011. XXIV, 304 Seiten. Geb. € 79,95

226 Sarah *Wolf*: **Unterseeische Rohrleitungen und Meeresumweltschutz.** 2011. XXIII, 442 Seiten. Geb. € 94,95

225 Clemens *Feinäugle*: **Hoheitsgewalt im Völkerrecht.** 2011. XXVI, 418 Seiten. Geb. € 89,95

224 David *Barthel*: **Die neue Sicherheits- und Verteidigungsarchitektur der Afrikanischen Union.** 2011. XXV, 443 Seiten. Geb. € 94,95

223 Tilmann *Altwicker*: **Menschenrechtlicher Gleichheitsschutz.** 2011. XXX, 549 Seiten. Geb. € 99,95

222 Stephan *Bitter*: **Die Sanktion im Recht der Europäischen Union.** 2011. XV, 351 Seiten. Geb. € 84,95

221 Holger *Hestermeyer*, Nele *Matz-Lück*, Anja *Seibert-Fohr*, Silja *Vöneky* (eds.): **Law of the Sea in Dialogue.** 2011. XII, 189 Seiten. Geb. € 69,95 zzgl. landesüblicher MwSt.

220 Jan *Scheffler*: **Die Europäische Union als rechtlich-institutioneller Akteur im System der Vereinten Nationen.** 2011. XXXV, 918 Seiten. Geb. € 149,95

219 Mehrdad *Payandeh*: **Internationales Gemeinschaftsrecht.** 2010. XXXV, 629 Seiten. Geb. € 99,95